The British Expeditionary Force of 1914 was de
the best trained, best organised, and best equip
The BEF proved its fighting qualities in the fierce battles of 1914 and its reputation has endured. However, the same cannot be said for many of its commanders, who have frequently been portrayed as old fashioned, incompetent, and out of touch with events on the battlefield.

Yet the officers who led the BEF to war were every bit as professional and hard-bitten as the soldiers they commanded. These officers had learned their craft in the unforgiving school of colonial warfare and honed their understanding of conflict in the period of reform that reshaped the army between 1902 and 1914. As this book reveals, when faced with the realities of modern combat, the officers of the BEF were prepared for the challenge.

This collection offers a broad picture of command at all levels of the BEF through a series of biographical essays on key officers. Drawing upon much original research, each chapter explores the pre¬war background and experience of the officer and assesses his performance in combat in the opening months of the First World War. The book features insightful reappraisals of famous figures including John French and Douglas Haig, fresh studies of staff officers such as William Robertson and Henry Wilson, and a thorough discussion of officers at 'the sharp end', with chapters covering divisional, brigade, battalion and company commanders.

The essays reveal an officer class that, despite certain weaknesses, provided highly effective leadership during the chaotic fighting of August to November 1914. Without their influence it is unlikely that the BEF would have been able to survive the difficulties of the 'Great Retreat', much less halt the German invasions of France and Belgium.

This book will be of great interest to anyone who studies the First World War, and of particular value to those who seek a greater understanding of the British Army of the era.

Spencer Jones received his PhD in 2009 and currently teaches War Studies at the University of Wolverhampton. His research focuses on the battle tactics of the Anglo-Boer War and the First World War. His previous publications include *From Boer War to World War: Tactical Reform of the British Army 1902- 1914.*

STEMMING THE TIDE

Wolverhampton Military Studies

www.helion.co.uk/wolverhamptonmilitarystudies

Editorial board

Professor Stephen Badsey
Wolverhampton University

Professor Michael Bechthold
Wilfred Laurier University

Professor John Buckley
Wolverhampton University

Major General (Retired) John Drewienkiewicz

Ashley Ekins
Australian War Memorial

Dr Howard Fuller
Wolverhampton University

Dr Spencer Jones
Wolverhampton University

Nigel de Lee
Norwegian War Academy

Major General (Retired) Mungo Melvin
President of the British Commission for Military
History

Dr Michael Neiberg
US Army War College

Dr Eamonn O'Kane
Wolverhampton University

Professor Fransjohan Pretorius
University of Pretoria

Dr Simon Robbins
Imperial War Museum

Professor Gary Sheffield
Wolverhampton University

Commander Steve Tatham PhD
Royal Navy
The Influence Advisory Panel

Professor Malcolm Wanklyn
Wolverhampton University

Professor Andrew Wiest
University of Southern Mississippi

Submissions

The publishers would be pleased to receive submissions for this series. Please contact us via email (info@helion.co.uk), or in writing to Helion & Company Limited, 26 Willow Road, Solihull, West Midlands, B91 1UE.

Titles

No.1 *Stemming the Tide. Officers and Leadership in the British Expeditionary Force 1914* Edited by Spencer Jones (ISBN ISBN 978-1-910294-72-7)

No.2 *'Theirs Not To Reason Why'. Horsing the British Army 1875-1925* Graham Winton (ISBN 978-1-909384-48-4)

No.3 *A Military Transformed? Adaptation and Innovation in the British Military, 1792-1945* Edited by Michael LoCicero, Ross Mahoney and Stuart Mitchell (ISBN 978-1-909384-46-0)

No.4 *Get Tough Stay Tough. Shaping the Canadian Corps, 1914-1918* Kenneth Radley (ISBN 978-1-909982-86-4)

No.5 *A Moonlight Massacre: The Night Operation on the Passchendaele Ridge, 2 December 1917. The Forgotten Last Act of the Third Battle of Ypres* Michael LoCicero (ISBN 978-1-909982-92-5)

No.6 *Shellshocked Prophets. Former Anglican Army Chaplains in Interwar Britain* Linda Parker (ISBN 978-1-909982-25-3)

No.7 *Flight Plan Africa: Portuguese Airpower in Counterinsurgency, 1961-1974* John P. Cann (ISBN 978-1-909982-06-2)

Stemming the Tide

Officers and Leadership in the
British Expeditionary Force 1914

Wolverhampton Military Studies No. 1

Edited by Spencer Jones

 Helion & Company Limited

To my First World War Studies MA students,
in appreciation of your kindness and support

Helion & Company Limited
26 Willow Road
Solihull
West Midlands
B91 1UE
England
Tel. 0121 705 3393
Fax 0121 711 4075
Email: info@helion.co.uk
Website: www.helion.co.uk
Twitter: @helionbooks
Visit our blog http://blog.helion.co.uk/

Published by Helion & Company 2013. Reprinted in paperback 2015.

Designed and typeset by Aspect Book Design (www.aspectbookdesign.com)
Cover designed by Farr out Publications, Wokingham, Berkshire
Printed by Berforts Ltd, Eynsham, Oxfordshire

Text © Spencer Jones and contributors 2013
Maps © Barbara Taylor 2013
Photographs © as individually credited

Cover: "Our 'Little Contemptibles, 1914", oil on canvas by William Barnes Wollen, c 1918
(Courtesy of the Council of the National Army Museum, London).

ISBN 978 1 910294 72 7

British Library Cataloguing-in-Publication Data.
A catalogue record for this book is available from the British Library.

All rights reserved. No part of this publication may be reproduced, stored in a retrieval system, or
transmitted, in any form, or by any means, electronic, mechanical, photocopying, recording or
otherwise, without the express written consent of Helion & Company Limited.

For details of other military history titles published by Helion & Company Limited contact the
above address, or visit our website: http://www.helion.co.uk.

We always welcome receiving book proposals from prospective authors.

Contents

List of Illustrations

List of Maps

General Key for all maps.

Red — German
Blue — Allied
FR — French
BE — Belgian

XXXX
Army

XXX
Corps

XX
Division

X
Brigade

I I
Regiment/Battalion

I
Company

Infantry

Cavalry

Artillery

117/XXVI — Battery/Brigade

How — Howitzer

HB — Half battery

RFA — Royal Field Artillery

RGA — Royal Garrison Artillery

RHA — Royal Horse Artillery

British Regiments

A&SH — Argyle & Sutherland Highlanders
Beds — Bedfordshire Regiment
BW — Black Watch
Border — Border Regiment
CH/Cam H — Cameron Highlanders
CGds — Coldstream Guards
DCLI — Duke of Cornwall's Light Infantry

DG — Dragoon Guards
Dukes — Duke of Wellington's
ES — East Surreys
GG — Grenadier Guards
GH — Gordon Highlanders
Glouc — Gloucester Regiment
Gr How — Green Howards
KO — King's Own
KOSB — King's Own Scottish Borderers
KOYLI — King's Own Yorkshire Light Infantry
KRRC — King's Royal Rifle Corps
LF — Lancashire Fusiliers
Linc — Lincolnshire Regiment
LNL — Loyal North Lancashires
Manch — Manchester Regiment
Middx — Middlesex Regiment
NF — Northumberland Fusiliers
Northants — Northamptonshire Regiment
RBks — Royal Berkshire Regiment
RF — Royal Fusiliers
RI — Royal Irish
RIF — Royal Irish Fusiliers
RIR — Royal Irish Rifles
RS — Royal Scots
RSF — Royal Scots Fusiliers
RWF — Royal Welch Fusiliers
RWK — Royal West Kents
SG — Scots Guards
SR — Scottish Rifles
SStaffs — South Staffordshire Regiment
Suff — Suffolk Regiment
SWB — South Wales Borderers
Wilts — Wiltshire Regiment
Worc — Worcestershire Regiment

Abbreviations

AA	Assistant Adjutant	GQG	Grand Quartier Général [General Headquarters of the French Army]
ADC	Aide de Camp		
AG	Adjutant General		
AQMG	Assistant Quarter-Master General	GS	General Staff
		GSO	General Staff Officer [numerical designation, indicates grade, e.g. GSO1]
BEF	British Expeditionary Force		
CAS	Chief of the Air Staff		
CB	Companion of the Order of the Bath	IGC	Inspector General of Communications
CFS	Central Flying School	IGS	Imperial General Staff
CID	Committee of Imperial Defence	KCMG	Knight Commander of the Order of St. Michael & St. George
CIGS	Chief of the Imperial General Staff		
		KRRC	King's Royal Rifle Corps
CinC	Commander in Chief	LNL	Loyal North Lancashire Regiment
CO	Commanding Officer		
CoS	Chief of Staff	LoC	Line of Communication
CRA	Commander, Royal Artillery	MGGS	Major-General, General Staff
CRE	Commander, Royal Engineers		
		MW	Military Wing [of the Royal Flying Corps]
DAAG	Deputy-Assistant Adjutant General		
		NCO	Non Commissioned Officer
DGMA	Director General of Military Aeronautics	OH	[British] Official History
		QF	Quick Firing [Artillery gun]
DMA	Director of Military Aeronautics	QMG	Quarter-Master General
		RA	Royal Artillery
DMO	Director of Military Operations	RAMC	Royal Army Medical Corps
		RE	Royal Engineers
DMT	Director of Military Training	RFA	Royal Field Artillery
		RFC	Royal Flying Corps
DSO	Distinguished Service Order	RGA	Royal Garrison Artillery
EEF	Egyptian Expeditionary Force	RHA	Royal Horse Artillery
		VC	Victoria Cross
GHQ	General Headquarters	WO	War Office
GOC	General Officer Commanding		

Notes on Contributors

Stephen Badsey PhD MA (Cantab) is Professor of Conflict Studies at the University of Wolverhampton UK, and a Fellow of the Royal Historical Society. An internationally recognised authority on military history and military-media issues, he has written or edited 25 books and more than 65 articles, his writings have been translated into five languages, and he appears frequently on television and in other media.

John Bourne taught History at Birmingham University for thirty years before his retirement in September 2009. He founded the Centre for First World War Studies, of which he was Director from 2002 to 2009, as well as the MA in British First World War Studies. He has written widely on the British experience of the Great War, including *Britain and the Great War* (1989; 1994), *Who's Who in the First World War* (2001), and (with Gary Sheffield), *Douglas Haig: War Diaries and Letters 1914-1918* (2005). He is currently editing the letters and diaries of General Sir Henry Rawlinson, again with Gary Sheffield.

Michael Carragher was born in South Armagh, Ireland, in 1953. Eighteen years later he rode an old motorbike to Trinity College, Dublin, and later graduated from the Writing Program of the University of Arkansas, Fayetteville, and the University of Birmingham's First World War Studies programme. He has published fiction and non-fiction, notably *A World Full of Places and Other Stories* (1997), and *San Fairy Ann: Motorcycles and British Victory 1914-1918* (2013). He lives in Dublin, where he teaches history and creative writing.

Mark Connelly is Professor of Modern British History at the University of Kent. His research interests focus on British military history and war and memory and commemoration. His publications include *The Great War: memory and ritual* (2002); *Britain Can Take It: Britain and the memory of the Second World War* (2003); *Steady the Buffs: a regiment, a region and the Great War* (2006) and (with Timothy Bowman), *The Edwardian Army: recruiting, training and deploying the British Army, 1902-1914* (2012).

Steven J. Corvi is a scholar with a Doctorate from Northeastern University in 19th-20th Century British Military History. His specialization is the First World War with particular expertise in military leadership & the emergence of modern warfare in the 20th Century. Publications include *Victoria's Generals* and *Haig's Generals*, both co-edited with Ian F.W. Beckett.

Brian Curragh graduated with distinction in 2012 from the University of Birmingham's Centre for War Studies MA in British First World War Studies programme. His dissertation was entitled 'The Queen's Own Oxfordshire Hussars - "agricultural cavalry" or an elite unit?'" He also won the Max Rosen Essay Prize for his essay "How important were tanks to British military success in the Hundred Days?" When not studying the First World War, Brian is the Finance Director of a property development company in Hertfordshire.

Peter Hodgkinson is a Chartered and Clinical Psychologist specialising in forensic work and trauma. A graduate of the University of Birmingham MA in British First World War Studies, he combined his professional and historical interests in a study of how soldiers of the Great War coped with the experience of death. He has also written on the subject of the post-war battlefield clearances. He is currently completing his PhD on the subject of infantry battalion command.

Spencer Jones completed his PhD in 2009 and currently teaches War Studies at the University of Wolverhampton. His research focuses on battle tactics of the Anglo-Boer War and the First World War. His previous publications include *From Boer War to World War: Tactical Reform of the British Army 1902 - 1914* (2012).

Michael Stephen LoCicero is an independent scholar who earned his PhD at the University of Birmingham in 2011. His thesis, 'A Moonlight Massacre: The Night Operation on the Passchendaele Ridge, 2nd December 1917', is scheduled for publication by Helion in 2014. He has, in addition to MA advisement for the University of Birmingham's respected War Studies programme, been employed by the National Archives of the United Kingdom and Soldiers of Oxfordshire Museum as a contracted researcher.

Richard Olsen is an amateur military historian. He read Law at Worcester College, Oxford and spent 35 years as a solicitor specialising in shipping accident law. After his retirement he was able to indulge his lifelong enthusiasm for the First World War, and studied for an MA in First World War Studies at the University of Birmingham. A retired Royal Naval Reserve officer, he is currently researching the activities of the RNVR during the Antwerp expedition of 1914.

James Pugh holds a BA (Hons) in Contemporary Military and International History (Salford), an MA in International History (Wales), and a PhD in Modern History (Birmingham). He is currently a visiting lecturer with the University of Birmingham, specialising in air power studies and the history of the First and Second World Wars. His thesis explored the conceptual origins of the control of the air in Britain between 1911 and 1918. He has also written on air power leadership and doctrine.

Simon Robbins, Senior Archivist in the Department of Research, Imperial War Museum, studied History at Nottingham University and War Studies at King's College London. He is the author of *British Generalship on the Western Front, 1914-18: Defeat Into Victory* (short-listed for the Templer Medal), *The First World War Letters of General Lord Horne, and British Generalship during the Great War: The Military Career of Sir Henry Horne* (1861-1929). He is co-author of *Staff Officer, the Diaries of Walter Guinness (First Lord Moyne), 1914-18* (with Professor Brian Bond) and *Haig's Generals* (edited by Ian F.W. Beckett and Steven J. Corvi).

Gary Sheffield is Professor of War Studies at the University of Wolverhampton. Educated at the University of Leeds and King's College London, he has taught at RMA Sandhurst and the UK's Joint Services Command and Staff College. His publications include *Douglas Haig: War Diaries and Letters 1914-18* (London, 2005), co-edited with John Bourne, and *The Chief: Douglas Haig and the British Army* (2011).

John Mason Sneddon trained as a biomedical scientist and pursued a research and academic career until retirement. He then focused on his life-long interest in the Great War through the University of Birmingham MA in First World War Studies. His interests focus on August 1914 to December 1915 and he has published on the Destruction of the Bridges at Mons; the Bombay Sappers and Miners at Neuve Chapelle in 1914; and in 2013 the book *The Devil's Carnival*, an account of the 1/Northumberland Fusiliers in 1914. He is currently preparing a book about the Trench Warfare Department.

John Spencer completed his MA in First World War Studies at the University of Birmingham in 2010; his dissertation on Sir William Robertson in 1915 won the Yorkshire branch of the Western Front Association's annual essay prize. He also has a BA in International Relations and History from the University of Lancaster. Since 1980 he has been a journalist and media executive. For 13 years he held the post of Managing Editor of the Press Association, the national news agency for Britain and Ireland. He is now a freelance travel writer, media policy consultant, and First World War enthusiast.

The Wolverhampton Military Studies Series
Editor's Preface

As series editor, it is my great pleasure to introduce the *Wolverhampton Military Studies Series* to you. Our intention is that in this series of books you will find military history that is new and innovative, and academically rigorous with a strong basis in fact and in analytical research, but also is the kind of military history that is for all readers, whatever their particular interests, or their level of interest in the subject. To paraphrase an old aphorism: a military history book is not less important just because it is popular, and it is not more scholarly just because it is dull. With every one of our publications we want to bring you the kind of military history that you will want to read simply because it is a good and well-written book, as well as bringing new light, new perspectives, and new factual evidence to its subject.

In devising the *Wolverhampton Military Studies Series*, we gave much thought to the series title: this is a *military* series. We take the view that history is everything except the things that have not happened yet, and even then a good book about the military aspects of the future would find its way into this series. We are not bound to any particular time period or cut-off date. Writing military history often divides quite sharply into eras, from the modern through the early modern to the mediaeval and ancient; and into regions or continents, with a division between western military history and the military history of other countries and cultures being particularly marked. Inevitably, we have had to start somewhere, and the first books of the series deal with British military topics and events of the twentieth century and later nineteenth century. But this series is open to any book that challenges received and accepted ideas about any aspect of military history, and does so in a way that encourages its readers to enjoy the discovery.

In the same way, this series is not limited to being about wars, or about grand strategy, or wider defence matters, or the sociology of armed forces as institutions, or civilian society and culture at war. None of these are specifically excluded, and in some cases they play an important part in the books that comprise our series. But there are already many books in existence, some of them of the highest scholarly standards, which cater to these particular approaches. The main theme of the *Wolverhampton Military Studies Series* is the military aspects of wars, the preparation for wars or their prevention, and their aftermath. This includes some books whose main theme is the technical details of how armed forces have worked, some books on wars and battles, and some books that re-examine the evidence about the existing stories, to show in a different light what everyone thought they already knew and understood.

As series editor, together with my fellow editorial board members, and our publisher Duncan Rogers of Helion, I have found that we have known immediately and almost by instinct the kind of books that fit within this series. They are very much the kind of well-written and challenging books that my students at the University of Wolverhampton would want to read. They are books which enhance knowledge, and offer new perspectives. Also, they are books for anyone with an interest in military history and events, from expert scholars to occasional readers. One of the great benefits of the study of military history is that it includes a large and often committed section of the wider population, who want to read the best military history that they can find; our aim for this series is to provide it.

Stephen Badsey
University of Wolverhampton

Acknowledgements

In any edited collection, the first acknowledgement must always be to the contributors. From the outset their enthusiasm for the project was inspiring. I am grateful for their willingness to contribute their time and for the quality of their scholarship. This is as much their book as it is mine.

I owe a special thanks to Duncan Rogers, owner of Helion & Company. The genesis of this book can be traced to a conversation with Duncan which took place in the late summer of 2011. In the midst of a wide ranging discussion on the BEF and military history in general, the idea of writing an edited collection on the officers of the Old Contemptibles was put forward. The concept had immediate appeal and the project soon took on a life of its own. I am sincerely grateful for Duncan's support of the book from its inception to its completion. His enthusiasm for the project was second to none and it has been a genuine pleasure to work with him.

I must thank an array of people who contributed to the project in some form. I would like to extend thanks to everyone involved with the Guild of Battlefield Guides' 'Mons to the Marne' tour of 2012, particularly Dudley Giles for leading the tour and Simon Worrall for kindly providing transport. This was an excellent trip that provided a new understanding of the battles of 1914 and also taught me a great deal about where to find a good cup of tea in France.

A number of individuals contributed to the book by sharing research and ideas. I am particularly grateful to Jim Beach, Stephen Harris, Alistair Hogg, John Lee, Andy Lonergan, Ross Mahoney, William Philpott and John Pratt. John Bourne provided valuable guidance at the outset of the project which shaped the selection of officers in the volume. Gary Sheffield and Stephen Badsey were instrumental in identifying potential contributors. Last but by no means least, my regular cross-Atlantic conversations with the erudite Michael LoCicero produced a constant flow of ideas.

I would like to offer a very special thanks to my MA students at the University of Birmingham. Their support for my work, particularly in the summer of 2012, has been deeply appreciated.

As ever, I owe particular thanks to all my friends, especially Leeann, Richard (and Alex), Andy and Jon, who politely endured my constant references to 'the book' with only the occasional roll of the eyes. Beyond lending sympathetic ears and moral support, they provided much needed levity, fun and laughter.

Finally, I could not have completed this work without the love and support of my parents. They shared my enthusiasm when the project was going well and supported me when the task became difficult. Their love is more appreciated than they can ever realise.

Introduction

Spencer Jones

The opening months of the First World War are a subject of enduring interest.[1] The fighting in this period was unique. Armies equipped with 20th century weaponry manoeuvred in a manner not unlike their Napoleonic forefathers had done one hundred years earlier. Colourful uniforms, marching bands and unfurled standards were still seen on the battlefield, although the ferocity of modern firepower would soon banish them to the realms of history. In contrast to the later years of the First World War, 1914 was marked by rapid manoeuvre and the tantalising possibility of a sudden war ending victory, as Germany launched the Schlieffen plan and hurled its forces into a swift invasion of Belgium and France.

Although the campaign in the west was predominantly a clash between French and German armies, the British Expeditionary Force (BEF) has established a distinct place in the historiography of 1914. Its time in action was brief, with its main combat involvement lasting just four months between August and November 1914. It was a small, professional force that consisted of six infantry divisions and a single cavalry division at the outset of the war, making it quite unlike the vast militaries of Europe or the great British citizen army that would take its place. However, its small size belied its fighting prowess. The BEF's volunteer composition, relatively long length of individual enlistment, and consequent standard of training meant that, man for man, it was the finest army in Europe.[2] The force took pride in its nickname of the Old Contemptibles, derived from an alleged order of the day issued by the Kaiser to his soldiers, urging them to "walk over General [John] French's contemptible little army."[3] Although many of its troops were recent enlistments rather than long service veterans, the BEF possessed a particularly hard bitten outlook on war that owed something to an earlier generation

---

1   For a detailed account of 1914 in its entirety, see Hew Strachan, *The First World War: To Arms* (Oxford, Oxford University Press, 2001).

2   Timothy Bowman & Mark Connelly, *The Edwardian Army. Recruiting, Training and Deploying the British Army, 1902-1914* (Oxford, Oxford University Press, 2012), p.216.

3   Spencer Jones, *From Boer War to World War: Tactical Reform of the British Army, 1902-1914* (Norman, University of Oklahoma Press, 2012), p.5.

of soldiers. This attitude was encapsulated in the A.E. Housman poem 'Epitah on an Army of Mercenaries' and captured in the darkly humorous memoirs of veteran Frank Richards.[4]

This unique army found itself fighting an unusual campaign. The nature of combat in 1914 was markedly different from the trench warfare of 1915 to 1918. August and early September 1914 were defined by fast moving operations and pitched battles in the open. Whilst machine guns and artillery proved their formidable killing power, the campaign also saw traditional cavalry playing a crucial role and engaging in cold steel combat.[5] It was not until the fighting at Ypres in October and November 1914 that the war assumed a more static character, but the hasty entrenchments and improvised obstacles deployed here bore little resemblance to the complex trench networks and dense lines of barbed wire that would come to define the Western Front.

Although its time in the field was comparatively short, the BEF exercised an important and arguably vital role in the 1914 campaign. Operating on the left flank of the French and advancing into Belgium, the BEF unexpectedly found itself facing the main thrust of the German invasion. Clashes at Mons (23 August) and Le Cateau (26 August) followed as the BEF was forced to undertake the Great Retreat in the face of overwhelming German forces. The retreat was covered by a series of fierce and sometimes costly rearguard actions. However, the main body of the BEF was able to break free from the pursuing Germans and was in a position to turn and counterattack alongside French forces at the Battle of the Marne (6 – 12 September). The battle ended in a decisive Anglo-French victory that left the German Schlieffen plan in tatters. Its strict timetable had been derailed by the friction of war, the unexpected recuperative powers of the French military and the resilience of the BEF.

However, the BEF's advance came to a bloody halt at the Battle of the Aisne (13 – 15 September) as British attacks stalled against dug in German defenders. A brief lull followed before the army was transferred to the Flanders front where both sides sought the open flank of their opponent. Anglo-French ambitions to drive into Belgium and liberate Brussels were stymied as they were forced onto the defensive by a major German attack that sought to capture Ypres, the last major Belgian town in Allied hands, and then drive onwards towards Calais. The clash of armies resulted in the Battle of Ypres (19 October – 22 November). The Allied line held off repeated German offensives but only at a heavy cost. Proportionately, the British Army suffered its highest rate of attrition for the entire war at First Ypres.[6] By the end of November 1914 the BEF had suffered some 89,000 casualties from an original force of approximately 120,000 men. As one survivor commented sadly, "the old army was finished."[7]

4   Frank Richards, *Old Soldiers Never Die* (London, Faber & Faber, 1933).
5   Stephen Badsey, *Doctrine and Reform in the British Cavalry 1880-1918* (Aldershot, Ashgate, 2008), p.239 – 248; Spencer Jones 'Scouting for Soldiers: Reconnaissance and the British Cavalry 1899 – 1914' in *War in History,* 18(4), pp.510-513.
6   I am grateful to Professor William Philpott for providing this information.
7   John Lucy, *There's a Devil in the Drum* (London, Faber & Faber, 1938) p.293.

However, the stubborn defence of Ypres cemented the reputation of the BEF. It had proven its fighting qualities, played a vital role in defeating the German invasion of France and then sacrificed itself defending the last free city of "Brave Little Belgium". The story of these victories became a focus for inspirational propaganda and was a subject of immense public interest. Lord Ernest Hamilton's *The First Seven Divisions*, an early history of the campaign, went through 14 impressions in 1916.[8] Such tales were tinged with poignancy, for the highly trained professionals of the BEF were essentially irreplaceable in the context of mass mobilisation. Indeed, the contrast between the training standards of the long service regulars of 1914 and the citizen soldiers of 1915 – 1918 posed numerous doctrinal problems for the army, as it struggled to adapt to the unexpected conditions of trench warfare and devise appropriate tactics for its inexperienced troops. This contributed to a degree of nostalgia for the old BEF, which in turn found expression through belief in the primacy of the regular army over citizen volunteers.[9] The image of the BEF was thus firmly established.

The subsequent historiography has built on this formative image and portrayed the army in a positive light. James Edmonds, in the first volume of the British *Official History*, described the force as "incomparably the best trained, best organised and best equipped British Army which ever went forth to war."[10] This interpretation has endured and been reinforced through subsequent work from authors such as John Terraine, Anthony Farrar-Hockley, David Ascoli and Richard Holmes.[11] The BEF has been singled out for its combat effectiveness, particularly its field craft and marksmanship, as well as its professional tenacity. The image of the BEF as a formidable fighting force has become so well established that it prompted one American historian to note in 2005: "Even today there is little, if any, criticism of the Tommies of the BEF. It seems unlikely this will change."[12] Despite some recent challenges, the historical consensus still holds the fighting qualities of the BEF in high regard.[13]

However, although the consensus on the BEF's tactical strengths remains strong, assessments of the army have been tinged with criticism of its commanders and resultant

8   Ian F.W. Beckett, *The Judgement of History: Sir Horace Smith-Dorrien, Lord French and 1914* (London, Tom Donovan, 1993), p.xiii.

9   Jones, *Boer War to World War*, p.49.

10   James Edmonds, *Official History of the Great War: Military Operations France and Belgium 1914*, Vol.1, (London, Macmillan, 1923), p.10.

11   John Terraine, *Mons: The Retreat to Victory* (London, Macmillan, 1960); A.H. Farrar-Hockley, *Death of an Army* (London, Arthur Baker, 1967); David Ascoli, *The Mons Star* (London, Harrap, 1981); Richard Holmes *Riding the Retreat: Mons to the Marne Revisited* (London, J. Cape, 1995).

12   Fred R. Van Hartesveldt, *The Battles of the British Expeditionary Forces, 1914-1915: Historiography and Annotated Bibliography* (Westport, Praeger, 2005), p.6.

13   For recent assessments on the strengths and weaknesses of the BEF in 1914, see Bowman & Connelly, *Edwardian Army*, pp.215 - 218 and Jones, *Boer War to World War*, pp.207 - 215. For a challenge to the consensus, see Terrence Zuber, *The Mons Myth* (Stroud, The History Press, 2010). Zuber dismisses the BEF's combat effectiveness as mythical. However, the argument is gravely undermined by its narrow approach to the evidence.

operational limitations. Even Edmonds was sharply critical of GHQ's non-influence at the Battle of the Aisne and its unrealistic orders during the Battle of Ypres.[14] Much recent writing has focussed on the weakness of BEF command, with works from Tim Travers, Martin Samuels and Nikolas Gardner highlighting the problems of education, training and culture that hampered the British Army's officer class in 1914.[15] The overall verdict of these critics is that the BEF suffered from fundamental command problems and was far behind the German military in terms of operational capability.

However, it is important to note the subtle difference between command and leadership. Many thousands of words have been written attempting to precisely define these terms, but a simple and effective definition has been offered by Gary Sheffield. Sheffield argues that command is a managerial function that emphasises direction, co-ordination and effective use of forces at the commander's disposal.[16] Leadership is concerned with inspiration and motivation, with skilled leaders able to persuade their troops to endure hardship and incur dangers that they would otherwise avoid.[17]

The distinction is an important one. The nature of the 1914 campaign meant that there were few opportunites for any senior British officer to exercise effective command.[18] The BEF was a junior partner to the much larger French army and by military necessity was obliged to conform to its movements and strategy. The opening weeks of the war gave little opportunity to implement schemes for independent action. The BEF spent August engaged in a fighting retreat, then in September played a relatively small part in the larger French offensive on the Marne. As Stephen Badsey shows in his chapter on Sir John French, it was not until the lull on the Aisne in mid-September that French was able to devise an efficient plan to redeploy the BEF to Flanders, but this imaginative scheme was undone when the Germans seized the initiative and launched an offensive of their own.

It is perhaps well that the BEF did not have an independent role in 1914, as attempts to command the force were seriously hampered by lack of experience in handling such a large number of troops. John French had commanded a cavalry division of approximately 9,000 men in the Boer War in 1900 but was now expected

---

14   Edmonds, *Official History*, Vol.1, p.465.
15   Tim Travers, 'The Hidden Army: Structural Problems in the British Officer Corps, 1900 – 1918' in *Journal of Contemporary History* 17 (1982), pp.522; Tim Travers, *The Killing Ground: The British Army, the Western Front, and the Emergence of Modern Warfare* (London, Unwin Hyman Ltd., 1987); Martin Samuels, *Command or Control? Command, Training and Tactics in the British and German Armies 1888-1918* (London, Frank Cass, 1995); Nikolas Gardner, *Trial By Fire: Command and the British Expeditionary Force in 1914* (Westport, Praeger, 2003).
16   G.D. Sheffield (ed.), *Leadership & Command: The Anglo-American Military Experience since 1861* (London, Brassey's, 1997), pp.1-9.
17   Ibid., pp.9-14.
18   John Bourne has argued that it is difficult to detect any of the senior officers of the BEF in the act of generalship in 1914, with the exception of General Sir Horace Smith-Dorrien. See John Bourne, 'Charles Monro' in I.F.W. Beckett & Steven J. Corvi (eds.) *Haig's Generals* (Barnsley, Pen & Sword, 2009), p.125.

to command an army of 120,000 soldiers. His subordinate commanders were similarly inexperienced. Douglas Haig and Horace Smith-Dorrien had held command of forces roughly equivalent to a corps at Aldershot in the pre-war years, but to lead the formation in war was very different from commanding it during manoeuvres.

Exacerbating the problem of command inexperience was the improvised nature of the staff arrangements, particularly in II Corps and the Cavalry Division. As a cost saving measure these formations had been denied a permanent peacetime staff, and on the outbreak of war the posts were hastily filled with officers who had no prior experience of working together. Smith-Dorrien was able to overcome this handicap through virtue of his own ability and the strength of his Chief of Staff George Forestier-Walker, but Simon Robbins' chapter on Allenby reveals that the weak staff arrangements played a major role in the disintegration of the Cavalry Division into its component brigades.

Overarching these problems was the relative absence of operational doctrine which could ensure unity of thought within the army. Although *Field Service Regulations* laid out important principles that proved of value in 1914, it emphasised flexibility of action and allowed wide room for interpretation. The result was that diversity of method in peacetime training was not merely tolerated, but actually encouraged.[19] Mark Connelly highlights the fact that James Grierson, although an otherwise innovative thinker and trainer, did not impose uniformity on those he commanded, whilst Brian Curragh shows that Henry Wilson's attempts to create a school of thought in the army had only achieved moderate success before the outbreak of war. The combined factors of inexperience in handling large formations, inadequate staff arrangements and an absence of operational doctrine seriously undermined command and control. This meant that the BEF tended to fight as individual components in August and September. II Corps fought the battles of Mons and Le Cateau with no significant support from I Corps, whilst at the Battle of the Aisne individual divisions attacked piecemeal and suffered heavy losses as a consequence.

However, while there were clear command failures during the 1914 campaign, the BEF ultimately acquitted itself well in battle and played a vital role in halting the German invasion. A key factor in this victory was the high quality of leadership within the army. These leadership skills had been developed and honed in conflicts around the British Empire. As the chapters in this collection reveal, the officers of the BEF possessed a tremendous fund of combat experience. Although action in the Anglo-Boer War was a common feature, the diversity of service was vast, particularly, as Peter Hodgkinson's chapter shows, at battalion level. There is a tendency for critics of the BEF to dismiss this experience on the grounds that colonial warfare was no preparation for the demands of a modern, industrial conflict.[20] This is unfair, for the skills of leadership developed in these imperial actions, namely the ability to make quick decisions, lead men in dangerous situations and endure the experience of being

19   Jones, *Boer War to World War*, pp.55-56.
20   G.R. Searle, *The Quest for National Efficiency: A Study in British Politics and Political Thought 1899 – 1914* (Oxford, Blackwell, 1971), p.50.

under fire, were of universal value. It should also be remembered that colonial warfare was an unforgiving school. Smith-Dorrien had barely escaped with his life after the British defeat at Isandlwana in 1879, Charles FitzClarence had been shot through the legs in the Anglo-Boer War in 1899, and as John Spencer reveals in his chapter, William Robertson had nearly been killed in what modern terminology would describe as a 'green on blue' attack in Afghanistan in 1895.

Tactical reform in the aftermath of the Anglo-Boer War had codified the British emphasis on leadership. *Combined Training* and its successor, *Field Service Regulations*, encouraged tactical flexibility and enshrined the authority of the man on the spot to make key decisions.[21] These regulations reflected confidence in the leadership of the army and the capacity of junior officers to rise to the challenges created by the chaos of battle.[22] Despite the occasional setback, the BEF did not disappoint in this regard. As Michael LoCicero's chapter on Edward Bulfin and my own on Charles FitzClarence reveal, the ability to make quick decisions without consultation to the chain of command was to prove vital in 1914. The speed of operations and the intensity of the fighting turned many engagements into "soldier's battles" where the intentions of higher command were rendered obsolete and decisions had to be made immediately.[23] The officers of the BEF were well prepared, through prior combat experience and pre-war doctrine, for dealing with this type of fighting. These leadership skills extended to the very top of the army, and even the much maligned John French was considered formidable in this regard. C.D Baker-Carr, who served as French's chauffeur in 1914 and later became a brigadier-general, felt that "Sir John French may not have been a great soldier in the modern sense of the word, but he was a great leader of men."[24]

There is thus a certain dichotomy about the BEF of 1914. It may be said that it was well led yet poorly commanded, tactically skilled yet operationally naive. However, its success in battle in 1914 suggests that its strengths ultimately outweighed its weaknesses. Major-General Thomas Snow, commander of 4th Division in 1914, commented on this issue: "the retreat of 1914 was not, as is now imagined, a great military achievement, but rather a badly bungled affair only prevented from being a disaster of the first magnitude by the grit displayed by the officers and men."[25]

Nevertheless, the role and performance of the BEF's officer class remains contentious.[26] This book aims to expand the debate through a series of biographical

---

21   *Field Service Regulations, Part 1* (HMSO, London, 1909), pp.27-28.
22   J.M. Bourne, 'British Generals in the First World War' in Sheffield, (ed.) *Leadership and Command*, pp.94-96.
23   Bourne, 'Charles Monro', p.125.
24   C.D Baker-Carr, *From Chauffeur to Brigadier-General* (London, E. Benn, 1930), p.27.
25   Quoted in Steven J. Corvi, 'Horace Smith-Dorrien' in Beckett & Corvi (eds.) *Haig's Generals*, p.194.
26   For recent scholarship on the issue, see Gardner, *Trial by Fire* and Niall Barr, 'Command in the Transition from Mobile to Static Warfare, August 1914 to March 1915' in Gary Sheffield & Dan Todman (eds.), *Command and Control on the Western Front: The British Army's Experience 1914-18* (Stroud, Spellmount, 2007). For valuable studies of the BEF's staff officers in 1914, see Brian Bond, *The Victorian Army and the Staff College, 1854-1914*

essays on key commanders. There are certain barriers when studying the army of 1914 which have shaped the selection of chapters. Some key officers remain largely unknown due to their untimely deaths, such as the divisional commanders Major-General Samuel Lomax (1st Division) and Major-General Hubert Hamilton (3rd Division), both of whom became casualties in 1914.[27] Other officers left no significant papers or otherwise provided little information about their 1914 experiences, a problem that becomes particularly apparent when studying mid-level and junior officers. Operating within these limitations, this collection offers a broad picture of command at all levels of the army. The work focuses on the career and conduct of officers in the pre-war years and 1914, examining how past experience had prepared them for the challenges of modern war and how they performed under the stress of combat. The collection is wide ranging, covering officers from General Headquarters down to the level of company command, with an additional chapter studying the role of the Despatch Rider Corps which provided communications between the formations. The chapters include new studies of familiar names, such as reinterpretations of the performance of John French by Stephen Badsey and Douglas Haig by Gary Sheffield, as well as discussion of lesser known figures such as James Pugh's chapter on David Henderson and Michael LoCicero's on Edward Bulfin.

Taken as a whole, these essays provide a fresh and illuminating portrait of the British officer class in the opening campaigns of the First World War. It has been remarked that, in the context of mass warfare, the importance of the individual officer is often neglected. The BEF of 1914 was far smaller than the army that was to follow, and individual decisions could exercise a disproportionate influence, for better or for worse, thus making the study of these commanders particularly interesting. Although there were errors and failures in the heat of battle, the picture that emerges from the essays is of an experienced, determined set of officers, as professional in their outlook as the Old Contemptibles which they commanded.

(London, Eyre Methuen, 1972) and Ian F.W. Beckett, *Johnnie Gough, V.C.* (London, Tom Donovan, 1989).

27   Hamilton was killed on 14th October 1914. Lomax was mortally wounded on 31st October 1914 and died on 10th April 1915.

GHQ

1

Sir John French and Command of the BEF

Commander-in-Chief, BEF

Stephen Badsey

As the BEF departed for the continent in August 1914, Lord Esher observed dryly that "whatever happens our military historians are in honour bound to show that Germany was vanquished or France saved by Sir John [French] and his gallant four or five divisions".[1] The BEF's reputation has stood so high since 1914 that recently historians have sought to highlight its defects, chiefly in doctrine, staffwork and generalship, contrasting these with its strengths at battalion level or below.[2] As part of this criticism, the failings of Field Marshal Sir John French as C-in-C have been taken almost for granted. French has been portrayed as never truly in command of the BEF during the retreat from Mons, as his GHQ repeatedly relocated without informing lower formations, and issued contradictory or confusing orders that were eventually disregarded. In the subsequent battles of the campaign he has been portrayed as an onlooker to events rather than as a commander. Credit for Mons, Le Cateau and First Ypres has been given to Smith-Dorrien and Haig as corps commanders, while the BEF's participation in the Battle of the Marne has been attributed to Joffre, or Kitchener.

While being given little credit for the BEF's achievements in 1914, French has mostly been blamed for its shortcomings, including for failing as CIGS 1912-14 to

---

1   Journal of Lord Esher, 6 August 1914, in Oliver, Viscount Esher (ed.), *Journals and Letters of Reginald Viscount Esher, Volume III 1910-1915* (London, Ivor Nicholson, 1938), p.175.

2   E.g. Nikolas Gardner, *Trial By Fire: Command and the British Expeditionary Force in 1914* (Westport Conn., Praeger, 2003), Ian F. W. Beckett, *Ypres: The First Battle 1914* (London, Pearson, 2004), Martin Samuels, *Command or Control? Command, Training and Tactics in the British and German Armies 188-1918* (London, Frank Cass, 1995), Holger H. Herwig, *The Marne 1914: The Opening of World War I and the Battle That Changed the World* (New York: Random House, 2009), and also, taking his argument far beyond the evidence, Terence Zuber, *The Mons Myth: A Reassessment of the Battle* (Stroud, The History Press, 2010).

Sir John French. (Editor's collection)

establish proper Army staffwork and doctrine. Popular expectations in 1914 were that a C-in-C in the Field should be a hero or great man, able to mould events and lesser mortals to his will, and beyond doubt French fell short of this. But more than any other individual, the BEF of 1914 was John French's army; victory or defeat was his responsibility. The emphasis placed on the more unattractive aspects of his personality has detracted attention away from the underlying causes of the BEF's failures in command and staffwork, including the issue of whether French or any other commander could have overcome them, as well as how he actually responded to them.

It is a sad fact that few commanders can have gone into their first battle of a war with their cards so heavily marked as Sir John French did in 1914. His relationship with Kitchener as Secretary of State for War was problematic, although not as bad as it was later portrayed, or became. Haig commanding I Corps made it clear in his diary (actually notes for his wife Doris, who was a lady-in-waiting to Queen Mary) that French was not fit to hold his command; and when Grierson commanding II Corps died, his replacement Smith-Dorrien informed French that he was also supplying his own version of events to King George V. At GHQ, French was criticised behind his back by Archibald Murray his CGS, Henry Wilson his Sub-Chief, and George MacDonogh his Chief of Intelligence. As for his French allies, Lanrezac and his staff were openly contemptuous of Sir John, and the attitude of Joffre and Foch was only slightly better. It is a vain search for anyone around him in 1914 who was prepared to put aside their own ambitions or concerns to help and support the BEF's C-in-C under the conditions of extreme stress in which he obviously found himself.

Removed from command of the BEF at the end of 1915, French then did much to destroy his own already shaky reputation with the publication in 1919 of his controversial memoirs, entitled *1914*, which in Barbara Tuchman's choice phrase "caused his countrymen to search helplessly for a polite equivalent of 'lie'".[3] Next year the publication of Kitchener's official biography revealed the extent of their disagreements, and added impetus to Smith-Dorrien's attempts behind the scenes to protect his own reputation over Le Cateau. The criticisms in Sir John's memoirs of French generals in 1914 also rebounded upon him. The head of the French mission to GHQ in 1914, Colonel Victor Huguet, described him at his famous meeting with Kitchener on 1 September as "but a spoilt child on whom Fortune had smiled prodigiously but who, the day she left him, seemed abandoned and forlorn".[4] Foch, who was appointed as an intermediate commander under Joffre on 11 October to improve co-operation with the BEF, claimed that during First Ypres French had panicked on 30 October at the news of the renewed German attack; while in the crisis of the next day a French staff officer depicted a broken Sir John pleading for reinforcements; French's memoirs say only that he, Foch and the staff "all went thoroughly into the situation".[5]

French came even more badly out of the two volumes of James Edmonds's official history of the BEF's 1914 campaign, which appeared in 1922 and 1925 (the year that French died), although Henry Wilson as Sub-Chief was Edmonds' main target. Edmonds had little first-hand knowledge of how French and GHQ had actually conducted themselves, serving as GSO 1 (chief of staff) of 4th Division in the retreat. On 27 August, GHQ issued orders that retreating BEF formations were to abandon *unnecessary* equipment and use the transport to carry their exhausted men, and Edmonds later promoted stories that these orders were evidence of panic by French and Wilson, and that they were torn up or suppressed at I Corps and II Corps headquarters.[6] Significantly, another officer's contemporary account relates that Edmonds himself went hysterical with strain on receipt of these orders, and threatened to shoot soldiers who disobeyed them. He was invalided home shortly afterwards, before returning in October to join GHQ, where he stayed for the rest of the war.[7] Edmonds became convinced by his own experiences as a staff officer that

3   Barbara Tuchman, *The Guns of August* (London, Folio Society, [1962] 1995), p.369.
4   General [Victor] Huguet, *Britain and the War: A French Indictment* (London, Cassell, 1928), p.84.
5   The contradictory evidence for this and other episodes involving French is admirably set out in Beckett, *Ypres 1914*, p.124 and p.140.
6   See e.g. Keith Jeffrey, *Field Marshal Sir Henry Wilson: A Political Soldier* (Oxford, OUP, 2006), pp.136-7; Ian F.W. Beckett, *Johnnie Gough V.C.* (London, Tom Donovan, 1989), p.184.
7   The account is from the war diary for 28 August of Aylmer Haldane, then commanding 10th Infantry Brigade, part of 4th Division, quoted in Simon Robbins, *British Generalship on the Western Front 1914-18: Defeat into Victory* (London, Routledge, 2005),

official documents and war diaries were of very limited value as historical sources, and he chose instead to rely heavily on the post-war verbal or written testimony of men very much like himself: well-placed staff officers or middle-ranking generals keen to explain what had *really* been going on. If a message or war diary was missing or misdated, then this must be due to a conspiracy to protect some general's reputation, rather than to the chaos of the BEF's retreat. This sort of information, given to or by Edmonds (and to Basil Liddell Hart), is the source of most of the anecdotes about French's conduct in 1914, always portraying him in a poor or even a bizarre light. Edmonds also had a malicious sense of humour: he boasted that during the war he had deliberately fed official correspondents at GHQ false stories as a test of their gullibility, and he continued the practice as official historian, misleading Liddell Hart, and making contradictory claims about the same event or general to different people at different times.

In 1934 the historian C.R.M.F. Cruttwell described French as possessing "that mercurial temperament commonly associated with Irishmen and cavalry-soldiers,"[8] and 'mercurial' meaning emotionally inconsistent and unreliable has been his character note among historians ever since. Unlike most senior British generals of the First World War he has no modern biography taking into account new evidence and changing perspectives on the war. A generation ago, his last biographer dismissed him as a dysfunctional personality, intellectually lazy, unoriginal, petty, unscrupulous and spiteful, adding that "I regret to say that before long I had, if anything, formed an even lower opinion of my subject".[9] Other historians have described French's behaviour in command in 1914 as foolish, panicked, or childish.

This view has become part of the wider criticism of the British Army before and during the First World War. The Army that could accept Sir John French as its commander, and the society that propelled him into such a position, were clearly both deeply flawed. This is an extension, in rather more sophisticated language, of the argument that the BEF were lions led by donkeys, good troops and battalions with incompetent commanders, with French as the outstandingly irredeemable example. The broad origins of these views, which have been greatly modified in recent years by new evidence, have been traced from the 1930s to the 1960s as essentially political and cultural rather than military in nature.[10] But in addition to this phenomenon, criticisms of Sir John French and British generalship also arose as an indirect consequence of attempts in the 1970s by American military analysts to apply history to what was then a pressing contemporary problem. At the time, mathematical combat models appeared to show that in both the First and Second World Wars

---

p.38. According to Edmonds, the destruction or suppression of these orders explained why copies could not be located for his official history.

8   C.R.M.F. Cruttwell, *A History of the Great War 1914-1918* (London, Granada, [1934] 1982), p.23. French came from Kent, but called himself Irish for family dynastic reasons.

9   George H. Cassar, *The Tragedy of Sir John French* (Newark, University of Delaware Press, 1985), preface (no pagination) and pp.66-7.

10   A good summary of present research is Dan Todman, *The Great War: Myth and Memory* (London, Hambledon Continuum, 2005).

the German Army was consistently superior to its enemies in inflicting casualties, a discovery which was used to prove that the German Army had "'won" the Battle of the Marne and many others.[11] (In what might be a satire on this methodology, it has even been calculated that in the course of the First World War the Central Powers spent $11,344.77 to kill each Allied soldier, compared with a rival Allied expenditure of $36,485.48 per enemy killed.)[12] This alleged German battlefield superiority was attributed in the later 20th century to two main institutional factors. One of these was the German General Staff, with its unified, written doctrine of battle, its training system used to inculcate that doctrine throughout the German Army, and its selection of a professional elite of staff officers to ensure this doctrine's proper application. The other was the German priority given to winning battles, with emphasis on the "operational level" of war, meaning broadly divisional and corps command, a concept that barely existed in British military thought in 1914.[13] In the late 1970s the main NATO armies began to copy this German system, and for the British Army this meant significant changes in its institutional culture, accompanied by a denunciation of the previous British doctrinal approach, which had been more Aristotelian than Clausewitzian in its pragmatism.[14] This in turn prompted criticisms of the British Army of 1914-1918 from historians, essentially for failing to be the German Army, whose champions accepted its own values and arguments almost in their entirety.

The German Army's system before 1914 was indeed much admired by the British. Admiral Sir John "Jacky" Fisher complained in 1904 that "all the Generals" (except French, who was interested in naval co-operation), "want to play at [being] the German army".[15] But whether the German Army possessed an intrinsically superior military system for its time is doubtful. Its emphasis on winning battles rather than on strategy produced institutional weaknesses in logistics and military intelligence, and a failure by its generals to grasp the wider political consequences of

---

11   The most influential of these studies has been Trevor N. Dupuy, *A Genius for War: The German Army and the General Staff 1807-1945* (Englewood Cliffs NJ, Prentice-Hall,1977) which on p.302 states that "Germany's involvement in, and loss of, the World Wars was in no way connected with the professional organization, indoctrination, or performance of the German General Staff," and on pp.330-1 shows a German 'victory' over the French and British in the Battle of the Marne by a margin of 3.86 to 3.48; see also the author's other most influential book, Trevor N. Dupuy, *Numbers, Predictions and War: Using History to Evaluate Combat Factors and to Predict the Outcome of Battles* (London, MacDonald and Jane's, 1979).

12   Niall Fergusson, *The Pity of War* (London, Allan Lane, 1998), p.336.

13   Dupuy, *A Genius for War*, pp.308-13; Martin van Creveld, *Fighting Power: German and US Army Performance, 1939-1945* (Westport Conn., Greenwood Press, 1982).

14   The need for such an institutional change is the main theme of Shelford Bidwell and Dominick Graham, *Fire-Power: British Army Weapons and Theories of War 1904-1945* (London, George Allen and Unwin, 1982), especially pp.292-5.

15   Quoted in John Gooch, *The Plans of War: The General Staff and British Military Strategy c.1900-1916*, (London, Routledge and Kegan Paul, 1974) p.49.

their actions, which eventually cost Germany both world wars.[16] Belief in an inherent German superiority was an argument for its time. As the era of the Soviet threat has passed away, and with it (although rather more slowly) belief in the primacy of the operational level of war in contemporary military thought, it should now be possible to see the BEF of 1914 in its own political, institutional and social context, including both its strengths and weaknesses, and those of its luckless commander.

The three great issues facing Sir John French and the British Army in the decade before the First World War were the creation and role of a General Staff 1904-1909, the creation of the BEF 1906-1914, and the training and doctrines of the BEF up to 1914. In September 1902, as he took over Aldershot Command, French's reputation was as one of the most successful British commanders of the Boer War, first under Lord Roberts as C-in-C in South Africa, and then under Kitchener, who was highly impressed by French, although he grumbled over the difficulties of the war's guerrilla phase (Edmonds, who served on Kitchener's staff, later exaggerated this into a story that Kitchener wanted to sack French).[17] French's lack of interference with the BEF's supply and communications staffs in 1914 may well have come from his experience commanding the Cavalry Division in the Boer War, when in January 1900 Kitchener as Roberts's chief of staff opted to change the army's transport system in the middle of a complex campaign of manoeuvre, with catastrophic results.[18] In 1905, French was made a permanent member of the new Committee of Imperial Defence (CID), in 1907 he left Aldershot to become Inspector General of the Forces, in 1912 he became CIGS, and a year later he was promoted to field marshal. In the course of this rise to prominence, French gained wide professional respect, including that of Admiral Fisher, Lord Esher, R.B. Haldane, Winston Churchill, Sir Edward Grey, Colonel Repington of *The Times* who described him in 1907 as "not only a fighting man but a real trainer, and all his people swear by him,"[19] and Prime Minister Herbert Asquith who became "impressed by his knowledge of war and his good sense".[20]

16   These weaknesses are recognised by some historians who have accepted the arguments of Dupuy and van Creveld; see e.g. Samuels, *Command or Control?* pp.2-3 and pp.24-5.

17   For evidence of Kitchener's view of French see André Wessels, *Lord Kitchener and the War in South Africa 1899-1902* (London, Army Records Society, 2006), especially p.70 and pp.227-8 and Richard Holmes, *The Little Field-Marshal: Sir John French* (London, Jonathan Cape, 1981), p.116; for Edmonds' claim see Andrew Green, *Writing the Great War: Sir James Edmonds and the Official Histories 1915-1948* (London, Frank Cass, 2003), p.211 note 30.

18   Ian Malcolm Brown, *British Logistics on the Western Front 1914-1919* (Westport Conn., Praeger, 1998), p.25, pp.48-51 and p.80

19   Repington to Moberley-Bell (his editor) 25 September 1905, in A.J.A.Morris (ed.) *The Letters of Lieutenant-Colonel Charles à Court Repington CMG, Military Correspondent of the Times 1903-1918* (Stroud, Army Records Society, 1999), p.67.

20   Journal of Lord Esher, 4 October 1911, in Esher, *Journals and Letters*, p.62; for Esher's own high opinion of French at an early stage of his rise see Gooch, *The Plans of War*, p.65.

After this record of achievement, French's failings in 1914 have sometimes been excused by increasing old age and illness.[21] But French was 61 at the Battle of Mons, almost exactly the same age as Joffre, Foch and Lanrezac (and also Ian Hamilton and Asquith). Kitchener was 64 and still hoping for a future field command, one precedent being Roberts's appointment as C-in-C in the Boer War aged 68. On the German side, von Moltke was 66, von Kluck was 68, and von Bülow was 69. French's health withstood the immense physical and mental strain of the campaign better than that of many younger men in addition to Edmonds, including John Gough (who as I Corps chief of staff became seriously ill), and Murray, who collapsed more than once, for the first time on 26 August, and was sent home temporarily in October, where he had the opportunity to give his version of events to Asquith before French.[22] Much later, Murray claimed that French's "health, temper and temperament, rendered him unfit, in my opinion, for the crisis we had to face".[23] Haig recorded in November that French had told him that he had been ordered by his doctors to rest after a "severe attack of the heart", but when Asquith saw French in December he looked fresh and well, younger than he had in August.[24]

The portrayal of French in 1914 as intellectually deficient in comparison with other generals is equally unconvincing. His contemporaries attested to his considerable personal charm, (including his *amours* even late in life), and to his deep friendships which could turn to hatred if he felt himself betrayed. Commissioned through the militia rather than Sandhurst or Woolwich, he was self-educated, with a reputation early in his career for "always reading books".[25] His eventual level of education is uncertain in a society that saw displays of knowledge or erudition as ostentatious. Although not inarticulate like Kitchener and Haig, he was impressive as a speaker only when addressing other soldiers, having in Asquith's judgement "no gifts of expression" with civilians.[26] His handwriting was notoriously indecipherable, partly because of a finger injury early in life. He authored *Cavalry Drill 1896* with Haig, and provided introductions to a few books, but it was normal at the time for senior officers to put their names to work done mainly by their staffs or secretaries; it is possible that even documents in his own hand had their origins with others, and his memoirs were written with the help of a ghost writer. As his career flourished,

21   This idea was advanced particularly by French's best biographer; see Richard Holmes, *Riding the Retreat: Mons to the Marne 1914 Revisited* (London, Jonathan Cape, 1995), p.260.
22   Michael Brock and Eleanor Brock (eds), *H.H. Asquith Letters to Venetia Stanley* (Oxford, OUP, 1982), p.287; Jeffrey, *Sir Henry Wilson*, p.135, repeats a story that Murray was given morphia injections to counteract his faints.
23   Quoted in George H. Cassar, *Asquith as War Leader* (London, Hambledon, 1994), p.244.
24   Haig diary entry for 21 November 1914 in Gary Sheffield and John Bourne (eds), *Douglas Haig War Diaries and Letters 1914-1918* (London, Weidenfeld and Nicolson, 2005), p.82; Brock, *Asquith Letters*, p.332.
25   Cecil Chisholm, *Sir John French: An Authentic Biography* (London, Herbert Jenkins, 1915), p.8
26   Esher's journal, 4 October 1911 in Esher, *Journals and Letters*, p.62.

French also acquired an entourage on which he relied heavily, with the result that he has become one of the rare generals who have been criticised for showing loyalty towards his subordinates. His biggest error was his increasing dependence on Henry Wilson, who cultivated French from 1906 onwards entirely for reasons of personal advancement, so that by 1912 Repington commented on "Wilson who now has Sir John in his pocket".[27]

The Boer War was French's second campaign, and recent experience of more than one war was normal among the senior officers of the BEF, unlike their German and French counterparts, who with the exception of Gallieni had not commanded combat troops since they were junior officers in the Franco-Prussian War (although Joffre had served as an engineer and in a minor command position in colonial postings). This made a large difference to the way that British generals viewed each other. Their personal courage and patriotism, their determination and qualities of leadership, were not in question among themselves. Their recent war experience had also taught them that the drill book, training and military intelligence were often wrong. Valuing practical war experience over theoretical staff training strongly coloured French's view of the debate that emerged after the Boer War as to whether an elite of "blue ribbon" General Staff officers should be modelled on the German system. The Army Staff College at Camberley, together with its Indian branch at Quetta after 1907, was not primarily an institution for trainee staff officers to be inculcated with an established official doctrine, but for rising stars with administrative and combat experience to share ideas and establish personal connections. In 1890 only seven per cent of serving generals had passed the Staff College course (distinguished by the letters *psc* after their names) although the number rose significantly to 39 per cent by 1910. Neither Kitchener nor French was *psc*, and French very strongly maintained that capable officers who had proved themselves were entitled to staff positions even if they were not *psc*, including Algernon Lawson, Philip Chetwode, and Henry Horne (later the only Army commander on the Western Front not to be *psc*). As Repington of *The Times* told Esher, French "if he thinks he sees a good man, [will] push him on regardless of opposition, precedents, or the custom of the Army".[28] In 1912 as CIGS, French told the Staff College that the General Staff should be indistinguishable from the Administrative Staff as it had evolved in the nineteenth century, "It is the duty of the Staff to present all the facts of the situation to the commander with perfect accuracy and impartiality and then to take the necessary measures for carrying his decisions into effect", rather than acting as a parallel or even superior chain of command on the German model.[29] French prided himself on being a regimental rather than a staff officer, and reserved particular venom in his

---

27   Repington to Haldane, 27 November 1912, in Morris, *Repington Letters*, p.192
28   Repington to Esher, 30 September 1907, in Morris, *Repington Letters*, p.122; Cassar, *Sir John French*, pp.64-5.
29   Quoted in Samuels, *Command or Control?* p.40.

memoirs for Lanrezac as "the most complete example" of "the Staff College 'pedant' whose 'superior education' had given him little idea of how to conduct war".[30]

French and all other senior British officers of the BEF also knew from recent military history of several cases of early plans being overturned by circumstances. The British studied the collapse of the French Army at the start of the Franco-Prussian War, and the unexpected successes of the Confederacy in the first years of the American Civil War, which together dominated the military history of the Staff College syllabus. French made conscious reference to both wars in his memoirs. He commented on Kitchener's political interference with his own authority over the BEF that "Stanton's interference with McClellan in the American Civil War should have been sufficient warning".[31] He also cited, as an influence on his decision not to fall back on the fortress town of Maubeuge at the start of the retreat from Mons, the disastrous decision of Marshal Bazaine to pull his army back to Metz in August 1870 in the face of the Prussian advance, quoting the assessment in Sir Edward Hamley's *The Operations of War* (the standard Staff College textbook of the 1880s) that "in clinging to Metz, he acted like one who, when the ship is foundering, should lay hold of the anchor".[32] This lesson from history was not foolishness on French's part. One phenomenon of several recent wars that generals on both sides in 1914 took to heart was that armies had repeatedly found themselves surrounded and besieged. To avoid this, both sides in the early months of the war either kept firm hold of the shoulders of each railhead town or pulled back to the next one, decisions which produced the characteristic sinuous curves of the Western Front as the year ended.

The principal function of the British Army was to provide contingents for its battalions policing the Empire, especially for the garrison in India. Even the changeover by infantry battalions in Britain in 1913 from eight small companies to four large ones, although partly to improve tactical flexibility in imitation of German practice, was made chiefly because the demand for drafts for India left the smaller companies too weak to fight effectively. Battalions of the Territorial Force, Indian Army, and British battalions serving overseas, did not make the same change until after the war's start.[33] Beyond this over-riding demand, the size of any expeditionary force that the British could send overseas was fixed in 1886-7 as at most three corps (six divisions, not all of them always regulars) and one cavalry division, and this size remained constant through to the second BEF of 1939 (with an incomplete armoured division replacing the cavalry), being unrelated to any strategic requirements.[34] The

30   [John] Viscount French of Ypres, *1914* (London, Constable, 1919), p.37.
31   French, *1914*, p.111; see also Brian Bond, *The Victorian Army and the Staff College 1854-1914* (London, Eyre Methuen, 1972), p.306.
32   French, *1914*, p.71, Edward Hamley, *The Operations of War: Explained and Illustrated* (Edinburgh, Blackwood, 1889), p.327; the first edition of Hamley's book appeared in 1866, and this passage comes from the 1889 edition; it was the sole Staff College military history set text until 1894, see Bond, *Staff College*, pp.87-9.
33   Bidwell and Graham, *Fire-Power*, pp.35-6.
34   W.S. Hamer, *The British Army: Civil-Military Relations 1885-1905* (Oxford, Clarendon Press, 1970), p.40; Stephen Badsey, *Doctrine and Reform in the British Cavalry 1880-1918*

war that broke out in 1914 was only one of several that the BEF might have been called upon to fight. In 1905 French raised the possibility of an expeditionary force being sent to aid Japan against Russia, and a year later as being sent to defend Egypt.[35] In 1908 (a year after the creation of the Triple Entente) Haldane portrayed the chief role of the BEF to parliament as reinforcing the Indian Army against a Russian invasion.[36] At the Imperial Conference in 1911, delegates were informed that the BEF existed if necessary to defend the Dominions against aggression from Germany or another country.[37] Finally, one of French's last papers to the CID, in July 1914 on the defence implications of a planned Channel Tunnel, noted that France might be a possible threat.[38]

By far the greatest factor in determining the BEF's organisation and training was the very severe financial stringency imposed on the Army by the Asquith government, the main concern of which was social reform.[39] 1911 may have been the year of the Agadir Crisis, but it was also the year of the Parliament Act and the start of the creation of the British welfare state. The Liberal Party and cabinet included important isolationists and anti-militarists, and the party as a whole much preferred the Royal Navy, as a protector of trade and creator of jobs, to the Army, whose higher command was mostly Unionist in sympathy. It was with some surprise that Lloyd George told C.P. Scott (editor of the *Manchester Guardian*) in late November 1914, "The Army which we regarded as capable of little has done wonders," while the Royal Navy's impact had been disappointing.[40] While trying to maintain six divisions and a cavalry division in existence, French as CIGS had to accept that much of the BEF's organisation would be incomplete in peacetime. Typical of pre-war problems was that the generals agreed that at four brigades (and a fifth independent brigade, but no permanent divisional headquarters) the Cavalry Division was too large, and that a sixth brigade was needed to create two divisions each of three brigades, but it was feared that if the matter was raised with the government the response would be to disband the fourth brigade instead as an unnecessary expense.[41]

In this political climate, there was very little that French could do. "Politics are not matters for soldiers to dabble in," he wrote in 1912 in the *Army Review*, "our

(Aldershot, Ashgate, 2008), p.40.

35   Gooch, *The Plans of War*, p.191 and pp.254-5.

36   Edward M. Spiers, *Haldane: An Army Reformer* (Edinburgh, Edinburgh University Press, 1980), pp.64-73.

37   Keith Jeffrey, 'The Imperial Conference, the Committee of Imperial Defence, and the Continental Commitment,' in Peter Dennis and Jeffrey Grey (eds), *1911: Preliminary Moves – 2011 Chief of Army History Conference* (Canberra, Big Sky Publishing, 2011), pp.20-40.

38   Elizabeth Greenhalgh, *Victory Through Coalition: Britain and France During the First World War* (Cambridge, CUP, 2005), p.11.

39   Spiers, *Haldane*, pp.72-4.

40   Quoted in Trevor Wilson (ed.), *The Political Diaries of C.P. Scott 1911-1928* (London, Collins, 1970), p.110.

41   Badsey, *Doctrine and Reform*, pp.197-8.

sole duty is to make the best use of our military resources".[42] He publicly supported the government position opposing conscription, but he remained concerned about the level of training of the Territorial Force, and in April 1913 he put his name as CIGS to a paper authored by Henry Wilson and Walter Kiggell which showed a preference for peacetime conscription if it were possible – which it was not.[43] The prevailing attitude in British and Dominion public opinion before 1914 has been well summarised as one of defensive patriotism; most people were willing to accept going to war if necessary, but efforts to promote conscription or even military volunteerism on any scale were political failures.[44] Like Kitchener, much of French's work during the 1914 campaign was spent in force generation, improvising from individual battalions the new formations that increased the BEF (including Indian Army formations) from four infantry divisions to ten by the end of the year, and the cavalry from one division to four, starting with 19th Infantry Brigade, improvised by French from lines-of-communications battalions, which fought at Le Cateau.

In addition to being understrength and under-resourced, the BEF of 1914 was also under-trained in large-scale manoeuvres, something that French as CIGS worked hard to address. As French's most sympathetic biographer Richard Holmes ruefully observed, "[British] First World War generals can no more win the historiographical battle than they could achieve clean breakthroughs on the Western Front,"[45] and French's pre-war efforts to train the BEF's generals and staffs have been criticised by historians as "umpiring", with French spending too much time adjudicating between subordinate formations rather than mastering the skills of commanding the BEF himself.[46] In fact the recommendation of staff officers following the 1913 exercises, in which French commanded one side as well as acting as exercise director, was exactly the opposite: that in future he should keep to being exercise director only.[47] The training of the BEF had to begin with smaller units, building up to divisional and corps levels, and French as CIGS had only two years and one large-scale exercise in which to improve its staff deficiencies. But his approach to operations may indeed be criticised as not having moved sufficiently away from his methods as a cavalry commander: advancing on a broad front with all his forces spread out, rather than

---

42   Quoted in Gooch, *The Plans of War*, p.123.

43   Spiers, *Haldane*, p.181 and p.185; the standard work, R.J.Q. Adams and Philip P. Poirier, *The Conscription Controversy in Great Britain 1900-18* (n.p., Ohio State University Press, 1987), p.271 note 12, states that French changed his mind in favour of conscription as late as October 1915.

44   A.J.A. Morris, *The Scaremongers: The Advocacy of War and Rearmament 1896-1914* (London, Routledge and Kegan Paul, 1984), pp.224-50; Adams and Poirier, *The Conscription Controversy*, pp.16-48, Catriona Pennell, *A Kingdom United: Popular Responses to the Outbreak of the First World War in Britain and Ireland* (Oxford, OUP, 2012).

45   Holmes, *Riding the Retreat*, p.259.

46   This was first suggested by Martin Samuels in 1990, and expanded upon in Samuels, *Command or Control?* pp.49-60.

47   Gooch, *The Plans of War*, pp.121-3.

keeping a reserve and concentrating his main effort on one point; this was his style both in training exercises and in the advance to the Aisne in September 1914.[48]

The British Army of 1914 was very much like other large and well-established British institutions. Its structure and approach to doctrine paralleled the British Constitution: improvised but sophisticated, largely unwritten, constantly evolving to reflect different interests and pressures, baffling to outsiders, and able to cope flexibly with considerable and sudden changes. The behaviour of the senior officer corps also was like that of a political party of the period, consisting of several unofficial and often changing factions, bound together by a common sense of identity. These factions or associations included the informal patronage typical of British professions, such as the 'firm' of a senior hospital surgeon or the chambers of a law practice, and functioned as a substitute for any strong central institutionalised system for promotion and doctrine. One consequence of this was that, despite the chain of command, officers of major general's rank or above were highly independently-minded, and viewed each other as essentially equals. To modify official tactical doctrine was an important part of any general's authority in peace, largely because it was often essential to do so quickly and confidently in war.

French was particularly involved in the debate over cavalry tactics following the Boer War, and his championing of swords, lances and mounted charges used to be cited by historians as evidence of his foolish or hidebound thinking. More recently, research into French's actual pronouncements on the cavalry, and into both its strengths and limitations in 1914, have revealed a much more complex case study of the many factors that shaped British military doctrine of the time.[49] French's views were quite consistent, from *Cavalry Drill 1896* onwards: an active reformer, he promoted new cavalry tactics including the use of carbines and rifles long before this became fashionable. But after the Boer War, he opposed Roberts's official doctrine that made the rifle the cavalry's *primary* weapon, partly because fire from the saddle was ineffective, partly because of the value of swords in colonial warfare, but chiefly because this doctrine reflected Roberts's claim that the failure to end the war decisively in early 1900 had been the fault of poor cavalry tactics, for which French could be held responsible. The debate was as much about a factional power struggle within the Army as about tactics, and it largely ended with Roberts's retirement as C-in-C in 1904, although it was briefly reignited in 1910 by the polemical book *War and the Arme Blanche* by Erskine Childers. By the time French became CIGS matters had calmed down: *Field Service Regulations I 1909*, *Cavalry Training 1912*, and all senior British cavalry officers, including French, stressed the importance of cavalry rifle fire, and French may have let slip the view that he *did* think rifles were more

---

48   Paul Kendall, *Aisne 1914: The Dawn of Trench Warfare* (Stroud, Spellmount, 2012), p.342; Badsey, *Doctrine and Reform*, p.200.

49   See David Kenyon, *Horsemen in No Man's Land: British Cavalry and Trench Warfare 1914-1918* (Barnsley, Pen and Sword, 2011), pp 1-38; Richard Holmes, *Tommy: The British Soldier on the Western Front 1914-1918* (London, HarperCollins, 2004), pp.435-50, and Badsey, *Doctrine and Reform, passim.*

important than swords.[50] The cavalry, like the rest of the BEF, performed extremely well in low level tactics in 1914, including fighting very well dismounted, but suffered problems above brigade level.

The real lesson of this cavalry doctrinal debate was that senior generals, including corps commanders such as Ian Hamilton, Smith-Dorrien, and French himself when at Aldershot, could openly and successfully defy War Office doctrine with which they did not agree, and that the consequent and often bitter arguments harmed the Army far more than they could be worth. When in 1911 a similarly potentially divisive debate started over whether artillery fire in support of an infantry assault should be chiefly direct or indirect, and the extent to which artillery and infantry fire should be a preliminary or a support to the infantry assault, it was quietly allowed to fade away, in the belief that only the next war could show which side was right.[51] In 1912, Sir Charles Douglas (who would succeed French as CIGS after the Curragh Incident) noted as Inspector General that his "personal observation of three divisions of the Expeditionary Force" (the 2nd, 3rd and 4th Divisions) "has led me to conclude that each of the commanders of these divisions usually employs a definite [different] method of deploying his division and conducting an offensive action".[52] The strengths and weaknesses of this approach to doctrine were evident particularly in the fighting on the Aisne in September 1914, in repeated small incidents of British artillery shelling their own infantry, GHQ's request to its corps to issue instructions for newly arrived formations on the tactical situation (including such elementary points as not deploying on forward slopes), and the speed with which the adjustment in tactics was made.[53] But a problem that could not be as readily addressed in war was that this level of independence hampered the development of ideas on how to move formations larger than a division, a critical skill which was only starting to be addressed under French as CIGS in 1914.[54]

Although French had been designated as C-in-C of the BEF in 1906, in 1914 his command was not actually guaranteed; Esher wrote prophetically in 1910 that "it would be very difficult, if a big war broke out tomorrow, to prevent the General [French] being succeeded in command by Lord K[itchener]".[55] He resigned as CIGS in April 1914 on an issue of personal integrity over the Curragh Incident, although Asquith's wife Margot hinted at a political deal to a lady friend, writing that French "is a hot Liberal & of course comes back to a high place in a very short time".[56]

50   This at least is what Haig believed he heard French say in 1909, see Badsey, *Doctrine and Reform*, p.203.
51   Bidwell and Graham, *Fire-Power*, pp.11-15.
52   The National Archives (TNA) WO 163/18 Minutes of the Proceedings and Précis Prepared for the Army Council 1913' report of the Inspector General of the Forces for 1912. I owe this reference to Dr Spencer Jones.
53   Gardner, *Trial By Fire*, pp.92-5.
54   Brown, *British Logistics on the Western Front*, pp.30-1, and 48-51.
55   Esher to Maurice Brett (his second son) 30 September 1910, in Esher, *Journals and Letters*, p.24
56   Roy Jenkins, *Asquith*, (London, Collins, 1964), p.313. Jenkins's perspectives as a

He remained a permanent member of the CID, and no announcement was made regarding the BEF, although Churchill remembered later that in early July Sir John was frustrated that he would be left out of a forthcoming European war.[57] On 28 July (the day on which Austria-Hungary declared war) French was re-appointed by Asquith to his former post of Inspector General of the Forces; his memoirs state that two days later Douglas told him privately that he would indeed command the BEF; and although he appears to have been uncertain of his appointment as late as 2 August, it was officially confirmed on 4 August.[58]

French's appointment to command the BEF was a matter of political expediency for Asquith, who was principally concerned to limit the number of resignations from his cabinet, and to hold both his party and the country together as it went to war. His appointment of Kitchener as Secretary of State for War in the interval between his two council of war of 5 and 6 August was made with very much the same objective in mind. Asquith had kept the War Office himself after Colonel J.E.B Seely's resignation over the Curragh Incident, but his first idea of maintaining this position with Haldane as his advisor and *de facto* minister proved politically unacceptable. (Seely claimed after the second Downing Street council of war that Asquith had offered him one of two vacant cabinet posts, implying that this meant the War Office, but that he felt it was his duty to serve at the front, adding in his memoirs that French had pressed upon him his appointment as a supernumerary at BEF headquarters, but neither story seems very likely.)[59] As a member of the House of Lords, Kitchener could hold government office without the need for an election (by the conventions of the time, a cabinet minister appointed from the Commons would resign his seat and stand for re-election), and politically he was the perfect choice for the War Office. Although he held no military command, as a field marshal he also remained on the active list and habitually wore uniform (something not even Wellington had done while prime minister), and he was senior to French. The timing of both their appointments placed French in a difficult position in his relationship with Kitchener from the start. Speaking in the House of Lords in 1916 on the occasion of Kitchener's death, French related that "when at the outbreak of the present war I had reason to believe that I had been selected for the Chief Command in the field, I went to Lord Kitchener very early one morning" when Kitchener was still planning to return to Egypt, "and urged him to approach the Prime Minister and endeavour to arrange that he himself should take the place and that I should

professional politician on the Curragh Incident are of great value, although he notes on the same page that Margot Asquith's comment was "certainly unauthorised and probably inaccurate".

57   Winston Churchill, *Great Contemporaries* (London, Odhams, [1937] 1939), p.61.
58   Brock, *Asquith Letters*, p.129; [G.A. Riddell], *Lord Riddell's War Diary 1914-1918* (London, Ivor Nicholson and Watson, 1933), p.6.
59   [G.A. Riddell], *Lord Riddell's War Diary 1914-1918* (London, Ivor Nicholson and Watson, 1933), pp.9-10; J.E.B. Seely, *Adventure* (London, William Heinemann, 1930), p.173.

accompany him as his Chief of the Staff".[60] The story sounds incredible, but French had no reason to lie, especially in so public a forum. He may perhaps have wished to cast himself in the role that Kitchener had originally played for Roberts in the Boer War, but if French did indeed offer to serve under Kitchener, then the suggestion was about to rebound upon him.

An important aspect of the authority of a C-in-C in the Field was the right to appoint and remove his own staff and lower-level commanders, as Roberts had done in South Africa; although like much else about the Army that authority was undefined and depended on circumstances. One of French's reforms while at Aldershot Command after the Boer War had been to insist that "the staff I work with in peace shall be the staff which I take to war,"[61] and this reform meant that in 1914 the Aldershot I Corps under Haig had the only staff above divisional level (or brigade level for the cavalry) that had trained together. But on mobilisation in 1914, French was confronted as C-in-C BEF with exactly the same issue. The existing plan was for Grierson to be French's CGS, but he was instead appointed to command II Corps; French then requested Wilson as CGS, but was told by Douglas that Murray, the designated BEF QMG (and French's former chief of staff at Aldershot) was being given the position, and Wilson was to take BEF Operations, a post for which he was too senior. This left the post of BEF QMG open, and Robertson was appointed almost by chance.[62] French's response was to invent the post of Sub-Chief for Wilson, and to work through him rather than Murray, with resulting confusion when Wilson and Murray issued conflicting orders, Murray refused to make decisions without French and Wilson present, and Wilson failed to inform French of crucial events.

French's behaviour was not only predictable given the conventions regarding the authority of a C-in-C in the Field, it also closely paralleled his response in South Africa when in February 1900 Roberts had attempted to impose an unwanted chief of staff on him in preference to Haig, an arrangement which French was able to reverse after a few days.[63] Anyone who knew this, including Kitchener who had been a witness, would have known of French's likely response to any attempt to impose officers on him. On Grierson's death, Ian Hamilton wrote to French asking for command of II Corps, and assuming that this had Kitchener's backing French wrote a polite and formal note pointing out that Hamilton was too senior, and requesting

60   (Hansard) House of Lords Debates 20 June 1916 volume 22 cc. 315-22; French, *1914*,
      pp.333-4.
61   Quoted in Samuels, *Command or Control?* p.54.
62   Wilson was a major general and Operations was a brigadier general's post. Keith Jeffrey
      points out correctly that there is no *contemporary* evidence for Murray being imposed on
      French, or for the belief that Wilson's appointment was blocked because of his behaviour
      over the Curragh Incident; however, the creation of the Sub-Chief post for Wilson
      and French's attitude towards Murray and Wilson is at least very highly suggestive that
      later accounts for French's opposition to Murray's appointment are correct; see Jeffrey,
      Sir Henry Wilson, pp.132-3, and also William Robertson, *From Private to Field Marshal*
      (London, Constable, 1921), p.196.
63   Badsey, *Doctrine and Reform*, pp.101-5.

Plumer. Kitchener's imposition of Smith-Dorrien (whose long-standing feud with French was well known) in command of II Corps, and his generally provocative behaviour towards French, has been excused on the grounds that Kitchener was a former Royal Engineer officer who had spent 20 years in Egypt and India, and so was unfamiliar with the complexities of the British Army. But Kitchener had dealt closely with British Army officers since at least the Boer War, including in his last posting in Egypt, where he had shared his residence with Julian Byng, and there were many officers in the War Office who could have advised him. French's conclusion from Kitchener's behaviour on 1 September that he had "assumed the air of a Commander-in-Chief", [64] and was trying to revive for himself the defunct post of C-in-C of the Army was neither emotional nor irrational; making Kitchener C-in-C of the Army was in fact suggested by Esher in 1915.

In his dealings with French, Kitchener largely by-passed Douglas as CIGS, described by Esher as "honest, incapable of subterfuge or of misplaced enthusiasm".[65] French was the first C-in-C to hold an independent overseas command while simultaneously being within a day's travel of Whitehall and in close telegraph contact with his government superiors. Before 1914, the British Army had expected to fight its wars far overseas, with delayed and inadequate communications, and the powers of a British C-in-C in the Field reflected this. By an arrangement dating from 1858, a C-in-C received campaign 'instructions' from the Secretary of State for War to whom he reported, by-passing the C-in-C of the Army in Whitehall, and it was up to a C-in-C in the Field to plan his own campaign.[66] This system was supported by successive governments on the grounds that the country could not predict its requirements for future wars, as well as by French and Ian Hamilton in 1901, and continued after the creation of the General Staff.[67]

Kitchener gave his formal 'instructions' to French on two occasions in the course of the campaign. The first, widely quoted by historians, was issued at the start, specifying that the BEF was an independent command (the document was reproduced in its entirety in Kitchener's official biography in 1920, and in Edmonds's official history two years later).[68] An important light was cast on Sir John's relations with his allies when in April 1915 Esher told him that the French War Minister, Allexandre Millerand, had recently been "thunderstruck" to learn of Kitchener's instructions, and that he and Joffre had believed up to that date that Sir John was being obstructive by resisting his government's orders to subordinate the BEF to GQG.[69] The second occasion was their meeting of 1 September, when Kitchener copied to French his telegram to Whitehall which specified that "French's troops are

64   French *1914*, pp.99-100.
65   Journal of Lord Esher, 13 August 1914, in Esher, *Journals and Letters*, p.178.
66   Bidwell and Graham, *Fire-Power*, pp.43-8.
67   Samuels, *Command or Control?* p.38.
68   Sir George Arthur, *Life of Lord Kitchener*, *Volume III* (London, Macmillan, 1920), pp.25-26.
69   Imperial War Museum, French Papers, Esher to French, 3 April 1915, and quoted in Holmes, *The Little Field Marshal*, p.202.

now engaged in the fighting line, where he will remain conforming to the movements of the French Army, although at the same time acting with caution to avoid being in any way unsupported on his flanks," adding to French "please consider it as an instruction," but that "By being in the fighting line you of course understand I mean dispositions of your troops in contact with, though possibly behind, the French as they were today; of course you will judge as regards their position in this respect".[70] Criticisms by historians of French for the slowness of the BEF in its advance in the Battle of the Marne and up to the Aisne have ignored not only its exhaustion and severe supply problems (and also some appalling weather), but the fact that French was simply obeying Kitchener.

French's dependence on Wilson and on his own aides-de-camp contributed to the breakdown of GHQ staffwork in the retreat from Mons, and also possibly to the bafflingly poor writing style of his telegrams of 30-31 August announcing that he intended to pull the BEF out of the line altogether, in response to which Kitchener was sent out to France, in Asquith's words, "to unravel the situation and if necessary put the fear of God in them all".[71] Asquith's anxiety was understandable, since on 19 August, after a thorough briefing by Kitchener to the cabinet, he had been left with the impression that the BEF would advance "in the rear of some 5 French Army Corps, and ought to give effective support,"[72] rather than being placed in the path of the strongest German forces. Kitchener's journey was prompted not only by French's statement that he intended to pull the BEF out of the line and leave the battle to the French, but also by his claim that he had repeatedly pressed to take the offensive, a confusing contradiction that was interpreted as instability or panic. A little thought in Whitehall at the time would have shown his probable meaning, since Sir John had been pressing the *French* to attack while he tried to preserve the BEF; but in such a moment of drama this simple explanation was missed.[73]

Famously, Kitchener arrived for his meeting with French in his field marshal's uniform, and French over-reacted, complaining to Asquith of "Lord Kitchener's apparent assertion of his right to exercise the power and authority of a Commander-

---

70   The original telegram from Kitchener to Whitehall is TNA WO 159/6, Kitchener Papers, 1 September 1914; the version given to French is in the Imperial War Museum, French Papers, Kitchener to French 1 September 1914, also first published in Arthur, *Life of Lord Kitchener, III*, pp.55-6; for the supply problems of the BEF in the advance see Brown, *British Logistics on the Western Front*, pp.61-3.

71   Brock, *Asquith Letters*, p.213.

72   Brock, *Asquith Letters*, p.179; for Asquith's lack of understanding of the BEF's position see George H. Cassar, *Asquith as War Leader* (London, Hambledon, 1994), pp.46-8. Lanrezac's Fifth Army was composed of four corps and a cavalry corps, but since the French had five armies in the field at the start of mobilisation, it is also possible that Asquith confused armies with army corps.

73   French's telegrams to Kitchener on 30 and 31 August are in TNA WO 33/713 series. They are open to interpretation in a variety of ways, a point which I owe to Stephen Harris.

in-Chief in the Field".[74] Esher's judgment was that "If he is not very careful [French] will be superseded. He has shown temper, there is no doubt about it. Very stupid thing to do. His telegrams have been full of inconsistencies".[75] But French soon realised his mistake, writing to Churchill on 10 September that "I fear I have been a little unreasonable about K[itchener] and his visit," but that "we have been through a hard time and perhaps my temper is not made any better for it".[76] Churchill came out to speak to French, as did Esher on 26 September, recording that "I have never seen the Field-Marshal look better in health and spirits. Throughout the retreat from Le Cateau he remained unperturbed and cheerful," and telling French that "Kitchener had taken the episode quite humorously and good-naturedly".[77] The root of the problem was that Asquith and his ministers could only wait anxiously for news from across the Channel, and listen to stories from any returning senior officer. Esher, who as always was keen to promote harmony, noted in November that "When Lord K[itchener] first asked me to go over to France it was with a view to smoothing out these constantly recurring difficulties that were invariably the work of tittle-tattlers and mischief-makers. Sir John's impulsive, warm-hearted nature, affectionate but suspicious, makes him open to easy attack".[78]

Whatever his skill in English, Sir John's inability to learn French has been the subject of repeated humorous anecdotes about his dealings with his allies. He became tongue-tied and embarrassed when trying to speak in French; although both Churchill and Kitchener spoke the language at least as badly, if more confidently. Descriptions of conferences with French officers in 1914 make it clear that he could follow a conversation, and he could probably read papers adequately (his memoirs reproduce some French documents without translation). There was also no shortage of interpreters on either side with the BEF, including Huguet, Edward Spiers, and Wilson; Grierson was fluent in French, and Haig was at least competent.[79] In contrast, neither Joffre nor Foch (or his chief of staff Weygand) could hold a conversation in

74   French, *1914* pp.99-100.
75   Esher to Maurice Brett, 2 September 1914, in Esher, *Journals and Letters*, p.182.
76   Quoted in Brock, *Asquith Letters*, p.229.
77   Journal of Lord Esher, 26 September 1914, in Esher, *Journals and Letters*, pp.187-8.
78   Journal of Lord Esher, 11 November 1914, in Esher, *Journals and Letters*, p.195; the role of Major General F.S. Robb, IGC of the BEF in shaping Kitchener's view of French's intentions on 30 August appears to have been particularly significant, see Cassar, *Kitchener's War*, pp.88-9. There is a parallel to be drawn between French's experience commanding the BEF in 1914 and Sir Bernard Montgomery's experience commanding in the Battle of Normandy in 1944: in the problems and misunderstandings caused with Montgomery's political and military superiors by communications back and forth across the English Channel (although under far more favourable conditions than those faced by French); the way that American popular history relegates Montgomery to the position of the ineffectual man at the top rather than the victor of the battle; and an obsession with his private and personal failings rather than his skills as a general.
79   Interestingly, Edward Spears, *Liaison 1914: A Narrative of the Great Retreat* (London, Eyre and Spottiswode, 1930), p.298 note suggests that "General Wilson did not speak French as well during this stage of the war as he did later".

English, and before their first conference at GQG on 16 August 1914 Joffre had never even troubled to meet Sir John.[80] Despite the planned role of French Fifth Army in co-operation with the BEF, there is no evidence that Lanrezac learned or understood English. Delightfully, French is credited with playing on both languages that "*au fond* they are a low lot, and one always has to remember the class these French generals come from".[81]

The chief complaint against French from other BEF generals in 1914, particularly during the retreat from Mons, was that he had not given them the bigger picture, the "general idea" as the term was emerging in British doctrine, within which they could improvise and act. The first of several consequences of this was his decision to leave I Corps and II Corps to co-ordinate the start of the retreat between themselves, leading to the separation of the corps by the Forest of Mormal. The simplest explanation for French's behaviour is that, from the BEF's concentration on 20 August through to the end of the retreat, he did not himself know what was happening, but was not prepared to admit this openly. His own solution to the problems of making command decisions with inadequate information was:

> [A] life-long experience of military study and thought had taught me that the principle of the tactical employment of troops must be instinctive. I knew that in putting the science of war into practice, it was necessary that its main tenets should form, so to speak, part of one's flesh and blood. In war there is little time to think, and the right thing to do must come like a flash – it must present itself to the mind as perfectly *obvious*.[82]

One consequence of this approach was that in 1914 French did not need to set out his thinking systematically, in the manner of a staff appreciation necessary for a large conscript army. This puts historians in the frustrating position of having to guess from his behaviour the motivations and plans that he may not have articulated fully even to himself. French's command style was at first largely dictated for him by the highly uncertain strategic situation and the failure of the BEF to communicate properly within itself. But by the time of First Ypres he appears to have adopted consciously the role of concentrating on politics, reserves, and offering reassurance, leaving his corps commanders to fight the battle. The line that subordinate generals might not cross with French in making these decisions was broad and somewhat elastic. He exacted no penalty when Haig disregarded his orders on 24 August by withdrawing I Corps from the Mons area without co-ordinating his move with II

80   French, *1914*, p.34; for the language skills of various French and British figures see Greenhalgh, *Victory Through Coalition*, pp.9-10.

81   Quoted in Greenhalgh, *Victory through Coalition*, p.8. What the reliable original source might be for this often-quoted little quip is uncertain; but if accurately attributed this wordplay (*au fond* – profoundly or ultimately – means literally 'at lowest') has been missed by historians who believe Sir John's skills in French were poor.

82   French, *1914*, p.11

Corps; or later when Rawlinson disregarded orders by halting IV Corps' advance on Menin on 16-18 October.[83] French only reacted badly when he felt that a subordinate had completely usurped his authority and had placed the BEF in jeopardy, contrary to Kitchener's original instruction, which warned that "In minor operations you should be careful that your subordinates understand that risk of serious losses should only be taken when such a risk is authoritatively considered to be commensurate with the object in view," and that "officers may well be reminded that in this their first experience of European warfare, a greater measure of caution must be employed".[84] So, French reversed Haig's promise to Lanrezac on 28 August to commit I Corps to the Battle of Guise because he felt that this could endanger the whole BEF. This approach was consistent with French's anger at Smith-Dorrien after Le Cateau, the outcome of which was due to German mistakes as much as British achievements, and which could have resulted in the BEF being destroyed in detail.

French's confident wider pronouncements have been taken, when compared with his worried telegrams, diary entries, and conversations, as evidence of indecision or inconsistency. But in Army culture, "cheerfulness", the maintenance of morale through an outward show of confidence and agreement, was one of the most treasured traits of a general, with its absence ("funk") being immediately remarked upon; and increasingly as C-in-C French's most important role became its maintenance. On 26 August as Le Cateau was being fought one of the GHQ staff noted French as looking "fit and quite cheery"; on 30 August (the day of the "panicking" telegrams) Spiers as a young liaison officer remembered "The impression that Sir John made on me that morning was very reassuring. He was one of the coolest and calmest people at G.H.Q. It was wonderful how he kept up his spirits in spite of the prevailing atmosphere of gloom";[85] and such examples may be multiplied many times. Even Haig recorded, when French visited I Corps HQ at White Chateau on 31 October to hear that the line was broken and the battle almost certainly lost (shortly before the counterattack at Gheluvelt), that French "could not have been nicer at such a time of crisis".[86]

William Robertson wrote shortly after French's death that "Sir John was extraordinarily popular with the troops, and I doubt if any other General in the Army could have sustained in them to the same extent the courage and resolution which they displayed during the trying circumstances of the first six months of the war".[87] French's high reputation among the ordinary soldiers of the BEF lasted at least throughout the First Battle of Ypres. From the war's start, local newspapers in Britain encouraged their readers to send in letters they received from soldiers

83   These episodes are discussed by Gardner, *Trial By Fire*, pp.48-9 and pp.152-3.
84   Quoted in Arthur, *Life of Lord Kitchener, Volume III*, p.26.
85   C.R. Woodroffe, the BEF's DAAQMG, quoted in Jeffrey, *Sir Henry Wilson*, p.136; Spears, *Liaison 1914*, p.281; Spiers anglicised his name to Spears after the war.
86   Quoted in Beckett, *Ypres 1914*, p.138.
87   William Robertson, *Soldiers and Statesmen 1914-1918; Volume I* (New York, Charles Scribner's Sons, 1926), p.71.

serving with the BEF, from which anonymous extracts were published. In early 1915, the *Liverpool Weekly Courier* ran a story about French's supposed actions on an unspecified day of the battle:

> In the thickest of that day's fighting he left his motor-car and ran afoot to a wood, where a brigade was giving ground. As he rushed in a wounded private staggered back into his arms. General [sic] French laid him gently down and went on talking to his men, encouraging them, and rallying them until they held.[88]

If something like this incident did take place, then it is highly likely that the general involved was a more junior figure misidentified as French; but the soldier who was the source of the story believed that French would behave in such a way, and so did the newspaper.

The critical days for French's philosophy of command were the first of the retreat, with soldiers hallucinating on the march from lack of rest in the August heat, commanders threatening to surrender their battalions, and morale and cohesion both plummeting. On 27 August Colonel Huguet telegraphed to Joffre that "conditions are such that for the moment the British army no longer exists".[89] On 28 August French spent most of the day visiting the troops on the road and delivering short speeches; "These glorious British soldiers," he remembered, "listened to the few words I had to say to them with the spirit of heroes and the confidence of children".[90] The experience convinced him that nothing but pulling the BEF out of the line altogether could preserve a nucleus of experienced officers and soldiers. Next day he ordered the BEF's first rest since Mons, the first troops of Pulteney's III Corps began to come up, and on 31 August French once more spent time away from headquarters to address as many units as he could find. He came to believe that by seeing for himself the desperate state of his soldiers, and by connecting with them at a personal level as only a C-in-C could, he had saved the BEF from disintegration, and his country from disaster. Colonel Huguet later recounted that Foch had told him that to put French in good humour it was only necessary "to tell him that he has just saved England," and that French's reply was "But my dear fellow, I know it only too well".[91] As the BEF recovered, almost every subordinate was ready to maintain that *their* particular unit had not been close to disintegration, but whether French's assessment was an over-reaction is a matter of judgement rather than fact.

The story that French (and Wilson) had panicked became the acceptable alternative to an examination of how well the individual battalions of the BEF, and their commanders, had really performed in the retreat. For some, French's behaviour

---

88   *The Liverpool Weekly Courier*, 20 March 1915, quoted in Michael Finn, 'Local Heroes: war news and the construction of "community" in Britain 1914-18,' *Historical Research*, Volume 83, Number 221 (2001) p.534.

89   Quoted in Gardner, *Trial By Fire*, p.60.

90   French, *1914*, p.88.

91   Huguet, *Britain and the War*, p.147.

had been an abnegation of command. Wilson in his diary on 1 September railed at both French and Murray as incompetent, complaining that "Sir John has not once taken command," and that French and Murray were leaving the work and responsibility to him.[92] Whether the BEF could have been pulled out of the line and the Battle of the Marne fought without it, as French himself believed, has also remained largely unexplored by historians.[93] But French was correct to think that committing the BEF to further battles would indeed destroy it. The legend of First Ypres as the graveyard of the old BEF must be modified by the fact that up to 4 October the BEF had already suffered 31,709 casualties, with some battalions being almost wiped out.[94] The long-term consequence of Kitchener's instruction to French on 1 September to keep the BEF in the line was the woeful lack of fit and surviving experienced officers and troops that beset the British Army for the next two years. In part, the failures at Gallipoli and in the early stages of the Battle of the Somme were the legacy of Kitchener's decision.

Once the BEF's line stabilised on the Aisne later in September, and French had time to think and plan, he showed a flash of the same generalship skills that had earned him praise as a cavalry commander in the Boer War. Between 4 and 17 October, the BEF in successive stages entrained to move northwards from the Aisne, with the cavalry moving by road. Briefed in advance about this move by Kitchener, Asquith on 29 September gave his understanding of French's ambitious new scheme as "to make with his whole force a great outflanking march via Amiens, Arras, Douai, Tournay [sic], to the line across Belgium from Brussels to Cologne. He thinks he could do it in a week or 9 days and the long march would be good for his troops. It would relieve Antwerp (which is going to be sorely pressed) take the Germans in their flank and rear, break up their communications, and if successful put an end to their invasion of France".[95] The whole manoeuvre resembled the swing of a weighted ball on the end of a rod and chain, with II Corps and III Corps, joining up with Rawlinson's IV Corps, forming the rod as they came into line, the Cavalry Corps forming the chain as it swung round into southern Belgium to envelop Lille from the north and north-east, and the concentrated I Corps – the best formation in the BEF – as the solid ball at the end of the arc. The manoeuvre came to a halt as the BEF began to encounter German troops at Messines and Armentieres during the second week of October, and Sir John expressed his frustration, declaring that it was impossible for him to plan his campaign properly since MacDonogh kept revising

92   Imperial War Museum, Wilson Diary, 29 August 1914.
93   Both Cassar, *Sir John French*, p.134 and Greenhalgh, *Victory Through Coalition*, p.19 assert in a sentence that the Battle of the Marne would have been lost without the BEF's contribution; French's view was that the French Fifth and Sixth Armies could have advanced joining their inner flanks.
94   E.g. in the course of I Corps attacks on 14 September, 1st Cameron Highlanders lost 600 casualties, and five other battalions lost approximately 350 casualties each; see Kendall, Aisne 1914, p.248, and Beckett, Ypres 1914, p.41.
95   Brock, *Asquith Letters*, p.256.

his estimate of the German divisions facing the BEF substantially upwards.[96] French also confessed in his memoirs that despite the static nature of the fighting on the Aisne, it was his "failure in the north to pass the Lys River, during the last days of October," that finally converted him to accepting the realities of defensive firepower and trench warfare.[97] Nevertheless, his manoeuvre had been well enough planned to cover all eventualities, and left the BEF positioned to fight First Ypres with its strong I Corps deployed exactly where it was needed, to defend the city and the route to the Channel ports.

French's decision to relocate the BEF from the Aisne to Belgium derived at least in part from his own view, dating from 1905, that in a war against Germany it was both politically and strategically better for the British Army to associate itself closely with Belgium (which it was widely assumed would be invaded), rather than becoming a small contingent under the domination of France. Preliminary negotiations with the Belgians took place in 1906, and French revived them unsuccessfully in 1912, led by G.T.M. Bridges.[98] While planning the purely military aspects of how to move the BEF from the Aisne to Ypres, French was also faced with considerable political issues, including that the BEF would be temporarily split in two as it moved, and that Rawlinson's IV Corps, as it fell back from the defence of Antwerp, was not actually placed under his command until 12 October. At one extreme, if Antwerp had held out Sir John might have got his preferred strategic result of association with the Belgians rather than the French; and at the other, the BEF might have been be further fragmented, or he might have lost command altogether. French's reaction to these possibilities was to show that he also could play at high politics. When on 5 October President Poincaré visited him to express concern about the BEF's role, French got Poincaré to press the British government to confirm his command of all British forces on the Western Front, and later berated Joffre for trying to express his own concerns about the BEF through Poincaré rather than addressing him directly as an equal.[99]

French's views while CIGS before 1914 were very close to those of Asquith on wider political issues, to "wait and see", and not to create problems before they actually arose. At the two councils of war on 5 and 6 August 1914, he raised the possibility of sending the BEF to Antwerp, but his general view was recorded as that the BEF should be sent to France, "a safe place" for concentration chosen and "events should be awaited".[100] The reasonable expectation, as the first of the BEF departed for France, was that it would play a subordinate role in a secondary part of the front, and that even if the Germans came through Belgium in strength north of the Meuse,

---

96   Beckett, *Ypres 1914*, pp.61-2 and pp.65-6 footnote 25 gives both versions of French's alleged comment, which do not differ substantially; the source for one version was MacDonogh himself.

97   French, *1914*, p.145.

98   Gooch, *The Plans of War*, p.281; Beckett, *Ypres 1914*, pp.9-10.

99   Huguet, *Britain and the* War, pp.122-3; Greenhalgh, *Victory Through Coalition*, p.20.

100   TNA CAB 22/1 Committee of Imperial Defence, Secretary's Notes of a War Council, 5 August 1914 and 6 August 1914.

the fortress system at Liege and Namur would delay their advance for some weeks, giving the British the chance to organise and prepare larger forces. When this failed to happen, Sir John French was thrust into a position of command of incredible complexity and danger, from which he and the BEF emerged victorious some four months later. As Asquith later remembered, French's last words to him on departing were that "we must be prepared for a reverse or two at the first".[101]

101   Brock, *Asquith Letters*, p.191.

2

Major General Sir Archibald Murray

Chief of Staff, GHQ

J.M. Bourne[1]

Archie Murray filled some of the most important posts in the British Army during the Great War: Chief of the General Staff [CGS] of the British Expeditionary Force [BEF] (August 1914-January 1915); Deputy Chief (then Chief) of the Imperial General Staff [CIGS] (February 1915-January 1916); GOC-in-C Egyptian Expeditionary Force [EEF] (January 1916-July 1917); GOC Aldershot Command (October 1917-November 1919). Despite this, his name is virtually unknown to the British public and he does not figure prominently in the recent scholarly historiography of the war. There are no modern studies of Murray in any of the posts he held.[2] He left no substantial body of personal papers.[3] He wrote no memoir and he has no biographer. He steered deliberately clear of wartime and post-war controversies, remaining loyal to the men with whom he served, notably Sir John French. Other major players in the events of 1914 were not so restrained. Sir John French and Sir Horace Smith-Dorrien wrote their memoirs, self-serving and highly unreliable in French's case. French and Sir Douglas Haig kept diaries and, most importantly, so did Sir Henry Wilson. Much of what we know about Murray in 1914 derives from Wilson's diary, a document that

---

1   I am grateful to Professor William Philpott for discussions about Murray and for lending me the notes for his lecture on 'Sir John French and his Chiefs of Staff' delivered to the University of Birmingham on 20 March 2004.
2   The fullest treatment of Murray's wartime career remains the volume of the British Official History covering his command of the EEF: Lieutenant-General Sir George Macmunn and Captain Cyril Falls, *History of the Great War based on official documents by direction of the Historical Section of the Committee of Imperial Defence. Military Operations. Egypt and Palestine:* [Vol. I] *From the outbreak of War with Germany to June 1917* (London: 1928)
3   The main collection of personal papers is in the Imperial War Museum: Department of Documents [IWM: 79/48/2.] The National Archives has a small number of 'Murray Papers' [TNA: WO 79/62-65] and the Churchill Archives Centre has some correspondence with Sir E.L. Spears.

Sir Archibald Murray. (Editor's collection)

is very much a tainted source where Murray is concerned. Sir William Robertson, Murray's successor as CGS, left a substantial collection of papers. All have modern scholarly biographies, several in the case of Haig. Murray's reputation was destined to wither and die in the shadows cast by his contemporaries.

Archibald James Murray was born in Sutton, Surrey, on 21 April 1860.[4] He was the fourth child and second son of nine children of the marriage of Charles Murray (1818-1879) and Anna Graves (1830-1917). Murray's father is described in the *Dictionary of National Biography* as a "landed proprietor", which sounds rather grand. He is more prosaically described in the 1871 Census as a "farmer of 209" acres, at Woodhouse Farm, Ashford Hill, Kingsclere, Hampshire.[5] Archie Murray was educated at Cheltenham College, from where, in 1877, he went to the Royal Military College, Sandhurst. There is no evidence of a family military connection or any indication of how free Murray was to choose his own career. Nor does his commission in the 27th Foot (later the Royal Inniskilling Fusiliers), an unfashionable regiment, on 13 August 1879 suggest that the

4   The *Dictionary of National Biography* gives Murray's birthplace as 'Woodhouse, near Kingslere, Hampshire', but this is contradicted by the *The Peerage* and by the 1891 Census.

5   The Murray family evidently also had an Indian connection. Charles Murray's first child, Charles Templeton Warden Murray, was born at Bangalore, in India. Anna Murray was the daughter of an Irish judge who had served in Ceylon.

Murray family had access to military patronage. Murray's pre-war military career is that of a man making his way on the basis of his abilities alone.

Brigadier-General Sir James Edmonds, the British Official Historian, dismissed Murray as "a complete nonentity" in the pre-war army.[6] This seems not only unfair but also absurd. Murray's rise through the ranks and positions of the Edwardian army was impressive, if unspectacular. His entry to the Staff College in 1897 indicates a serious commitment to his profession and a degree of personal and professional ambition. His fellow students at Camberley included not only Sir Douglas Haig and Sir William Robertson but also Murray's successor as GOC EEF, Sir Edmund Allenby. It was at Staff College that Murray seems to have gained the nickname "Old Archie". Generals' nicknames are worthy of consideration. "Old Archie" might imply 'good Old Archie', a decent and reliable chap. These were character traits much valued in the late Victorian and Edwardian army. But it might also mean 'bit of an old woman Archie', a nitpicker, fusser and worrier. Haig, for one, was prone to dismissing Murray as an "old woman".[7] Murray's manner throughout his career was thoughtful and reserved and he appeared to his contemporaries to be old beyond his years, which in Murray's case does not seem to have been a compliment, 'prematurely aged' rather than 'wise'.

The outbreak of the South African War, however, gave Murray the opportunity to unveil himself as a man of action and courage. He was appointed intelligence officer on the staff of Sir William Penn Symons, GOC Natal. Murray was with Penn Symons when he was killed at Talana Hill, the first major battle of the war (20 October 1899). Penn Symons's chief of staff was also killed. The second in command, the aged and unwell Brigadier-General J.H. Yule, appointed Murray to be chief of staff and it was Murray who skilfully extricated the British forces from contact with the enemy and brought them back to their base in Ladysmith.

Talana Hill was the making of Murray. Trained staff officers were at a premium in South Africa. Many of the leading field commanders were not themselves staff trained and they valued officers who could write clear and concise orders that did not result in troops getting lost or attacking the wrong objectives. Murray became sought after. He served on the staff of Sir George White during the siege of Ladysmith (November 1899 - February 1900) and was then senior staff officer to Sir Archibald Hunter (GOC 10th Division). Hunter was a protégé of Kitchener, which probably did Murray's chances of professional advancement no harm. On 29 October 1900 he took command of 2nd Battalion Royal Inniskilling Fusiliers, who were stationed in India. This meant that Murray had ticked another important box in his professional career and he was still only forty years old. His battalion was deployed to South Africa in February 1902 and it was while leading his men during an attack in the northern Transvaal that Murray suffered a serious stomach wound in April 1902.

6   See Nikolas Gardner, *Trial by Fire: Command and the British Expeditionary Force in 1914* (Westport, CT. & London: Praeger, 2003), p.5.
7   See, for example, Gary Sheffield & John Bourne (eds), *Douglas Haig: War Diaries and Letters 1914-1918* (London: Weidenfeld & Nicolson, 2005), p.58.

Murray's health has been at the centre of debates about him. There is a persistent undercurrent in contemporary memoirs suggesting that Murray never recovered from his wounding and that as a result he lacked the physical energy and robustness so necessary for a soldier in the field. There is no doubt that an abdominal wound was serious. Precise details of Murray's wound and the treatment he received are not known, but there was reluctance at the time to operate on the abdomen for fear of introducing infection that would result in peritonitis. (This reluctance was rapidly abandoned during the First World War, when it was realised that without surgical intervention soldiers wounded in the stomach would die long before they had the chance of developing peritonitis.) It is not inconceivable that Murray was left with a persistent and enervating condition.[8]

During his convalescence, if Murray was inclined to reflect on the state of his career, he would surely have concluded that once he was fit again his career was in a good place. He had passed staff college. He had shown initiative, decision and leadership in the field. His name had become known among senior officers and his services valued by them. He had commanded a battalion of his regiment in combat. He had been decorated and mentioned in despatches. Murray's career duly prospered. He was Assistant Adjutant-General 1st Division, Aldershot (1905-7), Director of Military Training at the War Office (1907-12), a key posting in an army that was undergoing substantive reform, and Inspector of Infantry (1912-14). He was made KCB in the Birthday Honours of 1911. On 1 February 1912 Sir Archibald Murray was appointed GOC 2nd Division, one of the formations that would become part of the BEF in any future war.

Following the South African War the British Army underwent a period of self-analysis, followed by structural, doctrinal and equipment reform. This was in the context of a re-ordering of British diplomacy that put Anglo-French and Anglo-Russian friendship at its centre. In order to give the government the ability to intervene in a continental war an Expeditionary Force was established. The size and composition of this force bore no relationship to Britain's actual or potential military obligations, but consisted of the largest number of troops available once the demands of imperial policing had been met. This amounted to c.100,000 troops, formed into six infantry divisions and five cavalry brigades.[9] Each infantry division had a designated commander, though the majority of the formations existed mainly on paper. The exceptions to this were the 1st and 2nd Divisions and 5th Cavalry Brigade, based at Aldershot, whose GOC would become the commander of I Corps in time of war. On the eve of war the designated commanders of the six infantry divisions of the BEF, besides Murray, were Major-General S.H. Lomax (1st Division), Major-General H.I.W. Hamilton (3rd Division), Major-General T.D'O. Snow (4th Division), Major-General Sir C. Fergusson Bt. (5th Division) and Major-General J.L. Keir (6th Division). Murray was the only one of these men who did not take his formation to war.

---

8   I am grateful to Dr F.G.A. Noon for discussions about contemporary abdominal surgery.
9   In the event the BEF deployed a Cavalry Division, commanded by Major-General Edmund Allenby.

Murray was instead removed from command of 2nd Division and appointed Chief of the General Staff of the BEF. The last minute nature of Murray's appointment is indicative of how *ad hoc* were the BEF's staff arrangements. In November 1912 Sir John French (then CIGS) was assured that in the event of a European war in the near future he would become Commander-in-Chief of the BEF. French, in turn, assured Sir James Grierson that Grierson would become his Chief of the General Staff.[10] This is the nearest the BEF got to having a designated staff and by the summer of 1914 even these limited and flimsy agreements had more or less disintegrated. Two events were instrumental in this. The first was the British Army autumn manoeuvres of 22 - 25 September 1913, which took place near Daventry in Northamptonshire. Their purpose was to give Sir John French the opportunity to practise commanding two corps against a skeleton force. French did rather badly and was subjected to a hostile press, led by the military correspondent of *The Times*, Colonel Charles Repington.[11] French typically laid the blame at the door of his chief of staff, Grierson, who was equally unimpressed with French's performance. From that moment, the post of CGS of the BEF was effectively vacant. The second event was the so-called Curragh Incident (or Mutiny) of 20 March 1914, when a group of officers of 3rd Cavalry Brigade, based at the Curragh Camp in Ireland, threatened to resign if ordered to participate in coercing Ulster into accepting Irish Home Rule. One of the results of this furore was French's resignation as CIGS, leaving in doubt who would command the BEF in the event of war. There was certainly doubt in French's mind. He was not informed that he was still the government's choice to command the BEF until 30 July 1914, when he was summoned to a meeting with the Chief of the Imperial General Staff, Sir Charles Douglas,[12] and at that moment it was still uncertain whether Britain would go to war.

Once assured that the command was his, French's most pressing need was for a Chief of the General Staff. It is far from clear how the appointment process worked. The British Army did not operate a 'new football manager' system, whereby the newly-installed commander is allowed to replace the existing staff with his own tried and trusted lieutenants. Later in the war, French's successor as Commander-in-Chief of the BEF, Douglas Haig, proved unable to choose his own Chief of the General Staff on either of the two occasions that the post became vacant. There is no paper trail to indicate why Murray was chosen in August 1914, who chose him or whether French expressed a preference for Murray or for anyone else.[13] Some commentators, notably Nikolas Gardner, have averred that French wanted Henry Wilson.[14] There is no contemporary evidence for this and it seems to be a reading backwards of French's

---

10   D.S. MacDiarmid, *The Life of Sir James Moncrieff Grierson* (London: Constable, 1923), p.250.

11   See Andrew Whitmarsh, 'British Army Manoeuvres and the Development of Military Aviation', *War in History*, 14 (3) (2007), pp.325-46.

12   The government does not appear to have considered an alternative to French, which in the circumstances is rather surprising.

13   Edmonds, in the original DNB entry on Murray, believed that French had asked for Murray.

14   Gardner, *Trial by Fire*, p.5.

apparent preference for Wilson to succeed Murray in January 1915, a preference that had no effect on the actual choice of successor. French offers no explanation in his memoirs for Murray's appointment. A CGS was urgently needed. Murray was to hand. He had the necessary seniority. He was staff trained. He had known Sir John French for ten years, working quite closely with him when French was GOC Aldershot and then CIGS. Unlike Wilson, Murray brought with him no political baggage and no professional enemies. His was a sensible, sound and safe appointment. Murray was, in short, unobjectionable.

Murray was appointed CGS on 5 August. He found himself head of a staff that had been formed from scratch and whom he first met at the Polygon Hotel, Southampton, shortly before embarking for France. On 14 August he sailed on board HMS *Sentinel*, landing at Boulogne. The BEF's headquarters were established at Amiens the same day before removing to Le Cateau on 16 August. A week later the BEF found itself in battle at Mons in Belgium; the following day there began a precipitate retreat. To use an old motoring expression, Murray had no time to 'run in' the organisation of which he was head before the BEF as a whole ran into the main forces of the German army. It should occasion no surprise that things began to unravel remarkably quickly.

What would now be called the 'job description' of a Chief of the General Staff was set out in the British Army's *Field Service Regulations. Part II. Organization and Administration. 1909 [FSR]*:

> The power and responsibility of co-ordinating staff work at general headquarters is vested in the C.-in-C., but, since it is not desirable that the C.-in-C. should himself be burdened with this duty, *he will delegate it to such extent as he may think fit to the C.G.S.*,[15] who is his responsible adviser on all matters affecting military operations, through whom he exercises his functions of command, and by whom all orders issued to field units, except as hereinafter specified, will be signed.[16]

To this general definition was added a list of specific duties: "The C.G.S. is responsible to the C.-in-C. for the working out of all arrangements, and for the drafting of detailed orders regarding:

> All military operations, including the general control, in co-operation with the navy, of embarkation and landings within the theatre of operations.

> War organization and efficiency of the troops.

> Selection of lines of operations.

---

15   My emphasis.
16   *Field Service Regulations. Part II. Organization and Administration. 1909* (London: General Staff War Office, 1914), p.38.

All plans for the concentration, distribution and movement of troops and material by rail, road or inland waterways in the theatre of operations.

The general allotment of areas in which divisions and brigades are to be quartered; security, marches and battle.

Intercommunication in the field.

Special reconnaissances.

Policy connected with raising new units.

Provision of guides and interpreters.

Acquisition and distribution of information about the enemy, the country and its resources.

Questions of policy in connection with international and martial law, including, in the case of martial law, advice as to the necessity for and scope of its enforcement.

Flags of truce and correspondence with the enemy.

Censorship over communications, i.e., the post, telegraphs, telephones and cables.

Control of the press and press correspondents.

Secret services, cyphers, care and disposal of captured documents.

Provision, distribution, and revision of maps.

Charge of foreign attachés.

Preparation of reports, despatches, and diaries relating to the above.[17]

Like much of *FSR*, this delineation of responsibilities and list of duties was opaque and left much to circumstances and to the interaction of personalities. In reality, Murray's effectiveness and success would depend on his ability to manage and to satisfy three constituencies. The first was his commander-in-chief; the second was the army as a whole, beginning with his own staff, but also encompassing relations with the senior formation commanders, especially Haig (I Corps) and Smith-Dorrien (II Corps); and third Britain's allies, especially the French. These constituencies were problematic from

17   *Field Service Regulations. Part II*, pp.38-9.

the outset and events were to make their management even more difficult until, by the end of the year, Murray had lost the confidence of all three.

The relationship between a commander-in-chief and his chief of staff is of fundamental importance to the effectiveness of military organisations. The relationship is a kind of professional marriage and, as with real marriages, there is no infallible recipe for success. Some marriages succeed (or fail) because the partners are temperamentally similar; other marriages succeed (or fail) because the partners are temperamentally different. Some commanders (like Haig) are very 'hands on'; others (like Montgomery) prefer to leave the day-to-day management of the army to their chiefs of staff, freeing themselves to think clearly about the "big decisions".[18] Some commanders (like French) need advice, whether they know it or not; some (like Plumer) seek advice and encourage discussion; others (like the imperious Franchet d'Espèrey) do not solicit or permit 'suggestions', but expect their decisions to be executed without demur.

What did Sir John French want from his CGS? William Philpott has spoken of French's ambivalence towards the staff system. French had not supported the establishment of a General Staff in 1904, even though Lord Esher, the principal mover, wanted French to be the first CGS. French ran into conflict with the War Office when he was GOC Aldershot over his appointment of officers who had not passed staff college to staff posts.[19] In a lecture to the Staff College in January 1912 French made clear his view of the "strictly" subordinate nature of staff officers:

> if you endeavour to comprehend clearly the definite line of demarcation which exists between the function of the commander and the function of the Staff. It is the duty of the Staff to present all the facts of the situation to the commander with perfect accuracy and impartiality and then to take the necessary measures for carrying his decisions into effect.[20]

French therefore seemingly wanted as his CGS a combination of an executive officer and a PA, someone who would deal with annoying distractions, manage the staff on a day-to-day basis, provide him with the wherewithal to make decisions and ensure that those decisions were conveyed to others. Whether, as the dramatic events of the late summer and autumn of 1914 unfolded in France and Belgium, this is what French really needed from his CGS remained to be seen, but it was a role to which Murray seemed not only temperamentally suited but also professionally inclined. There appeared to be potential for a fruitful collaboration between French's 'warrior' and Murray's 'worrier'.

---

18   Montgomery's celebrated "chief of staff system" that he employed at 8th Army was very similar to the command style of George Gorringe, to whom Monty was chief of staff (GSO1) at 47th (London) Division during the last six months of the war on the Western Front in 1918.

19   Richard Holmes, *Little Field-Marshal: A Life of Sir John French* (London: Weidenfeld & Nicolson, 2004), pp.127-8.

20   Holmes, *Little Field-Marshal*, p.136. French's view was the generally held one. It was repeated by Sir William Robertson in his farewell speech as Commandant of the Staff College in 1913. I owe this point to Professor Gary Sheffield.

The possibilities of the French-Murray relationship succeeding depended, however, on each man being able to deliver his half of the bargain: French to 'command' and Murray to 'manage'. Each man was destined to disappoint the other.

French was given some uncomfortable surprises even before the first clash of battle. The first surprise was the appointment to the government of Lord Kitchener. The Curragh Incident had resulted in the resignation not only of French but also of the Secretary of State for War, Colonel J.E.B. Seely. Prime Minister Asquith decided to delay a re-organization of his Cabinet by taking on the post himself. He occasionally strolled down to the War Office, made sure that the clerks had not absconded with the furniture, declared himself delighted and told everyone to carry on. Once Britain went to war this arrangement became unsustainable. Asquith personally chose Kitchener, who happened to be at home on leave from his duties as British Agent and Consul-General in Egypt, as the new Secretary of State. It was probably the most important and fateful decision Asquith made in his political career. Kitchener was the Empire's greatest still-serving soldier. He was bound to have views on the conduct of the war, but no one had the slightest idea what they would be. Little wonder that Asquith himself described the choice as a gamble. Within a few days of his appointment Kitchener persuaded the government to raise a mass volunteer army to fight a war that would last at least three years. This decision fundamentally changed the nature of the war from a British perspective. It also changed things for Sir John French, who now had a serving field-marshal as his immediate political master. This was a situation ripe with contention.

French's second surprise was supplied by Kitchener, who decided to hold back two of the BEF's designated six infantry divisions. French's command, even at full strength, was puny in comparison with the armies of France and Germany, but he would begin the war with only two-thirds of his infantry. This decision made Kitchener's "Instructions" to French even more problematic. French was instructed to co-operate fully with his allies, but he retained responsibility for the safety of what was Britain's only army. Kitchener stressed that "while every effort must be made to coincide most sympathetically with the plans and wishes of our Ally, the gravest consideration will devolve upon you as to participation in forward movements where large numbers of French troops are not engaged, and where your force may be unduly exposed to attack."[21] Within a few weeks of the outbreak of war French was to find these instructions less of a practical guide to action and more the horns of a dilemma.

French's third surprise was the sudden death of the GOC II Corps, his old CGS Sir James Grierson. Grierson died of a heart attack on the train taking him to the front on 17 August. Although French's relationship with Grierson was strained since the 1913 manoeuvres, he remained something of an old comrade. This could not be said of Kitchener's choice of Grierson's successor, Sir Horace Smith-Dorrien, with whom French had a combustible relationship that would take only a spark to reignite. Smith-Dorrien was a man with a volcanic temper and this soon alienated the chief of staff he

---

21   Kitchener's 'Instructions' to French are reprinted in Sheffield & Bourne (eds), *Douglas Haig*, pp.512-3.

had inherited from Grierson, George Forestier-Walker, who attempted unsuccessfully to resign. The BEF high command was hardly a 'band of brothers'.[22]

French's military instincts were aggressive. Unlike Kitchener, he also thought that the war would be short. Both instinct and judgement predisposed him to attack. This was reinforced by the French Commander-in-Chief, General J.J.C. Joffre, during their first meeting on 16 August. Joffre pressed French to advance as quickly as possible so as to join in the offensive of the French Fifth Army on the British right. But it did not take long for caution to set in. Events in Belgium were discouraging. Liege, last of the Belgian fortresses, fell on 16 August and the remains of the Belgian Army were bottled up in the port of Antwerp. On 17 August French had a difficult and inauspicious meeting with the commander of the French Fifth Army, General Charles Lanrezac, at Rethel. The acerbic and arrogant Lanrezac did not share Joffre's bullish optimism. He thought that the French war plan, with its concentration of forces in Lorraine, would end in disaster and was not shy of sharing this view with all and sundry. His discovery that Fifth Army was confronted by thirty German divisions, intent on a great flanking movement round him and his British ally, converted his pessimism into defeatism. His only response when confronted with disaster was to say "I told you so". Grave doubts about the reliability of the French were sown and grew speedily in Sir John's suspicious mind. French, however, remained committed to his promise to Joffre. The result was that the BEF soon found itself nine miles ahead of the French, with a five mile gap between the British and Fifth Army. The BEF was faced with the prospect of encirclement and annihilation.

These initial events established a pattern that was to repeat itself throughout 1914. French's attacking instincts, usually encouraged by Wilson, continually ran into battlefield realities. The most compelling of these realities was the overwhelming numerical superiority of the German army. The second was the failure of the French Army's strategy that had resulted in a series of shattering defeats right across its front. The third was the inadequacy of the BEF's communications system, which meant that French was unable, for much of 1914, actually to command the forces under him. The first battles of the war, Mons (23 August), the stand of II Corps at Le Cateau (26 August) and the retreat to the Marne were conducted almost without control from the top. I Corps and II Corps were left to fight their own battles in their own way. There were times during the retreat when Murray issued no orders at all, leaving corps and divisions to fend for themselves as best they could. Murray's reputation with the corps commanders, never high in the case of Haig, was badly damaged by the apparent inertia and chaos of GHQ in these early, dramatic days.

22   The dysfunctional nature of the BEF's GHQ in 1914 is a common theme in Gardner, *Trial by Fire*, Dan Todman, 'The Grand Lamasery Revisited: General Headquarters on the Western Front, 1914-1918', in Gary Sheffield & Dan Todman (eds), *Command and Control on the Western Front: The British Army's Experience 1914-18* (Staplehurst: Spellmount, 2004) and Simon Robbins, *British Generalship on the Western Front 1914-18: Defeat into Victory* (London: Frank Cass, 2005).

These problems were exacerbated by Sir John French repeatedly leaving his HQ to "get around the army". During these frequent visits he was totally out of communication with his HQ, including his CGS, and with subordinate formations. He commanded no one beyond his driver. The frequent and sudden moves of GHQ itself were very disruptive. After the battle of Mons GHQ fled from St Quentin to Noyon without informing either corps. In the aftermath of Le Cateau, Smith-Dorrien had the greatest difficulty finding the new location of GHQ so that he could brief French on the situation. The move of GHQ from Dammartin on 1 September was so sudden that the Adjutant-General Nevil Macready was inadvertently left behind![23] French's "gadding about" and the movement of GHQ meant that much good aerial and cavalry intelligence on the enemy's strength and movements, co-ordinated by the BEF's able and prudent intelligence chief, George Macdonogh, did not get through and French became reliant on Wilson's frequently bad advice.

For much of 1914 it is difficult to detect Sir John French in the act of generalship. His failure to command had serious consequences for Murray, whose view of his own role as CGS was dependent upon Sir John doing his job properly. Given Murray's self-effacing personality and his view of his role, it was unlikely that he would be able to fill the command vacuum that French often left. Murray seems to have accepted the appointment as CGS out of a sense of duty and a desire to help Sir John. Sir John certainly needed help. He was not staff trained. He was certainly charismatic, not least with ordinary soldiers, undoubtedly a leader at his best but never a manager. French was also temperamental, prone to bouts of irrational optimism and equally irrational despair. Haig described him as like a bottle of soda water, given to frothing uncontrollably when shaken. The course of the war would have shaken more equable characters than Sir John. French's personality gave Sir William Robertson, a much more ambitious and formidable man than Murray, reason to think twice about taking the post of CGS in January 1915, doubting whether he had the ability to control Sir John and concerned that his own career might go down in flames with that of his chief.[24] If Murray was to prove an effective CGS to such a difficult and problematic commander, he would need to establish his own authority over the General Staff. This he never did. His failure undermined his self-belief, the confidence in him of his chief, of the army as a whole and of his French allies.

Murray's problems were inherent in the nature and timing of his appointment. Just as French seems to have had limited influence over the choice of his chief of staff, so Murray had no influence in the choice of his own subordinates. In so far as the British Army carried out any pre-war staff planning, this concerned the mobilisation and deployment of the BEF. These plans were drawn up and repeatedly practised by the Directorate of Military Operations [DMO], under the superintendence of its head,

23   E.L. Spears, *Liaison 1914* (London: William Heinemann, 1930), pp.541-2, prints an
      account of the departure of GHQ from Dammartin written by the Medical Officer at
      GHQ, Colonel Lyle Cummins.
24   Field-Marshal Sir William Robertson, *From Private to Field Marshal* (London:
      Constable, 1921), p.218.

Major-General Henry Wilson. A BEF staff had to be improvised from somewhere and it is hardly a surprise that its main source was to be the DMO. A staff exercise involving officers from the DMO took place at the RMC Sandhurst in January 1914 with the aim of testing the operation of the BEF's headquarters. Wilson acted as CGS. This seems to be the only practice session that the potential staff of the BEF had. It was a disaster. Sir William Robertson, Commandant of the Staff College, who umpired the event, was heard to remark to French "if you go to war with that operations staff, you are as good as beaten".[25] Even so, thirty-one of the DMO's sixty-four officers did go to France on the general staff in August 1914.[26] Wilson was among them, intruded into the command structure as Sub-Chief of the General Staff. This put Murray into an invidious position from the outset. He knew nothing of the pre-war planning and liaison with the French, in which Wilson had been a key player. He was not familiar with the DMO staff, many of whom, not least the GSO1 at GHQ, Colonel Montague Harper, continued to look to Wilson as their leader, something that Wilson did nothing to prevent. Murray and Harper rowed constantly, which led Harper on 24 August to refuse to do anything for Murray.[27] Wilson had to intervene to prevent French from sacking Harper. Murray was a like a cuckoo in his own nest. This ensured that the top of the BEF was not a duumvirate but a triumvirate. It was a recipe for disharmony and confusion that was made even worse by the personal staff that French surrounded himself with and who acted as a further obstacle to effective co-operation between the C-in-C and his CGS.[28]

The closest Murray came to a briefing about his role was a meeting he had with Lord Kitchener. Murray left a note of the conversation:

> He [Kitchener] began by giving me caution as to not wasting rashly the lives of the 1st troops of the Expd. Force, material almost impossible to replace. Later when more troops were available greater risks might be taken. He said whatever happens to the force we must never be shut up like the French were in Sedan and before such a situation should arrive we must fight our way out of it. He further said we might have to retire to the coast, he did not intend that we should leave [the] continent. We should hang on till he send reinforcements. He did not intend to leave the continent till the Germans are completely crushed.[29]

Murray did not record his response to Kitchener's views, but he cannot have been much encouraged by their pessimistic tone. Like French, he was left in no doubt that the BEF might soon be placed in a precarious position and of his own responsibility for ensuring the army's safety. This understanding constrained Murray as much as it

---

25   Quoted in Holmes, *Little Field-Marshal*, p.127.
26   I owe these figures to Mr Michael Orr.
27   Robbins, *British Generalship*, p.116.
28   Robbins, *British Generalship*, p.117.
29   TNA: PRO WO 79/62, quoted in George Cassar, *Kitchener: Architect of Victory* (London: William Kimber, 1977), p.231.

did French. A more ruthless man than Murray might have demanded changes to the composition of GHQ, targeting the officers most disloyal to him. He might even have demanded the removal of Wilson or threatened to resign himself, but with the fate of the BEF at least partly in his hands and with battle commenced he had no option but to soldier on. These difficult, indeed impossible, circumstances would have tried any man, but a few days into the war Murray suffered another blow when he was betrayed by his own health.

From the moment the BEF clashed with the German First Army at Mons the pressure on the GHQ staff had been unrelenting. The weather, which was stupefyingly hot, was also very trying. Murray confided to his diary on 24 August, the day after Mons, that he had spent twenty-four hours without undressing.[30] Field-Marshal French himself witnessed at first hand the trials of the staff at Bavai on 24 August, recalling with admiration in his memoirs:

> In a close room on the upper floor of the Mairie I found Murray... working hard, minus belt, coat and collar. The heat was intense. The room was filled with Staff Officers bringing reports or awaiting instructions. Some of the Headquarters Staff had not closed their eyes for 48 hours, and were stretched out on forms or huddled up in corners, wrapped in that deep slumber which only comes to brains which, for the time being, are completely worn out.[31]

Murray's notorious 'collapse' on 26 August, the day of the battle of Le Cateau, undoubtedly undermined further his authority among his own staff and among the wider army. It has also blighted his reputation, both as a soldier and as a man. The implication is that Murray's collapse was a mental one, a failure of character, brought on by news of Smith-Dorrien's refusal to withdraw from Le Cateau as ordered.[32] This may be doubted. One compelling witness, Captain E.L. Spears, British Liaison Officer with the French Fifth Army, actually dates Murray's collapse to the previous evening:

> On the previous night [25 August] the strain had been so frightful that the Chief of Staff, Sir Archibald Murray, exhausted by anxiety and overwork, had had a temporary collapse from shock when false news arrived that the enemy had attacked and defeated the I Corps at Landrecies. Colonel Cummins, the M.O. at G.H.Q., was very anxious about him. He did not actually faint, but his pulse was very weak. He said to Colonel Cummins in a whisper: "They have got in between the I and II Corps. I have just heard, and it has been too much for me".[33]

---

30   IWM: Murray Diaries 79/48/2.

31   Field-Marshal Viscount French of Ypres, *1914* (London: Constable, 1919), p.69.

32   See, for example, Keith Jeffery, *Field-Marshal Sir Henry Wilson: An Irish Soldier* (Oxford: Oxford University Press, 2006) p.135.

33   Spears, *Liaison 1914*, p.239.

This account fits well with the bald statement in Murray's diary, on 26 August, that he was "fairly done up by 6 am";[34] in other words that it had been the previous night's news that had caused his distress, not the news of Le Cateau. Murray's diary then states that the "Doctor injected something that pulled me round for the day". The nature of the injection has been the subject of much speculation. It was before the development of amphetamines, such as Benzedrine, which were used during the Second World War. Morphine would almost certainly have been available, but it is an analgesic rather than a stimulant. Cocaine is another possibility and much more likely to have produced an improvement in alertness and a sense of well-being.

Whatever Murray was given, there is no evidence that he was given it more than once. Nor was there anything unique about his collapse. Colonel G.F. Boileau, GSO1 3rd Division, broke under the strain on 26 August and shot himself. The future official historian, James Edmonds, had to be replaced as GSO1 4th Division on 4 September. Brigadier-General R.H. Davies (GOC 6th Brigade) was sent home on 23 September suffering from exhaustion.[35] Even Haig's customary imperturbability slipped under physical and mental duress at Landrecies during the night of 25 August. Sir John French, himself, experienced perhaps the most spectacular and worrying crisis, when on 30 August he telegraphed Joffre that the BEF would have to withdraw from the allied line and retreat behind the Seine for up to ten days to refit. It took a celebrated and controversial visit from Kitchener on 1 September at which the Secretary of State decided that the BEF would not leave the line, a decision he conveyed to the Cabinet and which he told French to regard as an "instruction". French had equally to be persuaded to take part in the battle of the Marne by an emotional Joffre, a consummate actor who could turn on tears at will, providing a fine demonstration of how to play effectively on French's sensibilities, a task beyond a reserved man like Murray. Again, during the savage fighting round Ypres in October and November, during which the BEF was once more threatened with destruction, French repeatedly drank at the bottomless well of optimism and courage that was General Ferdinand Foch. Even Wilson, whose star rose as Murray's fell, was not always the paragon of "cheerfulness and moral courage" that he was portrayed by his first biographer.[36] Wilson signally failed to cover effectively for Murray on 26 August. He believed that the BEF was beaten and that the best course was to head for the Channel ports and home, even wiring his friend Major-General Snow (GOC 4th Division) "Henry to Snowball: Throw overboard all ammunition and impedimenta not absolutely required, and load up your lame ducks on all transport, horse and mechanical, and hustle along",[37] an order that had a damaging effect on the morale of 4th Division. As for Murray himself, he soon rallied. Spears

34   IWM: Murray Diaries 79/48/2.
35   Two of the BEF's more successful commanders later in the war were also sent home in 1914 for perceived failures: Ivor Maxse, GOC 1 (Guards) Brigade and Sir Charles Fergusson, GOC 5th Division.
36   Major-General Sir C.E. Callwell, *Field-Marshal Sir Henry Wilson: His Life and Diaries Volume 1* (London: Cassell, 1927), p.170.
37   Spears, *Liaison 1914*, p.254.

recalled an incident on 30 August when a "senior artillery officer" burst into GHQ, "seemingly on the verge of collapse":

'All the guns in the division are lost,' he almost sobbed. Sir Archibald Murray took a step towards him and getting hold of his shoulders shook him roughly. 'To my knowledge you have seven left,' he said sternly.[38]

But Spears' account was not published until 1930 and for Murray the damage had been done. Those, like Haig, who had doubted Murray's suitability from the outset had more ammunition to use against him. There is more than a grain of truth in the judgement of one of Wilson's biographers, Basil Collier:

In the past [Murray] had won a reputation as a calm, reflective, hard-working staff officer of the old school. But his breakdown during the retreat from Mons had shaken his self-confidence and had made him ill at ease with subordinates who witnessed it.[39]

Even so, French continued to rely on Murray to undertake huge volumes of work, while increasingly relying on Wilson for "ideas". To borrow William Philpott's felicitous phrase, Murray was "the donkey" at GHQ and Wilson was the "lion". Wilson had the better of this division of labour, which was, in effect, a position of influence without responsibility. Murray, in contrast, continued to bear the weight and the responsibility. Wilson became the man who brought French solutions, Murray brought only problems. French's initial admiration for Murray faded. Murray was eventually even excluded from Sir John's mess, an extraordinary state of affairs that soon became public knowledge, further undermining Murray's credibility.[40] Murray's replacement had been under discussion for weeks before the decision was finally made.

Murray's final perceived failure was in relation to inter-allied relations. There is a certain paradox in this because Murray's initial scepticism about the French was actually closer to the views of his Commander-in-Chief than were those of the Francophile Wilson. It is difficult to know what Murray's feelings were about the French before the war or even if he had any. He had played no part in the pre-war Franco-British staff talks and had no prior knowledge of the deployment contingency plans developed by Wilson. The evidence of Murray's actions in the early days of the war suggests, however, that he was committed to maintaining British military independence. If he

38   Spears, *Liaison 1914*, p.289.
39   Basil Collier, *Brasshat: A Biography of Field-Marshal Sir Henry Wilson 1864-1922* (London: Secker & Warburg, 1961), p.201.
40   Sir Henry Rawlinson (GOC IV Corps) makes reference to Murray's exclusion from Sir John French's mess in his diary for 4 December 1914, commenting that Murray's subordinates resented having him foisted on their mess. Churchill Archives Centre [CAC]: Rawlinson Papers, RWLN 1/1. Robertson, when he succeeded Murray as CGS, was also relegated to a junior mess, while Wilson continued to dine at French's personal table, see General Sir James Marshall-Cornwall, *Haig as Military Commander* (London: Batsford, 1973), p.138.

had not been so committed before he was appointed CGS this was certainly the import of his discussion with Kitchener, during which Kitchener had even flagged up the possibility that "[BEF] might have to retire to the coast" if its survival was threatened. This attitude was fully shared by Sir John French. There is a tendency to read backwards French's undoubted later reliance on Wilson to the start of the war and to see French as being always in Wilson's pocket. This was not the case. At the extraordinary council of war called by Asquith on 5 August French made it quite clear that he was not prepared to accept as a *fait accompli* the arrangements Wilson had made with the French to deploy the BEF on the left of the French line. Sir John raised the possibility of the BEF being landed on the Belgian coast to operate against the German lines of communication, a suggestion that provoked a characteristic outburst in Wilson's diary.[41] When it was eventually agreed that the BEF should deploy to France, French contested Wilson's planned forward concentration, at Maubeuge, arguing for a more rearward concentration, at Amiens, a view that was shared by Kitchener and by Murray. Significantly, and for Murray perhaps ominously, it was Wilson, with the support of the French general staff, who prevailed.

The opening moves of the war did nothing to convince French and Murray to share Wilson's belief in the leadership of the French army and the fighting power of the French nation. Everywhere along the line the French had been defeated. The French Fifth Army seemed to have little concern for the fate of the BEF, retreating without informing the British and leaving the BEF's right flank in the air. Wilson looked to have hitched his wagon to the wrong horse. But two things changed this state of affairs and ensured that Murray would have enemies outside the camp as well as within it.

The first was the decision taken by Kitchener on 1 September that the BEF would not bolt for the coast, but would stay in the line. The fate of the BEF now became inextricably linked with that of the French army. The second was the fighting at Ypres in October and November. After the Aisne battles in September, Sir John French had prevailed upon Joffre, no easy matter, to agree that the BEF should move to the far left flank of the fighting, close to the Channel ports and to its lines of supply and, if necessary, of retreat. This was perhaps French's most important achievement as commander-in-chief, perhaps his only achievement. However, in the short term it made the BEF more, not less, reliant on good relations with the French. Despite its iconic status in the history of the British army, the 1st Battle of Ypres was largely a French affair,[42] but one in which allied formations and units became intermingled under the pressure of German attacks. This made effective liaison with the French a priority for the BEF. It was a role to which Murray was unsuited and where his authority was trumped by Wilson who was meeting on an almost daily basis with the French commanders to arrange the practical co-operation between the allied forces

---

41   Callwell, *Wilson Volume 1*, pp.158-9. Haig was also dismayed by French's suggestion, deeming it proof of French's unfitness for command: Sheffield & Bourne (eds), *Douglas Haig*, p.54.

42   Ian F.W. Beckett, *Ypres: The First Battle 1914* (Harlow: Pearson, 2004) clearly demonstrates the dominant role played by French forces.

on which the survival of the BEF would depend. It also gave Wilson an unmissable opportunity to intrigue against Murray.

Wilson was well-known to the French. He was on terms of considerable intimacy with leading French soldiers, especially Foch, who was to play a key part in the successful defence of Ypres. Wilson spoke French well; Murray did not; French's ability in the language was even worse. As William Philpott has argued, by September Sir John French effectively had two chiefs of staff, one (Murray) for managing his army, and another (Wilson) for managing relations with his allies. One of the consequences of this was that Murray developed a reputation with the French for being a Francophobe. The only references to Murray in Joffre's memoirs are of instances when Murray raised objections to Joffre's proposals and wishes.[43] Murray certainly did not share Wilson's admiration for the French. During a period of leave in London in October 1914 Murray reported to Asquith, who described the meeting in a typically indiscreet letter to his confidante, Venetia Stanley:

> General Murray, who is Sir J. French's chief of staff, is over here for the day. He said a very good thing to K.[itchener] this morning, K having asked him what he thought of Joffre: 'Joffre is a very good man – capable, phlegmatic, equable; he has only 2 defects: the first is, that he is always 2 days too late, and the second, that he is always 2 divisions too few.'... He [Murray] says (as everyone does) that our infantry & cavalry are immeasurably superior to both the French & Germans: the French always give us the difficult things to do; with the result... that our casualties are very heavy.[44]

These were fairly commonplace views, but not everyone who held them was Chief of the General Staff of the BEF. By the autumn it was clear to Sir John French that Murray was increasingly *persona non grata* with his allies and he came under increasing pressure to remove Murray and replace him with Wilson. Murray was aware of his predicament and discussed with Wilson whether he should go:

> This morning Archie spoke to me about his position as C of S. He said it was becoming very difficult. He asked for my opinion as to whether he should resign. I replied that, for the moment, I thought there ought to be no change, that I knew of no one who could take his place with greater success, and that I thought we ought to tide over the present and watch developments. This was agreed to.[45]

43   I owe this point to Professor Bill Philpott.
44   Michael and Eleanor Brock (eds), *H.H. Asquith: Letters to Venetia Stanley* (Oxford: Oxford University Press, 1982), p.287.
45   Callwell, p.182. The date is 10 October 1914. Callwell edited this account. The passages he omitted make it clear that Wilson thought he could do a better job and that if Murray went Wilson would succeed him. In the latter view, at least, he was deluded. His appointment was anathema both to Asquith and Kitchener.

Despite Wilson's insincere disavowal, Murray's days were numbered. Sir John French was a bad enemy, but he retained an affection and regard for Murray that made sacking him something of a trial. French was also uncomfortably aware that he was abandoning a faithful lieutenant under external pressures. One way out was provided by the expansion of the BEF, which was about to be divided into two Armies, to be commanded by Haig and Smith-Dorrien, and the addition of another corps (V Corps), to the command of which Murray could be moved. In the event, however, it was Murray's health that provided the excuse. Murray returned to London on 5 January 1915. On 21 January he fell ill with influenza. On 24 January Sir John French "wired that I would be unfit for work for at least a month & had appointed Robertson to do my work".[46] This apparently temporary arrangement was, of course, permanent, as French made clear when Murray replied that he was ready to take up his duties at once. French also made it clear that he was prepared to have Murray back as a field commander, possibly of the about-to-be formed Third Army, but on 10 February Murray accepted from Lord Kitchener the offer of the post of Deputy Chief of the Imperial General Staff with special responsibility for training the New Armies. His career on the Western Front was over. Murray's admittedly sparse diary shows no sign of bitterness or betrayal. He was a man with a great sense of duty and his duty now lay elsewhere.

The French liaison officer, Victor Huguet, offered a reasonably generous post-war assessment of Murray from the French perspective in his less than generous account of Britain's role in the war:

> His character was … calm, balanced and reflective. His capacity for order and method, his prodigious powers for work, made him the ideal peace-time Chief of Staff. But delicate health was inclined to make him pessimistic and his own personal character led him to decisions where there was least risk and where there would be least responsibility. In fact during the six months he was with his Chief, he acted as a kind of brake. Nevertheless, the two men were bound by sincere friendship and mutual esteem and the Field-Marshal parted with him at the beginning of 1915 with a heavy heart.[47]

Quite often during the First World War removal from a position in the British Army was the first step on the road to professional oblivion. However, the British Army as an institution did not appear to hold Murray responsible for the failures of GHQ in 1914. He was given a series of high level and responsible jobs. A harsh judgement would be that he continued to fail in all of them. There is little doubt, however, that as GOC Egyptian Expeditionary Force he laid the logistical and administrative foundations of Allenby's later success, something Allenby recognised in his final despatch. One of the most common themes of British military history is that it is better to be in a position of high command at the end of a war rather than at the beginning. Sir Archibald Murray was an able, honourable, dedicated man who was in the wrong job, with the wrong

46   IWM: Murray Papers 79/48/2.
47   General Huguet, *Britain and the War: An Indictment* (London: Cassell, 1928), p.47.

commander, in the wrong place, at the wrong time. The reticence that characterised his career and that he carried into retirement and the lack of private papers make it difficult to offer a fundamental reassessment of his role in 1914, where he remains to some extent elusive. Murray died on 23 January 1945 at his home in Reigate. There may be a terse and wistful comment on his life and times in the name he chose for his house – "Makepeace".

3

Henry Wilson's War

Sub-Chief of Staff, GHQ

Brian Curragh

Henry Wilson is often portrayed as a mischievous political manipulator whose incessant use of intrigue was solely devoted to furthering his own ambitions. This ignores the fact that Wilson was an intelligent soldier who had thought long and hard about the forthcoming war and the role that a British force would play in it. He identified a lack of strategic clarity within the political and military hierarchies combined with unpreparedness for the conflict and attempted to correct the situation. His achievements while Commandant of the Staff College (1907-1910) in developing a "school of thought" and then in overhauling Britain's military readiness when Director of Military Operations (DMO) (1910-1914) enabled the deployment of the British Expeditionary Force (BEF) within days of the outbreak of war.

Wilson provoked conflicting views on his character: to F.E. Smith, Wilson possessed "an arrogant mind" and held "heavily discredited opinions";[1] to Winston Churchill he was a "subversive force";[2] J.F.C. Fuller saw him as "a Harlequin of the Mephistophelean type.";[3] while Maurice Hankey described Wilson as an "arch-intriguer".[4] Yet Churchill also described Wilson as "an expert adviser of superior intellect, who could explain lucidly and forcefully the whole situation and give reasons for the adoption or rejection of any course"[5] and Hankey acknowledged that he was "a profound student of war".[6] This is the Wilson enigma: a knowledgeable and inspiring soldier who thought deeply

---

1   2nd Earl of Birkenhead, *The Life of F.E. Smith – First Earl of Birkenhead* (London: Eyre & Spottiswoode, 1959), p.368.
2   Violet Bonham-Carter, *Winston Churchill as I knew him,* (London: Weidenfeld & Nicolson, 1995), p.294.
3   Anthony John Trythall, *"Boney" Fuller – the Intellectual General,* (London: Cassell, 1977), p.59.
4   S.W. Roskill, *Hankey: Man of Secrets Vol.1 1877-1918,* (London: Collins, 1970), p.238.
5   Roskill, *Hankey,* p.444.
6   Roskill, *Hankey,* p.458.

Henry Wilson. (Bain collection, Library of Congress)

about the impending conflict but whose political views and use of intrigue restricted the role he was able to play.

Wilson's impact on the war was most prominent in its opening and closing years. In 1914, he went to France as Sub-Chief of Staff of the BEF and was part of General Headquarters (GHQ) from the retreat from Mons in August through to the onset of static trench warfare in November. Wilson was removed from this role at the end of 1914 and spent three years in a series of unproductive posts before he returned as a member of the Supreme War Council and then as Chief of the Imperial General Staff (CIGS) in February 1918.

Wilson has been poorly treated by the historiography. In the *Official History* (OH) volumes that cover 1914, Wilson is mentioned just six times in the index of the first volume and not at all in the second. The OH notes his involvement in the pre-war development of the thinking behind the BEF; his telephone conversation with General Sir Horace Smith-Dorrien in the early hours of 26 August and his three meetings with the French - a lightweight treatment for a senior member of the BEF. Unlike his military counterparts, his premature death in 1922 removed the opportunity to present his view of the war through his memoirs. It was left to Major General Charles Callwell, Wilson's successor as DMO, to transform Wilson's very personal diaries into something fit for public consumption – an attempt that did not succeed if the reaction to their publication is anything to go by. Wilson's reputation was left undefended in the subsequent "battle of the memoirs" as others sought to stake out their own importance, frequently at the expense of their rivals. It was not until the 1960s that two biographies of him were published. Rex Taylor's *Assassination* focused on his killing and while written from a Nationalist angle, depicted Wilson as an honourable man. This work was followed by Bernard Ash's *The Lost Dictator*, which imaginatively set out to portray him as a potential fascist leader of a rebel political group. It was not until Keith Jeffrey's *Wilson - A Political Soldier* in 2006 that a more considered view became available.

Recently the BEF's commanders have come under criticism from Nikolas Gardner in *Trial by Fire*. His thesis is that the "gallant sacrifices" of the BEF actually mask a failure at the command level. While acknowledging Wilson's "considerable intelligence, energy and charisma" and his "unconventional, but nonetheless formidable intellect", he repeatedly refers to Wilson's "intellectual dominance" of Sir John French achieved through his "surreptitiously undermining Murray's position". He sees this "dominance" of the BEF's Commander-in-Chief (C-in-C) as having both positive and negative aspects: positive in that his vision of the BEF's role in fighting on the left flank of the French proved correct and also his initiative in requesting tactical notes from corps staff officers based on their experience of the early months of the war to assist newly arriving formations. But Gardner states that Wilson's dominant position had a negative impact, as he was a key source of the outbreak of "premature cognitive closure" - a process described as a state of mind where information is interpreted in such a way so as to only fit existing preconceptions or ignored if this cannot be achieved. If this does describe the mindset within GHQ, its decisions will have been made on incorrect interpretations and may have had a detrimental effect of the BEF's performance.[7]

The family history of military personnel does not normally constitute a major part of their biographies but in Wilson's case his origins are relevant to the role he came to play. His belief in the importance of the Union of Great Britain and Ireland came to influence and direct his behaviour during the Curragh Incident. The political damage to his reputation that arose from this intervention lead to his military career being held back so that it was not until he became CIGS in 1918, that he achieved a role that his political and military aptitude would have warranted.

Henry Hughes Wilson was born on 5 May 1864 at the family home, Currygrane, in County Longford, Ireland - the second son of a Protestant family that had prospered in the Belfast shipping industry. Wilson's grandfather had invested the family wealth in landed estates in Ireland with his father inheriting the Currygrane estate. As his elder brother would inherit the estate in due course, Henry appeared destined for a military career. However, despite private schooling and three years at Marlborough, he struggled to gain entrance into the Military Colleges at Woolwich or Sandhurst, failing the entrance examinations twice and three times respectively. His parents' employment of a series of French governesses was however to give him a grounding in a language that would prove useful in later years.

Wilson eventually joined the military through "the back door" by joining the Longford Militia (6th Battalion, Rifle Brigade) and was gazetted as a lieutenant on 20 December 1882, aged eighteen. After two years of training, he sat the examination for a direct commission in July 1884 and passed, coming 58th on the list.[8] Having been

7   Nikolas Gardner, *Trial by Fire*, (Westport: Praeger Publishers Inc., 2003), p.5-7, 40-41.
8   Major General Sir C.E. Callwell, *Field Marshal Sir Henry Wilson – His Life and Diaries*,

posted to 1st Battalion of the Rifle Brigade, Wilson sailed for India with the battalion on HMS Malabar on 12 February 1885. After twenty months' service, the battalion was posted to Burma in November 1886.

It was whilst in Burma that Wilson received the facial wound that left a permanent scar. He was leading an attack on a large entrenched camp "unarmed but for a bamboo walking-stick" when he came upon two *dacoits*[9] who attacked him with a concealed *dah*.[10] Wilson parried the blow with his stick and while his right eye was undamaged, the blow chipped the bones around it. Years later, the wound was still visible and notorious: John Cowans had a letter delivered successfully to Wilson by addressing it to "The Ugliest Officer in the Army, Victoria Barracks, Belfast".[11] Following the attack, Wilson spent a period of sick leave in Calcutta before a medical board recommended that he be sent home for convalescence. He spent the majority of 1888 in Ireland before being passed fit for duty again the following year and rejoining the Rifle Brigade, this time the 2nd Battalion at Woolwich. During this posting, Wilson successfully sat the entrance examinations for the Staff College.

Wilson's two-year course commenced in January 1892 and he moved into Grove End, two miles from the College, whose four acres of land allowed him to indulge his hobby of gardening. Camberley would introduce him to many of the officers with whom he would work in later years. These included Aylmer Haldane, later General Officer Commanding (GOC) 3rd Division and VI Corps; Hubert Hamilton, GOC 3rd Division; Launcelot Kiggell, Haig's Chief of Staff; Henry Rawlinson, GOC Fourth and Second Armies, and Thomas Snow, GOC VII Corps. Rawlinson was to prove Wilson's closest friend from this period with a friendly rivalry that continued after the college. Rawlinson was also to introduce him, in May 1893, to Lord Roberts, Rawlinson's C-in-C while in India. Wilson took this opportunity to present a paper to Roberts on the defence of India, which was well received. Roberts was to prove a strong supporter and patron as Wilson's career progressed. Outside professional circles, the Wilson and Roberts families were close and Wilson was at Roberts' bedside when he died in November 1914 while visiting the BEF in France. In the second year of college in 1893 Wilson visited the battlefields of the Franco-Prussian War, something he was to repeat over the years in the run-up to the Great War.

Following graduation from Camberley, Wilson was promoted to Captain within the Rifle Brigade but spent less than a year in this role as in November 1894 he was attached to the Intelligence Department at Queen Anne's Gate. Wilson would spend the next three years in his first War Office (WO) role as Staff Captain in Section A collating information and intelligence on France, Belgium, Italy, Spain and Portugal.

After this posting, Wilson spent two years as the Brigade Major of 2nd Brigade at Aldershot before the outbreak of the Boer War offered him the chance of war service

(London: Cassell and Co, 1927), Vol.1 p.3-4. (References are to volume 1 unless indicated.)

9   Hindustani for armed bandit.
10   Callwell, *Diaries*, p.7. *Dah* is Burmese for knife.
11   Callwell, *Diaries*, p.10.

as Brigade Major of the 4th (Light) Brigade. The brigade departed for South Africa on 24 October 1899 aboard the SS *Cephalonia*, forming part of the British forces in Natal that were attempting to break the Boer siege of Ladysmith. After being held in reserve during the Battle of Colenso in December, the brigade finally saw action on 23 January 1900 when it took part in the Battle of Spion Kop, with part of the formation capturing two smaller peaks to the east of the main kop. More costly action was encountered in February when the brigade seized Vaal Krantz ridge at a cost of sixteen officers and 253 other rank casualties. Unfortunately, despite the efforts of the officers and men on the front lines, both battles ended in British defeat. Even at this early stage of his military career, Wilson was forming his own opinions as to why the war was not proceeding to plan - before the relief his diaries record that "we have lost heavily, fought heavily, marched heavily, and are no nearer Ladysmith....our entire failure is due to two causes...[insufficient troops and] bad generalship".[12]

In September 1900, Wilson was appointed as Deputy Assistant Adjutant General before becoming Roberts' Assistant Military Secretary. His year in South Africa was to give him "a wonderful insight into the inner workings of the War Office, and to my mind it is exceedingly unsatisfactory" - his main complaint being that a civilian ran the department.[13] The position meant that Wilson would leave South Africa at the end of the year and return to England in time to take part in Queen Victoria's funeral procession on 2 February 1901. For his service in the Boer campaign, Wilson was to be mentioned in Roberts' Despatches before being awarded the Distinguished Service Order in April 1901. After a short spell back in the War Office, Wilson was given a command position in February 1902 when appointed as Commanding Officer of 9th Provisional Battalion, Rifle Brigade at Colchester. However, this position was short-lived as within the year the battalion was disbanded as part of the reduction of the Army following the end of the Boer War.

Wilson returned to the War Office in April 1903, taking a position at the Department of Military Education and Training, serving initially under Rawlinson before being appointed as Assistant Adjutant General for Education in June. In the next four years, Wilson was involved in initiatives including the drafting of a *Manual of Combined Training*, a *Staff Manual* which formed the basis of *Field Service Regulations, Part II* and the organisation of an annual conference for General Staff officers. Wilson was also approached by Hugh Arnold-Forster, Secretary of State for War, for his views on a General Staff. His suggestion that it should be formed of the ablest men in the army with a view to forming a school of military thought to ensure a "continuity of thought and action" was taken up by Arnold-Forster in his creation of a General Staff following the War Office (Reconstitution) Committee's *Esher Report* in 1904.[14] With the incorporation of his ideas, Wilson was optimistic that the Committee would have an effect on what he saw as "the appalling story of our unpreparedness for war" before the Boer War where a "rotten system of having our army run by politicians" would be

12   Callwell, *Diaries*, p.34.
13   Callwell, *Diaries*, p.47.
14   Callwell, *Diaries*, p.62.

addressed through the creation of a military equivalent of the Admiralty. However as the Committee's work continued, Wilson became concerned that the Treasury would financially cripple the proposed General Staff, with his anger being focused on the Committee's triumvirate of Lord Esher, Admiral Sir John Fisher and Colonel Sir George Clarke who he saw as a "vacillating ignorant crowd", commenting "the 'Treasury will beat us…and I think we deserve it".[15] Wilson's views may have changed the following day when the Committee offered him the role of Commandant of the Staff College, and it was also the Committee's setting up of the directorates of Military Operations, Staff Duties and Military Training that enabled him was to take on the role of DMO in 1910.

At this early stage in his career, Wilson was already being noticed through his almost daily meetings with Roberts and was making waves. Ten years before he came to serve under him at GHQ, French remarked that Wilson and Rawlinson "did much harm in Roberts' time. They are very clever and were R's special "Pets". They are now trying it on again and if the Army Council are to retain the confidence of the Army these two young gentlemen must have their wings clipped."[16] As it was, Wilson left the War Office on New Year's Eve 1906 "without a single regret, except that of incomplete and unsatisfied endeavour to get a number of useful and necessary reforms carried out" - but he was to carry on with the development of his beliefs in his next role.

At the start of 1907, Wilson took up his post as Commandant of the Staff College at Camberley. He was to hold the role for over three years. In addition to commanding the College, Wilson gave lectures to the junior and senior divisions, the notes for which are contained in his papers. These lectures - under titles such as "Standard of Efficiency" and "How to obtain and make a School of Thought" - set out Wilson's responses to the challenges he saw facing the post-Boer War army. He wanted cadets to examine "the elements & causes which go to make success" and thereby put themselves into "a position to know where our energies should be directed to insure improvement. With knowledge comes power & with power comes optimism, the true optimism."[17] His views as to what constituted the "assets of a nation" were firmly based in traditional Victorian values. In his "Efficiency" lecture, he saw those qualities from which a people derived superiority or "high moral" [sic] as comprising: religion; patriotism; education; physical development and bravery. While traditionally grounded, he also examined the practical issues that represented "the problem of war as it affects us" - these centred on the state of preparation for war and covered organisation; mobilisation; equipment, training; discipline and "superior command". On the latter, Wilson specifically highlighted the issue that "none of our generals ever command more than 10,000 to 12,000 men in peace" - preempting the criticism that Gardner makes in Trial by Fire.[18]

15   Callwell, Diaries, p.57.
16   Richard Holmes, Little Field Marshall, (London: Cassell, 2005 edition), p.127.
17   Imperial War Museum, HHW 3/3/5, Wilson lecture "Standard of Efficiency 1" given annually 1907-10.
18   Gardner, Trial by Fire, p.1.

Wilson saw the Staff College as "a training school for <u>war</u> & incidentally for peace", placing the emphasis on the offensive.[19] He stressed this in a speech to Cambridge undergraduates: "I pointed out far too much heard on public platforms and in public press of the word "defence" – anathema of the soldier. This Empire never won by defence – this Empire will never be kept by defence."[20] He repeated the point in his lecture on "Empire Building":

> We are an island and have no frontiers to look across, with an enemy armed to the teeth facing us, we are apt to talk of peace and to forget war; yet it is by war, by bitter desperate war that empires are won, and are lost – never forget this.[21]

Wilson inculcated the importance of the "offence" through his instigation of a training exercise entitled the "Belgian Scheme" to be run annually for the Senior Division. This study looked at "the employment of the British Expeditionary Force on the Continent of Europe" and was introduced with this premise:

> It is to be assumed that Germany has aggressive designs...Great Britain is assumed to have a secret understanding with France to support her against German aggression. She is prepared to uphold the neutrality of Belgium...She will fight to maintain the status quo and the balance of power in Europe.

The class was broken up into syndicates who were "to prepare a memorandum setting forth their views as to the most effective means of employing the British Expeditionary Force". The exercise developed into a scenario where "Germany intended to violate Belgian neutrality during the impending operations." The syndicates were asked to appreciate the general situation, write orders for the British forces, and write despatches to the Allied Secretaries of State for War.[22] The scheme indicates Wilson's early identification of the role he felt the BEF could be most effective in. The scheme meant that the staff officers in August 1914 had already considered, planned and carried out this precise scenario in a training environment.

Wilson's time at Camberley allowed him to develop his closeness with his French counterparts. His visits to the *Ecole Superieure de Guerre* in Paris to study their training methods and Foch's reciprocal visits lead to the adoption at the College of a French method that became known as "*Allez, allez* exercises". These consisted of the students being subjected to a series of brisk questions, which had to be answered without hesitation. In January 1910, the political dimensions of the BEF's involvement in the forth-coming war were clarified in a conversation with Foch. In response to Wilson's question: "What would you say was the smallest British military force that would be of any practical assistance to you in the event of such a contest as we have been

19   IWM, HHW 3/3/8, Wilson Lecture, 23rd Jan 1907.
20   IWM, HHW 3/3/21, Wilson Lecture, 3rd Feb 1909.
21   IWM, HHW 3/3/37, Wilson Lecture, 17th Jun 1912.
22   IWM, HHW 3/3/17, Senior Division scheme, 23rd Nov 1908.

considering?", Foch simply responded: "One single private soldier and we would take good care that he was killed."[23]

Not everyone agreed with his methodology. Kitchener visited the College in 1910 and attacked Wilson's attempts to set up a "school of thought" but "he got no change out of me, and he really talked a great deal of nonsense" thereby laying the foundation of a mutual distrust.[24] Wilson was to leave Camberley frustrated at being unable to develop the school more fully, but nevertheless he eagerly anticipated the opportunities offered by his next role.

On 1 August 1910, Wilson took up his appointment as DMO. He had wanted a brigade command and had been offered the Bordon Brigade at Aldershot by Smith-Dorrien, but General Sir William Nicholson had overruled this as he wanted Wilson at Military Operations.[25] Lloyd George and Liddell Hart subsequently came to see Wilson's arrival "as a key factor in the shift towards involvement in mass Continental warfare", but in reality talks had been going on between the recently established British General Staff and the French since 1906.[26]

After three months in the role Wilson was dissatisfied with his Department's lack of preparedness for war "in every respect". His concerns ranged from the lack of rail arrangements for concentrating and transporting the BEF, issues over the supply of horses through to the security of the Woolwich arsenal. The effect of the unreadiness was that "no one knows how long it will take us to mobilise" which he found "a disgraceful state of affairs".[27] The poor transportation arrangements to get troops to the embarkation points were compounded by a lack of staff arrangements at the ports and there was little planned liaison with the Navy to get them over to France. As Wilson accelerated the mobilisation plans, his aims were given greater urgency by the Agadir Crisis in July 1911 with the result that the planning process now focused on getting all six divisions into action.

Wilson's thinking about a future war began to further consolidate around the role of the BEF as fighting alongside the French. By October 1910, Foch had expressed his view to Wilson that "France must trust to England and not to Russia".[28] By August the following year, when Wilson lunched with Haldane, Grey and Eyre Crowe, he was forthright in his views: "First, that we *must* join with the French. Second, that we *must* mobilize the same day as the French. Third, that we *must* send all six divisions."[29] The next day, Churchill tabled "a ridiculous and fantastic paper on a war on the French and German frontier, which I was able to demolish. I believe he is in close touch with Kitchener and French, neither of whom knows anything at all about the subject."[30] Wilson was given the stage to set out his views when asked to present to

23   Richard Holmes, *Riding the Retreat*, (London: Pimlico, 2007 edition), p.78.
24   Callwell, *Diaries*, p.84.
25   Callwell, *Diaries*, p.82-3.
26   Peter Simkins, *Kitchener's Army*, (Barnsley: Pen & Sword, 2007), p.4.
27   Callwell, *Diaries*, p.91.
28   Callwell, *Diaries*, p.88.
29   Callwell, *Diaries*, p.99.
30   Callwell, *Diaries*, p.100.

the Committee of Imperial Defence (CID) on 23 August alongside the Admiralty. In front of an audience, which included Asquith, Lloyd George, Haldane, Churchill, Grey and French, Wilson lectured the Committee for almost two hours. His planning for the deployment of a BEF was detailed enough to include "*dix minutes pour une tasse de café*" at Amiens".[31] Wilson thought "everyone very nice" and won the day over his Naval counterpart, as the CID's focus switched from the traditional naval role onto the part the BEF would play in any Continental war. While Wilson was successful, historian Peter Simkins sees the presentation as forcing his view to such an extent that he "diverted attention from what were the logical corollaries of a Continental commitment - the necessity of raising a mass army and the corresponding need of a blueprint for industrial mobilisation to keep that army supplied."[32] Nonetheless the focus of the emphasis and planning was now the BEF.

By early 1913, another political debate began to dominate Wilson's thinking, which ultimately affected his wartime career. The Government's proposals for Home Rule in Ireland and the reaction of the Ulster Protestants had a resonance with Wilson through his family background. The topic appears in his diaries from March onwards, and throughout the year Wilson remained concerned at the implications that the Ulster crisis might have on the Army. On 4 November, Wilson - now a Major General "at 48½ with 28 years service" - told French "that I could not fire on the North at the dictation of Redmond".[33] The issue remained prominent over Christmas with the Roberts at Englemere. A Boxing Day round of golf with Rawlinson and John Gough provided the occasion for further discussion, with Wilson reporting to Roberts that "Johnnie had definitely made up his mind to join Ulster if the crash came.[34]

The New Year saw Wilson asked by French to stay on as DMO for another year with the promise of a divisional command - 4th Division was suggested - in 1915. Wilson accepted reluctantly: "of course, I could do nothing but agree though I hate the idea of an extension."[35] Two days later Wilson was back to canvassing senior officers' opinion over Ulster while attending a conference at Camberley.

On his return to London after a four-week skiing break at Gstaad, Wilson gloomily noted in his diary: "Ulster is abandoned."[36] With the subject continuing to dominate Parliament, his politicking went on throughout March with a trip to Belfast and several meetings with Andrew Bonar Law, Edward Carson and French – "it appears that they are contemplating scattering troops all over Ulster, as though it was a Pontypool coal strike."[37] Meanwhile to his frustration, the CID's attention remained overseas: "usual rubbish talked, but especially about the Channel Tunnel; I gave my opinion as being

31   Holmes, *Little Field Marshal*, p.146.
32   Simkins, *Kitchener's Army*, p.5.
33   IWM, HHW 1/22, Diary, 4th Nov 1913.
34   IWM, HHW 1/22, Diary, 26th Dec 1913.
35   IWM, HHW 1/23, Diary, 10th Jan 1914.
36   IWM, HHW 1/23, Diary, 21st Feb 1914.
37   IWM, HHW 1/23, Diary, 18th Mar 1914.

that, if we are going to take part in European wars the more tunnels the better, if not, then the fewer we have the better."[38]

Wilson continued to push Bonar Law into forcing the issue of army use in Ulster - he told him that he "must ask Asquith the point-blank question, "Are you going to use the army to coerce Ulster or are you not?" "There are three ways of answering the question, i.e. Yes - No - No answer".[39]

The crisis came to a head on 20 March 1914 when Sir Arthur Paget, GOC Ireland, issued deployment orders for "active operations in Ulster". As a result Hubert Gough and fifty-seven other officers based at Curragh Camp offered their resignations. Asquith was forced to back down and the officers duly reinstated but the political fallout became clear and Seely resigned as Secretary of State for War on 30 March. With French debating whether he should resign over the issue, Wilson's advice was clear - "I told him that in my opinion he must go" - which he did seven days after Seely.[40] Wilson's involvement came with a heavy personal price that was to severely restrict his career: in December Asquith would overrule French's choice of him replacing Murray as Chief of Staff with Churchill describing Wilson's actions as a "gross dereliction of duty" when he "betrayed the Government secrets to Bonar Law."[41]

Back at the War Office, Wilson carried out a Staff Tour at Amiens in June, designed to test the train arrangements for deployment within France. While noting on the 29 June, the "awful tragedy at Sarajevo in Bosnia, the Archduke Franz Ferdinand & his wife were assassinated yesterday", Wilson remained focused on Ulster.[42] With fears of civil war looming, he attended a conference in July at Buckingham Palace to bring the parties together but this broke up after three days with no agreement reached. By the end of the month with war becoming a serious possibility - although Wilson's views as to its likelihood fluctuated on a daily basis - he was informed by General Sir Charles Douglas that his role in the BEF was to be that of Brigadier General of Operations under French as C-in-C and Murray as Chief of Staff. Wilson was unimpressed and by 3 August had managed to convince French to change it to that of Sub-Chief of Staff, thereby creating the organisational structure that was to cause issues with Murray.

Some indication of Wilson's priorities may be gathered from the fact that even whilst preparing for deployment to France, he continued his involvement with Carson in the Ulster crisis, proposing to use the men gathering under the banners of the Ulster Volunteer Force to form a partially trained body of men to be offered to the British Government aimed at creating a feeling of British indebtedness towards Ulster.[43]

The following day, the debate within the War Office concentrated on the timing of the BEF's transfer to France. While both French and Wilson wanted an immediate

38   IWM, HHW 1/23, Diary, 3rd Mar 1914.
39   Callwell, *Diaries*, p.138.
40   IWM, HHW 1/23, Diary, 28th Mar 1914.
41   Randolph S Churchill, *Young Statesman – Winston S Churchill 1901-1914*, (London: Minerva, 1991), p.492.
42   IWM, HHW 1/23, Diary, 29th Jun 1914.
43   IWM, HHW 2/73/40, Carson to Wilson, 4th August 1914.

embarkation, Haig pushed for a delay of two to three months to enable development of "the minimum resources of the Empire". Wilson was unimpressed: "Haig asked his ridiculous questions & this lead to our discussing strategy like idiots", describing it as "an historic meeting of men, mostly entirely ignorant of their subject."[44] Wilson then met with Kitchener on 7 August but the two men did not agree on priorities:

> I answered back, as I have no intention of being bullied by him, especially when he talks such nonsense as he did to-day. The man is a fool. He is bringing the 6th Division to England [from Ireland] and sending troops from Aldershot to Grimsby, thus hopelessly messing up our plans. He is a d**** fool.[45]

This diary entry is interesting as it shows the editing decisions that Callwell took when working on the diaries in 1927. The published diary omitted the two references where Wilson described Kitchener as a "fool" (underlined above). Unsurprisingly, also dropped from publication were Wilson's views three months later when a proposal was made to replace French with General Sir Ian Hamilton that "K ought to be shot."[46] The diaries were to cause upset on their publication – how that reaction would be magnified had Wilson's true feelings been disclosed can be imagined.

The same day, Roberts wrote to Wilson to express his views on his impact on getting the BEF ready for war:

> Let me tell you how much those, who have been associated with you for the last three years, feel their indebtedness to you for all you have done as the Head of the Military Operations Section at the War Office. I know, perhaps better than anyone how hard and how intelligently you have worked, and the great difficulties you have had to overcome… But for your persistence we should have been quite unprepared for the great struggle now before us…You have laid the foundation for the success which – with God's help – we firmly believe will be achieved by our troops.[47]

Rawlinson was more pointed: "When all you lucky ones have gone to France it will be perfectly horrible to be left behind here…I shall shoot myself if left in the War Office. It's awful & I can't stand it."[48] Having said goodbye to Churchill - "he began to tell me he was sure I would 'lead to victory' and then he completely broke down and cried, so that he could not finish the sentence. I never liked him so much" - Wilson and GHQ departed for France on 14 August.

Apart from the significant issue that GHQ was carrying out tasks with which it was largely unfamiliar, the internal workings were further tested by strained relations between the personnel involved. Wilson was friendly with George "Uncle" Harper,

44   IWM, HHW 1/23, Diary, 5th Aug 1914.
45   IWM, HHW 1/23, Diary, 7th August 1914.
46   IWM, HHW 1/23, Diary, 7th November 1914.
47   IWM, HHW 2/73/45, Roberts to Wilson, 7th August 1914.
48   IWM, HHW 2/73/46, Rawlinson to Wilson, 8th August 1914.

GSO1 Operations, from their days at Staff College and in his role as Deputy DMO but his relationship with George Macdonogh, GSO1 Intelligence, was cold. Although partially due to Macdonogh's diffidence and aloofness, his religious upbringing as a Catholic had lead him to stand against Wilson over the Curragh Incident. Wilson's subsequent favouring of Harper and Operations over Macdonogh and his Intelligence team had the inevitable result of marginalising the latter's impact. An example of this came on 23 August when Wilson was estimating the enemy forces that lay in front of them. Although he claimed that he had carried out "a careful calculation", he convinced French and Murray that "we only had one corps and one cavalry division (possibly two corps) opposite us", when in reality the BEF was facing elements of five German corps.

On 26 August, Smith-Dorrien telephoned Wilson at 6 a.m. to inform him that he had decided to make a stand at Le Cateau despite the risk of being surrounded. Wilson was alarmed and responded that this risked another Sedan; Nikolas Gardner has alleged that Wilson's subsequent despondency "spread rapidly among senior staff officers" and lead to GHQ hurriedly withdrawing to Noyon.[49] In his diary, Wilson recorded his concern at Smith-Dorrien's decision and his worry that French "did not quite grasp what it involved. He would not wake up Murray, and in spite of all I could say about separation of Ist and IInd [*sic*] Corps…he agreed to S-D's proposal. This will lead to disaster, or ought to."[50]

Nevertheless, the stand at Le Cateau achieved Smith-Dorrien's objective and the BEF broke away from close German pursuit. With Wilson arguing successfully with French and Murray against a plan to withdraw the BEF "for at least ten days" to refit, the force returned to the offensive on 6 September alongside the French in a morale-lifting advance of eleven miles. This action had been ordered reluctantly by French, despite the fact that Wilson advocated "pushing like the devil in pursuit" - a response that matched the desires of both Kitchener and Joffre. Further advances were achieved on the following three days but progress began to slow through poor co-ordination and caution on the part of both French and Haig. By the evening of 12 September, the BEF's pursuit had come to a halt on the banks of the Aisne. Wilson saw this as having driven the German troops over the river "without any trouble" but this ignores the tactical reality that the Germans had identified the river as providing an opportunity for a defensive stand on the northern bank.

As the advance stagnated and casualties mounted, GHQ's ability to call for replenishments was restricted by Kitchener's retention of troops in Britain to train the New Armies and provide home defence against a potential enemy landing. In a letter from late September, Wilson was outspoken in his criticism: "we are deteriorating quicker than we need to, because many excellent officers, non-commissioned officers and men are being kept back to train, or try to train, these fantastic armies which are now being put to paper". He continued:

---

49   Gardner, *Trial by Fire*, p.58.
50   IWM, HHW 1/23, Diary, 26th Aug 1914.

These laughable paper armies…are not only useless but positively dangerous in that they give an ignorant, but patriotic people an entirely erroneous idea of the situation and of their power to alter it for the better…Never forget that it took the Germans 40 years and conscription to make their army.

Wilson concluded with a note that "further comment would be an impertinence."[51] While the recipient of this letter is unidentified, it may not be coincidental that Wilson received a letter from Leo Maxse four days later that broadly agreed with his sentiments:

It is really cruel that all this energy, personnel and material should be wasted on the impossible creation of amateur forces which can exercise no possible influence so far as one can see on the present war, which should be decided one way or another during the next few months. Squiff's speeches make one positively ill.[52]

Wilson was also dissatisfied with aspects of the BEF in France. By October he was openly questioning Murray's fitness for his role. A long talk with Billy Lambton, French's personal secretary, on 7 October appeared to reach common ground - "Billy thinks Murray should be removed. He thinks he is a real danger where he is & he says that Murray's jealousy & dislike of me increases every day" - with Lambton agreeing to speak to French. While Lambton's preference was for him to take up Murray's role, Wilson disingenuously replied "this was a thing I cared very little about, my chief concern being to keep the show going for Sir John as best I can."[53] Three days later, Murray approached Wilson with his self-doubts, possibly revealing Murray's naivety to the situation, although the move can also be interpreted as Murray probing Wilson's motives. Murray said that his position "was becoming very difficult" and asked him if he should resign. Wilson replied: "I thought there ought to be no change; that I knew of no-one who could take his place with greater success, & that I thought we ought to try & tide over the present & watch developments." But Wilson confided in his diary: "I could not tell him that I thought I could do better than he so I had no option. I was sorry for him…Archie said if he were to go, I would succeed him. This made my advice still more difficult to give."[54]

With growing dissatisfaction over the lack of thrust in the attack, Wilson's irritation now spread to French who he felt "quite unable to come to any decision involving fighting…it really fills me with despair to have such a man as C-in-C. He has gusts of childish passion but otherwise no sign of life, knowledge or decision."[55] Later that week at a meeting with Foch and Huguet, "Sir John talked arrant nonsense and was so stupid…that Foch apparently said to Huguet that Sir John might be sent home at once

51   IWM, HHW 2/73/57, Wilson to unknown recipient, 22nd Sep 1914.
52   IWM, HHW 2/73/59, Maxse to Wilson, 26th Sep 1914.
53   IWM, HHW 1/23, Diary, 7th October 1914.
54   IWM, HHW 1/23, Diary, 10th October 1914.
55   IWM, HHW 1/23, Diary, 14th October 1914.

& I ought to replace him. I was absolutely ashamed at Sir J's ignorance & incapacity... the man really has no brains."[56]

By the end of October, Murray's shortcomings as Chief of Staff were the subject of general conversation within GHQ. French told Wilson that "he realizes that Murray is not now the man for the place" while when Rawlinson met with Wilson and Henderson the next day Murray's performance was discussed: "whether Sir John will keep him on or send him somewhere else I don't know but if Murray goes H.W. sees a very good chance of succeeding him."[57]

The Machiavellian intrigues at GHQ were briefly interrupted by the death of Lord Roberts. Roberts was visiting the front when he caught a chill and died with Wilson at his bedside. Wilson took consolation from the fact that "the story of his life is thus completed as he would have wished himself, dying in the middle of the soldiers he loved so much & in the sound of the guns."[58] Wilson accompanied the body back to England and took part in Roberts' funeral at St. Paul's Cathedral.

Wilson's discussions with French continued on his return:

I repeated what I had said to him some weeks ago that if he gets tired of Murray that he must take his army first & pick the best man he could find & point [sic] him as Chief of Staff. He said he had done so, his mind was quite clear about that & he would have nobody but me. He said he would resign rather than take anyone else.[59]

However French returned to London for discussions with Kitchener and Asquith and it became obvious that any suggestion that Wilson should succeed Murray was going to be over-ruled. With Wilson puzzling as to why French was still in London on 22 December, the news was broken to him by Lambton who "told me that neither K nor Asquith liked me nor liked the idea of my being appointed C. of S. This is very flattering. For myself I really care very little and find it difficult to get up any enthusiasm" - a reaction that does not ring true.[60]

Wilson had the matter out with French on Christmas Eve:

He said the Government and Kitchener were very hostile to me. They said my appointment would be very repugnant to the Cabinet and would shake confidence in the army! That I was the principle cause of all the Ulster trouble and was, therefore, dangerous. In short, neither Kitchener nor Asquith will have me. I feel highly complimented, and told Sir John so. I care not a rush for the opinion of either of these men...I might go to Russia & see what they were doing there! How funny. When I remember Sir J's conversation with me a week ago I can't help laughing. The poor weak little devil. He knew he was on difficult ground so was as <u>charming</u> as he could be & said little till the end when I said I

56   IWM, HHW 1/23, Diary, 17th October 1914.
57   Churchill Archive Centre, RWLN 1/1, Rawlinson war journal, 30th October 1914.
58   IWM, HHW 1/23, Diary, 14th November 1914.
59   IWM, HHW 1/23, Diary, 16th December 1914.
60   IWM, HHW 1/23, Diary, 23rd December 1914.

was prepared to go 'at any moment' and had several times discussed the matter with Billy [Lambton] & that I was rarely of use or of value for my pay except occasionally when things were going all wrong and also in our work with the French...I cannot feel any sorrow at not serving him or Squiffy or K. as Chief of Staff. He said this Government would soon be out & then it would be all right.

So there are politics in our Army. One of these days I may be a bother to Squiff & his lying Cabinet.

The whole thing is a pantomime![61]

French informed Joffre of the decision at Chantilly on 27 December. Joffre reacted by describing the Cabinet's decision as *affolé*, which Wilson notes, can be translated as: "mad, frantic, distracted, bewildered, flighty, flickering, deranged".[62]

On 31 December, Wilson wrote in his diary that he had analysed the reasons why he had not been given the position and had gone through them with French. While he accepted that Kitchener's "objections were a matter of opinion viz. personal dislike & a belief that I was a rather mischievous fellow, Asquith's objections were political because of Ulster & this war & that it was a question of principle." In his own inimitable way, he told French "that in my judgment he <u>must</u> remove Murray, he <u>must</u> beat Asquith on the question of principle and he <u>must</u> offer me the appointment." But to alleviate any fears, Wilson continued: "to make matters easier for him, when he offered me the post, I would refuse it. He could then appoint whomever he pleased. I can do no more than refuse the appointment I have worked for & dreamed of for years."[63]

On 25 January 1915 William Robertson was confirmed as the BEF's Chief of the General Staff. Six days later, Wilson met with French to discuss three options for his future: to stay on as Sub-Chief (this was ruled out by Robertson), to return home, or to be the principal liaison officer to the French Army. The latter role was to suit Wilson and continued throughout 1915. French offered him command of a corps in August only to have Wilson reject it. A further reminder to him of the damage his political views had caused him came in February when he was taken off the KCB list in the Honours Gazette. Wilson's disappointment is clear from his diary: "Asquith hates me after the Ulster pogrom and says that Wilson is the sort of man who would head a revolution" concluding with the ominous comment "I'm not sure that he isn't right."[64]

As part of the reorganisation following Haig's replacement of French as C-in-C, Wilson was again offered a corps command and this time accepted. His eleven-month command of IV Corps was uneventful and regarded by many as a waste of a potential valuable resource. Esher thought Wilson's posting "a waste of fine material leaving

61   IWM, HHW 1/23, Diary, 24th December 1914.
62   IWM, HHW 3/8/16, Wilson papers, 27th Dec 1914.
63   IWM, HHW 1/23, Diary, 31 Dec 1914.
64   Callwell, *Diaries*, p.208.

him in command of a Corps."[65] Similarly, Moyne visited IV Corps and echoed Esher's opinion: "a man of great brilliance and width of view and it seems a pity that he should be wasted...It is said that those above him are afraid or jealous of his brilliant tongue."[66] Wilson's next role was as part of a Russian mission in 1917, an appointment upon which Lloyd George was to comment: "there is no other General available who had the necessary qualifications." He added cryptically: "he was a man of brilliant gifts but he had obvious defects which gave the impression of unreliability."[67]

Returning from Russia, Wilson was again able to use his close relations with the French when he took up the role of Chief of the British Mission to the French Army. His time in France however, only lasted until June when he returned to England. Being home allowed him to further his relationship with Lloyd George by expounding his vision of an inter-Allied body to "draw up plans for the whole theatre from Nieuport to Baghdad".[68] With their mutual aims coalescing, Lloyd George asked him to sell the idea to the War Cabinet and in November 1917 he was appointed as the British Permanent Military Representative to the Supreme War Council.[69]

Wilson finally achieved a position commensurate with his own perceived abilities when Lloyd George broke up the Haig/Robertson alliance by replacing Robertson with his old rival in February 1918. Despite Wilson's unsubtle courting of Lloyd George over the preceding year, he was an obvious candidate for CIGS. In terms of pre-war service within the War Office, Wilson had more than eleven years' experience, initially as AAG, Education and Training, then as Commandant of the Staff College and finally four years as DMO. This compared to Robertson's six years as Assistant Quarter Master General, three years also as Commandant of the Staff College followed by a year as Director Military Training. Outside of Robertson and Wilson, there were no obvious candidates with directly relevant experience. Foch's appointment as Supreme Commander of the Allied Armies, then reunited the two old friends and "inserted an additional level of authority above his [Haig's] head".[70] In reality, Haig and Wilson got on amicably with the task of holding the German Spring Offensive and then bringing the war to a conclusion through the Hundred Days Campaign.

As the Armistice approached, Lloyd George was growing weary with Wilson but any cooling in the relationship did not however prevent them dining together with Churchill and F.E. Smith in Downing Street on the evening of the 11 November. Following the Versailles Peace Conference, Wilson received his Field Marshal's baton

65   Viscount Esher, *Journals and Letters of Reginald, Viscount Esher*, (London: Ivor Nicholson & Watson, 1938), p.62.

66   Brian Bond, *Staff Officer: The Diaries of Lord Moyne, 1914-1918*, (London: Leo Cooper, 1987), p.129.

67   David Lloyd George, *War Memoirs of David Lloyd George*, (London: Odhams Press, 1938), p.928.

68   Callwell, *Diaries*, Vol.2, p.10.

69   Keith Jeffery, *Field Marshal Sir Henry Wilson: A Political Soldier*, (Oxford: Oxford University Press, 2008), pp.198-200.

70   Paddy Griffith, *Battle Tactics of the Western Front: British Army's Art of Attack, 1916-18*, (London: Yale University Press, 1996), p.36.

in July 1919 and a month later an award of £10,000 in recognition of his wartime services. However, the amount paled in significance compared to the £100,000 awarded to Haig; the £50,000 to French and the £30,000 awards to Horne, Plumer, Rawlinson and Byng, and possibly indicated again the personal cost of his political interferences. As his military career concluded, Wilson accepted the offer of a Westminster seat for North Down and stepped down as CIGS on 20th February 1922. In his maiden speech to the Commons, Wilson took the opportunity to attack plans to reduce Britain's military capability by noting the potential catastrophe of having "an army not sufficiently strong to prevent war and not sufficiently strong to win war, but just sufficiently weak to lose the war."[71] On the same day, in the Northern Irish parliament, it had been announced that Wilson was "coming over to advise how to crush out the murder-gang", a move that was to link Wilson with the new regime in Northern Ireland and bring him to the attention of the Republicans with fatal consequences.[72]

On Thursday 22 June 1922, Wilson unveiled the Great Eastern Railway's war memorial in Liverpool Street Station. In his last public speech, he gave a moving address, stating "in doing what they thought was right, they paid the penalty".[73] On returning home, Wilson was approached by two men who fired several shots, hitting him six times with two of the wounds proving fatal. He collapsed on the steps outside his home and died shortly thereafter. The two men were later identified as Reginald Dunne, IRA London commander, and Joseph O'Sullivan. With Wilson's strongly held Unionist views and his role as security adviser to the Northern Ireland Parliament, he had been earmarked in 1921 as an IRA assassination target but the attack was the result of a personal decision by Dunne to carry out the attack in an attempt to reinstate his falling standing within the IRA.[74] Four days after his death, Wilson was effectively given a state funeral at St. Paul's Cathedral where his body was laid to rest next to his old "chief", Lord Roberts.

ooooo

On the evening of Thursday, 31 December 1914, Wilson was in a melancholy mood. His diary entry for the day concluded:

> And so the year goes out in wind and rain and sobs. Uncle and I had a good gallop in spite of the weather and heavy going. Foch came to see me and to wish me a happy New Year. I dined with the French Mission, they were all so nice. I stood outside my house

---

71   http://hansard.millbanksystems.com/commons/1922/mar/15/sir-l-worthington-evans-statement - accessed 26th November 2012.
72   Callwell, *Diaries*, Vol.2, p.330.
73   Callwell, *Diaries*, Vol.2, p.345.
74   Peter Hart, "Michael Collins and the Assassination of Sir Henry Wilson", *Irish Historical Studies*, Vol. 28, No. 110 (Nov., 1992), pp. 150-170.

here (7 Place Victor Hugo) listening to the old church clocks beating midnight. What a year – Ulster & the War.[75]

Wilson's career was not where he might have imagined it. The war he had foreseen, thought about and planned for was underway but at that point, he appeared to have an uncertain role in its prosecution. His lack of discretion in expressing his views of the abilities of his colleagues - both political and military - combined with his role in fermenting unrest within the Army over its potential use in a Home Rule crisis had cost him his job as Sub-Chief of Staff in the BEF.

Wilson had certainly made mistakes in 1914. His effectiveness as Sub-Chief is questionable. His unswerving belief in French military effectiveness blinded him to the dangers that faced the BEF in August, and subsequently prompted an unrealistic assessment of the BEF's opportunity for offensive action in October. However, to paint Wilson as the villain of BEF's campaign is overly simplistic. British GHQ as a whole was inexperienced and poorly organised. Although Wilson's machinations contributed to the dysfunctional atmosphere, GHQ's numerous problems cannot be attributed to a single man. It is certainly true that Wilson plotted against Chief of Staff Archie Murray, but Murray's weaknesses were already known and manifested themselves as early as his physical collapse on 26 August. Similarly, the effect of Wilson's optimism on John French can be overstated; French was a strong willed C-in-C with a reputation for his "undisciplined intellect and mercurial personality" that manifested in sharp mood swings.[76] Furthermore, despite Gardner's claims that Wilson exercised undue influence at GHQ, it must be noted that John French rarely took up his often-offered advice. Wilson's direct influence was decidedly limited if James Edmonds' *Official History* is accurate in its sparse description of his activities. Much of the later criticism of Wilson comes from Edmonds' conversations with Basil Liddell Hart in the 1930s and should be treated with caution.

Yet ultimately, Wilson was a part of the team that brought the war to a successful conclusion. This was a conclusion that had been enabled by his long held belief in the importance of Britain's role as a partner to the French on the Western Front. His influence in 1914 is best measured by his pre-war role in establishing this idea and ensuring that the British Army was capable of fulfilling such a role. His time as Commandant of the Staff College and then as DMO gave him the opportunity to promote these beliefs and to focus the resources of the War Office and the Army into a position where they could place an Expeditionary Force into theatre within days of the outbreak of war thereby playing a key part in stopping the German advance. Wilson clearly was a "political soldier" who intrigued and agitated throughout his career, but he was also an intelligent officer who had the foresight to see the true nature of the forthcoming conflict and was determined to do whatever was necessary to improve Britain's chances in the war. He was an operational thinker at a time when the Army did little operational thinking and thus did not fit the traditional mold of the senior

75   IWM, HHW 1/23, Diary, 31st Dec 1914.
76   Holmes, *Little Field Marshal*, p.367.

staff officer. The early death of this intellectual outsider removed any chance from him to defend his role and his activities and allowed the establishment to characterise him as a controversial and convenient maverick.

Five years after Wilson's death, Foch contributed an introduction to Callwell's collection of his diaries:

> I can affirm without the slightest exaggeration that it was entirely due to his prevision, to his convictions at once shrewd and consistently maintained as to what was required, to his tenacity in insisting that preparations for a possible conflict must be made, that the British Army was enabled to disembark rapidly in France in August, 1914 and to take part with effect in the campaign.[77]

Without Henry Wilson, the British Army would not have been prepared for a continental commitment and would not have been ready for war in August 1914. The fact that it was is the true measure of Wilson's legacy.

77   Callwell, *Diaries*, p.ix.

4
"*The* big brain in the army": Sir William Robertson as Quartermaster-General

Quartermaster-General, GHQ

John Spencer

Sir William 'Wully' Robertson is well known to historians of the First World War as the unbending and resolute Chief of the Imperial General Staff (CIGS) who, along with Douglas Haig, promulgated the strategy of attrition and the primacy of the Western Front. Perhaps unsurprisingly, the historiography concentrates on his two years in the War Office, a period which saw the battles of the Somme and Passchendaele, or Third Ypres; for many the defining encounters of the conflict. He received a single substantive mention in the two-volume Official History for 1914[1] and the main Robertson biographies rush through the first three decades of his career like an impatient diner gulping the appetisers before gorging on the main course.[2] This is a mistake. William Robertson did not simply rise, as if from nowhere, to assume the mantle of the British government's chief military advisor. Had he done so, it is unlikely he would have retained the position for so long or in the face of strong political pressure. When Robertson arrived in the War Office in November 1915 the Whitehall life of his predecessors had been, if not nasty and brutish, certainly short. A stern manner and straight talking cannot alone account for his longevity in the post nor the influence he exercised on war policy. William Robertson was no overnight success. He had been working up to the task for more than 35 years, quietly and persistently, rarely putting a foot wrong. A study of Robertson's career, including his performance in the first 18 months of the war, reveals a consummate staff officer, one who applied the regulations but was not subservient to them. Even Robertson's ultimate nemesis, David Lloyd

---

1   Sir James E.Edmonds, *Official History of the Great War Based on Official Documents, Military Operations France and Belgium 1914* (2 vols., London, Macmillan, 1922 and 1925).

2   Victor Bonham-Carter, *Soldier True: The Life and Times of Field-Marshal Sir William Robertson* (London, Frederick Muller, 1963) and David R Woodward, *Field-Marshal Sir William Robertson: Chief of the Imperial General Staff in the Great War* (Praeger, Westport & London, 1998).

Sir William Robertson. (Bain collection, Library of Congress)

George, while deriding his intellect as "sound but commonplace" acknowledged that: "He understood the army better than any of his rivals".[3] A more admiring colleague believed he had: "The big brain in the army."[4]

The BEF's administrative unit in 1914 comprised three branches, the General Staff (GS), under its own chief (CGS), the staff of the Adjutant-General (AG), and that of the Quartermaster-General (QMG). These were known as 'G' Branch, 'A' Branch and 'Q' Branch respectively.[5] The GS, Lieutenant-General Sir Archibald Murray, dealt with the training, operations, intelligence and military policy, the AG, Major-General Sir Nevil Macready with recruitment and most other personnel related issues and the QMG, Robertson, with arming, clothing, feeding and housing those personnel, and moving them around the army's theatre of operations.[6] All were responsible directly to the Commander-in-Chief of the BEF Field Marshal Sir John French. A newly-created post of Sub-Chief of Staff was held by Major-General Henry Wilson, who as

3   David Lloyd George, *War Memoirs of David Lloyd George* (2 vols., London, Odhams, 1938) I, pp.466-7. Lloyd George's memoirs, notoriously unreliable on many points, nonetheless helped shape the traditional view of Robertson.

4   Liddell Hart Centre for Military Archives, (LHCMA), Maurice Papers, 3/1/4/92B, Major-General Sir Frederick Barton Maurice, letter to wife, 13 February 1915.

5   Dan Todman, 'The Grand Lamasery Revisited: General Headquarters on the Western Front 1914-1918' in Gary Sheffield and Dan Todman,(eds.) *Command and Control on the Western Front: the British Army's Experience* (Staplehurst, Spellmount, 2007 [2004]), p.41.

6   Sir William Robertson, *From Private to Field-Marshal* (London, Constable, 1921) pp.197-8.

Director of Military Intelligence had done much in the years before the war to define the role of the British force alongside its much larger French ally.[7]

At the beginning of the war, the whole General Headquarters (GHQ) staff numbered no more than 30 officers.[8] French and GHQ have come in for much criticism, their performance in 1914 compared unfavourably with that of the men doing the actual fighting. A general lack of experience in their new roles has been held up as one reason for the apparent confusion and lack of cohesion at GHQ in the first months of the war.[9] While this might have been true of some staff officers, Robertson had undertaken plenty of QMG work during his career. This familiarity, combined with no small amount of professional competence, meant that during the first six months of the war the BEF was, within the bounds of available resources, efficiently supplied in both retreat and advance. Shortages of all materials hampered effectiveness, but the problems were systemic and centred on the slow pace in which Britain's industry moved to a war footing rather than operational shortcomings in 'Q' Branch. The statistics illustrate the size of the challenge. The initial contingent of the BEF which went to France in early August 1914 comprised four infantry divisions, formed into two corps and one cavalry division; approximately 100,000 men. By the end of January 1915, the month in which Robertson was promoted to French's Chief of Staff, it had grown to five corps (twelve divisions), almost 350,000 men.[10] During this rapid expansion and the inevitable pressure it created, Robertson kept his head, even when some about him were losing theirs. He took a hands-on approach to commanding his branch and persistently harried his colleagues at the War Office to supply the resources the BEF needed. While these day-to-day activities might be classed as 'tactical' in nature, Robertson also devoted effort to 'strategic' matters. Early in the campaign he relocated the BEF's supply bases. Later he laid the foundations of a logistical infrastructure, both physical and managerial, to handle the enormous expansion to come.

Robertson's appointment to the post of QMG to the nascent BEF in August 1914 came as little surprise to his colleagues. As a major-general since 1910 it was a logical next step for a man who had followed a competent if largely uneventful staff officer career. Like many of his peers who set sail for France that month, he had seen service in India and attended the Staff College at Camberley. Efficient work, aptly demonstrated during a range of staff jobs overseas, including service in the Boer War, and a posting at the War Office (1900-1907) saw him climb the ladder of seniority. Three years (1910-1913) as commandant of the Staff College was followed by another Whitehall job as Director of Military Training in 1913 until the outbreak of war.

7   Keith Jeffery, *Field-Marshal Sir Henry Wilson: A Political Soldier* (Oxford, OUP, 2006), pp.85-105.
8   Todman, 'The Grand Lamasery', p.41.
9   Nikolas Gardner, *Trial by Fire: Command and the British Expeditionary Force in 1914* (Praeger, Westport & London, 2003), pp.36-7.
10   Edmonds, *Official History: 1914* (vol II) p. 8 and *Statistics of the Military Effort of the British Empire During the Great War 1914-1920* (London, HMSO, 1922).

While William Robertson's steady rise as an officer was to that point unremarkable, his military career as a whole was far from the norm. Unlike his fellow officers on the General Staff of the BEF Robertson had not been privately educated at one of the country's public schools. His *alma mater* had not been Clifton, Eton or Wellington College but rather the village school in the small Lincolnshire village of Welbourn where his father was both postmaster and jobbing tailor. Like his classmates he had left at the age of thirteen, his formal education apparently over. Unlike the vast majority of the senior officers in the British Army in 1914 Robertson had not joined as a commissioned officer. Instead he had taken the Queen's Shilling as a private, just short of his eighteenth birthday, at a recruiting station in Worcester, not far from the stately home where he had been employed as a footman. William Robertson's military career was truly unique. He retired in 1921 as a Field Marshal. He remains the only man in the British Army to rise from private to the highest rank.

Beginning as a trooper in the 16th Lancers in 1877, William Robertson combined an appetite for hard work, an ability to identify opportunities when they arose and a willingness to seize them with both hands. Deep self-confidence, a robust athletic physique and a reserved but assured manner meant he stood out. In just four years he rose to sergeant, the youngest in his regiment, and three years later to troop sergeant-major. During this period Robertson qualified as a regimental instructor in musketry, signalling and elementary intelligence work. It was an experience which meant that uniquely among the members of the General Staff of the BEF in 1914 Robertson truly understood the needs and concerns of the rank and file. Other senior officers undoubtedly concerned themselves with such matters, but Robertson had real empathy with the professional troops who made up the British force in France and Flanders at the start of the war.

Despite his rapid rise to senior NCO rank, Robertson was determined to obtain a commission. In 1888 he passed the officers' entrance exams and despite severe financial hardship was gazetted a 2nd lieutenant in the 3rd Dragoon Guards. Robertson had been determined to stay in the cavalry, despite the additional financial burden, and it was no coincidence that the Dragoons were at that time posted to Muttra in India as pay was higher and living costs lower on the sub-continent. Abstemiousness forced by economic circumstance suited Robertson, who devoted his time to study, exercise and career development. Nothing illustrates the sheer hard work for which Robertson was noted than his mastery of six local Indian languages, followed by competence in German and French. No doubt he had a gift for languages, but application driven by ambition was a fundamental factor. He expected his subordinates to match his capacity for work. One Robertson staffer noted when transferred to his command: "I shall come directly under Sir WR, which will be an education, if a strenuous one."[11] Enthusiasm for sporting pursuits, particularly equine, was widespread amongst British Army officers of the period.[12] Robertson was no exception, but like some others including Douglas Haig, he took care to balance such activities with the most up-to-date military thinking.

11   LHCMA, Maurice Papers, 3/1/4/91, letter to wife, 11 February 1915.
12   Gardner, *Trial by Fire*, p.22.

In 1890 Robertson got his first taste of the supply responsibilities he would face as QMG in 1914, supervising the government grass farm in Rawalpindi. The 11,000 acre (4,500 hectare) facility supplied fodder to the Indian Army's horses and thus formed a central part of the supply chain. Robertson demonstrated his flair for organisational management in this important post and as a result was selected for active service the following year. An expeditionary force was sent to suppress a tribal uprising on the North West Frontier. Robertson, appointed Railway Transport Officer, was put in charge of the terminus at Hasan Abdal: "The important thing seemed to be to hurry up to the front all the men, animals, and material arriving at the base, and send back to Rawal Pindi with equal despatch everything arriving from the front."[13]

His hard work learning local languages paid off when, in 1892, he joined the newly reorganised Indian Army Intelligence Branch in Simla. The unit was a subdivision of the Quartermaster-General's department, allowing Robertson to observe the QMG role at close quarters. It was a vital learning experience that gave Robertson experience beyond logistics work. At that time the QMG's department in India had responsibility not only for providing the army with supplies of food and equipment, but also had responsibility for the management of field operations.[14] In 1895, as intelligence officer, he joined the Chitral Relief Force charged with suppressing another uprising on the North West Frontier. While on a reconnaissance patrol Robertson, now a captain, was attacked and severely wounded by one of his guides. Despite his injuries he drove off his assailant with his bare hands, a feat which earned him a mention in despatches and the Distinguished Service Order.[15] Having gained combat experience and attendant reputation, Robertson chose to further his career by applying for entry to the Staff College at Camberley. After much 'cramming', in January 1897 he became the first former ranker to join the College. On 21 December 1898 he graduated with the second highest marks in his year.[16] Reflecting on the experience Robertson acknowledged the value of both the learning and the contacts he made: "Haig, Allenby, Murray, Milne, Capper, Haking, Barrow, Forestier-Walker, and others who filled important posts in the Great War were amongst my contemporaries, and this personal acquaintance was very useful to me, as no doubt it was to them."[17]

Following Staff College Robertson continued his rise up the staff hierarchy. At the start of 1899 he joined the Intelligence Division of the War Office, at that time the only branch of the British Army primarily concerned with operational planning.[18] One authority has likened the Intelligence Division at this time to "a kind of substitute for a British General Staff".[19] Working in the Colonial section at the time of the Boer War

---

13   Robertson, *Private to Field-Marshal*, p.47.
14   Robertson, *Private to Field-Marshal*, p.69.
15   An interesting lesson of history, this event would now be known in modern parlance as a 'green on blue' attack.
16   Bonham-Carter, *Soldier True*, p.49.
17   Robertson, *Private to Field-Marshal*, p.88.
18   Bonham-Carter, *Soldier True*, p.52.
19   Thomas G. Fergusson, *British Military Intelligence 1870-1914: The Development of a Modern Intelligence Organisation* (Arms & Armour Press, London, 1984), p.107, quoted

he was posted to South Africa at the end of the year carrying out intelligence duties on the staff of the Commander-in-Chief Lord Roberts.

After completing his service in South Africa, he returned to the Intelligence Division at the War Office and was promoted to Assistant Quartermaster-General (AQMG) and head of the Foreign Section. He held this post until 1907, restructuring the section and producing a range of reports on the military capabilities and ambitions of the major powers. Robertson's methods "derived logically form a shrewd mind and elephantine memory, fanatical attention to detail, and common sense that never faltered."[20] This was the period in which he made his mark and positioned himself for the most senior staff appointments. He met and became friends with the future King George V at this time and the two corresponded on military policy throughout the war.[21] One piece of insightful analysis caught the attention of Robertson's superiors. At the time some establishment figures still believed France to be Britain's principal opponent with Germany as a potential ally in a European war. Lieutenant-Colonel Edward Altham, head of the Imperial Section with responsibility for planning the defence of the Empire, wrote a paper suggesting that Germany might wish to ally with Britain in a future war with Russia. Robertson disagreed. Robertson's department had been studying German military development and he had visited that country while a pupil at the Staff College. He responded with a memorandum of his own in which he stated:

> Instead of regarding Germany as a possible ally we should recognise her as our most persistent, deliberate, and formidable, rival...It is not an exaggeration to say that in no other European country is hatred of England so general or so deep-rooted as in Germany...the most potent cause is the rivalry in trade and colonial enterprise, and in this respect Germany is the aggressor. Indeed, the hope of superseding us in the commercial and naval supremacy is the governing idea of the national imagination... it [this antipathy] has existed in every grade of society for many years past, and it has come to stay.[22]

Robertson's argument impressed his commanding officer Sir William Nicholson, Director-General of Mobilisation and Intelligence, who passed it on to both War and Foreign Offices: "This seems to me a remarkably able paper by Col. Robertson, and I am afraid that the unfavourable view which he takes of the attitude of Germany towards England is correct."[23]

in Jeffery, *Field Marshall Sir Henry Wilson*, p.22.

20   Bonham-Carter, *Soldier True*, p.56.
21   Robertson was not the only senior officer to correspond directly with the King. Sir Douglas Haig, Sir Horace Smith-Dorrien and others had similar access. Sir John French and Henry Wilson did not. Ian Beckett, 'King George V and His Generals', in Brian Bond, *The First World War and British Military History* (Oxford, OUP, 1991).
22   LHCMA, Robertson Papers 1/2/4, 10 November, 1902.
23   LHCMA, Robertson Papers 1/2/4, covering note by Sir W. G. Nicholson, Director-General of Mobilisation and Intelligence, 11 November, 1902.

Robertson's next billet was AQMG to the Aldershot Command where he gained: "valuable experience in the whole field of supply and administration of a large body of troops; and this was to stand him in good stead in the fierce days ahead, when QMG to the BEF in France."[24]

He soon became Chief of Staff at Aldershot, then the Army's principal training command and in 1910 Commandant of the Staff College, succeeding Sir Henry Wilson and before him Sir Henry Rawlinson. In this role Robertson was able to give full rein to his personal approach to teaching the science of warfare: "The flaw in instruction which struck me most was…the aptitude to dwell too much upon the theoretical aspect of a problem and the neglect to realise the difficulties which beset its solution in practice." Referring to his two more flamboyant predecessors he added: "Details, so-called, were thought to be petty and beneath the notice of the big-minded man, and yet they are the very things which nine hundred and ninety times out of a thousand make just the difference in war between success and failure."[25] Although they might have disagreed on methodology, Rawlinson, Wilson and Robertson represented a significant modernising cadre within the British Army of the period.

In the autumn of 1913 Robertson became Director of Military Training at the War Office and in the early summer of 1914 planned the army's annual manoeuvres. Instead of the usual simulated pitched battle, Robertson devised a scenario in which a force would retire in the face of a stronger adversary. The exercises were scheduled for September:

> Before then we were engaged in the real thing in France, and were being driven back by overwhelming masses of Germans. The study of the manoeuvres we had planned was most helpful to me during the first few weeks of the war, when I was hard put to it to keep the troops supplied with what they needed.[26]

With the BEF in 1914

During his time as QMG, which ended in January 1915 when he was promoted to be Sir John French's Chief of Staff, Robertson's role took on two chief characteristics. His fundamental responsibility was to keep the troops well supplied and the war machine fuelled with all it needed. Quite literally he was responsible for every bomb, bullet, belt buckle and bully beef tin. As the BEF grew so did the pressure on the supply chain. The demands on suppliers were unprecedented. With few exceptions, there was a shortage of everything. At the same time Robertson concerned himself with the machinery of supply; bases, advanced bases, lines of communication and the command structures which made them work. These too faced unique circumstances. Britain had never fought a war of such magnitude before. Everything was new and untested. Robertson's respect for regulations was tempered by flexibility and a readiness to flout

24   Bonham-Carter, *Soldier True*, p.65.
25   Robertson, *From Private to Field-Marshal*, p.175.
26   Robertson, *Private to Field-Marshal*, p.195.

the rules where he believed it necessary. The British army officer's 'Bible' *Field Service Regulations, Part I (Operations)* emphasised the primacy of the 'man on the spot' using his initiative should circumstances require it.[27] William Robertson acted, particularly in the early days of the war, in a way which suggested he believed the advice was as relevant to staff officers as it was to those commanding in the field.

The unique scale of the challenges facing the BEF meant that all pre-war organisational assumptions were on trial. Creative and decisive thinking were required. Robertson believed the duty of the QMG was to think ahead and "introduce such elasticity into the supply arrangements as would promptly afford the Commander-in-Chief the greatest possible choice of action."[28] This included options in the event of a withdrawal. On 22 August, the day before the Battle of Mons, Robertson made contingency plans to relocate the BEF's main supply bases, then at Le Havre and Boulogne. He calculated that, in the event of a withdrawal, these Channel ports could be seized by rapidly advancing German forces, thus severing the British cross Channel supply line. Planning for this unpleasant possibility, he replaced them, temporarily as it turned out, with St Nazaire on the Atlantic. At the same time he moved the BEF's main advanced base from Amiens, north of Paris, to Le Mans, to the south-west. This was a prudent decision as Amiens fell to the Germans on 31 August. These contingency plans were executed quickly with 20,000 men, 7,000 horses and 60,000 tons of stores being moved from Le Havre to St Nazaire in four days.[29] The move aptly demonstrated Robertson's intelligence and willingness to seize the initiative. Although far from perfect in execution - Robertson himself later admitted that lack of time had meant supplies were jumbled up and thus delayed[30] - the operation crucially preserved the BEF's logistical infrastructure for its future advances on the Aisne and the Marne:

> There are not many other instances in military history I imagine, if any, of measures having been taken before the first battle of a campaign to change the base of an army which has been deliberately selected after long and careful consideration. It was fortunate they were taken on this occasion.[31]

According to the historian John Terraine:

> It was as well that Sir William Robertson had laid his plans for a change of bases so well in advance: even so, the speed and efficiency with which the switch was made deserves all praise. But the high standard set by the QMG's department does not alter the fact

27   *Field Service Regulations Part I 1909: Operations* (London, War Office, HMSO, 1912), hereafter FSR I.
28   Robertson, *Private to Field-Marshal*, p.205.
29   Edmonds, *Official History: 1914* (I), p.287.
30   Robertson, *Private to Field-Marshal*, p.209.
31   Robertson, *Private to Field-Marshal*, p.206.

that GHQ as a whole was now in the grip of despondency which, left to run their course, would have spelt ruin for the allies.[32]

Robertson, his fellow members of the General Staff, and the BEF as a whole faced their first test at Mons. The details of the fighting do not concern us here, but the aftermath revealed Robertson's command abilities. Heavily outnumbered, the BEF's subsequent retreat could easily have turned into a rout were it not for excellent leadership and the professionalism of the BEF's regular troops. The QMG's role was to ensure the men were supplied with food and ammunition. The troops were moving quickly and information about the whereabouts of specific units was hazy. The pace of the retreat and the inherent confusion made traditional supply arrangements ineffective. Seizing the initiative, Robertson instead ordered large quantities of food to be dumped beside roads and at junctions for the men to help themselves when and if they marched past. The supply dumps also had the inadvertent effect of misleading the Germans into believing that the BEF was demoralised and abandoning much needed food and ammunition.[33] This unorthodox approach was not to be found in British regulations, but the army's hide-bound bureaucracy was not, in Robertson's view, best suited to spur of the moment decision making: "Compliance with routine regulations, and the extra expense incurred by issuing double or treble the normal allowance of rations, were not considerations to be taken into account."[34]

He took a similar view when it came to re-supply when the BEF regrouped in September. A lot of equipment had been abandoned and Robertson was frustrated by Treasury rules requiring 'vouchers' to replace every item. His no-nonsense style brushed such considerations aside and he acknowledged later that the staff officer responsible:

> Must have thought me most irrational and unsympathetic, for I would listen to nothing about his regulations so long as officers and men were going about bareheaded for want of a cap...I insisted that the missing articles must be replaced at once, whatever the regulations might or might not be.[35]

Despite these efforts the ongoing shortages were keenly felt by the men: "Our rations were very scarce at this time. Bread, we never saw; a man's daily rations were four army biscuits, a pound tin of bully beef and a small portion of tea and sugar."[36]

The stresses of Mons and the retreat that followed placed a heavy burden on the nerves of some senior members at GHQ. As discussed elsewhere in this volume, Murray suffered some form of emotional collapse. Robertson's aide-de-camp Captain CE Woodroffe noted in his diary:

32   John Terraine, *Mons* (London, Batsford, 1960), p.167.
33   Terraine, *Mons,* p.151.
34   Robertson, *Private to Field-Marshal*, p.210.
35   Robertson, *Private to Field-Marshal*, p.208
36   Frank Richards, *Old Soldiers Never Die* (London 1933 [Naval & Military Press reprint]), p.27.

The Chief of the Staff is dead beat – found him fainting at 5am and poured whisky down his throat – don't think he will last long. However pray that the moment is near where they will appoint Sir W[Robertson] Chief of the Staff. I firmly believe he is the only man capable of getting us safely out of this. Sir H Wilson is also splendid, keeping cheery all the time.[37]

Robertson kept his nerve but Wilson was unimpressed by his Commander-in-Chief's despondent mood: "Sir John and Murray ought to be ashamed of themselves."[38]

Despite the efforts of the QMG's department, the impoverished state of the British army's supplies was evident in the first few weeks. When he inspected his men after taking temporary command of 4th Division at the end of September, Major-General Sir Henry Rawlinson found that: "The men are getting their equipment gradually and the great majority have got greatcoats now, but there are still a good many discrepancies to be made up."[39]

The First Battle of Ypres, which began on 19 October, exposed the BEF to not only the determination of the German infantry but also the strength of their artillery. The British response was restricted by a shortage of shells. As discussed in other chapters, the BEF line ultimately held against tremendous German pressure, but only at great cost in lives and the loss of important higher ground. As the battle drew to a close Robertson pleaded with Major-General Sir Stanley Von Donop, Master General of Ordnance at the War Office to improve the supply of ammunition:

The stock of 18 pounder on the L[ine] of C[ommunication] is becoming very small indeed and I hope that it will be possible for you to send us this week a larger amount than you did last week. Even an allowance of ten rounds per day means a total of rather more than 35,000 rounds a week, and we have not received that amount during the past week. It really is causing very great anxiety ...as to 4.5" [howitzer] ammunition I can say nothing. The figures speak for themselves and it seems hopeless. But it is a terrible drawback being short of this ammunition, having regard to the nature of the artillery which the enemy brings to bear on our troops, and the topographical conditions.[40]

Although an allowance of ten shells per gun per day may seem modest, five days elapsed before the War Office responded that it would be "another fortnight at least" before such volumes were available. As for 4.5-inch shells, "we are sending every one we can lay our hands on", including supplies from the Channel Islands and India.[41] As a result Robertson recalled that at one point during this period he was forced to restrict

37   Imperial War Museum (IWM), CR Woodroffe Papers, diary entry, 26 August 1914.
38   IWM, Henry Wilson Papers, diary entry, 29 August 1914.
39   Churchill Archive Centre (CAC), Rawlinson Papers, (RAWLN 1/1), Journal, 29 September 1914.
40   LHCMA, Robertson Papers 2/1/2, Robertson to Major-General Sir Stanley Von Donop, Master General of Ordnance, 16 November 1914).
41   LHCMA, Robertson Papers 2/1/4, Von Donop to Robertson, 21 November 1914.

guns to two rounds each per day.[42] The shortage of shells would continue to haunt British commanders for the next 18 months.[43] With a foreboding of what was to come he wrote to London:

> We must continue to do our best with the ammunition we get, but of course the best will be but very indifferent. It is sad to think that we have provided guns which fire ten or more rounds a minute while our output is less than ten rounds in twenty-four hours. Artillery is dominating this war, and without plenty of artillery ammunition commanders feel themselves very handicapped... Total stock in the country [of 18 pounder shells] is still only about half the regulation allowance, and that allowance, as we already know is much below what is required for a war of the present nature.[44]

It was a similar story with small arms. Britain's weapons industry struggled to cope with demand and all manner of items were in short supply. Towards the end of November, Von Donop reminded Robertson of the need to recover rifles from dead and wounded men and even to utilise any German weapons they might obtain. Robertson replied that more than 30,000 rifles had already been recovered and either redistributed or were being refurbished.[45] Despite this, a spat erupted when Major-General Henry de Beauvoir de Lisle, commander of the 1st Cavalry Division told the Secretary of State for War, Lord Kitchener, that he had "no idea" that weapons should be recovered and that he had done nothing in this regard.[46] Robertson was furious:

> I also am rather surprised at the statement ...as a General Officer commanding he ought to know it, whether any orders are issued or not, and as a matter of fact orders have been issued, and I am quite sure that they have been received by him. It is well known throughout the army. I am taking up the matter officially because I cannot allow irresponsible and incorrect chatter of this kind to be passed on to the Secretary of State for War. Every effort is made to get rifles and all equipment of casualties back to the Base, but if you will recall the number of times we have fought and lost ground you will realise the difficulty of recovering lost equipment. If we always advanced after the fighting there would be no difficulty, but I am afraid we retire sometimes, to say nothing of the retirement during the first fortnight of the campaign when of course we could recover nothing and lost a very great deal.[47]

Von Donop attempted to pour oil on troubled waters, reassuring Robertson that he had independent evidence that rifles were indeed being recovered and re-used.

---

42   Robertson, *Private to Field-Marshal*, p. 217.
43   See Edmonds, *Official History of the Great War Based on Official Documents: 1914*, (I) pp.11-17.
44   LHCMA, Robertson Papers 2/1/6, Robertson to Von Donop, 24 November 1914.
45   LHCMA, Robertson Papers 2/1/5, Von Donop to Robertson, 24 November 1914 and 2/1/8 Robertson to Von Donop, 30 November 1914.
46   LHCMA, Robertson Papers 2/1/9, Von Donop to Robertson, 1 December 1914.
47   LHCMA, Robertson Papers 2/1/10, Robertson to Von Donop, 3 December 1914.

Robertson, in an example of the no-nonsense style for which he was already well known, was not to be mollified:

> I hope that your statement about what De Lisle said will cause a little trouble. I think it entirely unpardonable for him to make the statement he did. It is not only absolutely contrary to the facts but shows that he does not know the regulations, quite irrespective of any special orders that might have been issued.[48]

To increase infantry firepower and to help offset the shortage of small arms, Von Donop reassured Robertson that he was working hard to obtain more Vickers and new pattern Maxim machine guns, the models favoured by Sir John French and his commanders, leaving the less popular Lewis Guns for the New Armies: "I quite recognised from the first that in ordering the Lewis guns we were adopting a gun that had not been fully tried, but I faced the fact that unless we did that we should stand a chance of running short of machine guns."[49]

The usefulness of machine guns was already apparent. Robertson wanted sufficient to provide four per battalion, and create batteries of six machine guns per brigade:

> The Chief [Sir John French] is also very anxious to get out some mortars. I know you are doing all you can in the matter...they really are badly wanted now that the opposing trenches are so close together. We are doing our best to produce some ourselves. The Indian Corps has made six for which we provide 200 rounds of ammunition a day... [and] is also making 400 hand grenades a day.[50]

Although most famous for their marksmanship, the Old Contemptibles were not averse to favouring the hand grenade to the rifle if they were available. The 'cult of the bomb' began in the first static lines of 1914:[51]

> Now that the trenches are so close to each other, in many cases only about 20 yds apart, grenades are in great request. In fact it seems to be the chief form of attack and defence, and without them it is considered to be practically impossible to hold trenches. The Germans have a large number of them and are constantly using them.[52]

Despite these entreaties, supplies of grenades continued to be sporadic and a month later Robertson vented his frustration, demanding to know when more would be available:

48   LHCMA, Robertson Papers 2/1/12, Robertson to Von Donop, 5 December 1914.
49   LHCMA, Robertson Papers 2/1/9, Von Donop to Robertson, 1 December 1914.
50   LHCMA, Robertson Papers 2/1/7, Robertson to Von Donop, 28 November 1914.
51   Paddy Griffith, *Battle Tactics of the Western Front: The British Army's Art of Attack 1916-18* (New Haven, Yale University Press, 1994 [1996]), p.51.
52   LHCMA, Robertson Papers 2/1/8, Robertson to Von Donop, 30 November 1914.

Our troops really are very greatly handicapped in this matter. Every corps without exception has several times reported that their men are simply bombed out of their trenches and other localities. No sooner do they capture them than the Germans bomb them out.[53]

Rudimentary attempts to fashion grenades from jam tins failed, "apparently they are not much use for killing purposes."[54]

The British Army's unpreparedness for the scale and duration of the conflict is summed up by the fact that, despite his organisational skills, it took until late November for Robertson to recognise the value of producing a weekly statement for the War Office, detailing the BEF's current supplies and outlining what would be required in future.[55] Robertson had a modest staff at this time but in any case it was his style to involve himself in the smallest details. His official correspondence shows he devoted as much attention to the clothing and other comforts of the troops as to concerns about munitions supplies. In early December he agreed with his opposite number at the War Office, Quartermaster General to the Forces, Major-General Sir John Cowans that the officers' Sam Browne belt should be replaced with webbing in order to avoid them being "picked off" by German snipers.[56] As winter approached the two worked hard to make up for the inadequacies of the clothing issued to the BEF. A cold snap in November meant warm coats were needed in great numbers. Cowans turned to Oxford Street's grandest department store: "I haven't had a definite promise but Selfridge says 30,000 in 24 hours. I can't trust any of these contractors or makers. You see I have Lord K's New Army to throw an occasional bone to!"[57]

A few days later, recording many cases of frostbite among the men, Robertson painted a graphic picture of life in the British trenches:

As regards boots in general they must be very large sized, and so must jackets and trousers. The men simply stuff on all the clothes they have, and they are becoming pretty numerous in view of the large amount of gifts sent up, and a great deal of room is required both in the boots and in the clothes.[58]

Gifts from home boosted the standard issue kit but they were not always welcomed with open arms. Queen Alexandra commissioned leather belts for the troops, complete with a letter of support, but apparently they were not distributed as efficiently as they might, and nor had a letter of appreciation been sent by the army. Robertson, clearly

53   LHCMA, Robertson Papers 2/1/18, Robertson to Von Donop, 24 December 1914.
54   LHCMA, Robertson Papers 2/1/22, Robertson to Von Donop, 23 January 1915.
55   LHCMA, Robertson Papers 2/2/3, Robertson to Major-General John Cowans, Quartermaster-General to the Forces, 28 November 1914.
56   LHCMA, Robertson Papers 2/2/14 and 2/2/31, Robertson and Cowans 22 November and 3 December 1914.
57   LHCMA, Robertson Papers 2/2/7, Cowans to Robertson, 17 November 1914.
58   LHCMA, Robertson Papers 2/2/10, Robertson to Cowans, 21 November 1914.

exasperated by what he considered a minor matter at such a fraught time, responded with characteristic bluntness:

> All that I know of the matter is that a very large number of belts have been sent up, and that considerable numbers have been returned as the men decline to have them. As you know many men will not wear these belts.[59]

Nonetheless, the QMG saw to it that French wrote to the Queen and thanked her. Cowans told Robertson: "I saw the Queen the other day and she seemed quite pleased at the belts having been received. I did not tell her that most of them were being worn round the necks of natives probably."[60]

As Christmas approached Robertson's irritation with trivia finally boiled over, as he told his ally at the War Office:

> We have recently had several demands for additions to or changes in the daily ration. You will be interested perhaps to know what some of the recommendations have been. They have included kippered herrings, findon [sic] haddocks, kippered mackerel, chestnuts, pork for Christmas, treacle, and last but not least, peppermint bullseyes. The bullseyes constituted the last straw and I proposed a rather acrimonious reply pointing out that the quality and variety of our present rations, were not equaled in any other armies; the extent to which additions and alternatives had already been approved; discouraged the idea that luxuries are necessaries, and finally remarked that the main object in view is the destruction of the enemy's armies; that the general exigencies of active service must govern all recommendations of the above nature, and wound up by saying the attainment of the object in view would not be materially expedited or rendered more easy by the issue of peppermint bullseyes or the substitution of marmalade for plum jam. The Chief thought the memo a little too hot and perhaps ill-advised and so it did not go forward.[61]

It is ironic to know that Sir John French, famous for his mercurial temper, had to intervene to calm the normally reserved Robertson. His temper had not improved the following day when questioned about the efficacy of hand warmers, items similar to those used by the Japanese in their recent war with Russia:

> I know nothing more about the wretched things than you do yourself. What I do know is that we are collecting an enormous amount of clothes, equipment, and toys of all sorts, and honestly I feel some difficulty in taking much interest in them because all this presupposes we are continuing to sit still whereas we ought to get on.[62]

59   LHCMA, Robertson Papers 2/2/32, Robertson to Cowans, 6 December 1914.
60   LHCMA, Robertson Papers 2/2/39, Cowans to Robertson, 11 December 1914.
61   LHCMA, Robertson Papers 2/2/46, Robertson to Cowans, 16 December 1914.
62   LHCMA, Robertson Papers 2/2/47, Robertson to Cowans, 17 December 1914.

Although he carried out his QMG duties efficiently and at times with inspiration, Robertson's judgement was sometimes flawed. In late 1914 he was convinced that the static nature of the war was temporary and that the campaign would soon return to one of movement. At the end of November he rejected requests for the troops to be provided with a second overcoat, firstly because he did not believe they needed them and: "If we could only get on the move these numerous requests for all kinds of new and different things will automatically disappear."[63] Other senior members of GHQ were even more optimistic and expected the war to soon be over. Rawlinson, like Haig and Kitchener, did not and wrote in his diary when he arrived in France: "I think the war will go on until the K armies are fit to take the field - Henry [Wilson] does not agree with me. We shall see who is right in the long run."[64]

It is not surprising that faced with war on such a scale, with ever increasing demands on men and material, systems and nerves were strained. Kitchener's autocratic style meant he made little use of the Imperial General Staff (IGS) in London. Even if he had sought their counsel, many of the ablest staff officers had left their desks as soon as war was declared and were fighting at the front rather than carrying out the duties for which they had been trained. Those who remained were largely ignored by Kitchener. His first Chief of the Imperial General Staff, General Sir Charles Douglas, died from overwork in late October. His second, General Sir James Wolfe-Murray, was so overawed by Kitchener that Winston Churchill nicknamed him "Sheep".[65] The result was that for the most part Sir John French's staff were allowed to manage affairs on their own, for better or worse. This worked in Robertson's favour. Despite his reputation for pugnacity and rigour he engendered loyalty from both the men who served him and those he worked alongside.

One of his main allies was Cowans, one of the few IGS officers who stood out in Whitehall at that time.[66] The men developed a strong working partnership; Robertson shared his frustrations over supplies and Cowans passed on gossip about the military-political goings-on in London. Both were sensitive to the inevitable organisational tensions and frictions which develop in organisations under stress. Towards the end of November 1914 they were angered by the BEF's Adjutant General, Macready, who had brought to the attention of Kitchener his belief that some troops were arriving in France ill-equipped. Cowans wrote:

> This has absolutely nothing to do with him and is not the case. He has also apparently sent a wire saying demands [on ordnance and equipment] of Oct 15 have not been met...it really is intolerable and makes for nothing but confusion...it is your business and Maxwell's [the Inspector General of Communications] and mine.[67]

63   LHCMA, Robertson Papers 2/2/27, Robertson to Cowans, 30 November 1914.
64   CAC, Rawlinson Papers, (1/1), Journal, 21 September 1914. On 1 October.
65   CAC, Papers of Maurice Hankey, Hankey Diary, (HNKY 1/1) 23 September 1914.
66   Terraine, *Mons*, p.20.
67   LHCMA, Robertson Papers 2/2/26, Cowans to Robertson, 29 November 1914 (original emphasis).

A fortnight later Robertson and his colleagues faced unwanted political interference when Churchill, as First Lord of the Admiralty, attempted to pressure French into incorporating Royal Naval transport units into the BEF. The proposal, together with his suggestions for future military strategy, including Royal Navy artillery brigades being sent to the front, received short shrift from Cowans:

> Winston has received an absolute check in all his military [sic] ambitious schemes which he has been drawing up, by a letter [from the War Office] in which we have said we will have nothing to do with them: though we are quite willing to take his infantry to put in Coast Defences. All we are trying to guard against is that he does not let Lord K or ourselves in over this, for his ideas are absolutely crude (I need not comment on his Antwerp fiasco) on military matters. One would surely think that he had enough to do running his Naval affairs at the Admiralty...I quite understand how difficult your position is, as of course he is a very great friend of Sir John. [68]

Von Donop, with responsibility for munitions supply, took a similar view:

> If only we could squash Winston we should be saved very much trouble in this matter, but he will try and get his guns sent over. He makes out always that they have got any amount of ammunition and then when we ask where it is, we find there is scarcely any available. [69]

As QMG Robertson faced a fluid and constantly changing situation. It was one which required flexible responses. One key element of the BEF's organisational structure he wanted to change was control of the Line of Communication (L of C). This was the system by which the supplies and services for which the QMG was principally responsible reached the troops at the front. The Field Service Regulations relating to the operation of the Staff placed the L of C under the command of the Inspector General of Communications (IGC). [70] This added another officer to the supply chain, also a Major-General, also reporting to the Commander-in-Chief, but located far behind the lines at the main base at the port. The QMG feared he had responsibility without power. According to his memoirs, Robertson had been unhappy with this system before the war, convinced that it added complexity and that in the heat of battle poor communications were likely to result in disruption of supply. Finding his worst fears were proven, he set about changing the arrangement:

> With the approval of the Commander-in-Chief I swept away the regulations, and so far as the distribution of food and ammunition was concerned the responsibility of the IGC was made to end at the railheads, to be selected by me, the onward transport then becoming a matter for my staff and not for his. Later, his duties at the front were further

68   LHCMA, Robertson Papers 2/2/42 Cowans to Robertson, 14 December 1914.
69   LHCMA, Robertson Papers 2/1/17 Von Donop to Robertson, 16 December 1916.
70   *Field Service Regulations Part II 1909: General Staff* (London, War Office, HMSO, 1914).

restricted, and it was recognised that, instead of retaining the almost complete freedom of action assigned to him by the regulations, he must be guided by the instructions of the Quartermaster-General. [71]

Towards the end of 1914, as the BEF continued to grow, Robertson recommended a second L of C. Keen to retain control he told Cowans that this too should be co-ordinated by his office:

> There are some very important matters to be settled in regard to L of C, principles when we find it necessary to use more than one L of C, because we shall then require more than one IGC. I am thinking of entirely separate Lines of Communication… in the case of two or more lines of communication, the army or armies on each line would communicate direct with the L of C of that line, and it would for me as QMG to co-ordinate the work of the IGCs, so far as it is necessary to co-ordinate it out here at all. But the principle coordinating authority would be the War Office working in conjunction with me.[72]

Robertson successfully prevailed over his IGC colleagues, firstly Major-General F.S. Robb and then Major-General Ronald C. Maxwell, despite the latter's promotion to Lieutenant-General in October 1914. Force of personality must have been as much the reason for the accommodation as logical argument. While this approach overcame the regulations in 1914, its *ad hoc* nature meant that no matter how well it served the purpose the change was never formalised. The IGC retained its *de jure* independence until September 1916 when its responsibilities were finally split between the new Director General of Transport, Sir Eric Geddes, and the QMG.[73]

Robertson's influence was felt across the expanding logistical machine. In late November he appointed a new Director of Transport, Brigadier-General W.G.B. Boyce. His predecessor, Gilpin, had failed due to overwork and Boyce needed a deputy: 'The Transport business is a very extensive one in the present time, and the organisation of supervising transport needs to be considerably enlarged.'[74] In December he concluded that a senior-level post was required to control canal and river transport. This appointment, he argued, should come under the Director of Railways who would then have oversight of the movement of all heavy supplies. Cowans disagreed and pointed out that Chapter III of *FSR I* said the Director of Transport should control inland waterways. Railway officers, he claimed, knew nothing of such matters. Once again Robertson was prepared to set aside the regulations: "The whole question of railways and canals is generally regarded by French GHQ as one, and in this matter, as in several others, we have thought it best to conform to the French system and views."

71   Robertson, *Private to Field-Marshall*, p.200.
72   LHCMA, Robertson Papers 2/2/53, Robertson to Cowans, 23 December 1914.
73   Todman, 'The Grand Lamasery', p.56.
74   LHCMA, Robertson Papers 2/2/27, Robertson to Cowans 30 November 1914.

Cowans finally agreed with Robertson.[75] Around the same time Robertson asked for additional experienced Royal Engineers officers to support the railway system. The current team, including experienced men from the Indian Army was "barely sufficient, to say nothing of future expansion."[76] In January Robertson succeeded in persuading the War Office that Brigadier-General GH Fowke should be appointed the BEF's Chief Engineer: "We found it absolutely necessary to have such a man, as before he had no status and no power, and no mere advisers ever have."[77] While this appointment contributed to smoother running of the railway system, provision of transport remained a constant headache for the BEF. It was the responsibility of Robertson and Cowans but both realised that as the BEF grew the challenge would only become harder. In December Sir Archibald Murray, French's Chief of Staff, had complained to the War Office about the lack of lorries for the growing numbers of troops: "I have no doubt that Murray does remember that new organisations [i.e. new units] mean more transport, and therefore increases the difficulties of forming the New Armies. But I am afraid the matter ends there, as the Chief orders from time to time new organisations and they are made."

The same memorandum contained a prescient view on the role of the mounted corps:

> I quite realise that you cannot possibly go on supplying lorries at the rate you are now doing when we get another half million men out here, on the other hand I hope we shall not want nearly as many in proportion as we now do. We have been here for a long time now and a full ration of hay has to be distributed...this hay question is an enormous one, as we have at the front some 85,000 horses many of which are of no use at all because the cavalry have no opportunity of using their horses, and I am inclined to think that they never will have much during this Campaign. The nature of the operation will probably not admit of the employment of any considerable bodies of cavalry, any more than it now does.[78]

Further evidence, if it were needed, that not all former cavalry officers at GHQ held a blinkered belief in the efficacy of massed mounted assaults on the Western Front. In fact, William Robertson was far removed from the caricature of the clueless red-tabbed Staff Officer. In 1914 he brought valuable personal experience to the trials and tribulations of supplying a military machine which grew three-fold in six months. Although a master of regulation and procedure, Robertson refused to be hemmed in by either, seeing them as hand-rails to guide decision-making rather than barriers to creativity. Feeding and clothing an expanding army, which for at least part of 1914 was both mobile and engaged in fierce combat, required flexibility and imagination. Robertson demonstrated these attributes within days of arriving in France, firstly by moving the BEF's bases out of harm's way, and then adopting unorthodox methods

75   LHCMA, Robertson Papers 2/2/43, 2/2/43 and 2/2/52 14-20 December 1914.
76   LHCMA, Robertson Papers, 2/2/35 Robertson to Cowans, 9 December 1914.
77   LHCMA, Robertson Papers 2/1/19, Robertson to Von Donop 11 January 1915.
78   LHCMA, Robertson Papers, 2/2/45 Robertson to Cowans 16 December 1914.

to re-supply the army on the retreat from Mons. Thereafter he worked tirelessly, often bringing his forthright personality to bear, to ensure the troops were as efficiently supplied as limited resources allowed. At the same time he adopted a strategic approach to the QMG role, planning the expansion of the logistical infrastructure to cope with exponential growth. It is hard to disagree with the view that: "as an institution GHQ was hastily and imperfectly improvised during mobilisation and did not function properly as the "brain" of the army during 1914-15."[79] That said, 'Q' Branch performed satisfactorily in the circumstances, and its commanding officer made a series of changes to improve the efficiency of its operational systems.

In January 1915 Sir John French finally decided to replace the physically ailing Murray and Robertson was chosen ahead of Wilson. Despite being a close friend of the latter, Rawlinson wrote in his journal: "This will be a vast improvement and augers well for the future."[80] Robertson's new role allowed him to continue to impose his organisational philosophy on the BEF; a mixture of rigorous attention to detail leavened by creative strategic thinking. Throughout 1915 Robertson lobbied with Haig and others for the Western Front to remain the decisive battleground. Germany, he believed, was the principal enemy and must be defeated in the principal theatre. 'sideshows' in the Dardanelles and Salonika would not provide ultimate victory. It was a policy Robertson continued to espouse for the rest of the war, with no small measure of success. As Sir Maurice Hankey, Secretary to Lloyd George's War Cabinet put it:

> His greatest quality, transcending his great powers of work, his mastery of principle, his organizing capacity, and his judgement of men was "character". His was a dominating personality. He knew what he wanted, and he nearly always got his way.[81]

79   Robbins, *British Generalship*, p.116.
80   CAC, Rawlinson Papers, (RAWLN 1/1), War Journal, 25 January 1915.
81   Maurice Hankey, *Supreme Command: 1914-1918* (2 vols., London, George Allen & Unwin, 1961), pp.445-6.

Corps Command

5

The Making of a Corps Commander:
Lieutenant-General Sir Douglas Haig

I Corps

Gary Sheffield

Anyone writing about Douglas Haig as a commander in 1914 has to face the problem of hindsight and historical baggage. They may be influenced, consciously or not, by their opinions of his hugely-controversial conduct as Commander-in-Chief of the British Expeditionary Force (BEF) from the end of 1915. However, this is not comparing like with like. The scale of these later operations was vastly greater than those of 1914. Haig's job as a military strategic level *de facto* Army Group commander and 'war manager' was very different from his role in 1914. Then he was a subordinate commander acting at the operational level, occasionally reaching down to the tactical level. In 1914 Haig was regarded as a high-flyer, but his reputation was as a very competent staff officer and military administrator, rather than as a field commander. This chapter examines Haig as an operational commander in 1914, after establishing the context by examining his pre-war career. Generally, with a few exceptions, references to his post-1914 career are eschewed.

From his earliest days in the army Haig took the business of being an officer very seriously. In 1884 he was the top Gentleman Cadet of his intake at the Royal Military College Sandhurst.[1] As a subaltern in the 7th Hussars Haig acquired the nickname 'Doctor', because he had attended Oxford (although, through illness, he left without taking a degree), and probably because he was a thinking soldier.[2] Haig was a driven man, and took on a series of demanding jobs, beginning a pattern that would last until the end of his life. He had some important assets as an officer: a sharp, if not outstanding, mind; capacity for hard work; willingness to learn; and an excellent grasp of the essentials of soldiering. As early as 1892-93 Haig had caught the eye of senior officers, with the result that he carried out several staff jobs in India.

---

1   S.J. Anglim, 'Haig's Cadetship – A Reassessment', B[ritish] A[rmy] R[eview] (August 1992) p.13.
2   John Vaughan, *Cavalry and Sporting Memories* (Bala, 1954), p.3.

Sir Douglas Haig. (Editor's collection)

[3] It was not the case of a duffer getting on thanks to influential patrons. Haig's career was promoted by superior officers because they recognised him as an outstanding officer with huge potential. Moreover influential backers only advanced Haig so far. His career did not really take off until he had proved his competence on active service in South Africa. Haig was still a major in 1899, but by 1903 he had risen to major general.

In 1896 Haig entered the Staff College, Camberley. This has been seen as an important, and in some ways baleful, influence on his thinking.[4] A detailed examination of this claim would be out of place here, as it largely concerns his post-1914 campaigns, but a few comments about Haig's time at Camberley are appropriate. Although the course was primarily concerned with staff work, under the influence of Colonel G.F.R. Henderson, students were also taught the constituents of command through the study of military history, with stress on the operational level (referred to as "grand tactics" at the time). There was an emphasis on the Napoleonic Wars, as well as more recent campaigns such as the American Civil War.[5] These were in

3   National Library of Scotland (NLS) Acc.3155, Haig papers (HP)/1, Haig diary, 3 Jan. 1892; HP/6g, Wood to Haig, 1 Jul 1895; Haig to Wood, 7 July 1895 in Douglas Scott, *Douglas Haig: The Preparatory Prologue 1861-1914* (Barnsley, 2006) p.53; HP/6b, Haig to Henrietta, 4 Jul 1895.
4   Tim Travers, *The Killing Ground* (London, 1987), p.97. For a corrective, see Gary Sheffield, *The Chief: Douglas Haig and the British Army* (London, 2011) pp.25-8.
5   Brian Holden Reid, *War Studies at the Staff College 1890-1930* (Camberley, SCSI Occasional Paper 1, 1992) pp.8-9.

the main mobile campaigns, and as such relevant to Haig's experiences in August-September 1914. There was a belief that whatever the differences in technology the underpinning principles demonstrated in the previous campaigns remained relevant. (This justification for the study of military history by officers remains sound to this day).[6] Moreover, rather than a rigid, doctrinaire method,[7] at Camberley Haig learned – or more likely had confirmed – an adaptable, empirical, pragmatic approach to war. This gave him an overall framework within which he could work out his ideas. The army's command philosophy called for the higher commander to make clear his 'intent', and for subordinates to devise and execute plans within the overall structure. This devolution of command authority aimed to speed up the decision-making process by allowing the 'man-on-the-spot' to exercise his initiative. The flaw was that the man-on-the-spot was not always willing to exercise his devolved authority, and that superiors were sometimes unwilling to intervene decisively when things went awry, a practice that has been described as "umpiring".[8]

Haig saw active service in the Sudan in 1898. This reinforced his strong sense of the importance of logistics and of modern technology such as the machine gun.[9] He showed himself an effective leader on the battlefield, able to keep a cool head, while demonstrating considerable courage – some thought he deserved the VC for one particular action. The Sudan campaign reaffirmed his belief in the efficacy of cavalry. It is important to note that the received wisdom that horsed cavalry was an anachronism on late nineteenth century battlefields should be discarded.[10] Haig was a moderately progressive reformer in an arm evolving to meet the challenges of modern war. He was appalled by the costly and ineffective charge of the 21st Lancers at Omdurman.[11] Haig firmly believed that the mounted *arme blanche* charge had its place, but only as a part of combined arms tactics. During the fierce debates over the

6   In 1912, the Commandant of the Staff College made it clear that the purpose of the study of military history was to equip officers with intellectual tools, and campaigns of the past provided "warnings of the probable result of following a certain course of action" not "guide-posts showing the exact road to be travelled": Major-General W.R. Robertson, 'Final Address to the Officers of the Senior Division, Staff College', *The Army Review* Vol. IV (1913) pp.334-5. An influential modern historian at the UK's Joint Services Command and Staff College has made essentially the same point, that military history can provide "approximate precedents" for commanders: Andrew Gordon, *The Rules of the Game: Jutland and British Naval Command* (London, 1996) p.600.
7   Travers, *Killing Ground,* pp.95-7.
8   Martin Samuels, *Command or Control? Command, Training and Tactics in the British and German Armies, 1888-1918* (London, Cass, 1995), pp.49-53.
9   NLS, Acc.3155, HP/6b Haig to Henrietta, 29 May 1898; HP/6g, Haig to Wood, 26 Mar. 1898; HP/6b, Haig diary, 19, 20 Jan., 5 Apr 1898.
10   Antulio J. Echevarria II, 'Combining Firepower and Versatility: Remaking the "Arm of Decision" before the Great War', *J[ournal] R[oyal] U[nited] S[ervices] I[nstitute]*, Vol. 147 (2002) p.89.
11   NLS, Acc.3155, HP/6b Haig to Henrietta, 6 Sept. 1898.

role of mounted troops that followed, he was to champion the importance of the 'hybrid' cavalryman, equally adept at mounted and dismounted roles.[12]

In the South African War, as chief of staff to French's Cavalry Division Haig cemented his reputation as an excellent staff officer. Haig's name also gradually became familiar to the public: "one does not hesitate to predict a very distinguished career [for him]" wrote one journalist. [13] Haig also gained valuable command experience. Notably, having been a squadron commander under his command only three years earlier, in April 1901 Haig was selected by Lord Kitchener to inject dynamic leadership into a failing campaign in Cape Colony. [14]

In 1905 French told the Unionist Secretary of State for War. H.O. Arnold-Forster, that "no one in the army that I know of has greater Staff capacity" than Haig.[15] Indeed, following his return from South Africa in 1902, much of Haig's time was taken up with important staff posts: Inspector-General of Cavalry in India; Director of Staff Duties; Director of Military Training; and Chief of Staff, India. R.B. Haldane, Arnold-Forster's Liberal successor, relied on Haig as his principal military lieutenant in pushing through the eponymous reforms. Haig also played a major role in formulating doctrine for the cavalry and, in the form of *Field Service Regulations 1909*, for the entire army.[16] These built on previous manuals and were avowedly non-prescriptive, setting out "general principles – not rules – which will shall serve as guides, enabling subordinate officials to act in accordance with the views of the C.-on-C., under all ordinary circumstances, without the necessity of referring to him".[17] Robertson instructed Staff College students to "exercise your common-sense and act in accordance with circumstances and the spirit of Field Service regulations".[18]

Haig was evangelistic in his concern that officers should be thoroughly conversant with *FSR*.[19] Furthermore, he was insistent on the importance of training and combined arms tactics.[20] Thus the "principles" of all arms cooperation, a widely circulated memorandum declared, "which are distinctly laid down in Field Service

12   Haig's evidence to *Royal Commission on the War in South Africa*, vol. II, (HMSO, 1903) pp.403; Douglas Haig, *Cavalry Studies* (Hugh Rees, 1907); Stephen Badsey, *Doctrine and Reform in the British Cavalry 1880-1918* (Aldershot, 2008), pp.174-7, 210-12.

13   J.G. Maydon, *French's Cavalry Campaign* (London, 1901), pp.42, 108.

14   NLS, Acc.3155, HP/6c, Haig to Henrietta 11 Apr. 1901.

15   Quoted in John Gooch, *The Plans of War: The General Staff and British Military Strategy c. 1900-1916* (London, 1974) p.85.

16   Gooch, *Plans of War*, pp.113-17; Christopher Pugsley, *We Have Been Here Before: the Evolution of the Doctrine of Decentralised Command in the British Army 1905-1989* (Sandhurst Occasional Paper No.9) pp.4-9.

17   *Field Service Regulations* Part II (London, 1909), p.23; Gooch, *Plans of War*, pp.27-8.

18   Robertson, 'Final Address', *The Army Review*, IV p.340.

19   Liddell Hart Centre for Military Archives (LHCMA), Kiggell 1/9, Haig to Kiggell, 13 July 1911; Similarly, on becoming CIGS Sir John French publically emphasised the importance of a 'common doctrine' based on 'general principles': see his 'Memorandum', *The Army Review* Vol. II (1912) pp.vii, viii.

20   See e.g. NLS, Acc.3155, HP/40c, 'Notes on operations', 8 Dec. 1903; Sir George Barrow, *The Fire of Life* (London, 1942), pp.104-5.

Regulations, Part I", were to be "studied and thoroughly understood by all officers".[21] *FSR* has been criticised on the grounds that "confusingly", principles were not actually defined.[22] This is misleading. In the British army 'principles' in the modern, 'bullet point' sense only date from 1920, when they were introduced under the influence of J.F.C. Fuller. Before then they were regarded as broad precepts, much as in the way Clausewitz used them.[23]

Haig's dedication to reforming the army and training was driven by his belief that war with Germany was inevitable and coming soon.[24] On taking over Aldershot Command, consisting of 1st and 2nd Division and 1st Cavalry Brigade, in March 1912, he was given the opportunity to focus on preparing a major formation for active service. Major Eugene ('Micky') Ryan, a Medical Officer at Aldershot, later noted that after Haig succeeded Smith-Dorrien in this post

> it was noticed and talked of in the messes that the training of both officers and soldiers became much more strenuous. Regimental exercises, B[riga]de and Div[isional] training with long route marches were the order of the day. The manner of training changed frequently, especially during the hot weather the men worked without wearing their tunics and in the long route marches the men when they did wear their tunics did so with open necks (unbuttoned).[25]

In the 1912 manoeuvres, Haig was out-generalled and defeated by a force commanded by Lieutenant-General Sir James Grierson. The canard that this was caused by Haig's neglect of aerial reconnaissance has been convincingly refuted. Haig used aircraft and cavalry for scouting but both failed to locate the presence of an 'enemy' force on Grierson's flank (as did cavalry).[26] However, according to some witnesses Haig did not emerge well from these manoeuvres. The *Westminster Gazette*'s military correspondent was damning, asserting that "With regard to General Haig's

21   Memorandum on Army Training in India, 1910-11', *The Army Review* Vol. II (1912) p.57 (issued by Haig, this document nominally conveyed the views of the Commander-in-Chief, General Sir O'Moore Creagh).

22   Hew Strachan, 'The British Army, its General Staff and the Continental Commitment 1904-14', in David French and Brian Holden Reid, eds., *The British General Staff: Reform and Innovation, 1890-1939* (London, 2002), p.92.

23   Sheffield, *The Chief,* p.60; Antulio J. Echevarria II, 'Principles of War or Principles of Battle?' in Anthony D. Mc Ivor, ed., *Rethinking the Principles of* War (Annapolis, MD, 2005), pp.60-62. For Clausewitz's influence on Haig see Christopher Bassford, *Clausewitz in English* (New York, NY, 1994) pp. 77, 90-1, 107. On p. 84 Bassford points out that Clausewitz's British admirers tended to be military reformers. Haig fits this pattern.

24   LHCMA, Kiggell 1/2, Haig to Kiggell, 27 Apr. 1909; National Army Museum (NAM), Ellison papers, 8704-35-460, Haig to Ellison, 11 Sept. 1906.

25   Ryan papers (in private hands), Ms account of Mons campaign. Ryan was to become Haig's trusted friend and family doctor.

26   Andrew Whitmarsh, 'British Army Manoeuvres and the Development of Military Aviation, 1910-1913', *War in History,* Vol. III (2007), pp.335-8.

strategy, no particular brilliance could be claimed. He worked almost entirely by the training manuals, and his every move could be foreseen and met..." Haig was also criticised for failing to mount a "coup" with his cavalry.[27] However Charles à Court Repington, *The Times'* military correspondent, an army contemporary who personally disliked Haig, gave a rather more balanced critique of the manoeuvres. In his reports Repington criticised and offered some qualified praise of both Haig and Grierson. Repington mentioned that unlike Haig's force, Grierson had an "improvised" staff and troops without experience of working together, which perhaps implied that Haig might have done better. Although he identified an opportunity for Haig to make a bold attack on a Territorial force, Repington stated – fairly enough – that "it was bit of a gamble... [and t]here are not many generals who will take these risks" before slyly adding "and we must give up appointing Scotsmen at the head of our armies if we wish such risks to be run".[28]

Although the September 1913 Army manoeuvres have not gained such notoriety as those of the previous year, they were if anything even more contentious. Sir John French acted as both exercise director and commander of Brown Force, which consisted of two "Armies" (actually corps) under Haig and General Sir Arthur Paget. The opponent was a "skeleton" force under Major-General C.C. Monro. This dual responsibility contributed to French's lacklustre performance, which, to his fury, was criticised by Repington in print.[29] Repington's reports charitably opined that given the novelty of manoeuvres involving corps, the overall performance was "satisfactory", but he perceptively identified a number of problems that the exercise had revealed, such as problems of communication between formations and the slow transmission of orders.[30] Haig indirectly admitted that staff work in his corps had been a problem, stating that it was now "fifty percent more effective" as a result of the exercise. [31] Of course, one of the purposes of the exercise was to expose shortcomings that could then be corrected.

However, the foremost problem highlighted by Repington was that French's GHQ had failed to coordinate the activities of the two corps. [32] Haig's already sagging confidence in French's ability as a high commander suffered another blow. After the 1913 Aldershot Command manoeuvres Repington had predicted that Haig's force "will cover itself with much credit" in the forthcoming Army exercises.[33] In the event,

27   *Westminster Gazette*, 20 Sept 1912, quoted in Timothy Bowman and Mark Connelly, *The Edwardian Army: Recruiting, Training and Deploying the British Army, 1902-1914* (Oxford, 2012), p.181.

28   *The Times* 21 Sept 1912 p.8, 7 Oct. 1912 p.6.

29   Richard Holmes, *The Little Field Marshal: Sir John French* (London, 1981), p. 149. For an interesting if rather anodyne French perspective on the exercise, see Commandant de Thomasson, 'The British Army Exercise of 1913', *The Army Journal* Vol. IV (1914) pp.143-56.

30   *The Times* 16 Oct. 1913 p.14.

31   *The Times* 30 Sept. 1913 p.4, 20 Sept. 1913 p.10 .

32   *The Times* 10 Oct. 1913 p.7.

33   NLS, Acc.3155, HP/98, Haig Ts diary 13 Aug. 1914. For the differences between the

Haig did not escape without criticism, although not on the scale as that levied at French. Repington drew attention to the unwisdom of failing to exchange liaison officers between Haig's and Paget's Armies, although Haig had done so with Major-General E.H.H. Allenby's Cavalry Division and the coordination between these two forces had worked well. Haig was also criticised for allowing a sizeable gap (Henry Wilson claimed three miles) to develop between his two divisions in the advance to contact, and again in leaving a gap between formations in his final assault.[34] French's failure to coordinate his two corps; separation of formations; Haig's failure to liaise effectively with a neighbouring corps – in these three respects the 1913 Army manoeuvres foreshadowed the campaign of August 1914.

These criticisms notwithstanding, Haig's record in the 1912 and 1913 manoeuvres was not as poor as sometimes claimed.[35] Inexperienced at this level, Haig clearly benefited from the opportunity to practise command. His comments on Aldershot Command's 1913 manoeuvres provide a useful snapshot of him as a trainer and a tactician on the eve of war. Certain familiar themes emerge, such as the importance of training and all-arms cooperation. Some of his points are uncontroversial; the importance made in "establishing a uniform doctrine between staffs in the command"; for infantry to make maximum use of cover and to avoid "thick" firing lines to reduce casualties; and the "tremendous power" of correctly deployed machine guns. However his idea that artillery should press forward to support the infantry proved impractical under combat conditions in 1914 and was soon abandoned.[36]

Two of Haig's points deserve particular attention. He stressed the need to train "[s]killed leaders for war" part of which was the inculcation of necessity for plans to be "pursued with energy and decision". The latter point is Clausewitzian and could even, in Haig's view, compensate for weaknesses in the original plan. Also of note is the attention Haig paid to "manoeuvre in retreat". This involved making the best use of ground to delay an advancing force, but "resistance must be so calculated that no portion of the force is committed so deeply that it risks defeat..." The purpose of the "delaying action" was to force the enemy to deploy and then hit him with a "counter-stroke".[37]

Not surprisingly, this reflects *FSR* I's guidance, which Haig quoted. *FSR* declared that "The conduct of a rear guard, more perhaps than any other operation in war, depends for this success on the skill and energy of the commander". This statement underlines the importance with which Haig regarded the subject. He had told a senior

typescript and manuscript versions of the diary, see Gary Sheffield and John Bourne, eds., *Douglas Haig: War Diaries and Letters 1914-18* (London, 2005) pp.2-10; *The Times* 20 Mar. 1913 p.10.

34   *The Times* 30 Sept. 1913 p.4, Basil Collier, *Brasshat* (London, 1961) p.136; *The Times* 10 Oct. 1913 p.7.

35   See e.g., A.J.A. Morris, ed., *The Letters of Lieutenant-Colonel Charles à Court Repington* (Stroud, 1999), p.316.

36   The National Archives (TNA), WO 279/53 'Aldershot Command – Comments on Training Season, 1913' pp.3, 4, 6, 89, 11.

37   TNA, WO 279/53 pp.3, 19-22.

officer friend that the "manoeuvre of retreat" might be of the greatest importance in the coming war. Some of his staff rides in India had been concerned with this scenario.[38] *FSR* I shows a healthy awareness of the danger posed by an attack in flank or envelopment.[39] Thus, by September 1913 at the latest, Haig had a clearly thought-out concept of conducting a fighting retreat.

Haig was not alone among officers in paying attention to this subject. "Employment of Cavalry in a Retreat" was the title of a lecture given by Lieutenant-Colonel 'Bob' Greenly, to one of Haig's divisions, the 2nd, in January 1913. It was subsequently published in *The Army Review.*[40] Similarly, Smith-Dorrien had in June 1914 issued a memorandum that dealt with "retirement", both in its "tactical" and "strategic" aspects.[41] In his farewell lecture to students about to leave the Staff College, given on 30 November 1912, the Commandant, Major-General William Robertson spoke at some length, with historical examples, of the possibility of retreat. The object was to retire to "await a better opportunity", he gave his view that "there is practically no chance of successfully carrying out this operation in war unless we thoroughly study it and practise it beforehand in peace". This was important not least to avoid "demoralization" of troops previously trained in offensive operations.[42] Brigadier-General Aylmer Haldane had been thinking along similar lines, his views being reinforced by reading Robertson's address. In 1915 Haldane, who commanded 10th Brigade in the 1914 campaign, claimed that the retreat from Mons "caused me no anxiety" because he knew from his study of military history that retirement by British armies had often been the preliminaries to counter-attacks. However, he also said that before Mons few British officers contemplated being forced to retreat, which suggests that the views of senior officers such as Haig, Robertson *et al* had only limited impact in the wider army.[43]

In August 1914 Haig approached the commanding of I Corps, as Aldershot Command had become, with a mixture of pride and a keen sense of his awesome responsibility.[44] He was happy with his "first rate Staff" and his subordinates, but Haig had a low opinion of Sir John French and his Chief-of-Staff, Sir Archibald

38   TNA, WO 279/53 p.20; *FSR* I pp.96, 155; Sir George Arthur, *Lord Haig* (London, 1928), p.62; John Charteris, *Field Marshal Earl Haig* (London, 1929),pp.54, 91.
39   *FSR* I pp. 94, 154-55.
40   W.H. Greenly, ' Employment of Cavalry in a Retreat', *The Army Review* Vol. IV (1913) pp.379-90. Greenly was to hold the position of GSO 1 of 2nd Cavalry Division in 1914-15.
41   Imperial War Museum (IWM), 74/136/1, Lieutenant-Colonel L.L.C. Reynolds papers, 'Confidential Memorandum on Infantry Training, June 20, 1914 issued by General Sir Horace Smith-Dorrien'. I owe this reference to Dr Spencer Jones; for more details see his chapter in this volume.
42   Robertson, 'Final Address', *The Army Review*, IV, p.334 .
43   Aylmer Haldane, *A Brigade of the Old Army 1914* (London, 1920) pp.67-9. The book was written whilst Haldane was at the front in 1915 (p.v); the publication details for Robertson's address are slightly inaccurate.
44   NLS, Acc.3155, HP/98, Haig Ts diary 13 Aug. 1914; Duff Cooper, *Haig,* Vol. I (London, 1935) p.127.

Murray.[45] This mistrust underpinned some of the key decisions Haig made in August–September 1914.

Haig correctly deduced from the scanty intelligence available and from his study of German doctrine and military history that the Germans were seeking to turn the Allied left flank. On 20 August, sensing battle was near, he held a conference of his senior officers. At this time Haig was still anticipating taking the offensive, and was "particularly emphatic that all German teaching, strategy and tactics aim at envelopment".[46] However, in the encounter battle that unfolded at Mons on 23 August 1914, it was the Germans, not the British, who took the offensive. Lieutenant-General Sir Horace Smith-Dorrien's II Corps bore the brunt of the attacks, with I Corps on his right flank. Mons was a German operational success, with British II Corps eventually forced back, although it inflicted enough tactical damage on the attackers to also claim some success. I Corps' role had been distinctly secondary, suffering a mere 40 casualties throughout 23 August. Haig's troops did not face a serious infantry attack all day.[47]

In his diary Haig wished that he could have actively supported II Corps. He was certainly asked to do so, but ultimately did very little. Lack of accurate information, fear of encirclement, and mistrust of French's judgement induced a degree of caution.[48] French paid scant heed to aerial intelligence of substantial German forces in the Mons area given at a 5.30am conference on 23 August, before he departed for Valenciennes.[49] Such intelligence reinforced Haig's anxiety. He was "gravely concerned" that the threat to the BEF's flank posed by superior numbers of enemy troops was not being taken seriously by GHQ. Haig was well versed in German military doctrine, and the absence of a major attack on I Corps, in Charteris' words, "increased rather than diminished his anxiety." If indeed the Germans were attempting to envelop the BEF, as in fact they were, "they would not attack the inner flank in force".[50] The German bombardment of I Corps might have been intended to pin I Corps in place; Haig regarded it as "heavy", which of course in comparison to later in the war, it was not. Micky Ryan wrote that before I Corps could entrench, it was "peppered with shells, machine gun and rifle fire".[51]

Haig was given an additional reason to fear for his right flank when informed that Lanrezac's French Fifth Army was been pushed back.[52] Haig was fundamentally correct. On bumping into the BEF, the commander of German First Army's instinct

45   NLS, Acc.3155, HP/98, Haig Ts diary 13 Aug. 1914.
46   NLS, Acc.3155, HP/96, 20 Aug. 1914; Charteris *At G.H.Q.* p.13.
47   J.E. Edmonds, *Military Operations France and Belgium, 1914* Vol. I (London, 1933 [1922]), p.81-82 [hereafter *Edmonds, OH* I].
48   NLS, Acc.3155, HP/96, Haig Ms diary 23 Aug.1914.
49   NLS, Acc.3155, HP/96, Haig Ms diary, 23 Aug. 1914; Hew Strachan, *To Arms* (Oxford: 2001), p.220; Sewell Tyng, *The Campaign of the Marne* (Yardley, PA: 2007 [1935]), p.123.
50   Charteris, *Haig*, p.89.
51   Ryan papers, Ms account of Mons campaign.
52   NLS, Acc.3155, HP/96, Haig Ms diary, 23 Aug. 1914; *OH 1914*, I p.73.

was to get around the flank. However, the German left flank was weak on 23 August and Terence Zuber has recently criticised Haig for not taking advantage of this.[53]

All these factors influenced Haig's decision, taken at about 3pm, to turn down a request from Major-General Hubert Hamilton, GOC 3rd Division, for support. Haig was aware that 3rd Division was coming under heavy pressure, but at an earlier meeting with Hamilton he thought him "quite worn out with fatigue", and probably queried Hamilton's judgement. Moreover, according to one witness, Haig undertook a personal reconnaissance where he saw "masses of grey-clad figures advancing". If true, this is further evidence of the fear of being overwhelmed that influenced Haig during the Battle of Mons.[54] Stating that his "right was still being attacked" (this may refer to the shelling, or may indicate that Haig believed German troops were in contact with his forces) Haig sent two battalions to relieve two from 3rd Division. At 6.30pm Haig sent three further battalions to Smith-Dorrien, which suggests that by this stage he was less worried about the threat of envelopment.[55]

A major command and control problem was created by the Commander-in-Chief's absence, meaning two commanders of equal status were attempting to co-ordinate operations. The pre-war conception of a corps essentially as a post-box through which the C-in-C could deliver orders to divisions[56] broke down as both Smith-Dorrien and Haig were compelled to act as independent commanders. There was no higher 'command' at Mons, no one individual able to stand back and take an overall view of the situation, allocate reserves and resources, assert his authority and issue orders to both corps. Sir John French's absence was a major error that casts doubt on his judgement as a commander and supports Haig's unflattering views of his capability. Clearly, there was little if any attempt on the part of either corps commander to keep the Commander-in-Chief informed.[57]

That night Haig's Chief-of-Staff, Brigadier-General Johnnie Gough VC was summoned to a conference at Le Cateau, which eventually began at about 1am on the 24th. Sir John French had reluctantly decided to retreat, having discovered that Lanrezac was falling back. Murray passed on French's orders: the BEF was to fall back some eight miles to the south and "the corps were to retire in mutual co-operation, the actual order of retirement to be settled by the two corps commanders in consultation". Given the poor communications between the corps, this arrangement, by which Murray devolved to subordinates responsibility that was properly his, was highly unsatisfactory.[58]

53   Edmonds, *OH* I, pp.60-1, 86; Terence Zuber, *The Mons Myth* (Stroud, 2010) p.146.
54   Thomas Secrett, *Twenty-Five Years with Earl Haig* (London, 1929), pp.79-81.
55   NLS, Acc.3155, HP/96, Haig Ms diary 23 Aug. 1914.
56   Andy Simpson, *Directing Operations: British Corps Command on the Western Front 1914-18* (Stroud, 2006), p.42.
57   Imperial War Museum (IWM), 75/46/6, French papers, French to Kitchener, telegram F.23, 23 Aug. 1914, 12.20pm; French's dispatch, 7 Sept. 1914 in Tim Coates, *The World War I Collection: Gallipoli and the Early Battles, 1914-15* (London, 2001), p.281.
58   Edmonds, *OH* I, pp.97-8.

At about 2am on 24 August Haig received a telegram sent by Johnnie Gough from GHQ. It ordered I Corps to

> retreat at once on Bavai where a defensive position would be taken up. 1st Corps to cover retirement of 2nd Corps!...' (sic) This seemed impossible, as I was much further to East, and not being allowed to pass through Maubeuge had to make a flank march in the face of the enemy!

These orders aroused Haig's worst nightmare of envelopment. There were only two hours of darkness left, and Haig feared an attack at dawn while on the line of march. Instead, Haig formed a rearguard and marched the rest of I Corps south. As we have seen, before the war Haig had given considerable thought to manoeuvre in retreat, had practiced it on staff rides and manoeuvres, and had given doctrinal guidance on the matter in *FSR*. The purpose of doctrine is to provide commanders with 'handrails' to guide their decision making. In the aftermath of Mons Haig used *FSR* in precisely this fashion. He decided that that the BEF had to avoid battle, to out-march from their pursuers to give themselves a chance of regrouping and striking back, and to remain in contact with the French. To be forced into fighting a battle while on the retreat was to have failed.[59] As mentioned above, in 1913 Haig had stressed the importance of commanders carrying out operations with "pursued with energy and decision", arguing that this could even compensate for weaknesses in the original plan. This was precisely his approach now, single-mindedly aiming to save I Corps from what he regarded as a fatally flawed plan.

French acquiesced, apparently deferring to the 'man-on-the-spot' as recommended by contemporary doctrine.[60] French even paid tribute to I Corps' "excellent stand to cover the retirement" of II Corps, which suggests a rationalisation of the fact that his orders were disregarded as being unworkable as well as the desire to denigrate Smith-Dorrien, whom he loathed.[61]

Haig regarded the ease of I Corps' retreat as suspicious. As he pointed out to French, it might simply indicate that the BEF was being encircled further to the west.[62] Haig met French at Bavai. "All seemed much excited", Haig wrote in his diary, "but with no very clear plan beyond holding this wretched Bavai position. I pointed out strongly to Sir John that if we halted for a day at Bavai the whole force would be surrounded by superior numbers". According to Haig's post-war account, French replied that Smith-Dorrien had told him his men needed to rest on the next day. Smith-Dorrien vehemently denied that he had passed any such message on

---

59   NLS, Acc.3155, HP/96, Haig Ms diary, 24 Aug. 1914; Ian F.W. Beckett, *Johnnie Gough V.C.* (London, 1989), p.181; Charteris, *Haig*, pp.91-2.

60   IWM, 75/46/6, French papers, French to Kitchener, telegram F.28, 24 Aug. 1914.

61   Viscount French of Ypres, *1914* (London, 1919), pp.65-6; Ian F.W. Beckett, *The Judgement of History: Sir Horace Smith-Dorrien, Lord French and '1914'* (London, 1993) p.17.

62   Edmonds, *OH* I, p.99.

to GHQ.[63] Haig's assessment of the danger was a factor in French "order[ing] the [BEF] to continue its retreat. By Murray's request I arrange roads for retirement of my Corps on Landrecies, *giving the direct route to Le Cateau to the II Corps…*"[64] To march the entire BEF to either the east or west of the Forest of Mormal was extremely inadvisable for practical reasons. French therefore reluctantly decided to divide his force, sending II Corps to the west and I Corps to the east of the forest. Haig was consulted, and gave his consent.

French was tempted to order the BEF to retire into the fortress of Maubeuge. Charteris credits Haig with successfully arguing against this by stressing the importance of out-marching the Germans, and the dangers of fighting on the retreat.[65]

At the end of a long day Haig was taken ill with diarrhoea.[66] At this time Haig was challenged by a number of stressors: inadequate command arrangements, climatic conditions (it was very hot around the time of Mons); heavy workload; lack of sleep, physical danger; and difficult interpersonal relations. Up to the night of 24 August Haig had managed to cope and not allow these to affect his decision making, but a sudden bout of illness helps to explain his behaviour on the following day.

By the late afternoon of 25 August Haig's headquarters was in Landrecies, along with 4th (Guards) Brigade, at the southern tip of the Forest of Mormal. At 3pm Haig received a message from GHQ, asking whether I Corps would be able to support II Corps at Le Cateau. Haig was aware of the gravity of the situation, having received at midday reports from aerial reconnaissance that German troops were marching on Bavai. Orders were issued for I Corps to march to the flank of II Corps, but were later amended after the receipt – at 7.30pm – of orders from GHQ to retire to Busigny, about seven miles southwest of Le Cateau. Sir John French had decided that it would be too dangerous to stand and fight at Le Cateau. This conviction was to colour French's attitudes to the very different decisions of his two Corps commanders over the next 24 hours.

At 12.30am Haig issued his orders.[67] Abandoning the idea of marching to support Smith-Dorrien, he stuck to his original intention to retreat out of harm's way and he ordered I Corps to head for Guise. For the second time in three days, Haig exercised his initiative by ignoring GHQ's orders. Lacking accurate intelligence, he seems to have feared that he was about to be overwhelmed, an assumption that in the circumstances was wholly reasonable.[68] On 27 August, when informed that a French formation was demanding use of the main road to Guise, Haig anxiously noted that

63   TNA, CAB 45/129, Haig to Smith Dorrien, 18 Dec. 1919; John Charteris, *At GHQ* (London, 1931), p.16.
64   NLS, Acc.3155, HP/96, Haig Ms diary, 24 Aug. 1914 (emphasis in original).
65   Charteris, *Haig*, pp.91-2. Haig's writings are silent on this.
66   Charteris, *At G.H.Q.*, p.17 (29 Aug. 1914); Ryan papers, Ms account of Mons campaign.
67   TNA, WO 256/1, Haig Papers, Orders of 26 August 1914.
68   Edmonds, *OH* I, pp.139-40.

if this occurred, "it would be impossible for my Corps to escape". Therefore he "was prepared to fight them" for it.[69]

During the evening of 25 August a German advance guard attacked Landrecies. Charteris claimed Haig was surprised and shocked, saying "'If we are caught, by God, we'll sell our lives dearly'" and personally helping to organise the town for defence. Ryan however, said nothing of this, and remarked that during the night of 25/26 August Haig was "very observant, saw things that others missed, & always gave his orders in such a quiet and intelligent manner as if he had a thorough grasp of the situation in even the most trying circumstances"; indeed on the 27th he referred to Haig as "splendid – merry & bright" in a letter home, possibly in an effort to keep up morale. Late on the 25 August Haig and Charteris had a hair-raising drive to escape from the town for fear of being captured.[70] In the small hours of 28 August Haig's calm demeanour favourably impressed Ryan, who thought the contrast between Haig and Johnnie Gough (and other officers) was "very striking, he was calm and like Kipling's 'If'".[71] If Haig did panic, this state of mind was of short duration; but he was clearly very anxious.

Haig phoned GHQ from Landrecies at 1.35am on 26 August claiming to be under "heavy attack", and reported that the situation was "very critical".[72] French reacted with alarm. He signalled at 3.50am to II Corps asking Smith-Dorrien, to move to support Haig (Haig had requested reinforcements at 10pm the previous day), but Smith-Dorrien declined. Later Haig returned the compliment by refusing a request from French for I Corps to go to the help of Smith-Dorrien.[73]

At 6am I Corps received orders to "fall back southeast with the French and rejoin later by rail, or move on St Quentin". Having already set in motion a retreat south to Guise, Haig decided to let his orders stand. Both instructions divided the BEF and forced the two corps to operate as independent commands. Haig believed that GHQ had regarded I Corps "lost from their control!" The German attack at Landrecies was beaten off fairly easily, but in the confusion appeared more serious than it actually

69   NLS, Acc.3155, HP/96, Haig Ms diary, 27 August 1914.
70   Charteris, *At G.H.Q*, pp.19-20; Ryan papers, Ms account of 1914 campaign; NLS, Acc.3155, HP/96, Haig Ms diary, 25 Aug. 1914; TNA, WO 95/588, War Diary of I Corps HQ GS, 'Action at Landrecies' and 'First Army Corps' operations... to 5th September'.
71   Ryan papers, Ryan to wife, 27 August 1914 and Ms account of 1914 campaign.
72   Edmonds, *OH* I, p.135.
73   Holmes, *Little Field Marshal*, p.222; IWM, 75/46/6, French papers, French diary, 26 Aug. 1914.

was. The overrunning of I Corps HQ would have been a severe blow to the cohesion of the BEF.[74] French again acquiesced in Haig's decision.[75]

During the night of 25/26 August Smith-Dorrien decided it was less hazardous to fight at Le Cateau than to attempt to retire. Thus the II Corps commander also ignored French's orders. He had no realistic alternative. A factor in Smith-Dorrien's decision to fight at Le Cateau was his belief that Haig would support him on his flank, although it became clear during the night that this was unlikely to happen.[76] As a result II Corps had an open right flank that the Germans proceeded to turn.

On 26 August Haig decided he would not even attempt to support II Corps. The two corps were physically separated by the Forest of Mormal, and in a classic example of the 'fog of war' Haig was forced to make a decision based on fragmentary and incorrect information derived from rudimentary communications. If Haig had obeyed GHQ's original orders it would have brought I Corps squarely into the battle, but the subsequent orders (to retire on Busigny) would have carried I Corps beyond immediate support of Smith-Dorrien. Haig would then have faced the dilemma of whether to order his formations to retrace their steps and head north towards the battlefield, all the while fearing that I Corps was marching into a trap which would result in its encirclement and destruction.

Haig was out of direct contact with II Corps on 26 August. Haig telegraphed to GHQ twice (the second time to Smith-Dorrien via GHQ) offering help, but very late in the day; the first message, sent at 8.30pm, read "No news of II Corps except sound of guns from direction of Le Cateau and Beaumont. Can I Corps be of any assistance". Haig did not receive a reply to either message. It seems that having eluded the Germans on that day, and achieved his primary aim of avoiding disaster to I Corps, Haig believed he was in a position to offer support to Smith-Dorrien. However the tone of Haig's second telegram, sent at 11pm – "we could hear the sound of your battle, but could get no information as to its progress, and could form no idea of how we could assist you" – lends itself to a less charitable interpretation, that Haig was retrospectively (and unconvincingly) justifying his refusal to countenance even the possibility of marching towards the sound of the guns.[77]

John Terraine argued that Haig's oft-stated conviction that Smith-Dorrien was wrong to fight at Le Cateau suggests that the I Corps commander "was conscious of having fallen below his own standards".[78] More likely is that Haig genuinely believed that Smith-Dorrien took an unwarranted gamble, and the evidence suggests

---

74   NLS, Acc.3155, HP/96, Haig Ms diary and HP/98, Haig Ts diary, 26 Aug 1914; G.C. Wynne, 'The Other Side of the Hill: No. 12 The Night Attack at Landrecies: 25th August 1914', *Army Quarterly*, Vol. 28, (1934) pp.247-54. For differing views on the seriousness of the action compare John Hussey, 'Commentary' on 'Landrecies 25/26 August 1914', *Stand To!* No.46 (1996) p.16, and Zuber, *Mons*, pp.203-05.

75   IWM, 75/46/6, French papers, French diary, 26, 27 Aug 1914.

76   Edmonds, *OH* I, p.141; IWM, 75/46/6, French papers, French diary 26 Aug.1914; John Terraine, *Mons: The Retreat to Victory* (London, 1991 [1960]) p.142.

77   Edmonds, *OH* I, p.201.

78   John Terraine, *Douglas Haig the Educated Soldier* (London, 1963) pp.87-8.

that this belief was not wholly misplaced. In the aftermath of Le Cateau French, Wilson, Murray, Joffre and GQG all assumed that II Corps had been effectively destroyed.[79] Zuber's recent study based on German sources claims II Corps ceased to be "a cohesive combat-capable force" for a minimum of 48 hours as a result of the battle and concludes that Smith-Dorrien was no longer in command of events. However Zuber downplays, somewhat, the damage inflicted on the Germans during the battle.[80] Smith-Dorrien was able to deliver an effective "stopping blow", which did much to ensure the survival of II Corps, but according to Jack Sheldon, who has studied the battle from German sources, the British general was "lucky to be able to fight a delaying battle at Le Cateau and then to extricate II Corps [in] the way he did, especially when the result of the fighting at Landrecies was to widen further the gap between the British I and II Corps".[81] It is clear that the cohesion of II Corps was damaged in the short term. However by 28 August it was on the way to recovery; the wounds were beginning to heal, suggesting that the impact of the battle on the effectiveness of II Corps should not be exaggerated. Thereafter Smith-Dorrien who, as we have seen, had like Haig previously identified the importance of training for retreat, also followed the guidance of *FSR* in swiftly marching out of the grasp of the enemy.

Whatever one may think about Haig's failure to support Smith-Dorrien at Mons and Le Cateau, the accusation that he allowed rivalry and "professional jealousy" toward Smith-Dorrien to distort his decision-making can be safely dismissed.[82] This argument is based in part on a suspect source, consisting of information passed on to Basil Liddell Hart many years after the event. His informant was Sir James Edmonds, the British official historian, a fount of sometimes unreliable and malicious gossip. Both Edmonds and Liddell Hart had grudges against Haig. Douglas Haig was certainly ambitious, and probably saw Smith-Dorrien, who was senior to him, as a rival. This author, however, finds it unbelievable that Haig, who was acutely conscious of his responsibility as a commander, would risk the destruction of half of the BEF in pursuit of a personal ambition. Haig's decisions in August 1914 are perfectly explicable without recourse to conspiracy theories. They were decisions taken by a man under stress, groping around in the fog of war, a man above all aware that were he to make a mistake, it could have catastrophic consequences.

I Corps was to retreat until 5 September. A corps of two divisions was a small enough formation for Haig to dominate with his personality, and he led by example, riding whenever possible rather than going by car. On 29 August Mickey Ryan noted he had rode for 45 miles with Haig "all around his army".[83] On the evening of 28

79   Holmes, *Little Field Marshal*, pp.223-4.
80   Zuber, *Mons*, pp.257-9.
81   Nigel Cave and Jack Sheldon, *Le Cateau* (Barnsley, 2008) p.19.
82   Nikolas Gardner, *Trial by Fire. Command and the British Expeditionary Force in 1914* (Westport, CT, 2003), pp. 14, 48-9. Beckett, *Johnnie Gough*, p. 181, also uses Edmonds as a key source.
83   Ryan papers, Ryan to wife, 29 Aug. 1914.

August Lanrezac asked Haig to support French Fifth Army in an attack on the following day. He agreed, and asked GHQ for permission, only to be turned down. Offensive operations at this stage simply did not fit in with the pessimistic mental picture of the campaign held by French, Murray and Wilson.[84] Haig got into a spat with GHQ.[85] Perhaps Haig had decided that having out-marched the enemy it was now time to seize the initiative, even if only to buy time for a further retreat. Haig's decision to support Lanrezac was the right one. The battle of Guise was a strategic success.

Haig's command of I Corps in the Allied offensive that began on 6 September is controversial. It has been claimed that he was too cautious in the initial advance to the Marne, and that his timidity played a role in the Allies' failure on the Aisne. Haig displayed considerable wariness on the first day of the attack, 6 September, his anxiety about the possibility of German forces striking his flank as strong as ever. Next day as the enemy was in retreat, he motored to see both his divisional commanders to "impress on them [the] necessity for quick and immediate action".[86] Arriving at the Marne it was found that the Germans had left a bridge over the river intact. Haig was keenly aware of the need to drive on, to capitalise on the evident disarray of an enemy in retreat, but still full of respect for the German army and unwilling to take unnecessary risks. So, late on 9 September he found 5th Cavalry Brigade "moving at a walk and delay[ing] the advance of our infantry", and urged the brigade commander forward for "a little effort now might mean the conclusion of the war".[87] From Haig, who knew perfectly well that cavalry horses needed to be walked sometimes to keep them fresh, this was a significant comment. At about noon on 9 September with I Corps on the far bank of the Marne, Haig, received information from aerial reconnaissance of a large German force to his front, and he ordered a halt. News also reached Haig that caused him to suspect (erroneously) that the French had suffered a heavy defeat. Given the information he had, far from being "inexplicable"[88] Haig's decision to order a halt was perfectly understandable.

By 12 September the BEF was closing up to the River Aisne. Dominated by high ground on the north bank, this was an obvious place for the Germans to make a stand. However it was not clear whether the Germans were retreating in chaos or still intact. Fearing a hasty, improvised attack might be repelled, Haig chose to ignore GHQ's orders to seize the crossings of the River Aisne and occupy the high ground. Instead he halted short of the river and launched an attack on the following day.[89] This was a mistake, if an understandable one. By daylight on the 13th, the German defences had been strengthened, as retreating troops halted and regrouped

84   Tyng, *Marne*, pp.149-151.
85   TNA, WO 256/1, Haig papers, Haig to Murray, 29 Aug. 1914, 7 am; NLS, Acc.3155, HP/96, Haig Ms diary, 29 Aug. 1914.
86   NLS, Acc.3155, HP/96, Haig Ms diary, 6, 7 Sept 1914; Edmonds, *OH* I, pp.297-8, 310.
87   NLS, Acc.3155, HP/96, Haig Ms diary, 9 Sept 14.
88   David Ascoli, *The Mons Star* (London, 1981), p.160.
89   Edmonds, *OH* I, pp.367, 465.

and reserves were rushed to the Aisne. Haig still believed I Corps was faced only by a screen of cavalry, and he hoped to bounce forward "without making a formal attack". But the Germans had just enough to hold on. At the end of 13 September the BEF had three widely dispersed bridgeheads on frontage of all three corps, with Haig's the furthest forward.

On the following day Haig attacked the Chemin des Dames heights. 1st and 2nd Divisions inched forward in the face of German resistance. Haig spent the day moving around I Corps, visiting his commanders. He faced a crisis thanks to the failure of II Corps to get further forward, leaving a two mile gap on the left of I Corps. At 2pm 3rd Division was pushed back and he realised that this posed a serious threat to the left flank of 2nd Division. There were no reserves at corps or divisional level but he managed to scrape together dismounted cavalry which were sent to the left flank. Haig's intervention was potentially decisive, for if the German had mounted a major attack it might have had catastrophic consequences. A "general offensive" on I Corps' front at 4pm failed.[90] However the day's efforts had prevented a major German attack that could have pushed the Allies back across the river. At 11pm French ordered the BEF to entrench. In the official history there is some veiled criticism of Haig (as well as some praise), but Edmonds principally blamed GHQ for the failure to push on, and indeed, reading the GHQ diary, one gains little sense of urgency.[91] Haig undoubtedly made mistakes, and could have pushed his men harder but overall his generalship during the advance to the Aisne was prudent and sound.

Initially there was no reason to suppose that this period of trench warfare would be anything other than a temporary phase. By stages Haig changed his mind, noting on 4 October that "we are carrying on a kind of siege warfare". He adjusted his thinking accordingly, for example, rapidly grasping the advantages to be gained from marrying the aircraft to the gun battery.[92]

In mid-October the BEF was moved from the Aisne to Flanders. The BEF was plunged into confused semi-open warfare. Ordered to advance on 19 October, Haig was wary of French's optimism,[93] and sure enough I Corps soon found itself in a classic encounter battle. On 21 October Haig ordered I Corps onto the defensive, around Ypres. At Mons and Le Cateau, Haig and I Corps had played second fiddle to Smith-Dorrien and II Corps. The savage fighting around Ypres thrust the burden of "saving the BEF" on to Haig. His calm and resilient generalship greatly enhanced his standing as a commander.[94]

90   NLS, Acc.3155, HP/96, Haig Ms diary, 14 Sept. 1914; TNA, WO95/588, narratives.
91   Edmonds, OH I, pp.416, 65-6; TNA, WO 95/1, War Diary GHQ, entries for 12-13 Sept. 1914.
92   NLS, Acc.3155, HP/96, Haig Ms diary, 20, 23, 27, 28 Sept. 1914; NLS, Acc.3155, HP/141, Haig to wife, 21, 23 Sept., 4, 6 Oct. 1914; TNA, WO 95/588 'Notes on ... Employment of Aviators...' and 'Memorandum on ... Tactics' 28 Sept. 1914.
93   George H. Cassar, The Tragedy of Sir John French (Cranbury, NJ, 1985) p.162.
94   Churchill College Cambridge, DC 5/3, Duff Cooper papers, Edmonds to Duff Cooper, 1 May 1935.

The main focus of I Corps was the major road from Ypres to Menin. By "puttying up", shoving troops into the line to stave off short-term crises, Haig and his commanders limited the damage to the British position. [95] Late on 29 October, French ordered the BEF to attack on the next day, hoping for "a decisive result". That Haig prudently ignored him may "have saved the day on the 30th". [96]

On 30 October Haig began to think of a limited attack to retake positions lost the previous day. While the idea was sound in principle, it was based on an underestimation of German strength and the formidable firepower at their disposal. [97] It was probably just as well that the attack was overtaken by events, for on 31 October I Corps endured a series of major attacks. By 1pm the whole of the key village of Gheluvelt was lost; British defences on the main German axis were collapsing; and there were no reserves left. [98] Hooge Chateau, where 1st and 2nd Divisional HQs were co-located was shelled, fatally wounding Lomax of 1st Division. [99] A key link in the command chain had been destroyed at a critical time.

In his HQ at the White Chateau, some four miles behind the frontline, Haig was receiving only fragmentary snippets of information, and could do little to influence the fight.

He was anxious and had every right to be, but, as historian John Hussey has emphasised in his careful study of the events of 31 October, Haig remained calm throughout. There was no repetition of the supposed loss of nerve at Landrecies. [100] Edmonds told Liddell Hart after the war that Haig had panicked, issuing orders for I Corps to carry out a general retreat, but that this had been hushed up. [101] Hussey's work demonstrates conclusively that there is no evidence to substantiate this claim.

In reality Haig had prudently taken some preliminary steps to extricate his corps in the event of a major setback. On 29 October, he had sent his chief sapper, Brigadier-General Rice, to examine routes across the canal that ran near Ypres. Rice had identified two possible defensive positions closer to Ypres. [102] At 7am on 31 October, Haig had consulted with General d'Urbal, commanding French troops in Belgium, on arrangements should a retreat become necessary. When it became clear that 1st Division's front had given way, Haig opted to fall back to the first of Rice's alternative positions, and orders went out at about 1.30pm. [103] This was a dangerous manoeuvre, which could have led to the complete disintegration of 1st

---

95   Ian F.W. Beckett, *Ypres The First Battle, 1914* (Pearson, 2004), pp.118-19.

96   J.E. Edmonds, , *Military Operations France and Belgium, 1914* Vol. II (London, 1925])
      [hereafter Edmonds, *OH* II], p.279; Cassar, *Tragedy*, p.169.

97   Anthony Farrar-Hockley, *Death of an Army* (London, 1967), pp.147-8.

98   John Hussey, 'A Hard Day at First Ypres - The Allied Generals and their Problems: 31
      October 1914', *BAR*, No.107 (1994) p.77.

99   Sir George Barrow, *The Life of General Sir Charles Carmichael Monro* (London, 1931),
      p.44.

100   Hussey, 'Hard Day', pp. 83-4.

101   Beckett, *Johnnie Gough*, p.193.

102   TNA, WO 95/588, Rice to Edmonds, 6 Nov. 1922.

103   TNA, WO 95/588, war diary entry, 31 Oct. 1914.

Division. Haig presumably decided that ordering the troops to stay put was even less appealing. French arrived at I Corps HQ at about 2pm but he could offer nothing more than moral support. French then left, shortly before Rice arrived with the news that an attack by 2nd Worcesters had retaken Gheluvelt and restored the situation.[104] The orders to retire were cancelled; General Ferdinand Foch, Joffre's *adjoint* (deputy) in the northern sector of the Western Front with a coordinating role, also influenced this decision. As Elizabeth Greenhalgh has argued, Foch's helpful role during First Ypres contributed to making him acceptable to Haig as Supreme Allied Commander "when another crisis beckoned" in March 1918.[105]

Haig's subsequent ride to the front line on 31 October is controversial, with disputes about its timing, whether it was a publicity stunt or even whether it ever happened at all.[106] A rather more sensible criticism is whether Haig was wise to leave his HQ at this critical time, thus reducing his command span. Beckett has argued that "anxiety certainly clouded his [Haig's] judgment".[107] This is dubious. In his diary, Haig wrote "I got on my horse and rode forward to see if I could do anything to organise stragglers and push them forward to check enemy"; this was the instinct of an old regimental officer, to go forward and lead.[108] But there was more to it than that. Rice referred to Haig and his staff going forward "where we established a sort of advanced HQ".[109] This makes perfect sense. Haig went forward, to assess the situation for himself, to speak to commanders on the spot. As a result of these consultations, Haig gained a clear picture of the state of his forces and ordered some redeployment of troops, in part to create a reserve.

The British line held. The Germans did not make another major attack until 11 November. This too came perilously close to success. The situation was saved by a counterattack in which the 2nd Oxfordshire and Buckinghamshire Light Infantry played the primary role.[110] In a battle of this type the influence of the corps commander was inevitably limited, and Haig was in the position of a facilitator rather than a commander. He spent the day doing what he could: organising reserves, sometimes by withdrawing soldiers from the firing line to meet possible eventualities; keeping

---

104 This version differs slightly from the one in Haig's Ms diary, when he says that he found out about the Worcesters' action in the course of his ride to the front. As this fuller version of events, written when Haig had had time to collect his thoughts, largely agrees with other witnesses, this is probably an occasion when the later typescript diary is more accurate than the immediate hand-written version. See Charteris, *At G.H.Q.*, p.53; Hussey, 'Hard Day', pp.75-89.

105 Elizabeth Greenhalgh, *Foch in Command: The Forging of a First World War General* (Cambridge, 2011) pp.65-6, 67.

106 Gerard J. DeGroot, *Douglas Haig 1861-1928*, (London, 1988) pp.165-6; Denis Winter, *Haig's Command: A Reassessment* (London, 1991), pp.36-7; Gardner, *Trial*, pp.220-1.

107 Beckett, *Ypres*, p.140. See also J.P. Harris, *Douglas Haig and the First World War* (Cambridge, 2008) p.103.

108 NLS, Acc.3155, HP/96, Haig Ms diary, 31 Oct 1914.

109 Hussey, 'Hard Day', p.85.

110 TNA, WO 95 589, war diary entry, 11 Nov. 1914; Edmonds, *OH* II, pp.419-45.

subordinate commanders in touch with the situation on other parts of the Ypres front; impressing on Sir John French the gravity of the position; and preparing to pull back to a new defensive line should it prove impossible to dislodge the Germans from their gains. As on 31 October, Haig had no direct input into the decision to counterattack.[111]

Historians have mostly been sparing in their criticism of Haig's generalship in 1914, certainly in comparison to 1915-17. J.P. Harris is a recent exception. His military biography of Haig presents an extremely negative portrait overall, and he is particularly critical of Haig's conduct of operations in the mobile phase of 1914. According to Harris, Haig went "anxiously to war", "possibly" doubting his fitness to command. His response at Mons to Smith-Dorrien's request for support, to send two battalions "appears niggardly, perhaps disgracefully so". Haig's performance in the initial stage of the campaign was that of a "distinctly battle-shy commander", and during the Marne-Aisne phase he showed "at least his fair share" of "hesitancy and timidity". Harris sees the Aisne as "a watershed in Haig's mental state": he became less anxious about the ability of British troops and he grew more confident a s a commander. He is more complementary about Haig's performances in the trench phase on the Aisne and at Ypres, where I Corps commander showed appropriate "resilience and resolution".[112]

To the mind of this author, the documentary record does not support the idea that on the outbreak of war Haig doubted his ability to command. Certainly, he had no illusions about the scale of the task ahead of him. As his official biographer stated, in extravagant language, "It was the moment for which he had been preparing, but to which he had not looked forward with any emotions save those of awe and dread".[113] This was the reaction of a thorough professional, who understood through his study of military history and German doctrine the nature of the challenge posed by the enemy army. This influenced his advice at the council of war of 5 August when Haig argued for holding the BEF back from France for up to three months, building a mass army on the cadre and mobilising the resources of the Empire, in line with his long held and highly perceptive strategic vision. The realities of coalition warfare, which necessitated immediate support for the French, rendered this plan redundant - Haig was seemingly unaware of the full strategic picture until that day.[114] Moreover, Haig's

---

111   NLS, Acc.3155, HP/96, Haig Ms diary and HP/98, Ts Diary, 11 Nov. 1914.
112   Harris, *Haig*, pp.83, 86, 90-1, 105. This book has won prizes but has also come in for criticism. For measured criticism see this author's review in *English Historical Review* Vol.125, (2010) p.1568; for hostile reviews by Peter Hart and George A. Webster see http://www.amazon.co.uk/product-reviews/052115877X/ref=cm_cr_dp_see_all_btm?ie=UTF8&showViewpoints=1&sortBy=bySubmissionDateD. J.P. Harris with Niall Barr, *Amiens to the Armistice* (London, 1999) was much more favourable to Haig. One reviewer claimed that between the late 1990s and writing his biography, "It would appear that Paul Harris had a crisis of conscience and converted". http://www.amazon.co.uk/review/R2DGOXT4FIYWN, accessed 18 February 2013.
113   Duff Cooper, *Haig* I, p.127.
114   Sheffield and Bourne, *Douglas Haig* pp.5-7; NLS, Acc.3155, HP/40 Haig's paper on

sombre mood was influenced by his well-founded doubts about the competence of French and Murray, but not about his own capabilities.

As argued above, Haig's generalship in the initial phase of the campaign must be viewed in the context of his understanding of the German doctrine of envelopment, and finding in mid-August his Corps in just that position of danger that he had foreseen before the war. As recent scholarship has shown, at this time the BEF came closer to disaster than many realise. Haig's command decisions were not the product of a "battle-shy" mind, but reflected the conviction that to be brought to battle under such unfavourable circumstances would almost certainly result in defeat, while to retreat could lead to a successful counterstroke. As for the advance to the Aisne, Harris's criticisms are somewhat better founded, although exaggerated: the difference between prudent and timid generalship is a fine one.

What had Haig learned from the campaigns of 1914? Apart from reinforcing his healthy respect for the German army, and for the skill and resilience of his own men (Haig was fortunate in having his subordinate commanders, and the regimental officers, NCOs and ordinary soldier of I Corps, as he fully recognised),[115] several things stand out. The first is that his combat experience had validated pre-war doctrine and principles, which simply needed to be adapted to the new circumstances.[116] In 1918 Haig attributed the BEF's victories, in part, "to a steady adherence to the principles of our FSR Part I".[117] Historians such as Travers believe that this was a negative outcome. However Albert Palazzo persuasively argues that *FSR* provided the framework within which a successful approach to warfighting was eventually developed; the author has a great deal of sympathy with this thesis.[118]

Second, Haig was keenly aware how narrow the margin between survival and defeat had been at First Ypres. Had the Germans pressed their attacks on 31 October and 11 November, the BEF would probably have been defeated. This fed into his belief, encapsulated in *FSR*, that "decisive success in battle can be gained only by a vigorous offensive".[119] During Third Ypres in 1917, he cited the German failure of 31 October 1914, warning his Army commanders not to fall into the same trap.[120] The third was that his belief that Sir John French was unfit for high command was reinforced, and this opinion was to become of some consequence in 1915.

The importance of Haig's generalship, especially at Ypres, was widely recognised through the army.[121] A modern historian has concluded that the army has rarely

'National Defence', 20 May 1906.
115   Haig to Wood, 6 Nov. 1914, in Sir Evelyn Wood, *Winnowed Memories* (London, 1918), p.388; NLS, Acc.3155, HP/141, Haig to wife, 13 Nov. 1914.
116   LHCMA, Kiggell 1/36, Haig to Kiggell, 4 Oct. 1914.
117   Haig to Wilson 20 Sept. 1918, in Sheffield and Bourne, *Douglas Haig*, p.462.
118   Albert Palazzo, *Seeking Victory on the Western Front* (Lincoln, NE, 2000); Sheffield, *The Chief*, pp.147-8.
119   *FSR* I p.107 .
120   Sheffield, *The Chief*, p.98.
121   Home diary, 11 Nov.1914, in Diana Briscoe (ed.), *The Diary of a World War I Cavalry Officer* (Tunbridge Wells, 1985), p.38.

produced such a fine "defensive general".[122] In the eyes of some contemporaries Haig's performance during the defensive battle at Ypres eclipsed his role in the offensive on the Aisne and earlier. As late as 5 July 1916, in the context of the Somme offensive, a hostile witness, Henry Wilson, described Haig as a "good stout hearted *defensive* soldier", going on to imply that success in the defence required little but tenacity: "[Haig had] *no* had imagination, and very little brains and very little sympathy".[123] Be that as it may, Douglas Haig emerged from the fighting of 1914 with an immensely enhanced reputation.[124] He was now a clear rival to Smith-Dorrien as Sir John French's heir apparent. By the end of 1915, Douglas Haig was Commander-in-Chief of the British Expeditionary Force, a position he was to retain throughout the rest of the war.

The author would like to thank Lord Haig for granting permission to quote from the Haig papers, and to Professor Eugene Ryan for granting permission to quote from the Ryan papers. An earlier and somewhat different version of this chapter previously appeared in the author's book The Chief: Douglas Haig and the British Army *(London, Aurum, 2011). Thanks are due to Graham Coster for his assistance in this matter.*

122   Cassar, *Tragedy*, p.178.
123   Wilson to Foch, 5 Jul 1916, in Keith Jeffrey, *Field Marshal Sir Henry Wilson* (Oxford, 2006), p.165
124   French's Dispatch 8 Oct. 1914, in Coates, *World War I*, p.297; IWM, 75/46/6, French papers, French to Kitchener, telegram F.150, 15 Sept. 1914.

6

Lieutenant-General Sir James Grierson

II Corps

Mark Connelly

Sir James Grierson is the man who never was of the 1914 BEF. Long-since earmarked for a role in the expeditionary force, he died of a heart attack on 17 August 1914 whilst en route to the front in his role as commander of II Corps. Grierson's death deprived his peers and historians since of assessing whether this highly rated officer would live up to expectations in the field. His passing was certainly mourned by his contemporaries as a great blow to the BEF, but evaluating his career with the privilege of hindsight exposes a more complex picture than simply a great general tragically robbed of the crowning moment of his professional life.[1] Although Grierson's pre-1914 career indicated a general of great skill and insight, studying his progress creates the opportunity to explore him as a representative of the British army's high command and its preparations for future combat. Approached from this perspective, Grierson moves from being a wonderful example of history's propensity to throw up 'what ifs' to a highly valuable insight into the culture and values of an institution.

Born in Glasgow on 27 January 1859, the eldest son of a Glasgow merchant, Grierson was educated at the Glasgow Academy, in Germany and the Royal Military Academy, Woolwich. He proved an able candidate, passed out fourth in 1878 and joined the Royal Artillery. Within a very short space of time he began supplementing his income by writing newspaper articles on military matters, particularly on foreign armies, which also revealed his determination to take a wider perspective on his profession. This interest led him to accompany the Austrian armies during their occupation of Bosnia-Herzegovina in 1879, and a year later he covered Russian manoeuvres for the *Daily News*. In 1881 he joined his battery in India, but was soon attached to the Quartermaster-General's (QMG) department in Simla. This gave him the opportunity to return to the scholarly side of his military interests for here he wrote articles for *The Pioneer*, a volume on the Turkish army, an Arabic dictionary and a guide to Egypt.

---

1   For examples of obituaries see *The Times*, 18, 19 August 1914; *Manchester Guardian*, 18, 23 August 1914.

Sir James Grierson. (Editor's collection)

His rising reputation as an organiser and director was enhanced in 1882 when he took part in the expedition to Egypt as Deputy Assistant Quartermaster General where he witnessed the battles of Qassasin and Tel el-Kebir. On the cessation of operations he returned to India and soon entered the Staff College, but his time at Camberley was interrupted by the Sudan campaign of 1885 in which he served as Deputy Assistant Adjutant General (DAAG) and QMG.

On his return he passed the Staff College programme including honours in French and Russian, and completed a translation of Grodekoff's *Campaign in Turcomania*. He then served on the War Office's intelligence division Russian section which provided him with material for two further books, *The Armed Strength of Russia* (1886) and *The Armed Strength of Japan* (1886). Two years later he completed yet another work; this time a survey of the German army in *The Armed Strength of the German Empire*. Grierson's keen insight led Major-General Sir Henry Brackenbury to request that he return to the Russian section as its head, which entailed much time in Germany sharing and acquiring information about the Tsarist empire. In 1891 he completed *Staff Duties in the Field* and then moved to Aldershot where he spent a year as brigade major. His next posting was one of the most important of his career, being appointed military attaché in Berlin in 1896. Although an admirer of Germany, this role caused him to become suspicious of German intentions, and he was one of the earliest voices to warn the British government about the increasingly Anglophobic atmosphere in the Reich, but little of this can be detected in his 1897 study of the British army. Suspicions about German intentions were intensified in August 1900 when he was appointed chief of staff to the allied mission against the Boxer rebellion. Whilst his personal relationship with his German commander, Field Marshal Count von Waldersee, was entirely harmonious and he entered Beijing at his side, he detected an aggressive atmosphere in the German forces which he believed was mainly directed against Britain and Russia.[2]

His fears of Germany's intentions did not undermine his admiration for the German staff system, which made itself felt in 1900 when he was appointed Assistant Adjutant General to Lord Roberts in South Africa. Although deeply respectful of Roberts, he was dismayed by the lack of order surrounding his commander and felt it was hampering the war effort. He was particularly disgusted by the administrative chaos that led to the Poplar Grove debacle in which the cornered Boer leadership escaped through lack of a timely and well-directed British intervention. According to Grierson, the only way to profit from such disasters was to learn from them. In his diary Grierson identified the way forward. It was based on emulating German standards of efficiency in terms of rigorous staff practices and instruction. Crucially, he also noted that due to the restricted size and focus of the army British higher commanders lacked experience in managing large units:

> What a lot we have to learn from this war in every way! I think our first lesson is that we must have big annual manoeuvres and have staffs properly trained. We don't seem to grasp anything higher than a division. And we must have 'staff journeys' to teach the control of armies in the field. If we take the field with a force the size of this one against an [sic] European enemy and continue in our present happy-go-lucky style of staffing and staff work we shall come to the most awful grief. There is no system about it, and without a system a large army cannot be properly handled.[3]

On his return to Britain, Grierson found that his demand for reform was shared by many others including the Secretary of State for War, St John Brodrick, who had commenced a wide-ranging review of the army and its administration. Like Grierson, Brodrick was an admirer of the German system and wished to see the British army rebuilt on a corps-basis in order to provide large-scale, effective fighting units.[4] It was to the newly-established II Corps that Grierson was appointed Chief of Staff in September 1901. Bringing order to such a large new structure demanded that Grierson demonstrate all his skill and experience. The fruits of it were revealed in 1903 when I and II Corps undertook extensive manoeuvres in the first real test of British military organisation since the end of the South African War. Grierson was delighted that the

2   For biographical details on Grierson's early career see D.S. Macdiarmid, *The Life of Lieutenant-General Sir James Grierson* (London: Constable, 1923), pp.1-148. Macdiarmid's biography is based on Grierson's diaries and personal papers which were subsequently destroyed; R.W.A. Onslow (revised M.G.M. Jones), 'Grierson, Sir James Moncrief (1859-1914)', *Oxford Dictionary of National Biography*, http://www.oxforddnb.com/view/article/33574. Accessed, 30 September 2008.

3   Quoted in Macdiarmid, *Grierson*, p.271.

4   See D.M. Leeson, 'Playing at War: The British Military Manoeuvres of 1898', *War in History*, Vol. 15, No. 4, 2008, pp.432-461.

administrative elements unfolded smoothly and judged that the forces moved "in a way undreamt of in 1898".[5] This was a significant comparison, for 1898 was the year in which manoeuvres saw General Sir Redvers Buller throw a mass of infantry against well placed defensive positions contributing to the defeat of his side and much derisory comment in the press.[6] However, Grierson was concerned by the fact that too often commanders revealed an obsession with winning and occupying ground as an end in itself rather than as a means to destroy the enemy force.[7] This perceptive criticism was, unfortunately, never fully addressed by the army and played itself out it with appalling results on the Somme and at Third Ypres in 1916 and 1917.[8]

Having ensured another impressive achievement in organising II Corps, Grierson was given the role of Director of Military Operations (DMO) at the War Office.[9] His appointment was related to the latest stage in War Office reform which was paving the way for a general staff.[10] It was while serving in this post that Grierson played a hugely important role in the on-going process of reorienting British foreign and military policy towards an understanding with France in order to check German aggression in Europe. In hindsight it can be stated that appointing Grierson to this position was peculiarly apt for he was the embodiment of strands of British strategic thinking that had been gradually intertwining since the 1880s. But, understanding this process of evolution should not entail a determinist interpretation of British strategic policy starting with the given of an Anglo-French anti-German stance in 1914 worked backwards to identify positively its first signs of life. Instead, Grierson's career and developing thought processes show that ultimate outcomes were not necessarily the original intentions. Thus, Grierson's initial interest in the establishment of an effective general staff based on a German model was not to make a system capable of countering Germany, but merely to make the British army more efficient whatever its immediate task. This stance was similar to Wolseley and Roberts, both of whom were attracted to the idea of a general staff for imperial defence reasons rather than to fight a continental war.[11] Grierson's fears of Germany thus arose *after* his conversion to the idea of a general

5   Macdiarmid, *Grierson*, p.202.

6   See D.M. Leeson, 'Playing at War: The British Military Manoeuvres of 1898', *War in History*, Vol. 15, No. 4, 2008, pp.432-461

7   Macdiarmid, *Grierson*, p.202.

8   Shelford Bidwell and Dominick Graham identified this problem clearly in their ground-breaking study, *Fire-Power. The British Army Weapons and Theories of War1904-1945* (London: George Allen and Unwin, 1982). They note Haig's failure to appreciate that: "Ground is important only if it enables the killing business to be more efficient", p.71.

9   John Gooch, *The Plans of War. The General Staff and British Military Strategy, c. 1900-1916* (London: Routledge and Kegan Paul, 1974), p.49.

10   For further discussions of these processes see Williams, *Defending the Empire*, pp.41-58; Ian F.W. Beckett, '"Selection by Disparagement": Lord Esher, the General Staff and the Politics of Command, 1904-1914' in David French and Brian Holden Reid (eds), *The British General Staff: Reform and Innovation, 1890-1939* (London: Frank Cass, 2002), pp.41-56.

11   For a development of this argument see Hew Strachan, 'The British army, its general staff and the continental commitment, 1904-1914' in French and Holden Reid (eds),

staff. However, he quickly realised that the general staff was a crucial component for the planning of any serious continental commitment.

Influential authorities on military matters such as Lord Esher were convinced that they had made a good appointment in Grierson. He had a good knowledge of the German army and was on friendly terms with the French; this was complemented by a firm grip on the immediate security issues. Grierson identified his primary tasks as the establishment of suitable defensive arrangements for the empire and the creation of an effective expeditionary force of approximately two corps that could be raised in the UK. In terms of imperial defence, he brought decision and clarity especially over India where he remained a convinced sceptic on Russia's ability to invade. Kitchener's fears on this front were met by Grierson's firm insistence that Afghanistan's lack of a transport infrastructure, particularly railways, meant that any Russian force invading India would collapse within a very short space of time.[12] This led to a disagreement with the Committee for Imperial Defence (CID), which remained firmly convinced of the need to maintain high levels of manpower in India and it remained unmoved by Grierson's argument in March 1904 that there was a need to rebalance the armed forces towards an expeditionary force and home defence. The distaste for this option may also have been influenced by the fact that Grierson had been converted to the necessity of compulsory service as the solution to manpower deficiencies. He was afraid that the current situation would allow Britain to put more than 100,000 men into the field immediately, but only by denuding it of the cadre required for expansion purposes.

His sanguine stance over India was not, however, indicative of his attitude towards the whole empire. Grierson argued that the Suez Canal zone had been neglected and requested the detachment of more artillery units to its defence; he also believed Malta was vulnerable but, like India, considered the risks of attacking it outweighed the need to alter its existing defensive arrangements radically.[13] Looking to the Far East, he had doubts about the Japanese alliance. In his judgement the alliance was ill-considered for it was of far greater value to the Japanese than the British, and he also saw it as an example of politicians making commitments which the military might be unable to uphold. This had a direct impact on his interpretation of the Entente Cordiale, for, according to his logic, it demanded immediate interaction between the French and British armies in order to discuss the possible military implications of the understanding.[14] Grierson's commitment to this concept reveals that moves towards a firmer military link with the French pre-dated Sir Henry Wilson's arrival at the War Office, and he should not be regarded as the key architect of Anglo-French planning.

In pursuit of this objective Grierson was soon in communication with Colonel V.J.M. Huguet, who arrived in London in 1905 as French Military Attaché. The two men struck up a good working relationship and began informal discussions on military co-operation. Their conversations were so frank and wide-ranging that Huguet assumed

   British General Staff, pp.75-94.
12   Gooch, *Plans of War*, p.212.
13   Gooch, *Plans of War*, pp.187, 247.
14   Gooch, *Plans of War*, pp.188-190.

they were officially sanctioned and was rather surprised to find out later that they were initiated without the full knowledge of the government. Grierson's grip certainly impressed Huguet who recalled he "was happily surprised to find Sir James a listener, attentive and obliging" displaying from the start "the vivacity of his intelligence, the extent of his military knowledge, integrity and judgment".[15] In planning to counter German aggression, Grierson was careful to exclude the possibility of launching amphibious raids on the German coast. However, he did see much greater potential for intervening on the German flank in Belgium should its neutrality be violated, which he considered likely as the result of a strategic war game. It was this assumption which very probably formed the basis of the conversations he held with Huguet. These initial thoughts were taken up by Sir George Clarke, the secretary of the CID, who pushed for discussions of a wider range of options including direct intervention on the French frontier. Sir Edward Grey, Foreign Secretary in the new Liberal administration, was made aware of Grierson's conversations with Huguet in January 1906 and gave his blessing to their continuance and extension seeing "no objection to similar enquiries being addressed to our Military Attaché in Brussels to the Belgian Military Authorities as to the manner in which, in case of need, British assistance could be most effectually afforded to Belgium for the defence of her neutrality".[16]

Acting on this point with great alacrity and no doubt wishing to transform vague intentions into something firmer, on 16 January Grierson instructed the British Military Attaché in Brussels, Lieutenant-Colonel Barnardistone, to ascertain the nature of Belgian strategy and informed him of the most recent developments in British thinking:

> You tell the Chief of Staff what we are prepared to put in the field in this case, 4 Cavalry Brigades, 2 Army Corps, and a division of mounted infantry, and you know from our conversations the general lines on which you should go. The total numbers will be about 105,000 and we shall ferry them over to the *French* [original emphasis] coast – Calais, Boulogne, Dieppe and Havre, railing them afterwards if necessary to Belgium and then, when command of the sea is assured, changing our base to Antwerp.[17]

In reply Barnardistone stated the intention of the Belgians to mass around Brussels to protect Antwerp, their confidence in their fortresses at Namur and Liège and the possibility of a German southern sweep towards Sedan. This information chimed in with Grierson's thinking and led him to plan for the deployment of a British force on the right of the Belgian army. The intensity of this decision-making process was driven

---

15   Comments made to Macdiarmid, *Grierson*, pp.213-124. Author's translation from the original French. See also General V.J.M. Huguet, *Britain and the War. A French Indictment* (London: Cassell, 1928), pp.5-7. It is clear from Huguet's text that he did not believe Spencer Ewart, Grierson's successor as DMO, was in the same league in terms of insight and grip.

16   Quoted in John K. Dunlop, *The Development of the British Army 1899-1914* (London: Methuen, 1938), p.239.

17   Quoted in Dunlop, *Development of the British Army*, p.240.

by the first Moroccan crisis, and its successful resolution through concerted diplomatic action allowed the pace to slacken. Given some leeway over finalising schemes, Grierson remained in very close contact with Huguet and took the opportunity to observe Belgian and French manoeuvres. He was deeply impressed by the latter and deeply unimpressed by the former: "The infantry were of decidedly inferior physique, the artillery badly horsed, and the cavalry and engineers only made a good impression." As John Gooch has suggested, this negative assessment of the Belgians may well have been instrumental in pushing British military thinking towards direct support of the French as the wiser option.[18] This shift demanded detailed planning in order to turn the aspiration into reality, and much of it fell to Grierson. He produced excellent plans for the despatch of a force from south coast ports to Le Havre, but little was done to clarify the precise position of the BEF regarding its relationship with French forces once deployed on French soil. This vexed question was never unambiguously solved before 1914, and arguably only reached any sort of conclusion in March 1918.[19]

Much of Grierson's planning for the expeditionary force and his assumptions about German intentions looked as if they might come unstuck in January 1912 when the Navy revised its views. As a result of the 1912 manoeuvres, the Admiralty judged a German landing of up to 28,000 men on the east coast a possibility. Although this was still classified as a large-scale raid and not a full invasion, such an operation could force the retention of regular units for home defence and as a consequence tip the military balance against France on the continent. An atmosphere of consternation fell over the War Office, as the judgement was thought to be an attempt by the Navy to dictate military policy. A scramble to refute the scenario occurred in which the precise number, and type, of soldiers required for home defence were debated. The War Office was generally bullish and strove to keep numbers to a minimum. Even the most pessimistic general, Sir William Robertson, believed that the Territorial Force was the best deterrent and argued that its full manpower should be used for coastal defence. The final result was a report that differed little in its overall conclusions from those delivered after the first invasion investigation in 1908: for an invasion to be successful at least 70,000 men needed to be disembarked and that was highly unlikely. Where the report differed was in providing detail about the potential targets for raiders, which resulted in the General Staff agreeing to retain two or the six regular divisions if the situation demanded. Grierson's biographer, D.S. Macdiarmid, noted that Grierson "appended his signature to the report... not with any marked enthusiasm", but gave no reason why.[20] A possible explanation is Grierson's confidence that any German raiding force would be very small and that it should not undermine the central objective of dispatching as many regulars to France as quickly as possible.

18   See Gooch, *Plans of War*, p.283.
19   See Elizabeth Greenhalgh, "'Myth and Memory: Sir Douglas Haig and the Imposition of Allied Unified Command in March 1918'", *Journal of Military History*, Vol. 68, No. 3, July 2004.
20   Macdiarmid, *Grierson*, p.251.

Grierson reinforced his qualities as a staff officer in all his subsequent posts. When he moved on to Aldershot as commander of 1st Division in 1906, his first task was to oversee the restructuring of the division. With the abandonment of the army corps scheme, the division became the key all arms unit of the British army; an infantry core was made flexible through the addition of its own artillery and mounted units. Smoothing the transition from the somewhat unwieldy and unstable corps system to a divisional one required careful planning, and it required close attention to detail. It was vital to get the divisions of the Aldershot Command established on a robust basis, as they were both the models for the rest of the British army to follow and the spearhead of the expeditionary force. Lieutenant Charles à Court Repington, the influential military correspondent of *The Times*, believed Grierson carried out the transformation with great skill. When the restructured division was assembled and practised deployment for the first time, he praised the smoothness of the operation: "our modern division is not only well balanced and complete in all its parts, but also sufficiently mobile and flexible, if directed, as the 1st Division notoriously is, by a skilful commander and a well-trained staff".[21] Macdiarmid labelled it a "great achievement" and a "resounding success".[22]

On 9 May 1910 Grierson was promoted to the rank of Lieutenant-General and with that came the end of his tenure at Aldershot. He spent the next two years on half pay, but made little secret of his enthusiasm to return to his old command. Sir John French and the King certainly seemed keen on the idea, but Haldane was determined to ensure a fresh appointment and looked to Haig. Although disappointing for Grierson personally, this was a sound move by Haldane, for it ensured a greater spread of high command experience, a quality the British army desperately needed. In fact, Grierson's next appointment had a very important element to it, for he was given Eastern Command in the spring of 1912. Overseeing England's front door and the most likely region for a German raid required Grierson to consider closely plans for rebutting any incursion. Fortunately, he had a good base in the 1911 Eastern Command defence scheme, which in itself was based on his own initial forecasts while DMO. This document summarised the views of the CID: invasion was unlikely because of the Royal Navy; raids were the most likely strategy of an enemy and should be met by local auxiliary forces and then subdued completely by the despatch of swiftly concentrated regular forces using the advantage of interior lines of communication; and the most likely moment for such a raid would be in a state of heightened international tension, but before a formal declaration of war. Stressing the fact that the expeditionary force was not earmarked for home defence, but that units of it might be detached for that purpose, the main response would come from the Territorial Force with Eastern Command Territorial units providing the first line of defence.[23] Unsurprisingly, Grierson felt little need to revise this scheme and added only one or two extra details

---

21   *The Times*, 7 August 1909.
22   Macdiarmid, *Grierson*, p.225.
23   The National Archives, Kew (hereafter known as TNA) WO 33/2856 Eastern Command Scheme, 1911.

to the overarching concept in the 1913 revisions, but he did provide more attention to the nuts and bolts of local arrangements and the identification of defensive areas. The almost pedantic mind of the highly trained and confident staff officer shone through in this process.[24] Similarly, he and his staff fleshed out the intensely complex mobilization timetables with a comprehensive railway scheme completed.[25] It is perhaps a reflection of Grierson's disagreement with the proceedings of the CID's latest invasion enquiry that the 1913 scheme stresses much more firmly than the 1911 original that regular troops will only be available "in the somewhat improbable [situation] in which the Expeditionary Force is not required for service abroad".[26] Thus, Grierson's scheme very firmly placed the emphasis on the Territorial Force and other auxiliaries alone.

The final test of his strengths as an administrator came in the 1913 manoeuvres which he organised on behalf of the General Staff. The smooth unfolding of the grand exercise was certainly appreciated by Repington who noted in *The Times* that "General Grierson deserves the greatest credit for his organisation which, by its completeness and attention to the minutest details, enabled the changes of front to be made with perfect smoothness".[27] Somewhat ironically, it was just at this moment that Sir John French had second thoughts about Grierson's strengths and his allocated role as Chief of Staff to the Expeditionary Force. French told Sir Henry Wilson on 26 September that he was unhappy at certain aspects of the arrangements and was thinking of giving Wilson, who was critical of Grierson's work whilst he was DMO, the Chief of Staff role.[28] Ascertaining precisely what had irked French is not easy, and it may simply reflect his mercurial nature as he came more and more closely in contact with Wilson. It is possible that Repington detected this change of atmosphere and wanted to set the record straight in his report for *The Times*.

The result of French's shift in thinking was the allocation of field command in the expeditionary force to Grierson. Grierson's potential as a commander had been given a chance to mature through his tenure at Aldershot and Eastern Command, and his strengths and weaknesses in this role reflect not only on his own character, but also on the wider culture of the British army. His strengths were those of grip, vision and insight, which were clearly exhibited in pre-war manoeuvres. In September 1907 at the end of his first full season at Aldershot he took part in the Command's manoeuvres programme in East Anglia. Grierson was GOC First (Northern) Army working with Major-General T.E. Stephenson GOC Second Army; French directed the whole operation. Grierson was in command of the Blue Army which had invaded Redland (England). Grierson's knowledge of the German army was probably being utilised here for Blueland was identified as a continental power capable of putting 3 million men

24   TNA WO 33/2858 Eastern Command Scheme, 1913.
25   TNA WO 33/684 Eastern Command Railway Mobilization Timetable, 1914.
26   TNA WO 33/2858 Eastern Command Scheme, 1913, p.9. Compare and contrast it with WO 33/2856 1911 scheme p.7.
27   *The Times*, 27 September 191
28   See Keith Jeffery, *Field Marshal Sir Henry Wilson. A Political Soldier* (Oxford: Oxford University Press, 2006), p.63.

in the field. However, in this instance, it deployed a much smaller number due to fears about its own border security, which was a clear reference to Franco-Russian assaults.

The appreciation Grierson sent to his subordinates stressed the difficulty of working in the closely enclosed country of East Anglia and its many small waterways. On the plus side, he reminded them that this meant shock action by cavalry was unlikely. He then revealed the mentality of many commanders of his generation, for he believed that such a landscape would undermine the artillery. Artillery was still regarded as a direct fire support used in clear fields of vision. Stephenson was operating in Sussex and Grierson identified retention of the Downs as the key to his position. Believing Stephenson's force was more vulnerable to defeat in detail if it lost the Downs and that such knowledge might make it the more attractive force for the Red army, Grierson wished to see Southern Army re-embarked and transported round to the east coast in order to concentrate force and support his operations. He then argued that the best option was to march on London using Blueland navy to cover the coast. Logistics were to be assured by securing Harwich first, or if reconnaissance determined strong defences, he would seize a lesser harbour. According to Grierson's reasoning, the threat on London would draw Red army towards him and offer more chance of engaging on favourable ground. To find and fix the enemy army first was unattractive as it might lead to enormous expenditure of energy and material for little reward.[29] Grierson was opting to remain concentrated for a decisive march bringing about a decisive battle on optimum terms: this was a British General Staff-approved reading of Clausewitz.

Sir John French, as overall commander Blue Force and director of the manoeuvres, responded by stating that the Southern Army could easily distract a large Red force and any re-embarkation would be logistically very difficult, so this was not perhaps the wisest response. Secondly, although the drains and ditches of the fens would act as a useful aid to protecting the flank of the Blue Army, the further south it went, the easier it would be for a rival force to advance. This possibility did not seem to figure too highly in Grierson's planning. Although Harwich might be a highly useful base, the movement towards it might allow Red force to gather on his flank. In turn, Grierson provided criticisms of his own commanders' appreciations. He believed that Sir Henry Rawlinson, General Officer in Command 3rd Division, paid insufficient attention to the advantage of Red force's interior communications. Rawlinson shared French's bullish stance over Second Army, but Grierson maintained that it was vulnerable to defeat in detail. He reminded Rawlinson that its ration strength disguised its lack of front line troops. Despite French's doubts about the wisdom of re-embarking Stephenson's force, French thought this a well worked response to Rawlinson, and is perhaps revealing of his own capricious nature.[30] The Times was certainly impressed by Grierson's performance. Repington remarked that:

> General Grierson's division on September 19 gave a beautiful exhibition of these methods [concealed advance]; and, although little or nothing could be understood from

29   TNA WO 279/517 Aldershot Command Staff Tour and Manoeuvres, 1907.
30   TNA WO 279/517 Aldershot Manoeuvres, 1907.

the defender's position of what he was about, it was suddenly apparent, as the whole line began to leave their last cover and advance in perfect order, that the men in the firing line were almost shoulder to shoulder, and that every yard of front held a rifle with its magazine.[31]

Similar qualities were displayed a year later when Lieutenant-General Sir Horace Smith-Dorrien led the Aldershot Command manoeuvres. Once again, Grierson took command of invading Blue Army landing in the Bristol area and Stephenson commanded the Red defending force. Grierson's orders were to pin down the defending army as a prelude to the landing of the main force. On landing, Grierson made straight for the Marlborough Downs with the objective of inducing the enemy to fight him there. Here Grierson maintained the principles he had expressed at the II Corps manoeuvres in 1903 when he declared that ground was only important if it allowed for the destruction of the enemy force. His move went according to plan and he took the high ground around Stow-on-the-Wold and Maughersbury Hill. The positions were immediately entrenched strongly and made an excellent fire-base for beating off Stephenson's counter-attacks. Although concerned that he had massed his mounted units and given them a punishing schedule far from supporting troops, Smith-Dorrien praised Grierson for seizing every opportunity: "The Blue Commander acted quite rightly to-day when, on hearing of the further detrainment of Red troops at Bath and Trowbridge, he gave orders to the 13th Division to push on with all possible vigour and interfere with the detrainment. This was successfully carried out and the enemy must have suffered heavily."[32] Once again, the military correspondents were congratulatory with the *Manchester Guardian* stating that Grierson "had at this moment much the better of the situation and made the best use of it".[33] Smith-Dorrien had very little in the way of significant criticism to make of Grierson's planning and execution, which was in contrast to his more comprehensive, and less flattering, responses on Stephenson. By the evening of 11 September Grierson seemed to be getting the better of it. Smith-Dorrien remarked: "The appreciation of the situation rendered the Blue Commander on the evening of the 10th is quite sound, and his estimation of the enemy's dispositions and intentions are on the whole very good."[34] At the final conference on 12 September, Smith-Dorrien praised Blue force for being in a concentrated position and "have so far been victorious, their losses have been comparatively small, and they should be considerably fresher than Red's".[35] Although "no decisive result was obtained... Blue Commander must be regarded as having successfully carried out the instructions he received, namely, to draw Red's main Army towards Bristol and, having done so, to keep it employed until the Blue Southern Army could land on the south coast."[36]

31   *The Times*, 28 September 1907.
32   TNA WO 279/21 Aldershot Command Staff Tour and Manoeuvres, 1908, p.19.
33   *Manchester Guardian*, 16 September 1908.
34   TNA WO 279/21 Aldershot Command Manoeuvres, 1908, p.21.
35   TNA WO 279/21 Aldershot Command Manoeuvres, 1908, pp.21-22.
36   TNA WO 279/21 Aldershot Command Manoeuvres, 1908, p.23.

Grierson's most famous success, and the one that his admirers believed revealed the qualities lost to the BEF in 1914, came in the 1912 manoeuvres when he successfully outwitted Haig with some aplomb. During the course of the operations both Grierson and Haig proved that they were no technophobes for aircraft were deployed extensively for the first time. The attached aircraft were used whenever conditions allowed and both men took very careful note of the intelligence they gathered. In fact, as Andrew Whitmarsh has argued, perhaps too much attention was paid to their work, for it seemed to become the sole determinant of Haig's thinking to his ultimate detriment.[37] Each side consisted of two infantry divisions, a cavalry division, two aeroplanes and an airship. Grierson commanded Blue army and Haig, Red. Haig's subordinates were Major-General E. Allenby (cavalry), while Majors-General S.H. Lomax and Henry Lawson commanded the 1st and 2nd Divisions respectively. Grierson's cavalry was commanded by Colonel Charles Briggs, whilst Rawlinson and Major-General Thomas D'Oyly Snow commanded the 3rd and 4th Divisions. This time Grierson played the role of defender, which was apt given his new task at Eastern Command, while Haig was directed to attack the forces and capital of the enemy land.

Grierson was well aware that he had the cobbled together staff, while Haig had the established Aldershot team to assist him. The unsettling effect an improvised staff could have on the force under its control had been noted by Grierson when he witnessed the German manoeuvres of 1896, and he was keen to ensure a team spirit as quickly as possible. He was disadvantaged still further by the fact that his infantry was a motley assortment of regulars and territorials drawn from across Eastern and Southern Command and his cavalry was an equally patchwork collection consisting of the Scots Greys, Yeomanry, Cyclists and Household Cavalry units. Lieutenant-General Bruce Hamilton was chief umpire Red Force, and Smith-Dorrien performed the same role for Blue, with Sir John French in overall charge of the scheme.[38]

On 16 September Grierson remained in camp and pushed his cavalry forward to carry out reconnaissance. This allowed him to determine accurately Red Army's lines of march and halting places. He kept up his cavalry work on the following day using it to harry the advancing 2nd Division while all the time keeping his own options open. By skilful deployment of his troops, Grierson was able to choose both the location and timing of his main assault on 18 September. The battle was, nonetheless, a close fought affair, but by throwing in his reserves at the right moment, in particular the use of the 4th Division which appeared totally unexpected on the enemy flank, he checked Red Army decisively. Thorough instructions on concealment from aerial observation had been distributed by Grierson's staff, and this undoubtedly contributed to their success. Grierson had effectively negated the risk of a better trained force defeating his own army in detail through good reconnaissance, effective deployment and concealment of his own forces, and skilful interpretation of enemy intentions.[39] It was an even more

37   Andrew Whitmarsh, 'British Army Manoeuvres and Military Aviation, 1910-1913', *War in History*, Vol. 14, No. 3, 2007, pp.325-346.
38   TNA WO 279/47 Army Manoeuvres, 1912.
39   TNA WO 279/47 Army Manoeuvres, 1912.

remarkable performance given the fact that a large part of Grierson's force consisted of the much-derided Territorial infantry. Thanks to intelligent central leadership, these men put up an excellent performance against the regular forces of the Aldershot Command. Although the final outcome of the manoeuvres was inconclusive, Grierson's position was generally considered stronger in that he still had a cohesive force and had made better use of his available resources.

An effective headquarters team played an important part in ensuring success for Grierson, but this, too, was very much his creation which he had melded together from a scratch collection of officers. Furthermore, his staff was not simply an apparatus for his decisions, but a command forum, and he was prepared to trust the judgement of subordinates. One of his staff officers, Sir Percy Radcliffe, later recalled that he was detailed to deliver orders to a Territorial unit, but on arrival found that the situation had changed completely. Taking the initiative, he ignored the orders and instructed the unit to undertake a different mission. Radcliffe stated that he would not have taken such a step had he "not known that General Grierson would have backed me".[40] In stark contrast, the official report on the manoeuvres criticised the fact that Haig's instructions to Lomax left him with "little scope for the exercise of initiative".[41] Perhaps even more surprisingly, Grierson appeared to use his mounted units with more imagination and dash. It is even possible that Grierson's lack of cavalry training was an advantage, for, unencumbered by the fine points of mounted doctrine, he saw no problem in allowing Colonel Briggs to mix regular cavalry, yeomanry and cyclists in a variety of tasks. Blue army certainly made far more extensive use of cyclists; they screened the flanks of mounted troops and formed pivots of manoeuvre. "In both roles the Blue cyclists contributed materially to the successful results... and useful lessons as to the possibilities of co-operation between cyclists and cavalry in enclosed country were learned."[42]

On the conclusion of the manoeuvres Grierson reflected on his own role and performance and made some perceptive points. He averred that command was relatively straightforward when in the reactionary mode or preparing for an assault on a known enemy position. A much greater challenge was decision-making in a state of uncertainty, which was most likely to come in an encounter battle. Gaining the right intellectual and psychological skills to deal with these situations was crucial. He believed far too little attention was paid to this type of battle in higher command training and it had to be rectified. Very much alive to the fact that a commander would be forced to make decisions based on imperfect information and a range of possibilities, he wanted to ensure that all higher commanders were given regular practice in analysing scenarios from scraps of information in quick time in order to perfect the mental processes required to assess a fluid situation. He also stressed the importance of maintaining the offensive spirit in the encounter battle even when the enemy has the initiative, and that all training had to be directed to this end. Finally, unlike Haig in this instance,

40   Quoted in Macdiarmid, *Grierson*, p.246.
41   TNA WO 279/47 Army Manoeuvres, 1912, p.57.
42   TNA WO 279/47 Army Manoeuvres, 1912, p.61.

Grierson revealed that a general had to analyse the information in front of him then use his training and skills in a delicate act of reflection and refinement before reaching a decision. This he did when interpreting intelligence on Red Army's movements. Lacking the full picture, he *"had to act on probabilities"* [Grierson's original emphasis] and wrote his orders with the intention of taking the initiative from the enemy, which he achieved under difficult circumstances.[43]

Newspaper coverage of the manoeuvres was extensive, and the various military correspondents used it as an opportunity to weigh up the different qualities of Grierson and Haig. The *Westminster Gazette* celebrated Grierson's sudden deployment of the well-concealed 4th Division as his "Brilliant Achievement" and "the finest bit of strategy in the manoeuvres". Haig, by contrast, is portrayed as a prisoner of aerial observation. Convinced that it would reveal everything, he moved "in the orthodox fashion", and thus the "cavalry man trained" allowed himself to be stripped of dash by his thrall to the aircraft.[44] The other great Liberal newspaper, the *Manchester Guardian*, was equally glowing. In the run-up to the manoeuvres its editorial column had defined the event as a fascinating clash between two highly respected officers. Haig was praised for being "remarkably accurate in his appreciation of a situation", and Grierson was a "brilliant staff officer" with a high reputation among the rank and file. "I find, however, that many knowing ones believe that the result of the manoeuvres will be to display General Grierson as a scientific officer of the very highest order, and that General Haig will suffer by the comparison." Presciently, it was stated that: "General Haig is less tolerant of advice than his rival, and the value of the staff will therefore be more evident in the acts of General Grierson."[45] By the conclusion of the manoeuvres, the *Manchester Guardian* felt vindicated. While Haig "remains second to none as a staff officer, or as a man able to handle a unit which he can retain in his own hand. General Grierson seems to exhibit himself as the bigger man, more in the manner of Lord Kitchener, who can impose his will on circumstances, and whose mental ramifications are wider, who can set and keep machinery working without turning the handle himself."[46] Haig's reputation also suffered as a result of his notoriously incoherent verbal commentaries. The military correspondents present at the final conference noted how difficult it was to decipher his overarching comments.[47]

However, Grierson's performance was not perfect and nor does it reveal that he was above the systemic weaknesses of the British army. In fact, he successfully diagnosed his own problem, and by extension that of his fellow senior commanders, lack of experience and practice in handling large numbers of troops. General Sir Charles Douglas, the Inspector-General, commented in his 1912 report that Grierson had kept his two divisions widely separated which might have left them vulnerable to defeat in detail. Douglas stated that he referred to such incidents "not in the spirit of criticism,

43   TNA WO 279/47 Army Manoeuvres, 1912, p.175.
44   *Westminster Gazette*, 20 September 1912.
45   *Manchester Guardian*, 9 September 1912.
46   *Manchester Guardian*, 20 September 1912.
47   *Westminster Gazette*, 21 September 1912.

but in order to show that two of our most distinguished leaders, when put to the actual test, committed errors in the conduct of field operations which they would have been the first to detect and criticize in others. The obvious conclusion is that their failures, such as they were, were due to lack of experience in the actual handling of large bodies of troops".[48]

Along with many of his colleagues, Grierson questioned the precise relevance of the South African War. The most significant aspect of this was the assessment of firepower on infantry tactics. He was critical of what he deemed the over-extended infantry lines used in the 1903 manoeuvres. "I am afraid that in tactics the Boer War has had a baleful influence upon us", he wrote, "for certainly much that we did could not have been done in the face of an European enemy".[49] The fear of over-extension then explains Repington's description of Grierson's assaults in 1907: "the men in the firing line were almost shoulder to shoulder, and that every yard of front held a rifle with its magazine".[50] Although deploying such a densely packed final assault line was not necessarily a problem *if fire supremacy had been achieved*, the lack of clarity in British thinking about fire supremacy should have urged caution in the use of this formation. Grierson here reflected an institutional weakness in the British army: too vague a grip on the fine details of minor tactics. This is not to say that the subject was not discussed, far from it, only that unambiguous, simple-to-follow conclusions and guidelines were missing.[51] Grierson may well have been reflecting his own keen interest in, and knowledge of, the German army here for it was also debating the nature of formations and faced similar contradictory arguments. For some the intensity of the Prussian 'swarm' which had overcome French soldiers armed with the superior Chassepot rifle in 1870 and 1871 was still the tactical key to the battlefield, whereas others were considering devolution of authority and troops widely dispersed.[52]

Further weakening the grip of commanders at all levels on this matter was the difficulty of extrapolating lessons from exercises and manoeuvres. This point was made by the *Manchester Guardian*'s military correspondent when analysing the 1912 manoeuvres: "Once troops become closely engaged in mimic warfare the operations cease to become either instructive or – to the soldier – realistic, and nothing can be gained by continuing the exercise, whatever its nature may be."[53] According to this

48   TNA WO 27/508 Reports by the Inspector-General of Forces – submitted to the Army Council, (1903-1913), 1912, p.4.
49   Quoted in Macdiarmid, *Grierson*, p.202.
50   *The Times*, 28 September 1907.
51   For differing interpretations of this issue see Timothy Bowman and Mark Connelly, *The Edwardian Army. Recruiting, Training and Deploying the British Army, 1902-1914* (Oxford: Oxford University Press, 2012), pp.64-105 and Spencer Jones, *From Boer War to World War: Tactical Reform of the British Army, 1902-1914* (Norman, University of Oklahoma Press, 2012).
52   For further details see Eric Dorn Brose, *The Kaiser's Army. The politics of military technology in Germany during the machine age, 1870-1914* (Oxford: Oxford University Press, 2001), pp.152-154.
53   *Manchester Guardian*, 21 September 1912.

correspondent, the real value of the operations was the test of higher commanders rather than the minutiae of combat. This was flawed thinking, for without a good grip on what was actually achievable on the battlefield, all other decision-making processes were undermined. The difficulty of assessing the outcome of combat was freely admitted by the army itself: most manoeuvres reports stress issues with umpiring which clouded understandings of likely results. The 1912 report noted that: "Umpires also do not always realize that superiority of numbers is not the only factor to be taken into account in deciding upon the success, or otherwise, of an attacking force, and the importance of building up a good fire position is apt to be overlooked."[54] This admission is of particular importance for it implies that the umpires lacked basic tactical principles themselves. Further, it was also noted that umpires gave little consideration to the possibility of an extended fire-fight leading to stalemate and too often declared an action decisive.[55] The Chief Umpires were able to compensate for some of these shortcomings in their concluding reports and usually provided robust analyses. Stressing his belief that umpires did not emphasize the impact of firepower with enough force, the Blue Force umpire, Smith-Dorrien, said it allowed infantry and cavalry to ignore incoming artillery fire as ineffective.[56] He was also concerned by the field artillery's failure to make best use of cover, and noted that the heavily enclosed nature of the country stopped the artillery from engaging advancing infantry until it had reached decisive ranges.[57] He made a similar point in 1908 when commenting on the difficulty of using artillery in enclosed country: "we must take more risks with our guns, pushing sections forward with the advanced Infantry. Undoubtedly Mountain Artillery would be invaluable for this purpose."[58] Although he was a bit more subtle by 1912, he still failed to see his logic through to its conclusion; namely, the possibility of field artillery surviving when firing over open sights: the denouement of this omission came at Le Cateau when the artillery was placed well forward and suffered heavily as a result of facing an enemy armed with heavier guns and a longer reach.[59]

It is also clear that whatever Grierson's qualities as a team-builder, he did not impose uniform approaches on those he commanded. Again, this merely reflected a deep fault line in the British army, not an issue peculiar to Grierson as an individual commander. Douglas commented in his report for 1912 that the commanders of 2nd, 3rd, 4th Divisions each had their own subtly different approaches to the attack and so concluded that the *Field Service Regulations* had failed to achieve any kind of uniformity.[60] The weakness was not so much the advice contained in the regulations, but the seeming obliviousness of the army's highest ranks to the need for common practice. The explanation for such blind spots can be found in the double-bind of the

54   TNA WO 279/47 Army Manoeuvres, 1912, p.127.
55   TNA WO 279/47 Army Manoeuvres, 1912, pp.134-135.
56   TNA WO 279/47 Army Manoeuvres, 1912, pp.138, 152.
57   TNA WO 279/47 Army Manoeuvres, 1912, p.140.
58   TNA WO 279/21 Aldershot Command Manoeuvres, 1908, p.31.
59   See Shelford Bidwell and Dominick Graham, *Gunners at War. A Tactical Study of the Royal Artillery in the Twentieth Century* (London: Arms and Armour Press, 1970), p.29.
60   TNA WO 27/508 IG Report, 1912, pp.83-84.

army's small size and the strength of its regimental traditions. When combined, a very powerful parochial culture was created, which Grierson could never quite escape regardless of his other experiences. That it was a deep-seated aspect of Grierson's character, typical of so many of his immediate peers, can be detected in his comment, "I would rather command a battalion in war than be Chief of the General Staff!"[61] The veneration for regimental culture was shown in the fact that he kept a small notebook in which he scribbled details about each unit in the British army recording scraps of regimental history, types of uniform, and battle honours.[62] Thus, Grierson's victories in manoeuvres cannot be taken as absolute proof of his military prowess and qualities, and the performance in 1912 against Haig should not be taken as evidence of supreme authority in one and inferiority in another. Haig's undoubtedly ponderous and somewhat cautious approach meant he lost the initiative, but this did not necessarily mean that he would have lost the battles.

It is highly unlikely that the death of Sir James Grierson led the BEF to fight any less effectively in its opening battles of the conflict. Given his training, outlook and encompassing military culture, and in particular his affinity with Smith-Dorrien after their time at Aldershot, Grierson would probably have managed II Corps in a very similar manner to his successor. Grierson had many strengths: he recognised the need for rigorous staff work; he made realistic appreciations of German intentions and the defence needs of the empire; he had a good understanding of the Belgian, French and German armies; he was confident in the ability of the Territorial Force to perform its central task, and he recognised the challenges thrown down by higher command. On the downside, he failed to understand the true tactical implications of modern firepower and with it the likelihood of stalemate leading to a prolonged conflict, and never quite understood the distinction between the broader, almost abstract, plotting of strategy and the more prosaic, but nonetheless vital, command requirement of maintaining high tempo operations with a large field force for a prolonged period. Few of these weaknesses actually reflected fundamental flaws in Grierson himself; rather, they were symptoms of a wider cultural problem in the British army. The first was the obsession with corps and regimental identities. On the plus side this translated into a healthy concern for the well-being of the rank and file which was critical in the maintenance of morale and fighting spirit. Its weakness was the tendency to undermine truly broad perspectives. The second was the inability to define the precise role and function of a staff. Enthralled by the German system, the British tended to infuse it with an Olympian status in which the nature of war was dissected in an atmosphere of intense intellectual rigour and scientific detachment. In fact, the German Staff system was rather more prosaic and spent a good deal of time on 'nuts and bolts' issues of military management. Modelling itself on a misunderstanding, and unable to replicate the scale of the German army, the British staff and, more especially its Staff College, became stuck in a strange limbo. It was neither the finishing school for a military secretariat nor a training course for generals. Ideas aplenty were thrown around and discussed, but

61   Quoted in Macdiarmid, *Grierson*, p.224.
62   Macdiarmid, *Grierson*, p.226.

the ultimate intention and outcome was ill-defined.[63] The final issue was the failure to understand the likely drift of modern combat, a problem by no means confined to the British army. Grierson was, therefore, a product of his time and culture. He was a very fine officer reflecting every aspect of the professional society he adored and strove to serve to the best of his considerable abilities.

63   For further discussion of this point see Bowman and Connelly, *Edwardian Army*, pp.33-34, 64-65. See also Strachan, 'The British army, its general staff and the continental commitment, 1904-1914' in French and Holden Reid (eds), *British General Staff*, pp.86-88.

7

"A Commander of Rare and Unusual Coolness": General Sir Horace Lockwood Smith-Dorrien

II Corps

Spencer Jones and Steven J. Corvi

General Sir Horace Lockwood Smith-Dorrien is arguably the most important British general of 1914. His success in leading a heavily engaged formation through one of the most arduous of military manoeuvres, a retreat under close pursuit, has been widely praised.[1] The stakes were high, for had Smith-Dorrien failed in his task and II Corps been destroyed, the consequences for the British Expeditionary Force as a whole would almost certainly have been catastrophic. The achievement is all the more impressive due to the fact that Smith-Dorrien was a late replacement for the original II Corps commander, the unfortunate James Grierson, and had been in charge of the formation for less than a week before the Battle of Mons on 23 August 1914. A further problem that Smith-Dorrien overcame in this period was the lack of support from either GHQ or Douglas Haig's I Corps. Of the wider BEF, only the recently arrived 4th Division and elements of Edmund Allenby's fragmented Cavalry Division fought alongside II Corps during its critical engagement at Le Cateau on 26 August. For the most part, II Corps fought its own campaign in August. That it survived at all was an achievement, but that it survived with comparatively few casualties given the dangers it faced is testament to Smith-Dorrien's military skill and the quality of the soldiers he commanded. In 1933, Smith-Dorrien's handling of II Corps on the retreat, particularly the stand at Le Cateau, was singled out as an example of "great leadership" and thus ideal for study on the Staff College syllabus.[2]

However, Smith-Dorrien's career did not benefit from these achievements. He had endured a strained relationship with John French in the years before the war and the nature of his appointment in 1914 did nothing to improve matters. French had not

---

1   Fred R. Van Hartesveldt, *The Battles of the British Expeditionary Forces, 1914-1915 : Historiography and Annotated Bibliography* (Westport, Praeger, 2005), pp.8-11.

2   Major-General A.J. McCullough, 'Teaching in the Army' in the *Journal of the Royal United Services Institute*, 79(2), 1933, p.22.

Sir Horace Smith-Dorrien. (Editor's collection)

wanted him to replace Grierson in 1914, but had been overruled by Lord Kitchener who had insisted on giving Smith-Dorrien a command. From the outset French deeply resented his presence.[3] Smith-Dorrien's effective performance in 1914 did nothing to improve relations between the two men and may even have stoked deeper professional jealously between the commander and his subordinate. This unhappy relationship culminated when French removed Smith-Dorrien from command in May 1915 after the British had lost ground at the Second Battle of Ypres, a disproportionate punishment that owed more to French's vindictive personality than any military justification. Although subsequently appointed to take charge of the faltering campaign in German East Africa, a severe bout of pneumonia prevented Smith-Dorrien from taking any further combat postings, meaning that the British Army lost one of its most experienced and successful generals.

Historians have generally adjudged that Smith-Dorrien was treated unfairly and subsequent authors have done much to restore his reputation.[4] Much of this rehabilitation stemmed from the publication of John French's spectacularly ill judged

3   Ian F.W. Beckett, *The Judgement of History: Sir Horace Smith-Dorrien, Lord French and 1914* (London, Tom Donovan, 1993), p.viii.
4   C.R. Ballard, *Smith-Dorrien* (London, Constable & Company, 1931); A.J. Smithers, *The Man Who Disobeyed: Sir Horace Smith-Dorrien and his Enemies* (London, Leo Cooper, 1970); Steven J. Corvi 'Horace Smith-Dorrien' in Ian F.W. Beckett & Steven J. Corvi (eds.) *Haig's Generals* (Barnsley, Pen & Sword, 2006); See Beckett, *Judgement of History*, pp.x - xxi for contemporary reaction to the French and Smith-Dorrien feud.

memoir, *1914*.[5] Although the memoir aimed to destroy Smith-Dorrien's reputation, French ended up destroying his own and enhancing that of his intended target. Authors rallied to Smith-Dorrien's defence and exposed the exaggerations and outright fabrications in *1914*, whilst Smith-Dorrien maintained a dignified stance and steered clear of the controversy in his own memoirs.[6]

Indeed, Smith-Dorrien's reputation has been so firmly established in the historiography that it can prove a challenge to say anything new about the man. A biography published in 1931 caused the reviewer in the *Journal of the Royal United Services Institution* to question its relevance as the story was so familiar.[7] The last full length biography of Smith-Dorrien was published in 1970 and received a frosty review in the same journal, which dismissed the work as a "prolix and one-sided book" which did "nothing to either enhance or adorn a well known story."[8] Since then academic authors have revisited aspects of Smith-Dorrien's career, shedding fresh light on his achievements as a trainer of troops and his conflict with John French, but he lacks a modern biography.[9]

Although the story of Smith-Dorrien's career is well covered, no study of the BEF of 1914 is complete without some consideration of his role on the retreat from Mons. This chapter examines Smith-Dorrien's military background, detailing his pre-war experiences, his notorious temperament, and his difficult relationship with John French, before discussing his time in command of II Corps in August 1914. This chapter will reach an informed conclusion on his abilities and importance, and highlight avenues for future research on this important officer.

Formative Career

Horace Smith-Dorrien was born on 26 May 1858. He was the eleventh child of a brood of sixteen.[10] Following education at Harrow and Sandhurst, he was commissioned as a 2nd lieutenant in the 95th Foot in February 1876. His early career was marked by a vast amount of combat experience. He was one of the few officers to survive the infamous British defeat at Isandlwana in 1879; had won a DSO in Egypt in 1885; had

---

5   [John] Viscount French of Ypres, *1914*, (London, Constable, 1919).
6   A useful summary of this miniature battle of the memoirs is given in Beckett, *Judgement of History*, pp.viii-xxi.
7   'Reviews of Books: *Smith-Dorrien* by Brig-Gen. C. Ballard', *Journal of the Royal United Services Institution*, 76(1), 1931, pp.905-906.
8   'Reviews of Books: *The Man who Disobeyed: Sir Horace Smith-Dorrien and His Enemies* by Maj. A.J. Smithers', *Journal of the Royal United Services Institution*, 116(2), 1971, p.68.
9   Richard Ray Seim, *Forging the Rapier among Scythes: Lieutenant-General Sir Horace Smith-Dorrien and the Aldershot Command 1907-1912*, unpublished MA thesis, Rice University, (Houston), 1980; Steven J. Corvi, *General Sir Horace Lockwood Smith-Dorrien: Portrait of a Victorian Soldier in Modern War*, unpublished PhD thesis, Northeastern University (Boston), 2002.
10   Smithers, *The Man Who Disobeyed*, p.11.

fought in the Tirah campaign in 1897 and in the reconquest of the Sudan in 1898; and had commanded a battalion, a brigade, and finally an all-arms mobile column in the Boer War 1899 - 1902. Over the course of Smith-Dorrien's career he saw front line combat in its elemental form and fought on three different continents - Africa, Asia and Europe. His early career was largely defined by "small wars", but he experienced firsthand the implementation and effects of new and innovative weapon systems, including the magazine loading smokeless powder rifle, modern breech-loading rifled artillery, and the machine gun. Other elements of modern warfare were present in this battle environment, including defensive entrenchment, wire obstacles, the use of cavalry as light mounted infantry, and the use of artillery in close support of infantry. Smith-Dorrien's experience at the sharp end of battle shaped his views on warfare. Smith-Dorrien was not the paradigmatic theorist Douglas Haig was, but his consideration of tactics revealed an eye for the practicalities of combat.

The defining moment of Smith-Dorrien's pre-war career, was, like many of his contemporaries, the Boer War. The effectiveness of firepower in this conflict was undeniable and left a profound impression on the British Army. Smith-Dorrien was present at the Battle of Paardeburg (18-27 February 1900) and witnessed the difficulties of attacking an entrenched position. He recalled one such assault in his memoirs: "It was a gallant charge, gallantly led, but the fact that not one of them got within 300 yards of the enemy is sufficient proof of its futility."[11] Such revelations came as an unpleasant shock as, prior to the Boer War, the British Army had enjoyed an almost unbroken string of victories in colonial warfare and possessed considerable confidence in its tactics. However, the destructive capacity of modern weapons, particularly the magazine loading Mauser rifle of the Boers, prompted reconsideration. In the aftermath of the war, the army grappled with the lessons of South Africa and struggled to integrate new weapons and concepts into its tactics and training.[12]

The debate over the appropriate tactics for a modern battlefield began whilst the Boer War was still in progress and was ongoing when the First World War broke out in 1914. Within the context of this intellectual debate Smith-Dorrien developed a reputation as an independent thinker and an innovative trainer. Sir John Fortescque noted of him that "Never was a British soldier less hidebound by the traditions and prejudices of the Regular Army."[13] Smith-Dorrien's vast combat experience gave him a perceptive understanding of infantry tactics and the employment of firepower, and consideration of these issues defined his pre-war training methods. He planned and led an ambitious exercise in India in 1906, inspired by trench warfare in the Boer War and the Russo-Japanese War, which involved the construction of a triple line trench system

---

11   Horace Smith-Dorrien, *Memories of Forty-Eight Years' Service* (London, J. Murray, 1925), p.154.

12   For differing interpretations of the reform debate, see Timothy Bowman and Mark Connelly, *The Edwardian Army. Recruiting, Training and Deploying the British Army, 1902-1914* (Oxford: Oxford University Press, 2012), pp. 64-105 and Spencer Jones, *From Boer War to World War: Tactical Reform of the British Army, 1902-1914* (Norman, University of Oklahoma Press, 2012).

13   John Fortescue, 'Horace Smith-Dorrien', *Blackwood's Magazine*, June 1931, p.847.

that featured bunkers, command posts and machine gun positions. Once the trenches were constructed, the exercise moved from defensive preparation to solving the riddle of how to capture such a formidable set of earthworks. The attack was made in stages, with the simulated battle continuing through both day and night, and featured troops using innovative weapons such as mortars and "bomb throwers". Smith-Dorrien commented modestly in his memoirs: "It was a very impressive operation… Looking back on it now, it was quite a good forecast of the trench warfare in the Great War."[14]

In 1907, Smith-Dorrien moved to Aldershot Command, the premier training area for the home based British Army. He introduced a number of popular reforms to improve the lot of soldiers stationed at the post, demonstrating a common touch which endeared him to his men.[15] Henry de Beauvoir de Lisle, then serving as a staff officer at Aldershot, commented that "everyone loved S-D".[16] Smith-Dorrien also brought a fresh approach to training, emphasising realism with a particular focus on the ebb and flow of battle. Innovative exercises included the use of moving and "surprise" targets. These were cleverly incorporated into attack training. When the attackers had fought their way onto a position, they would face a counter attack simulated by the sudden appearance of moving targets. Units competed against one another to achieve the best performance in the exercise and the scheme was judged by Smith-Dorrien to have been "an unqualified success."[17]

However, his tenure at Aldershot became notorious due to his vigorous reform of cavalry training. Cavalry were expected to reach the same standard of marksmanship as infantry, but Smith-Dorrien was irritated to find that the horsemen at Aldershot were decidedly poor shots. He attributed this to an overemphasis on mounted training, with a particular focus on knee-to-knee charges.[18] Smith-Dorrien was further displeased by the mounted arm's performance at an otherwise successful field day in May 1908 which culminated with the cavalry launching a frontal charge against entrenched infantry. Smith-Dorrien denounced the incident as an example of "light brigade" tactics.[19] King Edward VII was a guest at the event and agreed with the scathing assessment.[20] Over the following months the cavalry failed to develop to Smith-Dorrien's satisfaction, and in August 1909, he assembled his cavalry officers and "gave them my views pretty clearly" on the need for improvement.[21] Although it did not make him popular, either with his cavalry subordinates or with senior cavalrymen like John French, it produced a marked improvement in musketry standards and dismounted work.[22]

14   Smith-Dorrien, *Memories*, p.338.
15   Ballard, *Smith-Dorrien*, p.126.
16   Henry de Beauvoir de Lisle, *Reminiscences of Sport and War*, (London, Eyre & Spottiswoode, 1939), p.214.
17   Smith-Dorrien, *Memories*, pp.358-359.
18   Ibid., p.359.
19   Quoted in Richard Ray Seim, *Forging the Rapier among Scythes*, p.93.
20   Smith-Dorrien, *Memories*, p.93.
21   Ibid., p.359.
22   Ibid., p.359-360.

During Smith-Dorrien's tenure at Southern Command he circulated a confidential training memorandum, dated June 20 1914, which covered tactical points on "Attack" and "Retirement".[23] Taken as a whole, the memorandum illustrated Smith-Dorrien's grasp of the tactical consequences of firepower and the problems inherent in moving troops under fire. This keen understanding had been obtained during his long and varied combat career and further refined during a decade of army training. The memorandum also revealed that Smith-Dorrien was considering the difficulties of retirement and retreat, a growing theme in the thinking of British senior officers which is discussed in detail by Gary Sheffield elsewhere in this volume.

Although he possessed a reputation as a tactical reformer and innovative trainer, Smith-Dorrien was also known for his short, ferocious temper. The origin of this temperament has variously been ascribed to a scrappy childhood amongst his boisterous siblings, or to niggling health problems, particularly tooth ache.[24] Sir Archibald Murray remembered this vicious temper, commenting "These storms swept over him all his life. They were like gout in the head. I don't think he realised them and forgot them immediately. As he got older they got worse."[25] In a similar vein, de Lisle recalled Smith-Dorrien's "quick temper which bubbled up in a moment and as quickly subsided."[26]

Smith-Dorrien's temper was twinned with a fiercely independent attitude that often manifested itself in the form of insubordination. As a junior officer in the Anglo-Zulu War he had risked his career when he refused to obey orders that he felt were foolish.[27] His award of the DSO in Egypt had come after he had ignored the remit of his orders and conducted a vigorous pursuit of a group of Arab river boats, but the success of this operation had stifled any criticism.[28] At the Battle of Paardeberg, he had resisted pressure from senior officers to launch a reckless frontal assault on the Boer position, laying out his reasoning and stating he would only make the attack if given a direct order to do so.[29] Smith-Dorrien's independent outlook continued in peacetime, and his forthright views were not always in tune with the doctrinal outlook of the army as a whole. A vigorous proponent of firepower, his strongly argued position made him something of an intellectual outsider and he was not closely involved with any of the influential cliques that formed in the Victorian and Edwardian era.[30] However, he did

---

23   Imperial War Museum (IWM), Lieutenant-Colonel L.L.C. Reynolds papers, 74/136/1, 'Confidential Memorandum on Infantry Training, June 20, 1914 issued by General Sir Horace Smith-Dorrien'.

24   Stephen Badsey, 'Dorrien, Sir Horace Lockwood Smith- (1858 - 1930), *Oxford Dictionary of National Biography*, http://www.oxforddnb.com/view/article/36169?docPos=1 accessed 27 February 2013.

25   IMW, Murray Papers, 79/48/2, Murray to Jasper [surname unknown], 28 December 1933.

26   de Lisle, *Reminiscences,* p.214.

27   Ballard, *Smith-Dorrien,* p.9.

28   Corvi, 'Smith-Dorrien', p.185.

29   Smith-Dorrien, *Memories,* p.155.

30   Nikolas Gardner, *Trial by Fire: Command and the British Expeditionary Force 1914,* (Westport, Praeger, 2003), p.14.

possess a powerful patron in the form of Lord Kitchener. The two had become friends in Egypt in the 1880s and Smith-Dorrien subsequently served under Kitchener in the Boer War and in India.

This combination of fierce temper and strongly held opinions did not always endear Smith-Dorrien to his fellow officers. He was a hard taskmaster. Murray recalled "He was a straight, honourable gentleman, most loveable, kind and generous, and never forgot those who served under him, but he gave them a Hell of a time."[31] Smith-Dorrien had a difficult relationship with George Forestier-Walker, who would serve as his chief of staff at II Corps. Forestier-Walker actually attempted to resign his post on the evening of the Battle of Mons because of Smith-Dorrien's temper - a request that was dismissed by Murray with the admonishment "to not be an ass" - although it is likely their uneasy relationship dated back to their shared time at Southern Command.[32] Nevertheless, the two men were able to forge a cool but professional working relationship and Smith-Dorrien appreciated the ability of his subordinate, commenting in February 1915 "I don't know how I should get on without him, for he always rises to the occasion. His work is of a very high order" and echoing similar sentiments in his post-war memoirs.[33]

However, there was precious little professionalism in Smith-Dorrien's relationship with John French. The precise origins of their notorious feud are difficult to determine. It has been suggested that French's suspicion of Smith-Dorrien can be traced back to the Boer War, but the two were on sufficiently good terms at the close of the conflict for French to write a glowing letter to Smith-Dorrien which recalled their time in action together, stating "There is nothing so glorious as to be fighting side by side with a man you thoroughly rely upon and believe in."[34] It seems that the feud ignited as a result of Smith-Dorrien's overhaul of cavalry training at Aldershot Command. French had been in attendance at the controversial field day in May 1908, and had been greatly offended by Smith-Dorrien's criticism of the cavalry.[35] French demonstrated his displeasure by breaking off all social contact with his former friend and refusing to visit Aldershot unless required to do so in an official capacity.[36] The relationship deteriorated further in 1909 after Smith-Dorrien had instituted his cavalry training reforms.[37] French appears to have taken this as a personal insult, perceiving it as both a condemnation of the arm of service of which he was a champion and an implicit criticism of his training methods during his own tenure in charge of Aldershot. French responded to this perceived

31   IMW, Murray Papers, 79/48/2, Murray to Jasper [surname unknown], 28 December 1933.
32   Ibid.
33   Imperial War Museum, Smith-Dorrien Papers, 87/47/10, Diary, 18 Feb 1915.
34   Badsey, 'Dorrien, Sir Horace Lockwood Smith- (1858 - 1930), *Oxford Dictionary of National Biography*, http://www.oxforddnb.com/view/article/36169?docPos=1; Ballard, *Smith-Dorrien*, p.104.
35   Richard Ray Seim, *Forging the Rapier among Scythes*, p.93.
36   Ibid., p.93.
37   Ballard, *Smith-Dorrien*, pp.127-128; Richard Holmes, *The Little Field Marshal: A Life of Sir John French* (London, Cassell, 2005 edition) pp.132-133.

slight with undue criticism of Smith-Dorrien's performance at the manoeuvres of that year. Interestingly, Beauvoir de Lisle claimed in his memoirs that he was the cause of the feud, relating that French and Smith-Dorrien had quarrelled over his appointment to command a cavalry brigade.[38] Ultimately, Smith-Dorrien had won the argument and secured the position for de Lisle, thereby earning the enmity of French. However, the dates for this event are unclear and it seems probable that this occurred after the Aldershot reforms that had sparked French's anger. This is particularly plausible given that de Lisle was a former commander of mounted infantry with views on cavalry tactics that echoed Smith-Dorrien's own, and thus an ideal candidate to support the training reforms that had been recently introduced.[39]

Regardless of its precise origin, the animosity between French and Smith-Dorrien was well known in the small world of the pre-war army.[40] It appears to have died down following Smith-Dorrien's completion of his tenure at Aldershot, but events in 1914 reignited the feud. At the outbreak of the First World War Smith-Dorrien was appointed to command the Home Defence Army. However, the death of James Grierson on 17 August left the BEF's II Corps without a commander. John French requested Herbert Plumer be placed in charge of the formation, but, for reasons that remain open to debate, Lord Kitchener chose to send Smith-Dorrien. Kitchener was well aware of the animosity between Smith-Dorrien and French, but he was also aware of his friend's military capabilities and may simply have seen him as the best man for the job. There is also an intriguing yet unproven suggestion that Kitchener wanted to deliberately introduce a tough, independently minded commander who was outside the circle of officers that formed French's clique.[41]

Smith-Dorrien was 58 years old when he assumed command of II Corps. He was a veteran officer who had a vast pool of combat experience, with the lessons further refined by innovative peacetime training. However, he faced a number of problems on arrival in France on 20 August. Unlike I Corps, II Corps was not a permanently constituted formation and had been assembled on mobilisation by combining 3rd Division from Southern Command with 5th Division from Irish Command. It did not possess a full strength staff in peacetime, and so its staff officers were hastily assembled and had to forge a working relationship in the field.[42] Beyond these serious organisational issues, Smith-Dorrien had a difficult relationship with his commander in chief, greatly exacerbated by the fact that he was an unwanted appointment; he had inherited a formation and a set of staff officers whom he would need time to familiarise himself with; and he was about to lead his men through one of the most trying campaigns in British military history. He would have just three days to prepare himself and his command before the British Expeditionary Force found itself fighting for survival against the German onslaught.

38   de Lisle, *Reminiscences*, pp.214-215.
39   Ibid., p.216.
40   Charles Callwell, *Experiences of a Dug-Out, 1914-1918* (London, Constable, 1920), p.57.
41   Gardner, *Trial by Fire*, p.14; Corvi, 'Smith-Dorrien', p.191.
42   Smithers, *The Man Who Disobeyed*, p.164.

Mons to the Marne, 1914

The events of August 1914 are deeply ingrained in the historiography of the British Army. John Terraine described the campaign from Mons to the Marne as "the retreat to victory", an apt phrase that has formed the basis for subsequent writing on the subject.[43] Whilst the retreat did ultimately lead to the BEF being in place to play a role at the decisive Battle of the Marne, it was a difficult manoeuvre that carried enormous risks. In the process, I and II Corps were separated and the latter became the primary target of German pursuit, who mistakenly believed that they were pursuing the entire BEF.

When considering the British campaign, it is important to remember that II Corps was engaged continuously between 23 and 26 August. The fighting began with the Battle of Mons on 23 August, followed by fierce delaying actions at Frameries and Audregnies the next day. The 25 August was marked by rearguard skirmishing at Solesmes, before II Corps fought a major action against its pursuers at the Battle of Le Cateau on 26 August. Early works on the subject sometimes referred to this period as a single battle lasting four days, although modern authors prefer to see each as a distinct engagement.[44] There then followed a gruelling retreat until II Corps was finally reunited with I Corps on 1 September. The pressure of the campaign on officers and men was immense, and it is testament to the physical and mental resilience of Smith-Dorrien that he was able to guide his formation through the retreat without suffering from the defeatism that gripped GHQ for much of the same period.

At the opening clash of forces, the Battle of Mons, it was Smith-Dorrien's II Corps that bore the weight of the German assault.[45] Smith-Dorrien had outlined in his diary on August 22, 1914, "The Mons salient, which is held by the 8th Brigade, is almost an impossible one to defend, but I gather it is not expected that this is to be treated as a defensive position."[46] The Mons salient was untenable for a variety of reasons. Although the British occupied the line of the canal, there were so many crossing points that it did not present a formidable obstacle to a German attack. Furthermore, both British flanks could be brought under enfilading fire from the enemy. Smith-Dorrien's assessment displayed his keen tactical awareness, but nevertheless he followed GHQ's orders and organised his position as best he could.

There was little time for preparation. Elements of German First Army began their attack in the morning, supported by heavy fire from their artillery. Smith-Dorrien was nearly struck by a high explosive shell whilst inspecting the British line in a staff car.[47] A fierce battle followed, but, as Smith-Dorrien had accurately perceived, the Mons salient was indefensible and the Germans were able to gain several lodgements on the

---

43   John Terraine, *Mons: The Retreat to Victory*, (London, Pan, 1960).
44   For an example of Mons as a four day battle, see Arthur St. John Adcock, *In the Firing Lines*, (London, Hodder & Stroughton, 1914).
45   For a concise account of the battle, see Terraine, *Mons*, pp.68-98.
46   IMW, Smith-Dorrien Papers, 87/47/10, Diary, 22 August 1914.
47   IMW, Smith-Dorrien Papers, 87/47/10, Diary, 23 August 1914.

British side of the canal. Nevertheless, Smith-Dorrien had always envisaged the battle as a delaying action and felt that this goal had been achieved, recording that he "was quite happy after the result".[48]

However, subsequent events were not to his satisfaction. The withdrawal from Mons marked the moment at which Smith-Dorrien believed GHQ began to lose comprehension of the situation, and consequently control over operations as a whole. GHQ lacked a direct line to II Corps and Forestier-Walker was forced to travel 35 miles by staff car on the evening of 23 August - not a simple process in dark and unfamiliar country - to receive orders to withdraw.[49] He returned to II Corps at around 2.00am and began work on sending withdrawal orders to the subordinate formations. This was a complicated business. II Corps had been disrupted by the fighting and the Germans remained in close contact.[50] Smith-Dorrien's diary gives a sense of the difficulties involved and is worth quoting at length:

> At 2.00am I received an Order from Headquarters that, in consequence of the French on our right having fallen back instead of advancing, both our flanks were exposed, and that, as several German Army Corps were engaged against us, it would be necessary to retire. Of course, before we could do so, all our baggage and impediments had to be cleared away. I saw Haig, and we settled on a course of action, as we both fully realised that we were in for a very heavy day's fighting and that the operation of withdrawal in the face of such numbers was a very serious and difficult one … But the Germans were checked, and nightfall saw us on the line Maubeuge-Bavai-Wargnies, the men tired, hungry, but extremely cheerful, and they all felt that they had done well…Bavai was the dividing point between the two Army Corps.[51]

At this stage, I and II Corps were on the move and in touch with one another, but under close German pursuit. II Corps was forced to fight a sharp and costly rearguard action at Audregnies as it attempted to break contact with German forces. The situation was dangerous but not yet critical. Unfortunately, the unexpected nature of the retreat and news of French defeats elsewhere on the front seems to have caused John French and GHQ to become overanxious and lose their grip on the situation.[52] Lord Loch, serving as a liaison officer between II Corps and GHQ, recalled that later that day:

> Sir John French went out to the various corps headquarters and about 6 p.m. returned to Le Cateau-Murray and the Liaison officers, staying at Bavai till 3 a.m. [Chief of Staff Sir Archibald] Murray has been very anxious all day and as he is by nature petulant - he is difficult for some people to work with.[53]

48   Ibid.
49   Ballard, *Smith-Dorrien*, p.161.
50   Ibid., p.162.
51   IMW, Smith-Dorrien Papers, 87/47/10, Diary, 23 August 1914.
52   Gardner, *Trial by Fire*, pp.48-52.
53   IMW, Lord Loch Papers, 71/21/1. Diary, 24 August 1914.

Whilst the basic principle of corps by corps consultation was fine, French and GHQ failed to impose their will on the formations when it came to moving off. Haig was naturally concerned with the survival of his own I Corps and French did not seem to take into consideration the needs of the whole BEF in approving the movement of this formation. Haig recorded:

> Monday 24 August 1914: I pointed out strongly to Sir John French that if we halted for a day at Bavai the whole force would be surrounded by superior numbers. He agreed and ordered the force to continue its retreat. By Murray's request I arranged roads for retirement of my Corps on Landrecies giving the direct route to Le Cateau to the Second Corps.[54]

Haig's belief that the BEF would be encircled if it remained as Bavai was perceptive and the need for a continued retreat was logical. However, GHQ did little to coordinate the movement of the two corps and does not seem to have understood the pressure which was being brought to bear on Smith-Dorrien's formation. Greatly exacerbating GHQ's failure to grasp the location of the respective corps and 'grip' the situation was the presence of the sizeable Forest of Mormal, which placed a serious geographic and operational barrier between I and II Corps on the retreat. Major-General Thomas Snow, commanding the recently arrived 4th Division, described it as "a huge forest about 10 miles through from east to west", noting that its presence meant that neither corps could assist the other.[55]

I Corps, passing on the eastern side of the forest, was not heavily engaged during this period. Haig recorded "In two actions, the casualties were [at] Maroilles 2 killed, 41 wounded and 101 missing [and at] Landrecies 17 killed, 86 wounded, and 23 missing."[56] Conversely, on the opposite side of the forest, II Corps was being hard pressed by pursuing German forces. Smith-Dorrien was frustrated by the dearth of information provided by GHQ and disappointed by the lack of support from Haig's troops, writing in his diary:

> A lot of fighting took place this day [25 Aug], and Haig's Army - in some ways of which I have no knowledge - instead of coming back in to line with my own, kept much further East and North and halted, leaving a gap of some ten miles between us.[57]

The 25 August was a difficult day for II Corps, which was now effectively fighting its own campaign. Under "a very hot sun" the formation had undertaken a forced march, which in some cases covered 30 miles, struggling along roads that were crowded with

---

54   National Library of Scotland [Hereafter NLS], Haig Papers, 3155, Diary, 24 August 1914.
55   IMW, Thomas D'Oyly Snow Papers, 76/79/1, p.16.
56   NLS, Douglas Haig Papers, 3155, Diary, 24-25 August 1914.
57   IMW, Smith-Dorrien Papers, 87/47/10, Diary, 25 August 1914.

civilian refugees and retreating French troops.[58] Yet despite this effort the Germans remained dangerously close behind.[59] Exacerbating the difficulties was the fact that II Corps was not retiring in a straight line, but was instead moving diagonally away to the west, "thus making our west flank very much difficult to cover, as well as complicating the movement of our impediments."[60] The danger to the flank was so severe that 5th Division detached an entire brigade, the 14th, to cover the exposed area.[61] Adding to the British woes, a thunderstorm had broken on the evening of 25 August and heavy showers fell throughout the night.[62] The one positive of the day was that 4th Division, recently deployed from England, had arrived at Le Cateau and provided a screen for tired rearguards to fall back on.[63] After observing the men of II Corps passing 4th Division, Snow recognised their exhausted state: "I gleaned that the 3rd and 5th Divisions had been retreating and fighting for 36 hours, and that they had had about as much as any troops could stand."[64]

At 7.30pm GHQ issued orders that II Corps should continue the retreat on the following day and, having received the message at around 9.00pm, Smith-Dorrien forwarded the instructions to his divisions at 10.15pm.[65] However, upon receipt of the orders at 11.00pm, Edmund Allenby, commanding the much disorganised Cavalry Division, reported that he could not guarantee an effective rearguard for the next day unless II Corps moved off before dawn.[66] This alarming revelation prompted Smith-Dorrien to assemble a crisis conference at 2.00am, inviting Allenby and the commander of 3rd Division, Hubert Hamilton, to discuss the situation.[67] At the meeting Allenby reiterated his inability to cover the retreat whilst Hamilton stated he considered it unlikely his division could move before 9.00am. Faced with these reports from his

58   Ballard, *Smith-Dorrien*, pp.168-169.
59   A.H. Hussey & D.S. Inman, *The Fifth Division in the Great War* (London, Nisbett & Co., 1921), p.9; Ballard, *Smith-Dorrien*, p.167; 'General Sir Horace Smith-Dorrien's Statement with regard to the first edition of Lord French's Book *1914*' in Beckett, *Judgement of History*, p.24.
60   IMW, Smith-Dorrien Papers, 87/47/10, Diary, 25 August 1914.
61   Hussey & Inman, *Fifth Division*, p.8.
62   Ballard, *Smith-Dorrien*, p.169.
63   IMW, Smith-Dorrien Papers, 87/47/10, Diary, 25 August 1914. It should be noted that 4th Division was not at full strength. It had recently arrived in France and although it had a full complement of infantry in its three brigades, it was short of its divisional cyclists, cavalry, signals company, field ambulances, Royal Engineers and heavy artillery, as well as its divisional ammunition column.
64   IMW, Snow Papers, 76/79/1, p.15.
65   Ballard, *Smith-Dorrien*, p.168.
66   Ibid., p.170.
67   James Edmonds, *Official History of the Great War: Military Operations France and Belgium 1914*, vol.I (London, MacMillan, 1922), p.140. [Hereafter *Official History*]; Notable by his absence was Sir Charles Fergusson, GOC 5th Division. Fergusson could not be located in the darkness and due to the urgency of the situation it was decided to begin the meeting without him. For a full list of officers at the conference, see Ballard, *Smith-Dorrien*, p.172.

subordinates and knowing that to be caught on the march by his pursuers would be fatal, Smith-Dorrien presented a case for making a stand and sought the opinions of the gathered officers. Having received a generally positive response to the suggestion, he asked Allenby if he would place his cavalry under II Corps command, and, having received an affirmative reply, stated "Very well gentlemen, we will fight."[68] This resolution would come to define both Smith-Dorrien's career and the BEF's campaign. As A.J. Smithers has argued, the temptation to blindly follow the orders of GHQ and thus absolve oneself of responsibility would have been too great for a weaker willed officer.[69] However, Smith-Dorrien's career had always been defined by his willingness to show the courage of his convictions.

Smith-Dorrien's intention at Le Cateau was to fight a large scale delaying action, bringing the German pursuit to a standstill and giving II Corps precious time in which to escape.[70] Yet to offer battle was not a decision that could be taken lightly. The plan was extremely risky. As at Mons, both flanks of II Corps were vulnerable. Its right flank was completely 'in the air'. Smith-Dorrien had hoped that I Corps could march to cover this position but received word that this was impossible at 3.30am.[71] The left flank was only covered by French territorial cavalry of uncertain quality. Unlike Mons, there was no physical obstacle to impede the German advance and no time to construct any fallback position. Indeed, there was little time to construct effective trenches for the front line infantry and in the darkness it was difficult for units to find the best ground to occupy for the coming battle. This problem extended to the artillery, with the gunners forced to locate firing positions in the pre-dawn light.[72]

As with any delaying action, the timing of the withdrawal was of critical importance. Following the emergency conference, Forestier-Walker had issued full orders for a retirement but the instructions were only to be followed when Smith-Dorrien gave the word.[73] However, Smith-Dorrien was not explicit on how long he planned to hold the position. He told Henry Wilson on the morning of the battle "I hoped to be able to hold on until evening and slip away in the dark."[74] However, in his later writing he merely stated that he intended to give the Germans "a stopping blow" and then "retire under the confusion caused by that blow."[75] It would seem that Smith-Dorrien planned to use his well honed tactical instincts to determine the correct moment to retreat,

68   Quoted in Ballard, *Smith-Dorrien*, p.173; Terrence Zuber, *The Mons Myth* (Stroud, The History Press, 2010), p.259 claims that Smith-Dorrien "had clearly lost control of the situation" on the night of 25/26 August. This is a spurious statement that is not supported by any of the available evidence.

69   Smithers, *The Man Who Disobeyed*, p.183.

70   Edmonds, *Official History*, Vol.1, pp.141-142.

71   Richard Holmes, *Riding the Retreat: Mons to the Marne 1914 Revisited* (London, Pimlico, 2007), p.174.

72   A.F. Becke, *The Royal Regiment of Artillery at Le Cateau* (Woolwich, R.A. Printing Institute, 1919), p.23.

73   'Smith-Dorrien's Statement', p.36.

74   Ballard, *Smith-Dorrien*, p.176.

75   'Smith-Dorrien's Statement', p.34.

but the timing for this decision had to be exact. Withdrawing too early would mean the pursuit would continue unchecked, whereas holding for too long ran the risk of destruction at the hands of superior German numbers.

Given the vulnerable position of II Corps and the lack of clear idea of when to withdraw, the stand at Le Cateau represented a grave gamble. However, it was a calculated one that was based on certain advantages. Smith-Dorrien noted that he "had gained great confidence in the shooting power of the infantry" at the Battle of Mons, and could rely on the quality of his troops and the experience of his officers.[76] He believed that the French forces on his left would cover that flank and he also possessed a small mobile reserve in the form of Allenby's cavalry.[77] Smith-Dorrien also had an understanding of the ground, as he had arrived at the battlefield in the early afternoon, giving him time to survey the area and reach the conclusion that it offered some advantages to the defender.[78] There were some rudimentary trenches in place which had been constructed by French civilians under GHQ orders.[79] It also seems plausible that Smith-Dorrien anticipated the engagement that would follow would pose problems for the Germans. If they chose to launch an immediate attack then they would have little time to reconnoitre the British position, thus running the risk of being drawn into a frontal assault which he believed his men could hold off. However, more thorough preparations would take time, and every hour that the British could delay the Germans was precious.

This assumption was the riskiest aspect of the plan. German operational art emphasised double encirclement, a fact that was well known in the British Army, and II Corps' vulnerable flanks presented a perfect target for such a manoeuvre.[80] *Field Service Regulations* was explicit on the dangers posed by fighting a delaying action in such circumstances, noting that it carried "the risk of crushing defeat" and advising against it.[81] It was concern over this possibility that provoked such alarm at GHQ when they received news of Smith-Dorrien's decision to stand at 5.00am. French was awoken to receive the message and initially responded with a vaguely positive reply that emphasised the need to retreat as soon as the opportunity arose.[82] However, after considering the issue further he changed his mind and decided the risks involved in making a stand were too great.[83] Wilson telephoned Smith-Dorrien at approximately 6.45am to urge him to retreat, warning of "another Sedan" if he chose to stand and

---

76   Ibid., p.34.

77   Ibid., p.34.

78   Anthony Bird, *Gentlemen, We Will Stand and Fight: Le Cateau, 1914* (Trowbridge, Crowood Press, 2008), p.46.

79   Ibid., p.46.

80   See for example, Captain F. Culman, 'French and German Tendencies with regard to the preparation and development of an action', *Journal of the Royal United Services Institution*, 52(1), 1908, pp.690-703.

81   *Field Service Regulations Part I*, (London, HMSO, 1909), p.161.

82   Holmes, *Little Field Marshal*, pp.222-223.

83   Ibid., pp.222-223.

fight.[84] By this time the battle had already begun and Smith-Dorrien was in no position to disengage. His confident reply to Wilson's message prompted the latter to state "Good luck to you; yours is the first cheerful voice I have heard for three days."[85]

Ultimately Smith-Dorrien's gamble paid off. The first German forces on the field were the horsemen of II Cavalry Corps. However, these cavalry failed to carry out an effective reconnaissance and instead became embroiled in local fighting. Over the course of the morning they were, in historian Jack Sheldon's words, "drawn progressively into a dismounted battle in unfavourable circumstances", thus failing to identify the true vulnerability of Smith-Dorrien's position.[86] Additionally, the French cavalry on the left proved their value and performed an important role in securing this flank.[87] As more German forces arrived on the field they began to turn the British right, but this did not become a serious problem until early afternoon, by which time the delaying action had achieved its objective.

The full story of the Battle of Le Cateau is beyond the scope of this work and can only be summarised here.[88] From dawn onwards, II Corps fought a ferocious delaying action against at least five German divisions.[89] Smith-Dorrien based his headquarters at the town of Bertry and strove to remain in contact with his divisional commanders via telephone and despatch riders. By midday, after some six hours of battle, the British position was becoming untenable.[90] German forces were lapping around the right flank and threatening to encircle the hard pressed 5th Division. This crisis prompted Smith-Dorrien to ride forward to consult with the divisional commander, Major-General Sir Charles Fergusson, passing beneath German shrapnel bursts that fortunately left him unharmed.[91] The crumbling British flank convinced Smith-Dorrien of the need to withdraw, an operation that was put into motion between 1.30pm and 3.00pm.[92] However, disengaging from battle in broad daylight was a difficult process. Not everyone received the order to withdraw, causing some troops to be left behind, and of those that did escape, many battalions were still seriously disorganised on the following day.[93] Yet despite the severe difficulties of breaking contact, the majority of II Corps had moved clear by 5.00pm. The Germans were left as masters of the battlefield, but their pursuit had been brought to an abrupt halt. German commander *Generaloberst* Alexander von Kluck believed that he had fought "The whole British Expeditionary

84   Quoted in Ballard, *Smith-Dorrien,* p.176.
85   Quoted in Ibid., p.176.
86   Nigel Cave & Jack Sheldon, *Le Cateau* (Barnsley, Pen & Sword, 2008), p.19.
87   Bird, *We Will Stand and Fight,* p.171.
88   Full accounts of the battle can be found in Cave & Sheldon, *Le Cateau* and Bird, *We Will Stand and Fight.*
89   Edmonds, *Official History,* vol.1, p.210.
90   Ballard, *Smith-Dorrien,* p.176.
91   Holmes, *Riding the Retreat,* p.187.
92   Ibid., p.191.
93   For a vivid account of the disorganisation, see John Mason Sneddon, *The Devil's Carnival: 1st Battalion Northumberland Fusiliers August - December 1914* (Brighton, Reville Press, 2012) pp.107-109.

Corps [sic], six divisions, a cavalry division and several French Territorial Divisions", a misapprehension born of the fog of war, which his cavalry's faulty reconnaissance had done little to dispel.[94] On the evening, German cavalry headed in a westerly direction due to the erroneous belief that the British were falling back on Calais, whilst the bulk of the German army halted on the battlefield overnight to lick their wounds, before marching off in a south-westerly direction the next day.[95] By this time II Corps was clear of danger and would not be seriously troubled by German pursuit for the remainder of the campaign.

The Battle of Le Cateau achieved Smith-Dorrien's purpose and was a crucial, albeit bloody, victory for the BEF.[96] The *Official History* noted "Smith-Dorrien's troops had done what GHQ had thought to be impossible."[97] British losses were comparatively heavy but, considering the difficulties of the situation, they were nowhere near as severe as they might have been.[98] Luck certainly played its part in the victory, but it was the luck that all gamblers sometimes need.[99] Furthermore, this should not detract from the fact that Smith-Dorrien's plentiful combat experience and understanding of tactics allowed him to weigh up the odds and decide that his chances were favourable. The stand at Le Cateau was a considered decision made by an experienced commander.[100] In the aftermath of the action, Smith-Dorrien seized the opportunity presented by the delay to the Germans, following the guidelines of *Field Service Regulations* and marching away as quickly as possible with a view to a future counterattack.[101] Alexander von Kluck had hoped that the British would hold their ground again on the 27 August and present another chance for an encirclement battle, but this opportunity had slipped away forever.[102]

Nevertheless, controversy followed the battle. On the evening of 26 August, GHQ came to the mistaken conclusion that II Corps had been effectively destroyed at Le Cateau.[103] John French seems to have retained this belief long after the evidence proved otherwise. In 1915 he confided to Haig that he regretted not putting Smith-Dorrien before a court martial for his decision to fight.[104] He subsequently took up the theme in his memoirs, where he argued that the battle "was to render the subsequent conduct of the retreat more difficult and arduous" and suggested that the "shattered condition

94   Quoted in Holmes, *Riding the Retreat*, p.195.
95   Ibid., p.195; Bird, *We Will Stand and Fight*, pp.142-145.
96   Edmonds, *Official History*, vol.1, p.182.
97   Ibid., p.182.
98   The exact losses at Le Cateau are a subject of dispute. For a useful summary of the debate, see Bird, *We Will Stand and Fight*, pp.145-153.
99   Cave & Sheldon, *Le Cateau*, p.8.
100   Smithers, *The Man who Disobeyed*, p.196.
101   *Field Service Regulations Part I*, p.160.
102   Alexander von Kluck, *The March on Paris and the Battle of the Marne 1914* (London, E. Arnold, 1920), p.64.
103   Terraine, *Mons*, p.143.
104   Holmes, *Riding the Retreat*, p.197.

of the Army" seriously hampered later operations.[105] This assessment is unfair. II Corps was severely disorganised during the night of 26 August and on the following day, and their fighting capabilities in this period may well be doubted, but the formation was still in sufficiently good order that it was capable of marching up to 35 miles on 27 August.[106] The only black spot on this day was the surrender of the 1st Royal Warwickshire Regiment and the 2nd Royal Dublin Fusiliers at St. Quentin. However, as Peter Hodgkinson argues elsewhere in this book, to judge the state of the BEF on such an atypical event is misleading. Furthermore, historians who have cited the St. Quentin incident as an example of the poor state of II Corps have sometimes omitted the fact that the battalions in question were actually rallied and marched on.[107]

However, the retreat that followed was exceptionally demanding on officers and men. Captain James Jack remembered a "ghastly queue" of disorganised troops with only a handful of formed units remaining.[108] Private Frank Richards related "We retired all night [26/27 August] with fixed bayonets, many sleeping as they were marching along. If any angels were seen on the Retirement, as the newspaper accounts said they were, they were seen that night."[109] Corporal John Lucy echoed similar sentiments, writing of "the frightful agony of sleeplessness" and remembering that "Men slept while they marched, and they dreamed as they walked… The brains of soldiers became clouded, while their feet moved automatically."[110] Brigadier-General Aylmer Haldane recorded being so exhausted that he could not trust himself to ride a horse, but even on foot he frequently found himself "asleep and walking into the ditches and fields that bordered the road."[111]

Although II Corps was clear of German First Army, Allenby's cavalry continued to skirmish with German horsemen, lending urgency to the retreat. False alarms that the Germans were nearby frayed nerves that were already stretched to breaking point.[112] The pressure on the staff officers charged with traffic control and road allocation for the retreat was crushing. Smith-Dorrien noted in his diary on 28 August "some of the Staffs of Brigades and Divisions are quite worn out and almost unequal to working out orders."[113] The strain caused casualties. The chief of staff for 3rd Division, Colonel Frank Boileau, shot himself and died of the wound, whilst the chief of staff for 4th Division and future official historian, Colonel James Edmonds, suffered a nervous breakdown and was sent home on 4 September.[114]

---

105   French, *1914*, p.79.
106   Bird, *We Will Stand and Fight*, p.166.
107   Holger H. Herwig, *The Marne 1914* (New York, Random House, 2011), pp.182-183.
108   John Terraine (ed.), *General Jack's Diary* (London, Cassel, 2000), p.42.
109   Frank Richards, *Old Soldiers Never Die* (London, Faber & Faber, 1933), p.19.
110   John Lucy, *There's a Devil in the Drum* (London, Faber & Faber, 1938), p.147.
111   Aylmer Haldane, *A Brigade of the Old Army* (London, E. Arnold, 1920), p.37.
112   Ibid., p.36.
113   IMW, Smith-Dorrien Papers, 87/47/10, Diary, 28 August 1914.
114   Gardner, *Trial by Fire*, pp.61-62.

However, Smith-Dorrien, ably assisted by Forestier-Walker, proved his abilities as both a commander and a leader in this difficult period.[115] His constitution was immense. He recorded in his diary on 28 August "I reckon that I myself have not averaged two hours' sleep during the last six days" but despite this lack of rest he maintained close control of his corps and the situation.[116] His efforts were not helped by GHQ, who, still labouring under the belief that II Corps was all but destroyed, failed to offer any meaningful guidance and allowed the gap between the corps to remain open. Indeed, GHQ worsened the situation through the notorious "*Sauve qui peut*" order issued on 27 August which instructed Smith-Dorrien's divisions to abandon all spare ammunition and other impedimenta and use the wagons to carry the troops.[117] This unnecessary order was ignored by 3rd and 5th Division but created serious alarm at 4th Division.[118] Smith-Dorrien was enraged by the incident and travelled via staff car to GHQ to confront John French over it, admitting later "I was angry and spoke with some heat".[119] French defended his order, claiming that Smith-Dorrien was overly optimistic about the state of II Corps, an unsustainable allegation given that Smith-Dorrien was in close contact with his troops and far more informed as to their condition that GHQ.[120]

Nevertheless, Smith-Dorrien did harbour concerns about the physical state of his troops.[121] He frequently took to the roads to encourage his men by making himself visible and talking to passing soldiers. He recalled one such incident in his diary on 28 August:

> I was able this day to see a lot of the troops on the march, and talked to them, and tell them that the true reason for retirement was not that we had been beaten, but that it was part of the French strategical plan to fall back and draw the enemy further from his base.[122]

John Lucy saw Smith-Dorrien on this day and the general's brief inspection left a profound impression:

> General Sir Horace Smith-Dorrien inspected us... He did not wear the hard and sometimes haughty look of other generals, and we liked him for it. Calm and kindly-eyed, he gazed from horseback on soldiers weary of marching and fighting.... [He] knew that he viewed a body of men aching in every limb, to whom the smallest action, even that of moving rifles to attention, was an added minor torture, and he excused us - the good old stick. He was our man.[123]

---

115   Ballard, *Smith-Dorrien*, p.187.
116   IMW, Smith-Dorrien Papers, 87/47/10, Diary, 28 August 1914.
117   'Smith-Dorrien's Statement', pp.50-52.
118   Ibid., pp.51-52.
119   Ibid., pp.52.
120   Ibid., pp.52-53.
121   Ballard, *Smith-Dorrien*, p.185.
122   IMW, Smith-Dorrien Papers, 87/47/10, Diary, 28 August 1914.
123   Lucy, *Devil in the Drum*, p.144.

Smith-Dorrien's frequent appearances on the march showed that he had the skills of leadership as well as an ability to command. His inspirational influence on exhausted troops left an impression on the survivors, and his actions were featured in the 1926 film *Mons*, where he played himself. He was the only senior officer portrayed in film, which focussed on individual heroism and Victoria Cross winners, an accolade which indicates his close association with the ultimately successful retreat.

The retreat would continue for several days and would tax the stamina of participants to the limit. However, in contrast to the 23-26 August, the absence of close German pursuit made the manoeuvre a trial of endurance rather than a struggle for survival. The situation improved at the beginning of September. II Corps was reunited with I Corps on 1 September, the retreat finally came to an end on 5 September, and the BEF turned and joined the French advance at the Battle of the Marne which followed. As the 1914 campaign continued, II Corps fought, with varying success, at the battles of the Marne, the Aisne and at Ypres. At the end of the year Smith-Dorrien was promoted to command the newly formed Second Army that included his original corps. However, it must be remembered that the survival, let alone success of II Corps in this period would not have been possible without the stand at Le Cateau.

Conclusions

Smith-Dorrien's reputation has come to rest on his gamble at Le Cateau; in general, the verdict of history has been in favour of his decision to stand and fight. The chief of staff for the Cavalry Division, Colonel John Vaughan, believed that the action at Le Cateau "made the rest of our retreat possible and easy."[124] Sir Frederick Maurice, who served as a staff officer in 3rd Division in August 1914, felt that the results of Le Cateau showed that "Smith-Dorrien's courage in accepting battle had been justified."[125] Writing in 1916, Arthur Corbett-Smith argued that the country owed Smith-Dorrien "an imperishable debt" for his command on the retreat.[126] In their respective post-war works, both A.F. Becke and James Edmonds saw the Battle of Le Cateau as essential for the survival of II Corps and the BEF as a whole.[127] John Terraine described it as "the most brilliant exploit of the BEF during the retreat."[128] Even John French, before his animosity towards Smith-Dorrien had robbed him of his good sense, paid tribute to the decision to stand and fight. In his dispatch of 7 September, he stated:

124   Quoted in Ballard, *Smith-Dorrien*, p.174.
125   Frederick Maurice, *Forty Days in 1914* (London, Constanable, 1920), p.111.
126   Arthur Corbett-Smith, *The Retreat from Mons, By One Who Shared in It* (London, Cassell, 1916), p.231.
127   Becke, *Artillery at Le Cateau*, pp.73 - 76; Edmonds, *Official History*, Vol.1, p.216.
128   Terraine, *Mons*, p.143.

I cannot close the brief account of this glorious stand of the British troops without putting on record my deep appreciation of the valuable services rendered by Gen. Sir Horace Smith-Dorrien.

I say without hesitation that the saving of the left wing of the army under my command on the morning of August 26th could never have been accomplished unless a commander of rare and unusual coolness, intrepidity, and determination had been present to personally conduct the operation.[129]

When assessing Smith-Dorrien's career there is the sense that he was a lucky officer. His insubordination in his early career went unpunished and was even rewarded in some cases. He was fortunate in battle, being one of only five officers to survive Isandlwana and then escaping the effects of German shellfire at both Mons and Le Cateau. Undoubtedly the success of the stand at Le Cateau owed something to luck, but as has been argued, it was a calculated gamble where the odds were adjudged to be at least partially favourable. However, generals cannot survive by luck alone and Smith-Dorrien's good fortune should not detract from the combination of courage, leadership and skill that was demonstrated during his direction of II Corps in August 1914. He proved to be the steadiest of the BEF's commanders in this fraught period. Although facing the greatest dangers of any of the senior British officers, he did not suffer from the mental defeat that clouded judgement at GHQ or from the panic that seized Haig during the early days of the retreat. For this he deserves the plaudits he has received.

His reputation has endured, partly through the post-war "battle of memoirs" previously discussed, and also because his abrupt dismissal in April 1915 meant that he was not tarnished by association with the costly trench battles that followed. However, his career did not end with the Battle of Le Cateau and his conduct in the latter stages of the 1914 campaign remains understudied. In particular, the performance of II Corps at the opening of the Battle of Ypres has drawn criticism from some historians and remains an area in need of further research.[130] John French claimed that II Corps never recovered from the casualties of Le Cateau and that this prejudiced its performance in the latter part of the campaign.[131] Such allegations require fresh research before they can be conclusively addressed. A definitive study of Smith-Dorrien's career, taking advantage of the plentiful primary sources now available, remains to be written.

129   Quoted in 'Smith-Dorrien's Statement', p.2.
130   Gardner, *Trial by Fire*, pp.137-138.
131   French, *1914*, p.79.

Divisional Command

8

The Bull and the Fox Terrier:
Edmund Allenby and Command in the BEF in 1914

Cavalry Division

Simon Robbins

In considering Edmund Allenby and his career, there has been an understandable tendency to concentrate on Allenby's participation in the controversial Battle of Arras on the Western Front in early 1917, which had initially been very successful but had then rather petered out into an attritional failure, and his subsequent more triumphant exploits in Palestine in 1917-18, which resurrected his career and established his long-term reputation.[1] As a result, Allenby is established as perhaps the greatest British general of the First World War. His earlier service on the Western Front as a Divisional Commander in 1914 and as a Corps Commander in 1915 has been rather overshadowed and neglected. What has been written recently has concentrated on Allenby's difficult relationship with his contemporary and rival, Douglas (later Field Marshal Earl) Haig, and the somewhat unfortunate results of Allenby's feud with Haig's protégé, General Sir Hubert Gough, one of his brigade commanders in 1914.[2]

Throughout his career, Allenby was governed by the ethos and 'culture' of the Army as an institution. The senior officers of the Army had a relatively uniform social and political outlook. As a result of its narrow social base of recruitment, which was drawn from an Anglo-Saxon, Protestant, rural, upper middle-class professional background, sharing not only a set of common experiences but also political affiliations, members of the army's hierarchy had a common social background and

---

1   See Matthew Hughes, 'Edmund Allenby' in Ian F W Beckett and Steven J Corvi (Editors), *Haig's Generals* (Barnsley, South Yorkshire: Pen & Sword Military, 2006) for an excellent introduction to Allenby's career.

2   See Nikolas Gardner, 'Command and Control in the "Great Retreat" of 1914: The Disintegration of the British Cavalry Division' *Journal of Military History*, Vol.63, No.1 (January 1999), pp.29-54 and Nikolas Gardner, *Trial by Fire: Command and the British Expeditionary Force in 1914* (Westport, CT and London: Praeger, 2003).

Edmund Allenby. (Bain collection, Library of Congress)

elaborate family ties. One of the most important factors behind this close sense of community was the fact that the officer corps came from the same class background, that of a privileged elite. It was from this elite and cohesive officer corps that the leadership of the British Expeditionary Force (BEF) was drawn. The senior staff and commanders of the British Army formed a particularly close knit and homogeneous community. Philip (later Brigadier General) Howell, a relatively junior officer, could remark that "I seem to know everybody & everyone me", attending a conference in September 1914 with "all the generals & staffs of the whole bally show", meeting "hundreds of old friends", and being taken to tea with the Commander-in-Chief (Field Marshal Sir John French), who explained "the whole situation on the map".[3]

Born on St George's Day (23 April) in 1861 at Brackenhurst Hall near Southwell in Nottinghamshire, the second child and eldest son of the six children of Hynman Allenby, a country gentleman and his wife, Catherine Anne, the daughter of a local clergyman, Edmund Allenby was typical of this officer corps. The military elite was traditionally drawn from gentry with a military tradition and continued to serve King and Country as officers in the armed services. Members of the British officer corps with its aristocratic and landed-gentry background and its respectable middle-class service families were of a privileged class enjoying social prestige based on

---

3   Liddell Hart Centre for Military Archives (LHCMA), Howell Papers IV/C/V308 and 66-67, Brigadier-General P Howell to his wife, 30 June 1916, 20 and 28 September 1914.

family origin and service to the state. The majority came from upper or middle-class homes since their fathers, if not gentry, were either professional men or serving officers. General Sir Walter Kirke's ancestors had been the squires of Mirfield Hall, East Markham, Nottinghamshire, for several centuries.[4] Similarly, Major General Sir Hereward Wake, Baronet, was one of the Wakes of Northamptonshire, who when they were not defending the Empire, resided at the family seat, Courteenhall,[5] while General Sir Sidney Clive's family home was Perrystone Hall in Herefordshire until it was destroyed by fire in 1959.[6] The Allenbys had been members of the Lincolnshire gentry for some three and a half centuries, never straying far from the family home of Kenwick Hall, near Louth.[7]

The British Army was a narrow, almost feudal world, the ethos and values of which remained those of the landed gentlemen, who moved in "county" circles. These officers still espoused the traditional lifestyle of the gentry and being a "Gentleman" was the status by which officers were judged. Although his family background and his initial preference for joining the Indian Civil Service did not suggest a military career, it was natural for Allenby to join the Army as "other openings were limited, for commercial business was not in those days considered a suitable occupation for a gentleman".[8] For example, in Scottish society of the mid-nineteenth century, Douglas Haig's mother was regarded as having married beneath her class by marrying into trade (his father sold the well-known whisky bearing his name). As a result Haig went to school in England and into an English cavalry regiment, the 7th Hussars, rather than into the Scots Greys.[9] Brought up as the son of a country squire, loving nature and enjoying a gentry life style based on outdoor activity, hunting and sport, Allenby looked like "a typical young English fox-hunting squire".[10] At Staff College in 1896 Allenby was chosen by fellow officers for the prestigious social position of Master of the Drag Hounds instead of Haig.[11] This marked the beginning of his uneasy and formal relationship with Haig, which would have a significant and unfortunate effect on events during the war.

4   Imperial War Museum (IWM), Kirke Papers, 'General Sir Walter M.St.G. Kirke, G.C.B., C.M.G., D.S.O., D.L., J.P.', pp.1-4.
5   See Professor Peter Gordon, *The Wakes of Northamptonshire*, (Northampton, Northamptonshire Library Service 1992) pp.174-197.
6   Obituary of Brigadier Archer Clive, *The Times*, 17 April 1995, p.17.
7   Brian Gardner, *Allenby*, (London: Cassell, 1965) p.2.
8   General Sir Archibald Wavell, *Allenby: A Study in Greatness*, (London: George G Harrap, 1940) p.35.
9   See Duff Cooper, *Haig*, (London, Faber & Faber, 1936) p.166; LHCMA, Liddell Hart Papers 15/2/23, Lord Geddes, 'Unworthy Apolgia', *National Review*, February 1953, p.109; and LHCMA, Liddell Hart Papers 1/90/36, Ca[ptain] Sir Basil Liddell Hart to Victor Bonham-Carter, 2 March 1964.
10   LHCMA, Edmonds Papers III/2/13-14, Brigadier General Sir James Edmonds, Memoirs, Chapter XIV.
11   LHCMA, Allenby Papers 6/3/3-6, Comments from [General Sir George] Barrow on Chapter 3.

The pre-war army enjoyed a style of life apart from the outside world which is almost incomprehensible to later generations. The officers of the Edwardian army were born and bred - or at least educated - as gentlemen. The regiment, the surrogate family for the officer and the lodestone for his loyalty, demanded that each member conduct himself in accordance with the customs, values and mores of the upper echelons of society. Officers served for honour, prestige, and to reconfirm their social status, and this was also a manifestation of the ideal of service in the aristocratic tradition. These were the days when it was *de rigeur* for a "Gentleman" always to carry a walking stick, which had replaced the sword as a symbol of his position amongst the gentry.[12] In 1914 Major General Sir Frederic Glubb reminded his son, later Lieutenant General Sir John Glubb, about to be commissioned, "that you are also a gentleman, a simple honest English gentleman - you cannot be anything better whatever you are."[13]

To be a gentleman was to fulfil the expectations of one's peers and often had little to do with professional competence. When discussing the possibility of his removal from command of Second Army, Haig decided that "Plumer is himself such an honest straightforward gentleman that I feel one ought to retain him if possible".[14] To many, Haig himself was the epitome of the traditional cavalryman and gentleman.[15] Those such as Brigadier General John Charteris, who "behaved in anything but a gentlemanly manner",[16] were compared ill-favourably with those, such as Field Marshal Viscount Byng, who was "a perfect old courtier & gentleman in every way",[17] or General Lord Horne, who was "a very parfait gentil knight",[18] and "a great-hearted Christian Gentleman".[19]

Loyalty to the Crown and religion were other bonds which kept the hierarchy bound together. A number of generals were close to the Royal Family, notably

---

12   IMW, Archibald Papers, Major General S.C.M. Archibald, Memoirs, p.38.
13   Major General Sir Frederic Glubb to his son, later Lieutenant General Sir John Glubb, 27 October 1914; quoted in Lieutenant General Sir John Glubb, *The Changing Scenes of Life: An Autobiography*, (London, Quartet Books, 1983) p.26.
14   LHCMA, Robertson Papers 1/22/24, LHCMA, Field Marshal Earl Haig to Field Marshal Sir William Robertson, 18 February 1916.
15   LHCMA, Liddell Hart Papers 1/499, General Sir Ivor Maxse to Sir Basil Liddell Hart, October 1927; LHCMA, Liddell Hart Papers 1/531, Sir Desmond Morton to Liddell Hart, 17 July 1961; LHCMA, Liddell Hart Papers 1/408, Guy Chapman to Liddell Hart, 24 June 1961; IMW, Kirke Papers, General Sir Walter Kirke to his wife, 6 August 1916; IMW, PP/MCR/107, Butler Papers, The Memoirs of Major General S.S. Butler, p.35.
16   National Library of Scotland(NLS), Haldane Papers, Acc.20249, General Sir Aylmer Haldane, War Diary, 8 March 1917.
17   LHCMA, Howell Papers IV/C/3/208, Howell to his wife, 15 August 1915; see also LHCMA, Beddington Papers, Brigadier Sir Edward Beddington, Memoir, p.25.
18   *The Brigade: The Official Organ of the Church Lads' Brigade*, Volume XXXVI, Number 9, September 1929, p.159, IMW, Horne Papers 124/1.
19   Foreword by Field Marshal Lord Milne to 'General The Lord Horne of Stirkoke', p.3 in IMW, Horne Papers.

Lieutenant General Sir William Pulteney (III Corps), who was "a personal friend" of the King[20] and Douglas Haig, whose marriage to the Queen's lady-in-waiting took place in the private chapel of Buckingham Palace.[21] Many officers believed, as a result, that "influential backing is more important than the possession of brains and professional ability".[22] For example, Allenby was accused of grovelling to seniors and titled people,[23] while Haig was accused of flaunting his royal connections.[24] Haig's rapid rise was attributed partly by contemporaries to his links with the Royal family.[25]

On the whole the British Army elite was overwhelmingly a Protestant group, supporting the established Church of England and advocating a muscular Christianity. Like Horne who was "strengthened by a steadfast faith in God, and complete devotion to duty",[26] Allenby took great solace and strength from his faith. He was not alone among senior British commanders on the Western Front such as Plumer, Byng, Rawlinson and Gough in drawing inspiration from religion and, like most generals, took a relaxed, Anglican view of Christianity. Allenby did not view the war in explicitly providential terms. In contrast, some did, notably Horne, who had read "the Bible from cover to cover including the dull bits",[27] and Haig, a Presbyterian and Covenanter, by persuasion and also upbringing, whose bedside books were the Bible, Bunyan's *Pilgrim's Progress* and a life of Cromwell.[28] Nevertheless, Allenby was one of three army commanders (with Horne and Gough) who in January 1917 wrote public letters in support of the Church of England's National Mission of Repentance and Hope on the Western Front.[29]

Although some officers such as Haig were personally well off, many lacked financial resources and social status was not necessarily synonymous with wealth. Once in the Army, Walter Kirke had to rely on his ability to buy and train horses for racing and polo, selling them at a profit to finance his life style.[30] Lieutenant General

20   IMW, French Papers 75/46/11, Field Marshal Lord Kitchener to Field Marshal Sir John French, 11 July [1915].

21   The Countess Haig, *The Man I Knew*, (London, The Moray Press, 1936) pp.36-37.

22   LHCMA, Edmonds Papers I/2B/6, Edmonds, Remarks on the Staff College, undated.

23   NLS, Haldane Papers, Acc.20249, General Sir Aylmer Haldane, War Diary, 29 November 1916.

24   LHCMA, Liddell Hart Papers, 11/1933/108, Lt Col William Vaughan to Sir Basil Liddell Hart, 21 February 1939; LHCMA, Edmonds Papers III/2/10, Edmonds, Memoirs, Chapter XIV.

25   LHCMA, Liddell Hart Papers 11/1928/1b,Edmonds, Diary Note, Liddell Hart, 1 February 1928; Lord Geddes, 'Unworthy Apolgia', *National Review*, February 1953, p.109; LHCMA, Edmonds Papers III/2/10, Edmonds, Memoirs, Chapter XIV.

26   Lieutenant General Sir Hastings Anderson, 'Lord Horne as an Army Commander', p.407.

27   Churchill College Cambridge (CCC), Bonham-Carter Papers, General Sir Charles Bonham-Carter, Autobiography, Chapter IX, pp.27-28.

28   LHCMA, Liddell Hart Papers 1/531Sir Desmond Morton to Sir Basil Liddell Hart, 17 July 1961; IMW, Butler Papers, The Memoirs of Major General S.S. Butler, p.33.

29   Michael Snape, *God and the British Soldier*, (London, Taylor and Francis, 2005) pp.67-70.

30   Brian St. George Kirke, 'General Sir Walter Kirke, Part I: Subaltern to Major - 1896 to

Sir Adrian Carton de Wiart was forced to seek active service abroad in Somaliland when his father crashed financially [31] and like Major General Sir Frederick Maurice, "a poor man" [32] with no allowance, had to live off his salary. Although as the son of a country gentleman he was probably better off than some of his poorer contemporaries, Allenby needed his army pay because he was always short of money. His private income was small as the sale of his father's Norfolk estates in 1878 left his widow and children in reduced circumstances. Allenby had to forgo playing polo in order to meet his son's school fees at Wellington. He also had to borrow from his mother to pay the mortgage on a London house. [33]

Owing to their financial circumstances, far from emulating the relaxed amateurism of the old imperial army, many senior officers on the Western Front, who were often from a lower income group than their predecessors, took their profession seriously. Thus, they were determined to develop and maintain professionalism and to keep abreast of the latest technology, weapons and tactics. For example, both Maurice and Wace were sons of Major Generals and had, therefore, to live off their own earnings and like Brigadier General Philip Howell, "a poor man and keen", [34] were driven by economic necessity to take their profession very seriously. Like many of his contemporaries, notably Henry Horne, his fellow Army Commander in 1916-17, who was reliant on his own talents to support himself and his family as the second surviving son of a laird, [35] Allenby was also dependent on his own abilities to support his wife and son. He joined the 6th (Inniskilling) Dragoons, which was one of the less fashionable regiments, in which an officer could live off a small allowance. [36] As Horne noted in 1891, "now-adays we are such keen soldiers that we devote every available moment to our profession". [37] Of necessity, therefore, Allenby also took his profession extremely seriously. This may have conditioned his response to those officers who took their profession less earnestly, notably some cavalry officers who were very independent in both attitude and wealth and were prone to flout regulations and dress codes when Allenby reached senior rank.

Passing out from Sandhurst in December 1881, and commissioned into the 6th (Inniskilling) Dragoons in May 1882, Allenby had attended Staff College during the 1890s along with many other future senior commanders and staff officers of

---

1914', *The Army Quarterly and Defence Journal*, Volume.115, No.4, p.447.

31   Lieutenant General Sir Adrian Carton de Wiart, *Happy Odyssey*, (London, Cape, 1950) pp.45-46.

32   LHCMA, Grant Papers C41/24, General Sir Charles Grant to Lord Rosebery, 20 May [1918].

33   Lawrence James, *Imperial Warrior*, (London, Weidenfield & Nicholson, 1993) pp.8, 28 and 54; Gardner, *Allenby*, p.8.

34   IWM, Home Papers, Brigadier General Sir Archibald Home, Diary, 15 March 1915.

35   Simon Robbins, *British Generalship during the Great War: The Military Career of Sir Henry Horne (1861-1929)*, (London, Ashgate, 2009) p.27

36   Matthew Hughes, 'Edmund Allenby' p.14.

37   IMW, Home Papers 164/1. General Lord Horne to Mrs Kate Blacklock (later Lady Horne), 23 February 1891.

the BEF between 1914-18, such as Byng, Gough, Haig, Haking, Kiggell, Lawrence, Macdonogh, Plumer, Rawlinson, and Robertson. At this time, the intellectual world of officers tended to be rather limited. General Sir George Barrow contrasted the single-minded concentration on professional studies by Haig with the wider accomplishments of Allenby. Where Haig had few outside interests except polo and thereby stunted the growth of his imagination and general knowledge, Allenby was an imaginative man of broad interests, being widely read in English literature, fond of classical music, and with a passion for ornithology, becoming a Fellow of the Zoological Society.[38] Where Allenby relied on intellect, Haig relied on a forceful and dominant personality.[39] Similarly, Horne, whose success was built on "strength of character rather than the intellectual attainments",[40] like his mentor, Haig, showed little interest in anything other than his professional duties and his off-duty sport. Moreover, in "marked contrast" to Haig, who was "as a rule intolerant of any opinion that differed from his own", Allenby was open to accepting advice and "always ready to listen to and give due weight to the opinions" of subordinates.[41]

Allenby's sole active service prior to the outbreak of the First World War, like many of his contemporaries, was in South Africa, where he arrived with his regiment in October 1899 as an unknown major.[42] Like many of his peers, such as Birdwood, Briggs, Byng, Haig, Plumer, Rawlinson, Allenby established his reputation within the army as an all-arms column commander during the South African War. The years after the Boer War would see many reforms within the British Army, notably the formation of a General Staff and of the BEF.[43] Learning the lessons of the South African War and the Russo-Japanese War, attempts were also made to reform the cavalry, improving education, horsemanship and musketry.[44]

Allenby was one of those officers who sought to learn the lessons of the Boer War and was associated with these improvements. Along with other cavalry officers such as Lieutenant General Sir Charles Kavanagh, Lieutenant General Sir Charles Briggs and Philip (later Field Marshal Lord) Chetwode who all became prominent in the Great War, Allenby participated in the rejuvenation of the British cavalry prior to the outbreak of war in 1914. He served as commander of 4th Cavalry Brigade (from October 1904) and as the Inspector General of Cavalry (from April 1910, having

38   LHCMA, Allenby Papers 6/VI/17, Barrow to Field Marshal Earl Wavell, 3 June 1938; LHCMA, Allenby Papers 6/VI/23-24, General Sir Noel Birch to Wavell, 11 and 15 December 1936; LHCMA, Allenby Papers 6/VII/36, J M Irwin to Wavell, 25 June 1937.
39   Barrow, *The Fire of Life*, (London, Hutchinson & Co., 1942) pp. 43-5.
40   Lieutenant-General Sir Hastings Anderson, 'Lord Horne as an Army Commander', p.407.
41   LHCMA, Allenby Papers 6/III/3, Barrow to Wavell, [3 June 1938] and Allenby Papers 6/I/6, R H Andrew to Wavell, 5 April 1937.
42   Matthew Hughes, 'Edmund Allenby: Third Army, 1915-1917', pp.53-5.
43   Thomas Pakenham, *The Boer War*, (London, Random House 1979) pp.573-4.
44   Marquess of Anglesey, *A History of the British Cavalry, 1816-1919*, Vol.4: 1899-1913, (London, Leo Cooper, 1986) pp.376-423.

been promoted to Major General in September 1909), commanding the Cavalry Division during cavalry tours and manoeuvres on Salisbury Plain and Lambourn Downs.[45] Such training and manoeuvres sought to establish a "New School of Learning",[46] and were often undertaken under the eagle eyes of senior generals, such as William Robertson, Douglas Haig, Horace Smith-Dorrien and John French, and liberal politicians, notably Lord Haldane and David Lloyd George.[47]

During Allenby's period as Inspector General of Cavalry, the cavalry reached a peak of tactical efficiency. Indeed, the success of the Great Retreat of 1914 has been attributed to the "massive superiority" of the British cavalry over its German rival, making the whole withdrawal possible.[48] Allenby deserves a great deal of credit for this, having as Inspector General of Cavalry emphasised training in the realities of modern warfare, with a focus on covering a retreat, reconnaissance, horsemanship and marksmanship, which "all paid dividends in 1914".[49] General Sir Beauvoir de Lisle noted later that Allenby as Inspector General of Cavalry had laid the foundations for the Retreat from Mons in August 1914.[50]

Nevertheless, the cavalry, in common with the army as a whole, suffered from certain operational and organisational weaknesses. Prior to the outbreak of war, the Cavalry Division had rarely trained as a division and did not have a permanent staff, so that on mobilisation in 1914 the staff lacked familiarity with each other and its unusually heavy organisation of four cavalry brigades lacked cohesion.[51] As one staff officer noted after the war, "the Division was never a unit, it was a collection of brigades" and "once in touch with the enemy the Division broke up into independent Brigades to a large extent".[52]

However, Allenby's own character was to play a significant part in the problems faced by the Cavalry Division in 1914. He had gained a reputation as a fiery martinet, displaying "almost demoniacal bursts of temper",[53] and in consequence acquired the nickname of "the Bull" prior to 1914.[54] He also gained an unfortunate obsession with petty matters which made him unpopular with both his subordinates and the troops. Hubert Gough, Allenby's chief staff officer when he was Inspector General

45   Barrow, *The Fire of Life*, pp.117-8.
46   Colonel Montague Cooke, *Clouds that Flee: Reminiscences*, (London, Hutchinson, 1935) pp.133, 140-141.
47   IMW, Horne Papers, General Lord Horne, Diary, 25-31 May, 1-10 and 21-23 June, 1 and 29 August, and 6-7 September 1909.
48   Stephen Badsey, 'Cavalry and the Development of Breakthrough Doctrine', in Paddy Griffith (Editor), *British Fighting Methods in the Great War* (London and Portland, Oregon: Frank Cass, 1996) p.147.
49   James, *Imperial Warrior*, p.49.
50   LHCMA, Allenby Papers 6/V/28, General Sir Beauvoir de Lisle to Wavell, 3 September 1936.
51   Gardner, *Allenby*, p.65.
52   LHCMA, Allenby Papers 6/VI/4, R Hutchinson to Wavell, 20 July 1938.
53   LHCMA, Allenby Papers 6/7/55-56, General Sir Thomas Snow to Wavell, 29 April 1937.
54   LHCMA, Allenby Papers 6/VI/16, Barrow to Wavell, 3 June 1938.

of Cavalry, remembered that Allenby had a "great regard for regulations and all sorts of detail" and was liable to explode if he came across any breach of detail or failure to implement orders.[55]

One staff officer noted that this tendency to concentrate on minor details continued in France where "Allenby paid too much attention to chin straps, number of buttons on uniform sleeves, colour of tie etc" and "tended to irritate commanders". In particular this provoked "the animosity of two B[riga]de commanders" (Gough and de Lisle) which "did not help Allenby in using the Division as a unit".[56] The same staff officer recalled that Allenby "was never popular with our Cavalry brigadiers & that fact was against the success of the Cav. Div."[57] Another, who served with the Cavalry Division headquarters, agreed that Allenby "was certainly not popular" and in some cases "was actually disliked" because of his "very abrupt manner" and rudeness and that this "made his task a far more difficult one than would otherwise have been the case".[58] As a result, Allenby was also unpopular with the front line troops while serving on the Western Front.[59]

Nevertheless, it is possible to exaggerate the impact of Allenby's obsession with petty details and his temper. As one subordinate, John Vaughan noted:

> I think that Allenby was in every sense a big man, he always had complete confidence in himself and inspired the same confidence in those under and above him.
>
> He had some little fads which were at times annoying but he was a good man to serve under or with in any capacity.[60]

Horne, who had been Inspector General of the Artillery at the same time as Allenby was Inspector General of the Cavalry, told his wife that "I always like him, although everyone does not",[61] believing that "he has a kind heart under his rough manner".[62] Thomas Snow agreed that Allenby "was at other times, gentle and kindly, with a grim sense of humour".[63]

Beyond his abrasive personality, Allenby's difficulties in controlling his subordinates were increased by the lack of a permanent, experienced and well-established staff for his Cavalry Division when it went to war in 1914. Instead, like

55   Gardner, *Allenby*, p.23.
56   LHCMA, Allenby Papers 6/VI/4, Hutchinson to Wavell, 20 July 1938.
57   Ibid.
58   LHCMA, Allenby Papers 6/VI/38, Home to Wavell, undated.
59   LHCMA, Allenby Papers 6/VI/26 and 6/VII/25-26, Chetwode to Wavell, 20 June 1938 and Grant to Wavell, 21 November 1936.
60   LHCMA, Allenby Papers 6/IV/27, Major General John Vaughan to Wavell, 15 October 1936.
61   IMW, Horne Papers, Horne to his wife, 3 November 1916.
62   IMW, Horne Papers, Horne to his wife, 8 August 1917.
63   LHCMA, Allenby Papers 6/7/55-56, General Sir Thomas Snow to Wavell, 29 April 1937.

the rest of the BEF, the divisional staff was largely improvised and its members had little previous experience of either working together or of handling large forces of cavalry in the field. Indeed, few British commanders or staff officers had any experience of handling large formations in warfare on a continental scale. During the chaotic retreat from Mons, Allenby's *ad hoc* and inexperienced staff proved unable to maintain control over the unwieldy and improvised organisation of the Cavalry Division, which before the war had essentially been a paper formation with each of its four brigades trained and organised separately.[64]

Gough argued that Allenby "had no grip on the situation" partly "because his Chief of Staff was John Vaughan who did not supply him with ideas".[65] Furthermore, Vaughan, although a "much admired cavalryman", had no staff training or experience. By 26 August he was "a passenger", "had gone to pieces" and "was a broken man". He had to be replaced by George Barrow, who himself was serving as a hastily improvised albeit effective Intelligence Officer,[66] who Allenby noted was "a good staff officer, & an old Staff College friend of mine".[67] Hampered by Vaughan's failings and the organisational problems previously discussed, Allenby's headquarters lost contact not only with GHQ, but also with its own brigades, as the system of communications collapsed during the Great Retreat and the division lost cohesion.[68]

John Vaughan was not the only staff who had problems adjusting to the pressures of war in 1914. It should be noted that Johnnie (later Brigadier General) Gough, Haig's Chief Staff Officer at I Corps was "a good deal handicapped" and not fully recovered from a "very severe operation" in June 1914.[69] Major General Sir George Forestier-Walker, Smith-Dorrien's Chief Staff Officer at II Corps, failed to telegraph ahead the orders for the retreat from Mons,[70] and was criticised for his performance as MGGS, Second Army in 1915.[71] At Vaughan's own, more junior, level, Colonel F.R.F. Boileau (GSO1, 3rd Division) was announced to have died of wounds during the retreat from Mons,[72] when in fact he had gone "quite off his head with strain

64   Gardner, *Allenby*, p.70 and Simon Robbins, *British Generalship on the Western Front 1914-18: Defeat into Victory*, (London, Psychology Press, 2005) pp.41-49.
65   LHCMA, Liddell Hart Papers 11/1935/72, 'Talk with Sir Hubert Gough', 9 April 1935.
66   LHCMA, Allenby Papers 6/VI/48, General Sir John Shea to Wavell, 8 December 1938; Allenby Papers 6/VI/37, Home to Wavell, 25 February 1937; and Allenby Papers 6/VI/10, Barrow to Wavell, 3 June 1938.
67   LHCMA, Allenby Papers 1/5/12, Field Marshal Viscount Allenby to his wife, 16 September [1914].
68   Nikolas Gardiner, 'Command and Control in the "Great Retreat" of 1914: The Disintegration of the British Cavalry Division', p.45.
69   Ian F W Beckett, *Johnnie Gough*, (London: Tom Donovan, 1989) pp.179-181.
70   Ibid., p.181.
71   Robbins, *British Generalship on the Western Front 1914-18: Defeat into Victory*, p.44.
72   IMW, Wollocombe papers, Lieutenant Colonel T S Wollocombe, Diary of the Great War, p.52,

& finally shot himself".[73] Similarly, Colonel James (later Brigadier General Sir) Edmonds (GSO1, 4th Division) broke down and had to be replaced.[74]

In accordance with the Schlieffen Plan, the German First and Second Armies had invaded Belgium on 4 August and, although held up by the Belgian defences around Liège, had by 20 August occupied Brussels and forced the main Belgian Army into Antwerp. Having moved from its concentration area at Mauberge to an area between Le Cateau and Wassigny, the BEF advanced on 21 August in support of the French Fifth Army (General Charles Lanrezac) and ran headlong into the German First Army (General Alexander von Kluck) which was advancing between Charleroi and Mauberge. Moving ahead of the BEF, Allenby's Cavalry Division made contact with the German advance guard on 21 August. Gradually, aerial and cavalry reconnaissance revealed the BEF's precarious situation and on 23 August Sir John French decided to offer battle along the Mons – Condé Canal. With II Corps (General Sir Horace Smith-Dorrien) in particular being attacked heavily and faced by overwhelming German strength, Sir John French ordered a withdrawal.[75]

In fact Allenby had been one of the first senior officers to ascertain that the small BEF was facing a massive German onslaught.[76] His Intelligence Officer, George Barrow, had telephoned from Mons railway station gathering information from the neighbouring Belgian towns about the location and direction of the German advance, discovering the advance of the German right wing under von Kluck towards Mons.[77] However, Allenby's discovery was greeted with scepticism by GHQ,[78] and Henry Wilson, the Sub-Chief, replied at 11.35 pm on the evening of 21 August that: "The information which you have acquired and conveyed to the C.-in-C. appears to be somewhat exaggerated. It is probable that only mounted troops, perhaps supported by Jäger battalions, are in your immediate neighbourhood."[79]

Within twenty-four hours Allenby was proved to be correct and a much better judge of the situation than the over-optimistic GHQ and, indeed very shortly, the BEF would be in full retreat. This withdrawal would be covered by the cavalry. During a retreat of nearly a hundred miles in less than a fortnight, Allenby lost control of much of his division as his brigades became scattered. His task was not aided by the splitting of his command during this critical period.[80] Operational Order No.7 issued by GHQ at 8.25 pm on 24 August stipulated that:

73   LHCMA, Maurice Papers 3/1/4/10, Major General Sir Frederick Maurice to his wife, 28 August 1914; see also IMW, Loch Papers, Major General Lord Loch, Diary, 28 August 1914.
74   NLS, Haldane Papers, General Sir Aylmer Haldane, War Diary, 28 August 1914.
75   Beckett, *Johnnie Gough*, pp.188-189.
76   LHCMA, Allenby Papers 6/VI/38, Home to Wavell, undated.
77   LHCMA, Allenby Papers 6/VI/10, Barrow to Wavell, 6 June 1938.
78   Gardner, *Allenby*, p.69.
79   Edmonds, *Official History of the Great War: Military Operations, France and Belgium, August – October 1914*, Appendix 12, (London, H.M.S.O., 1922) p.514.
80   Gardner, *Allenby*, pp.70-72.

Two brigades of the Cavalry Division with Divisional Cavalry of the 2nd Corps, under the command of a Brigadier to be named by G.O.C. Cavalry Division [Brigadier General H de B de Lisle], will cover the movement of the 2nd Corps. The remainder of the Cavalry Division with the 19th Inf. Brigade, under command of the G.OC. Cavalry Division [Allenby], will cover the western flank.[81]

I Corps retained its own Cavalry Brigade (the 5th under Chetwode).

Allenby's loss of control over his four brigades was exacerbated by his poor relationship with one of his brigade commanders, Hubert Gough. Gough (3rd Cavalry Brigade) took advantage of the chaos of the retreat to detach himself from Allenby's command and attach himself to I Corps under his patron, Douglas Haig. Gough's relationship with Allenby had been one of "some coldness" ever since Allenby's column in South Africa had rescued Gough, who had been captured but managed to escape after his column of mounted infantry "had been somewhat impetuously led to defeat by its dashing commander".[82] Gough, who had been one of the main instigators of the Curragh incident, relied on the support of his patrons, French and Haig to escape Allenby's command. Chetwode (5th Cavalry Brigade) attached to Haig's Corps remembered that

...I met Gough in a field and asked him what the devil he was doing there, and he told me he was getting as far away from the Bull [Allenby] as possible. It was a most scandalous affair, and he was almost in open rebellion against Allenby all the time.[83]

Gough also admitted to General Sir John Shea, a Liaison Officer at GHQ, that "he had ridden away on purpose and did not mean to go back".[84] As another staff officer noted, "Gough treated Allenby badly & always tried to attach himself to Haig".[85] Indeed, Gough "never lost an opportunity of indulging in common abuse of Allenby before his staff or any officer no matter how minor" and "had he not been a *persona grata* with French and Haig", Gough "would have been sent straight back to England".[86]

Gough never returned to the Cavalry Division, despite repeated orders from Allenby to do so, and on 31 August GHQ placed his Brigade under I Corps, while Allenby retained control of the other three brigades of the Cavalry Division.[87] Gough was further rewarded for his insubordination by being given command of the 2nd Cavalry Division on 16 September 1914, made up of his own brigade and Chetwode's 5th Brigade. Allenby was given command of the newly formed Cavalry

81   Edmonds, *Official History of the Great War: Military Operations, France and Belgium, August – October 1914*, Appendix 13, p.515.
82   Gardner, *Allenby*, p.49.
83   LHCMA, Allenby Papers 6/626, Chetwode to Wavell, 20 June 1938.
84   LHCMA, Allenby Papers 6/VI/48, Shea to Wavell, 8 December 1938.
85   LHCMA, Allenby Papers 6/VI/4, Hutchinson to Wavell, 20 July 1938.
86   LHCMA, Allenby Papers 6/VI/10, Barrow to Wavell, 3 June 1938.
87   Gardner, 'Command and Control in the "Great Retreat"', p.52.

Corps on 19 October 1914. One staff officer noted of the incident that Allenby "was not a popular man, but on the other hand, he should have had the required support of those under him, and this he certainly did not have".[88] Gough "was a short, thick-set man with a bronzed face and a rather large aquiline nose" who "was keen and very active" and resembled a "fox terrier" because of "his alertness".[89] However, Gough's over-enthusiasm tended to get him into trouble, not only in the Boer War but also during the Great War. As one cavalry officer noted, although "a dear little man", Gough was "excitable & thoughtless & impatient", "like a cat on hot bricks", and "can't help seeing red", and his rash and impetuous orders often got his troops killed unnecessarily.[90] It was felt by many that Gough "showed too much of the cavalry spirit".[91]

Allenby "never once lost his temper or showed any further resentment than to say 'it's only Gough's funny little way'". But Gough's insubordinate "behaviour and abuse" imposed a great strain and not long before Allenby's death "all the pent up feeling burst out with a vehemence". Indeed, "what he said of Gough there – quite unrepeatable – is a measure of the self control he showed when greater matters called for his attention".[92] Nevertheless, "the continuous responsible strain and physical fatigue together with a certain sense of impotence in face of disloyalty of subordinates supported by higher authority, which deprived him of the power of acting more vigorously" took a heavy toll. On one occasion Allenby for "a short while" during the retreat was "looking physically and mentally tired out".[93]

Yet despite these problems, Allenby still made a major contribution to the successful withdrawal of II Corps from a perilous situation following the beginning of the Great Retreat. The decision made by Smith-Dorrien to stand at Le Cateau on 26 August was made "after a full discussion of the situation" with Allenby and Major General H.I.W. Hamilton (GOC 3rd Division) at Smith-Dorrien's HQ in Bertry. In particular, Allenby had warned him that his Cavalry Division "was too much scattered and exhausted to be able to give useful assistance in covering the retreat". He also "expressed the opinion that the Germans being so close, unless the troops of II Corps and 4th Division could march "before daylight," the enemy would be upon them before they could start, and it would be necessary to fight". Allenby also readily placed himself under Smith-Dorrien's command.[94] This official version of events is supported by the recollections of the participants in the decision to stand and fight. In short, Allenby had warned of the possible dire consequences of failing to continue

88   LHCMA, Allenby Papers 6/VI/38, Home to Wavell, undated, Allenby Papers 6/VI/38, LHCMA.

89   The National Archives (TNA), CAB 45/208, Bernard Freyberg, *A Linesman in Picardy*, Chapter VII.

90   LHCMA, Howell Papers IV/C/3/75, Howell to his wife, 14 October 1914.

91   LHCMA, Edmonds Papers III/12/16, Edmonds, Memoir.

92   LHCMA, Allenby Papers 6/VI/10, Barrow to Wavell, 3 June 1938.

93   Ibid.

94   Edmonds, *Official History of the Great War: Military Operations, France and Belgium, August – October 1914*, pp.140-142.

the retreat before 5 am but had given his full support for Smith-Dorrien's decision to fight when it became clear that the troops were too tired to march before 9 am.[95] Allenby himself later recalled for Smith-Dorrien his memory of this momentous decision:

> As regards Le Cateau – you fought there in consequence of the report I made to you. I said that unless your troops could resume their retreat before daylight, it would be, in my opinion impossible to extricate them. You consulted with Hubert Hamilton [GOC 3rd Division] & Forestier-Walker [BGGS, II Corps] & they reported that the troops could not continue the retreat during the hours of darkness. You therefore decided to stand & fight. I think you had only these 2 alternatives – to march on during the night, or to fight.[96]

Refuting criticisms by Sir John French in his memoirs, Smith-Dorrien agreed that "I fought Le Cateau not in spite of what Allenby reported to me – but in consequence".[97] Vaughan, who had accompanied Allenby at his meeting with Smith-Dorrien, was adamant that the stand at Le Cateau "made the rest of our retreat possible" and that thereafter "the Huns gave us no trouble at all".[98] The stand made by Smith-Dorrien at Le Cateau at the cost of some 7,800 casualties stopped the German advance in its tracks and undoubtedly saved the BEF as a whole.[99]

On 5 September the long retreat from Mons ended and on 6 September the French and British armies began to advance once again until stalemate was reached on the Aisne. Following the transfer of the BEF to Flanders, the "Race to the Sea" during October also ended in stalemate during the First Battle of Ypres in which there was little opportunity for the cavalry to manoeuvre.[100] During the pursuit of the retreating German army to the Aisne, the High Command of the BEF was somewhat tentative in the first two days of its advance (6-7 September). Allenby received some criticism, notably from Haig,[101] for not launching a more vigorous pursuit by the cavalry but given the ordeals of the Great Retreat, the caution of GHQ and Sir John French's poor relationship with the French High Command his caution was understandable.[102] Nevertheless, Barrow, his senior staff officer, admitted after the war that Allenby could not be "held entirely free from criticism" and that "there was no definite effort as far as I could see, even to keep touch with the retreating

95   TNA WO79/62, Murray Papers, General Sir Horace Smith-Dorrien to General Sir Archibald Murray; 21 July 1919, TNA CAB 45/129, Shea to Edmonds, 19 October [1919]; and LHCMA, Allenby Papers 6/VI/48, Shea to Wavell, 8 December 1938.
96   TNA CAB 45/129, Copy of Allenby to Smith-Dorrien, 4 June [1919].
97   TNA CAB 45/129, Smith-Dorrien to Edmonds, 28 September 1919.
98   TNA CAB 45/129, Copy of Major General Sir John Vaughan to Smith-Dorrien, 24 June 1919.
99   Beckett, *Johnnie Gough*, p.183.
100   Wavell, *Allenby*, pp.116-123.
101   NLS, Haig Diary, Haig, Diary, 7, 8 and 10 September 1914.
102   LHCMA, Allenby Papers 6/VI/20, Wavell to Barrow, 9 July 1938.

enemy – surely the first duty of cavalry!"[103] The Germans were thus able to withdraw relatively unmolested.

In the fighting on the Aisne and during the First Battle of Ypres, which marked the beginning of trench warfare and an end to mobile conflict, Allenby and his cavalry were given little opportunity other than to show stubborn tenacity. Nevertheless, Allenby made some significant contributions as the cavalry were constantly employed as a mobile reserve to plug gaps in the line in support of the infantry. A typical instance was when Allenby, on 14 September, moved two of his brigades to Chavonne to support I Corps. As Haig informed him, this promptness prevented his "left flank from being turned and saved the situation".[104] Having driven the German cavalry from the high ground of Mont des Cats and Kemmel, south-west of Ypres, Allenby's Cavalry Corps advanced towards the Lys between 13 and 19 October.[105] Praising "very highly" the cavalry's participation in the First Battle of Ypres, Sir John French "laid special emphasis on the fact that, for 48 hours, on the 30th-31st Oct., the Cavalry Corps held a front of 7 miles against the attack of a whole German Army Corps – a record feat for Cavalry".[106] As one staff officer noted: "Allenby did a very good bit of cavalry work in covering the front Wytschaete through Messines to the Petite Douvre River for about 10 days – holding up very superior forces of German infantry & cavalry until Oct. 31st when we were forced out of Messines."[107]

31 October was a day of crisis with the Cavalry Corps being forced off the Messines Ridge after heavy fighting and the situation was, as Allenby noted, "decidedly critical".[108] But the Cavalry Corps held on and "in holding at bay so greatly superior a mass of enemy infantry, performed a feat of defence unrivalled in history by any other cavalry" and much of the credit was due to the "composure, personal example and iron resolution" shown by Allenby.[109] This was to be the last hurrah of the cavalry and indeed of the old regular army prior to stalemate on the Western Front and the subsequent dominance of trench warfare.

In conclusion, although the performance of the cavalry and Allenby himself in 1914 was mixed, it is somewhat harsh to allege that Allenby failed as a leader of cavalry. Many of the problems faced by senior commanders in 1914 merely reflected their inexperience of fighting on a continental scale and were to foreshadow the future problems of 1915-17 as the small, colonial army of 1914 expanded to take on the might of the German military. Allenby himself showed some realisation that the possibilities of employing cavalry *en masse* on the Western Front would be severely limited and would go on to develop new tactical methods which would make his reputation in Palestine. His experiences in 1914 were to form the basis for that

103 LHCMA, Allenby Papers 6/VI/15, Barrow to Wavell, 3 June 1938.
104 Marquess of Anglesey, *A History of the British Cavalry 1816-1919:* Vol.7 *The Curragh Incident and the Western Front, 1914*, (London, Secker & Warburg, 1996) p.199.
105 Ibid., p.207.
106 LHCMA, Allenby Papers 1/5/12, Allenby to his wife, 16 September [1914].
107 LHCMA, Allenby Papers 6/VI/4, Hutchinson to Wavell, 20 July 1938.
108 Marquess of Anglesey, *The Curragh Incident and the Western Front, 1914*, p.214.
109 Wavell, *Allenby*, p.299

journey which stuttered on the Western Front during 1915-17 but eventually ended in glory in Palestine in 1917-18.

Many of the command problems which emerged in 1914 related to the smallness of the pre-war British Army, which was a colonial police force rather than an army capable of fighting a war on a continental scale. In such a compact, tight knit army, personality clashes were inevitable and were exacerbated by the stressful conditions of 1914. Allenby's performance was not perfect but nevertheless he demonstrated many of the qualities, such as resilience, tenacity, an ability to learn, and a growing expertise, which would eventually pull the British Army through the war and make victory possible. Allenby's pre-war experiences and training of the cavalry would provide the basis for not only his relative success in 1914 but also for his greater triumphs in 1917-18.

9

An Inspirational Warrior:
Major-General Sir Thompson Capper

7th Division

Richard Olsen

On 1 October 1915, *The Times* announced the death on 27 September 1915 from wounds received the previous day of "one of the best and most promising of the younger generals of the British army", Major-General Sir Thompson Capper KCMG CB DSO. Capper's eccentric personality and outspoken belief in the power of the offensive mark him out as one of the most interesting characters of the British Expeditionary Force. This chapter explores his background, pre-war experiences and tempestuous spell in charge of the Staff College at Quetta. Yet, for all his eccentricities, his inspiring leadership as commander of 7th Divison at Ypres demonstrated his clear military talents and played an important role in halting the German offensive.

Thompson Copeland Capper was born on 20 October 1863 in Lucknow, India, the fifth of eight children and the third of five sons of William Copeland Capper and his wife, Sarah (née Copeland). Neither William nor Sarah came from a military family but, apart from their youngest son who died early, all their sons joined the army. The eldest, William, passed Staff College and held several appointments as a Temporary Brigadier-General before eventually retiring as a Colonel. The second son, John, joined the Royal Engineers, and, like Thompson, was awarded the CB, became a Major-General, commanded a division in the Great War and was knighted. Their fourth son, Alfred, was awarded the DSO and rose to command his regiment of Indian Cavalry, retiring as a colonel.

Thompson's sisters also made their contribution to this instant military tradition; Amy, the eldest daughter, married a Major-General and their sons included an Air Commodore, a Colonel and two Lieutenant-Colonels, while the two sons of her younger sister, Jessie, became an Air Vice Marshal and a Major-General respectively.

The inspiration for what would become a military dynasty seems to have been the siege of Lucknow during the Indian Mutiny in 1857. William Capper was amongst 153 civilian volunteers who fought with the garrison of 855 British and 712 loyal Indian soldiers against a large force of mutinous sepoys, estimated at up to 60,000 men. Surrender was not an option, as the massacre of the European inhabitants of Cawnpore, a mere 42 miles away, had proved. Reduced to 982 fighting men after 87

Sir Thompson Capper. (Editor's collection)

days, the Lucknow garrison was reinforced by a relief force under Sir Henry Havelock, which itself numbered fewer than 1,000 effective troops by the time it had fought its way into the city. This force was too weak to raise the siege, which continued for a further 61 days until a larger army led by Sir Colin Campbell arrived. Campbell was able by skill, daring, and a degree of luck, to evacuate the survivors, but was forced to abandon Lucknow to the mutineers until it was recaptured the following spring. Over 30 Victoria Crosses were awarded during the fighting, of which 24 were earned as the second relief column fought its way into the city on 16 November 1857, the largest number ever awarded on a single day. One of the recipients was William's Bengal Civil Service colleague, Thomas Kavanagh, one of only four civilians ever to be awarded the Victoria Cross, who disguised himself as a sepoy and passed through the enemy lines investing Lucknow with information for the relieving force. The siege was the stuff of legends, and was fêted as an unalloyed triumph of the army with a stiff-upper-lipped supporting cast of ordinary Victorian civilians in an otherwise somewhat ill-starred and embarrassing conflict.

William remained with Campbell until the end of the mutiny, fighting at the battles of Cawnpore and Fategahr, before returning to his civilian career in Lucknow where his sons John and Thompson were born in 1861 and 1863 respectively and his eldest daughter Amy was married in 1878. It is reasonable to assume that William's children would have been brought up amongst veterans of the siege and would have been regaled with tales of their adventures. The ruins of the buildings where the siege took place, such as the Residency, would also have been a constant reminder of the heroic events of 1857.

After spending his earliest years in Lucknow, Thompson was in due course sent "home" to England for a traditional public school education at Haileybury, before moving on to the Royal Military Academy at Sandhurst. The London Gazette of 9

September 1882 records the appointment of Gentleman Cadet Thompson Capper as a lieutenant in the East Lancashire Regiment, and the Army List shows that he joined the First Battalion which was then serving in India.

With its often enervating climate and lack of most forms of activity except sport and the occasional punitive expedition, life in the peacetime army in India could well have been somewhat frustrating for an ambitious and adventurous young man, but Capper saw action in 1895, when his regiment took part in the Chitral expedition, earning the Chitral Relief Force medal with clasp. He clearly had some aptitude for administration as he served as adjutant of his regiment from 1890 until 1894 and passed the competition for entry into the Staff College at Camberley in 1896.

To seek entry to the Staff College at that time was in itself an indication of ambition, commitment, and application. The entrance examinations were extremely competitive, requiring months of dedicated study, and the annual expense was discouraging, representing between £100 and £250 more than the pay of an officer serving in India.[1]

Nevertheless 1896 was a good year to enter Staff College, and that year's intake was a particularly impressive one, taking and holding the record for the largest percentage of officers recommended for staff appointments.[2] Colonel G.F.R. Henderson was the Professor of Military Art and History and imbued all who passed through Staff College not just with his enthusiasm for the moral and tactical lessons of the past, but also with the need to recognise how war was changing as a consequence of modern technology and firepower, requiring the exercise of initiative at all levels.[3] The appointment of Colonel (later Lieutenant-General Sir) Henry Hildyard as Commandant in 1893 had resulted in greater emphasis being placed on instructional exercises and discussions involving "a salutary friction with other brains" and less on written examinations.[4] Field Marshal Sir William Robertson, one of the 1897 intake, described the course as "more exclusively practical than at any other college in Europe",[5] and applauded the fact that "officers [were] enabled to rub shoulders with others of their own standing with whom they [might] have to work later in life", making particular reference to his contemporaries, "Haig, Allenby, Murray, Milne, Capper, Haking, Barrow, Forestier-Walker, and others who filled important posts in the Great War", and commenting that "the mutual agreement and excellent comradeship established between Staff College graduates during the twenty years previous to 1914 were of inestimable value to the Empire".[6] Robertson might also have added to his list of his eminent contemporaries the names of Generals Du Cane and Furse, and of the two undisputed 'brains' of

1   Brian Bond, *The Victorian Army and the Staff College* (London; Eyre Methuen, 1972) p.200.
2   Liddell Hart Centre for Military Archives (LHCMA), King's College, London, Edmonds Papers, III/2/6, Brigadier-General James Edmonds, Draft Memoirs.
3   Colonel G.R.F Henderson, *The Science of War – A Collection of Essays and Lectures 1892-1903* (London: Longmans, 1905), p.352.
4   Ibid., p.402.
5   Field Marshal Sir William Robertson, *From Private to Field Marshal* (London: Constable, 1921) p.171.
6   Ibid., p.90.

the 1896 intake, Lieutenant-General George Macdonogh, later Director of Military Intelligence and Brigadier-General James Edmonds, the Official Historian of the Great War. Edmonds wrote of the 1896 intake

> Of my batch of thirty-one, four (two generals) were killed in action or died of wounds... Of the remainder, two (cavalry) became Field Marshals and peers; fifteen became generals (of whom eight were knighted); one (the youngest) got no further than colonel; three retired for reasons of health before 1914; one resigned because he had come into a fortune; and one, 'the bravest of the brave' shot himself, his mother-in-law and her lawyer in une drame passionelle.[7]

Capper shone at Camberley, and General Sir George Barrow recalled in his memoirs that Capper was a "delightful companion ... admired for his brilliancy and ... popular for his humanity and unoffending wit", and looked back on the pleasure he derived from "early morning rides through the woods splashed with the colours of the rhododendrons, in company with Tommy Capper".[8]

As the 1896 intake reached the end of their two years at Camberley, the Adjutant-General, Sir Evelyn Wood, was asked by Herbert Kitchener, the *Sirdar* or Commander-in-Chief of the Egyptian army, to recommend three officers who had recently graduated from Staff College for his campaign to reconquer the Sudan and avenge General Gordon's 1885 defeat at Khartoum. The Mahdi, who had commanded the army which had taken Khartoum, had died before retribution could be visited on him, but Sudan had to be wrested back from his successor, the Khalifa. Wood selected Douglas Haig, Arthur Blair and Thompson Capper, who were given the rank of *Bimbashi*, the equivalent of major, in the Egyptian army. Such appointments were highly sought after by ambitious officers desirous of action, medals, recognition, and promotion; Winston Churchill, even after enlisting the combined influence of the Prime Minister and the Adjutant-General only obtained a supernumerary posting. Haig wrote to his sister about how lucky he was to be there; "The crowd of fellows who have asked to be taken and refused is very great... I hear that the cavalry is full as regards regular officers... Kitchener will only take the best now and picks and chooses from hundreds who are anxious to come".[9] The fact that Capper was included is indicative of the young officer's high reputation.

Capper was assigned to the 13th Sudanese Infantry Battalion, where he joined three other British officers who, like himself, were to become generals with CBs and DSOs, Ivor Maxse, Richard Gamble and Robert Whigham. At first, life for the infantry was frustrating, in contrast with the cavalry who, Haig wrote to his sister, Henrietta, were

7   LHCMA, Edmonds Papers, III/2/10,Edmonds, Draft Memoirs.
8   General Sir George Barrow, *The Fire of Life* (London: Hutchinson, 1941) p.45.
9   Letter to Henrietta Jameson, 6 February 1898, quoted in Douglas Scott, *Douglas Haig: The Preparatory Prologue; 1861-1914 Diaries and Letters* (Barnsley: Pen & Sword, 2006) p.69.

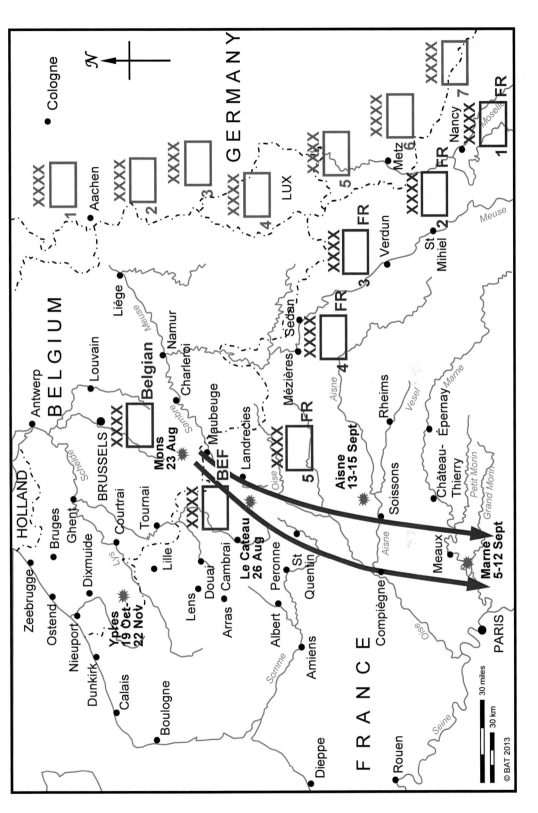

The course of the Great Retreat 1914.

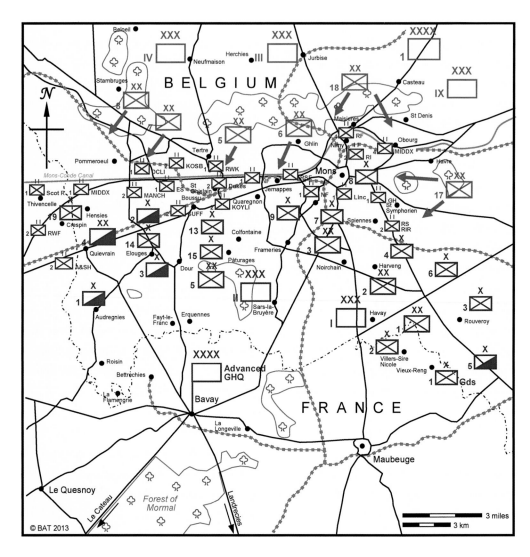

The Battle of Mons, 23 August 1914.

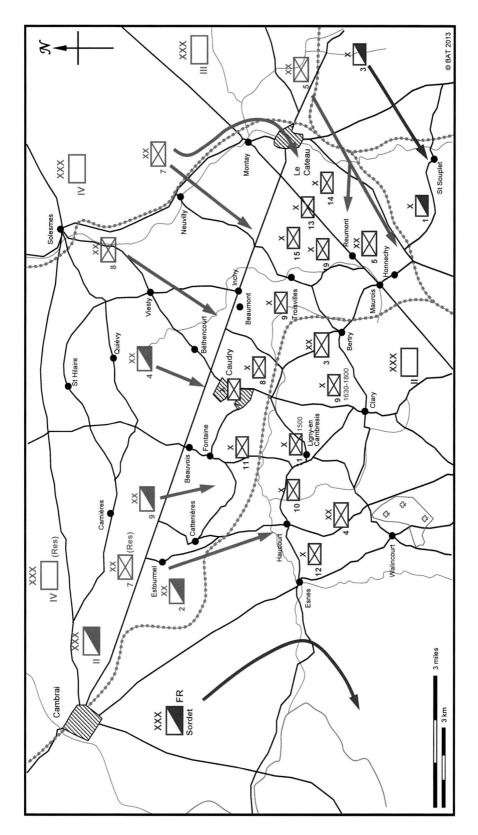

The Battle of Le Cateau, 26 August 1914.

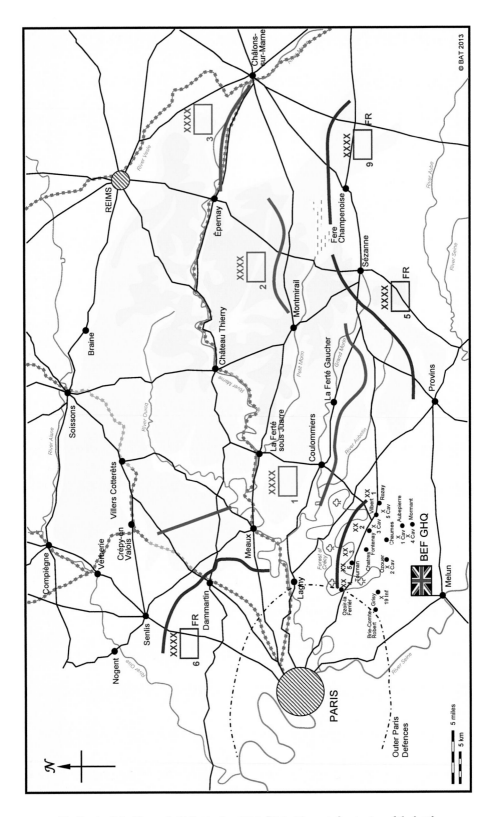

The Battle of the Marne 5–12 September 1914: Dispositions at the opening of the battle.

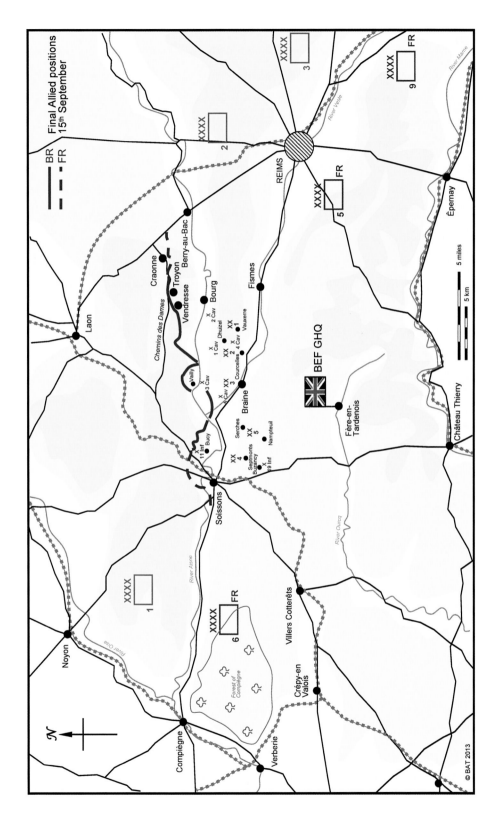

Final Allied positions 15th September

BR
FR

XXXX 3 FR

XXXX 9 FR

XXXX 2

REIMS

XXXX 5 FR

Épernay

Laon

Craonne

Berry-au-Bac

Troyon

Vendresse

Bourg

Chemins des Dames

X 2 Cav Dhuizel

X 1 Cav
XX 2
XX 4 Cav Vauxerre
X 1

X 3 Courcelles

Fismes

X 3 Cav

X 3 Cav XX 3

Vailly

Braine

BEF GHQ

Serches

X 11 Inf
Bucy

XX 5
Nampteuil

Fère-en-
Tardenois

XX 4
Septmonts
Buzancy
X 19 Inf

Soissons

Château Thierry

River Vesle

River Marne

River Aisne

River Ourcq

River Oise

XXXX 1

XXXX 6 FR

Villers Cotterêts

Forest of
Compiègne

Crépy-en-
Valois

Noyon

Compiègne

Verberie

5 miles
5 km

N

© BAT 2013

The Battle of the Aisne 13-15 September 1914. Dispositions at the opening of the battle and final British lodgements.

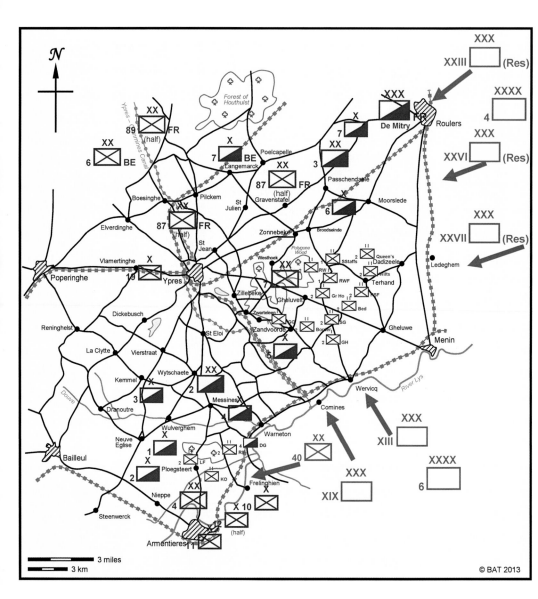

The Battle of Ypres, 19 October–22 November 1914: The opening of the German offensive, 19 October.

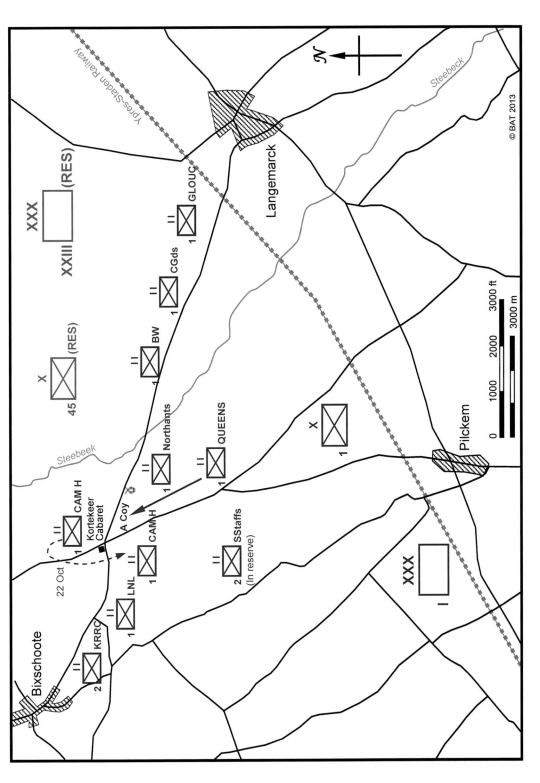

Counterattack at Kortekeer Cabaret, 23 October 1914.

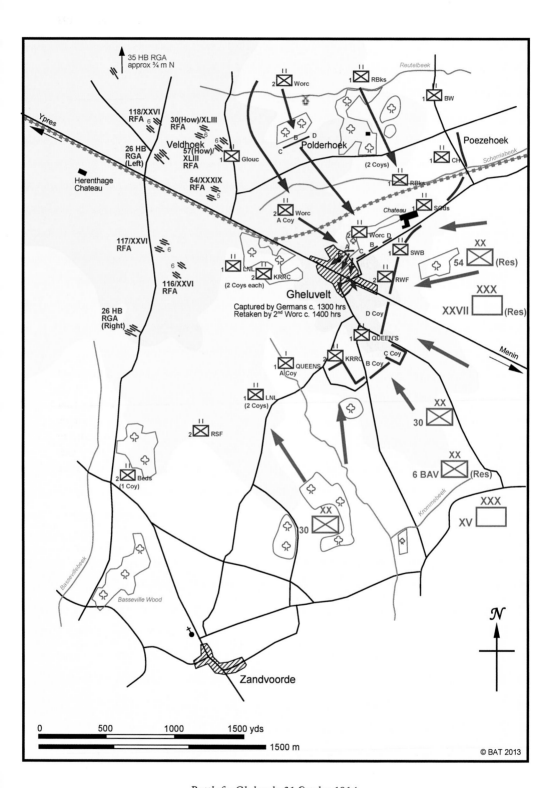

Battle for Gheluvelt, 31 October 1914.

"out every day and [getting] plenty of fun chasing Dervish horsemen".[10] Haig wrote in one of the regular reports he had been asked to send to Sir Evelyn Wood, a fellow guest of the King at Sandringham shortly before his departure for Sudan, that "most of my friends who were at the Staff College with me complain that they find it difficult to find work to do as their commanding officers do not allow them to do anything".[11]

Capper did however see action at the Battle of Atbara on 8 April 1898, when the Khalifa's subordinate, Mahmud, was defeated and captured in a surprise attack, and things looked up further on 16 July 1898 when Horace Smith-Dorrien arrived to replace his battalion's Egyptian commander. Smith-Dorrien, a Sudan veteran, had, like so many others, been angling to return there, and when eventually allowed to do so, was ordered by Kitchener to assume command of the 13th battalion, which he had in fact himself raised in 1886.

The Anglo-Egyptian army began moving south in July, and on 2 September, after weeks of marching by night and resting from the intense heat during the day, offered battle to the Khalifa's army near Omdurman on the western bank of the river Nile. Their backs were to the river with several gunboats behind them, one of which was commanded by Lieutenant David Beatty RN (later Admiral of the Fleet the Earl Beatty), and their front and flanks were protected by a *zeriba*, a barrier of thorns as effective as barbed wire, which the spear-wielding Dervishes found impenetrable. Before them was open desert, sufficiently undulating to hide the movements of the Dervish army from its base at Omdurman, some eight miles to the south west. High ground lay to the north of the Egyptian army, with, to the south, a steep hill, Jebel Surgham, rising some 200 feet above the plain, at the eastern end of a low ridge. From that hill there was a good view of Omdurman city itself as well as of the lower-lying ground beyond sight of Kitchener's main force, where the Khalifa's army was manoeuvring. Smith-Dorrien ordered Capper to clear Jebel Surgham, from where the enemy were firing, and recalled in his memoirs how he

> sent two companies ... under Captains (Tommy) Capper and R. Whigham, to turn them out, and right well they did it ... It was a pretty sight: the dash up the hill, occasional halts to fire, and Capper on his horse leading throughout. On reaching the top they found, immediately underneath them on the north-west side of the hill, enormous masses of Dervishes, evidently a reserve. These latter was so taken by surprise by the sudden appearance of troops above them, and by the heavy fire and Sudanese yells of these same troops, they bolted in confusion.[12]

After the battle Capper accompanied Smith-Dorrien who led the pursuit of the Khalifa to Omdurman, where they personally engaged in hand to hand fighting with

10   Haig to Henrietta, 1 April 1898,quoted in Scott, *Haig*, p.82.
11   Haig to Wood 15 March 1898 ; quoted in Duff Cooper, *Haig* (London: Faber & Faber, 1935), p.55.
12   General Sir Horace Smith-Dorrien, *Memories of Forty-eight Years Service* (London: John Murray, 1925) pp.111-2.

the Khalifa's personal bodyguard but were unable to prevent his escape. Smith-Dorrien recalled how, the following day, he "found time to gallop with Tommy Capper over the battlefield of the 2nd and saw enough horrors to last a lifetime."[13]

The defeat of the Dervish army did not bring Capper's time in the Sudan to an end. Kitchener had been informed of the arrival at a disused fort at Fashoda, 469 miles further up the White Nile, of a French expedition under Major Marchand after a remarkable 4,000 mile journey across Africa, and he needed to dispel any illusion they might have that the Sudan was no longer under British control. Accordingly, on 10 September, barely a week after the battle of Omdurman, he set off south with a flotilla of gunboats to confront them. Smith-Dorrien, Capper, Gamble and the 13th Battalion, together with a company of Highlanders, were embarked in the steamer *Fateh*, commanded by Beatty. Travelling by gunboat was infinitely preferable to marching, and Smith-Dorrien wrote that it was "a very happy party and we enjoyed ourselves enormously".[14] On the way, they encountered and attacked some Dervish troops, burning their boats and capturing their emir. The arrival of Kitchener and his men probably came as a relief to Marchand, who was somewhat concerned about the threat to his small force from the Dervishes, and he conceded *de facto*, if not yet *de jure*, that he was in a British sphere of influence and agreed to vacate the fort. While Kitchener, Smith-Dorrien and most of their troops returned to Khartoum, small forces were left at Fashoda and at a fort in the Sobat river, some 80 miles upstream, to ensure the French departed as agreed and to garrison the area against roving bands of Dervishes. Capper was in the second detachment under Gamble's command, which consisted of three companies, two guns, two Maxim machine guns, and a month's supplies. "It was a poisonous spot, this mouth of the Sobat;" Smith-Dorrien wrote in his memoirs, "heavy, rank vegetation, and the largest mosquitoes I have ever seen, so much so that curtains had to be sent out even for the black soldiers. I was sorry for Gamble and Capper…"[15]

Capper was soon back at Fashoda, from where he departed on 5 December as a member of a force consisting of half the battalion under the command of Maxse, who rejoiced in the title of Commandant of the Sobat sub-district.[16] They were embarked in two gunboats, under the command of Lieutenant (later Admiral Sir) Walter Cowan DSO RN, with orders to monitor Marchand's progress towards Abyssinia after he had left Fashoda, and to explore the course of the Sobat river. Gamble was once again left in command of Sobat fort, while the rest of the party proceeded to chart some 450 miles of the Sobat and its tributaries, work for which Maxse would later be elected a Fellow of the Royal Geographical Society. Capper received a clasp to the Egyptian Medal to add to the two clasps and a Mention in Despatches resulting from the Omdurman campaign, and was promoted to Brevet-Major.

13   Ibid., p.120.
14   Ibid., p.121.
15   Ibid., p.148.
16   John Baynes, *Far From a Donkey: The Life of General Sir Ivor Maxse* London: Brassey's, 1995), p.68.

After the Nile expedition, Capper served briefly as a Staff Captain (Intelligence) at Army Headquarters from 15 July to 12 November 1899, working alongside his Staff College contemporaries, Furse, Forestier-Walker and Robertson, before being appointed to the Staff of the 5th Infantry Division under the command of Lieutenant-General Sir Charles Warren. Warren was not one of the better generals of the Boer War. Sir Redvers Buller had little faith in him, and Lord Roberts wrote that "he has the credit of being a bad-tempered wanting-in-tact sort of man",[17] although his principal defect seems to have been a propensity to sluggishness. Capper saw at first hand Warren's conduct of the Tugela River crossing beginning on 16 January 1900; the delays that followed gave the Boers time to bring in reinforcements, and the subsequent fiasco at the Battle of Spion Kop resulted in retreat back across the river. The later crossing of the Tugela, which led to the successful relief of Ladysmith, owed much to careful reconnaissance by Capper and Buller's Intelligence Officer, Lt.Col. Arthur Sandbach, another Camberley contemporary, who together suggested a position where the river crossing could take place out of sight of the Boer positions on Pieter's Hill.[18]

Although only a captain and brevet-major, Capper had by then become became Chief Staff Officer of the 5th Division following the promotion of his chief to command a brigade. Major (later Major-General Sir) Charles Callwell, whose battery was attached at various times to 5th Division, contrasted Capper's orders, which "were at once clear, concise, and comprehensive", with those written by other staff officers who "although they were competent in peace … did not properly understand their duties in time of war".[19] Capper's orders for the Battle of Pieter's Hill on 28 February, which are quoted in the official *History of the War in South Africa*, show not only unambiguous clarity, but also an opportunistic eye. The special instructions for the 5th Division artillery, for example, read as follows;

1. Attention is specially drawn to the trench at head of donga in which the railway causeway arch is situated. Please shell this well.

2. Follow the infantry attacks up closely. When no longer safe to shoot at enemy's position, do not cease fire, but shoot over the enemy's trenches, pitching them well up ['intended and understood', as the author of the Official History rather pedantically interjects, 'as a cricketfield phrase'] so as to make the enemy think he is still being shelled, and also catch him as he runs down the other side.[20]

17   Roberts to Lord Lansdowne, quoted in Field Marshal Lord Carver, *The National Army Museum Book of the Boer War* (London: Sidgwick and Jackson, 1999) p.92.

18   Major-General Sir Frederick Maurice, *History of the War in South Africa 1899-1902: Vol II* (London: Hurst & Blackett, 1906) p.505.

19   Major-General Sir C.E.Callwell, *Stray Recollections, Vol.II* (London: Edward Arnold, 1923), pp.99-100.

20   Maurice, *War in South Africa: Vol. II*, p.509.

The assault was devastatingly successful. Boer Deneys Reitz wrote that the bombardment "was an alarming sight" and that "of our Pretoria men ... not one came back ... This day marked the beginning of the end in Natal".[21] Ladysmith was relieved the following day.

Capper was transferred from 5th Division on 8 July 1901 to command a mobile column attempting to suppress the activities of the Boer commandant, Manie Maritz, in Cape Province. Capper's exploits during that period involved a number of wild goose chases interspersed with occasional episodes of brisk action. On one occasion, his column marched 68 miles in two days to assist another British column which had been out-manoeuvred by Maritz and had lost the supplies it had been escorting.[22] On another occasion, Capper's column, hiding by day and marching by night, almost managed to surround Maritz's commando, and were only foiled by Maritz himself chancing on them as he returned to his force after leading a reconnaissance.[23] The boot was on the other foot some months later, when Capper found his column trapped in a defile by Maritz's entrenchments, but he managed to force his way out, with the loss of five men.[24]

Capper returned to England from South Africa as a Major and Brevet Lieutenant-Colonel having added a DSO and six Mentions in Despatches, the Queen's Medal with six clasps and the King's Medal with two clasps to his tally. After nearly five years of active service and much action, he had proved himself an effective staff officer and had gained considerable experience of independent battlefield command. He had also added to his circle of contacts, a matter of considerable significance in a still clique-ridden army in which appointments and promotion were strongly influenced by patron-protégé relationships.

Capper's experience led to his assignment to the Staff College as a professor in December 1902. His arrival at Camberley coincided with the appointment of Sir Henry Rawlinson as Commandant. Capper and he had served together in both Sudan and South Africa. Sir George Aston, who had been a student in 1889-91 and who also returned as an instructor, wrote in his memoirs

> The South African War had wrought a great change at the Staff College. There seemed to be a new spirit in the place, and staff and students were the most inspiring community I have ever had the good luck to come across. At a full muster at dinner in the mess four VCs and 23 DSOs sat down at the table.[25]

21   Denys Reitz, *Commando: A Boer Journal of the Boer War* (London: Faber & Faber, 1929) p.88.

22   Maurice Grant, *History of the War in South Africa 1899-1902: Vol.IV* (London: Hurst & Blackett, 1906) pp.455-6; Carver, *Boer War*, p.246.

23   Grant, *War in South Africa*, p.356.

24   Ibid., p.455.

25   Major-General Sir George Aston, *Memories of a Marine: An Autobiography* (London: John Murray, 1919), p.239.

In addition to Capper and Aston, the instructors during this time included Hubert Gough, Richard Haking, Launcelot Kiggell, John Du Cane, and later George Barrow, but of these it was Capper who seems to have made most impact. Hubert Gough wrote in his memoirs, *Soldiering On*:

> Capper revolutionised the teaching of staff duties. He never discussed the details of the duties of a junior staff officer in peace at Aldershot … on the contrary, he went thoroughly into the plans, orders, and arrangements which might be required for the success of some definite operations in war. Moreover he always inculcated a spirit of self-sacrifice and duty, instead of the idea of playing for safety and seeking only to avoid getting into trouble. This high-minded inspiration marked all the teaching under Rawlinson too, but it was due perhaps more to Capper than to anyone else. It was like a silver thread which ran through every problem we discussed and studied.[26]

Throughout his time as a professor, and later as a Commandant, Capper always stressed the fundamental importance of the contribution of each and every man – not just the officers. The increased accuracy and firing rate - and hence effectiveness - of the Lee-Enfield rifle had been a factor contributing to greater recognition of the value and importance of the individual soldier, and it was therefore increasingly necessary to ensure that training at all levels was of the highest quality, comprising not merely technical skills but also mental qualities. Amongst Capper's papers at King's College, London is the actual wording - not merely notes - of a lecture to Staff College students in 1908 with his manuscript underlinings and annotations showing where he placed particular emphasis. He quoted, with evident approval, Fortescue's words in his *History of the British Army*, that "it should never be forgotten that military discipline rests at bottom on the broadest and deepest of <u>moral</u> foundations; <u>its ideal is the organised abnegation of self</u>", and added,

> All strategy is based primarily on the <u>military value of the individual</u> ... The most able strategist, the most brilliant tactician, can make little of his army unless the hearts of the individuals composing it are in the right place ... We must instil into the minds of our potential soldiers such virtues as patriotism, devotion to duty, the loss of the sense of self in the interests of the community ... After all is said and done, the art of war consists almost entirely in the application of <u>one</u> principle; that principle never changes. It is the principle that <u>determination to conquer or die</u> must pervade all ranks from the leaders to the simple soldiers; and that principle must not be the mere enthusiasm of the moment, but it must be a principle nourished and cultivated by moral training and intelligent preparation throughout the whole of his military career.[27]

26   General Sir Hubert Gough, *Soldiering On* (London: Arthur Barker, 1954), p.93.
27   LHCMA, Capper Papers, 2/4/1 Lecture on a strategical exercise set to the Senior Division at Quetta 1908.

Enthusiasm and determination were obviously potent ingredients of success, but they had to be focused:

> The first essential object is to distinguish the enemy's <u>decisive point</u> ... You must <u>preserve that idea</u>, no matter how adverse circumstances seem, ... by keeping the initiative in your own hands; and ... to keep this initiative, you must maintain a vigorous and uncompromising <u>offensive</u> attitude. There, Gentlemen, lies the art of the strategist in a nutshell.[28]

The key problem with which military thinkers were grappling and for which Capper could provide no obvious solution was how to mount an attack against prepared defensive positions in the face of accurate firepower.[29] Capper had seen for himself the effectiveness of the accurate musketry at which the Boers excelled, and the fact that even the fanatical bravery of the Dervishes at Omdurman could achieve virtually nothing against machine-gun, artillery, and rifle fire. However his solution seems to have been to maintain the initiative by offensive action that would keep the enemy on the moral back foot before overwhelming him by élan and determination, aided if possible by a heavy artillery bombardment as at Pieter's Hill, rather than "a gradual building up of the firing line" usually involving "a prolonged and severe fire fight" as prescribed by *Field Service Regulations*.[30]

Nevertheless Capper recognised that this approach might not appeal to all, and required considerable moral courage from the commander. Disparaging half-heartedness and the "pernicious effects of a press expressing the voice of a people ignorant of war", he commented,

> It is too often the case that the slow cautious commander, who ventures nothing and gains nothing, is praised, decorated, and promoted as an able and <u>sound</u> leader, while the more audacious , who will accept risks in his efforts to attain decisive results, is condemned as a reckless butcher. Such evil influences it is our duty to counteract by all means in our power...[31]

He also preached what he himself had practised, notably at Omdurman, that an essential element of leadership was that those in command should lead from the front, and, by their example, demonstrate to their troops the highest level of bravery and acceptance of risk; "Men ... learn from example far better than precept".[32]

---

28   Ibid., p.11.
29   For a comprehensive discussion on doctrine and training in this connection, see Timothy Bowman and Mark Connelly, *The Edwardian Army: Recruiting, Training, and Deploying the British Army 1902-1914* (Oxford: OUP, 2012), pp.77-97.
30   *Field Service Regulations, Part I: Operations: 1909*, (London, H.M.S.O, 1909) pp.136-137.
31   LHCMA, Capper Papers, 2/4/1, p.14.
32   Ibid., 2/2.

Capper had been seen as a possible successor to Rawlinson as Commandant at Camberley, but, according to Edmonds, Henry Wilson secured the post for himself by underhand means:

> How Wilson became Commandant of the Staff College is typical of his methods. As Deputy Director of Staff Duties, he managed to dispose of the two strongest candidates, Lawson [later Lieutenant General Sir Henry Lawson] and Capper by offering them the Dublin Infantry Brigade and the Indian Staff College respectively. Then he put before the CIGS, Sir Neville Lyttelton, who told me, a list of several unsuitable persons so that Lyttelton said 'I couldn't face the army if I appointed any of them'. Then Henry mentioned, with becoming diffidence, 'my name comes next, Sir' and Lyttelton, in a kind of despair, ejaculated, 'Oh, you will do'.[33]

Considerable doubt has been cast on this story.[34] Wilson was the most obvious candidate, being the choice of both Rawlinson and Lord Roberts, and Edmonds's credibility is undermined by his intense dislike for Wilson, who, he wrote, "had no education, failed for Woolwich and Sandhurst and entered the army through the back door of the Irish militia, ... had no military judgement whatever, ... and engineered the downfall of even his dearest friends ... in order to advance himself".[35]

In fact Capper's move to the Staff College at Quetta as its first permanent Commandant was an inspired appointment. The Army Council had been unenthusiastic about the establishment of a Staff College in India for fear of fostering differing "Schools of Thought",[36] but Capper, as a member of the Directing Staff at Camberley, could be relied upon to ensure that the syllabus and teaching at Quetta would be identical to those at Camberley. He would also be very acceptable to Kitchener, then Commander-in-Chief in India, who placed considerable reliance on practical experience, and knew Capper personally from his service in the Sudan and during the Boer War.

Capper's appointment, with his promotion to the substantive rank of colonel, was gazetted on 12 June 1906, although there would be a break while the nascent College was moved from its temporary site at Deolali. By coincidence, his two elder brothers were also deeply involved in training around that time. William had been Kitchener's Director of Military Training in India, and was Commandant of the Royal Military College at Sandhurst between 1907 and 1910. His most significant and enduring contribution to British arms was probably his decision to grant leniency to a young cadet called Bernard Montgomery, despite the willingness of his regiment to decommission him, for setting fire to the shirt-tails of another cadet causing him to be hospitalised with serious burns.[37]

---

33   LHCMA, Edmonds Papers, III/15/11, Draft Memoirs, Chapter XX, p.11.
34   John Hussey, 'Appointing the Staff College Commandant 1906: A Case of Trickery, Negligence or Due Consideration?', *British Army Review*, 114 (Dec.1996), pp.99-106.
35   LHCMA, Edmonds Papers, III/15/11, Draft Memoirs, Ch. XX, p.28.
36   Bond, *The Victorian Army and the Staff College*, pp.200-2.
37   Nigel Hamilton, *Monty: The Making of a General* (London: Coronet, 1984) p.44.

The second brother, John, was at that time Commandant of the Balloon School and became something of a celebrity when he piloted the army's first airship, *Nulli Secundus,* on a flight over London in 1907.[38] As Commandant, and as Secretary of the Committee on Military Ballooning, he was in fact tasked to oversee all forms of aeronautics, not just ballooning, and was responsible for the earliest aircraft development by the Army, being considered at one time for the post of Director General of Military Aeronautics. He was subsequently Commandant of the School of Military Engineering at Chatham, Commandant of the Machine Gun Corps Training Centre, and Director General of the War Office Tank Directorate where he was deeply involved in the development of the tank, and in the planning for the 1919 campaign, (a contribution eventually recognised when he became the first Colonel Commandant of the Royal Tank Corps in 1923). Unfortunately, he lacked Thompson's ability as a communicator to such an extent that that, despite being at the forefront of aeronautical, machine gun, and tank development, his nickname amongst tank crews was "Stone Age". Like Thompson, however, he was regarded as a good fighting soldier, and after serving as Chief Engineer of 3rd corps and then of 3rd Army, he commanded the 24th Division on the Western Front in 1915-17 with sufficient success for Robertson to suggest him to Haig as a Corps Commander.[39]

Capper's youngest brother, Alfred, was already at Staff College in India and was one of a party of instructors and students, whom he led on a tour of the battlefields of the Manchurian War in 1907. This trip reinforced Capper's belief in the value of the offensive and he seized with relish on the Japanese Marshal Oyama's reported maxim that "One ought never to allow oneself to be forced onto the defensive, even by superior forces".[40] The tour also seems to have reinforced his views of the efficacy of a heavy artillery barrage as a precursor to attacking a strong position as at Port Arthur; in a passage of his notes that could be regarded both as harking back to his experience at the Tugela and anticipating the set piece attacks of the future, he wrote:

> Evidently the way to attack a fort of this kind is [with] covering fire from as much artillery as can be concentrated on the point of attack. Heavy artillery (11.2" howitzers) is worth all the rest put together. Covering infantry fire at trenches and loopholes. Infantry sapping at night. Destruction of obstacles. First assault under heavy artillery fire which must be kept up and pitched high as the infantry close in. It must not stop even when the height is carried until told it is no longer doing damage to the flying enemy.[41]

38   Alfred Gollin, *No Longer an Island: Britain and the Wright Brothers 1902-1909* (London: Heinemann, 1984), pp.267-9 & *passim.*

39   Robertson to Haig, 14 August 1916, quoted in David R. Woodward, (ed.), *The Military Correspondence of Field Marshal Sir William Robertson, Chief of the Imperial General Staff, December 1915-February 1918* (London: Bodley Head *for* Army Records Society, 1989) p.82.

40   LHCMA, Capper Papers, 2/2, pp.165-6.

41   Ibid., p.9.

It is interesting to note, in passing, that he applauded the boldness of both protagonists in placing their advanced trenches on forward slopes,[42] to obtain a better field of fire, albeit at the cost of exposing themselves to enemy shelling, an action that the 7th Division would emulate at Ypres and be heavily criticised by Haig and Rawlinson for so doing.[43]

Capper's time as Commandant of Quetta ended in January 1911 amid circumstances that illustrate well both the extreme and sometimes eccentric nature of his military philosophy, and his increasingly uncompromising and irascible character. One of the instructors at Quetta was Major Berkeley Vincent. An artilleryman, he had seen service in the Boxer rebellion and the Boer War. He was attached to the Japanese 1st Army as an observer during the Manchurian War and had written on the conflict for the Journal of the Royal United Services Institute.[44] He attended Staff College at Camberley in 1907-8. His confidential Staff College report was unfavourable stipulating that he should spend a year with a regiment before being considered for a staff appointment, but, after he had commanded a squadron of the Inniskilling Dragoons, Capper put his name forward for a lectureship at Quetta after Kitchener had rejected all the other candidates. Kitchener, who knew Vincent well, "said at once that he was the man" and "made the appointment in a most decided manner".[45]

Kitchener left India very shortly afterwards and his successor as Commander-in-Chief, General Sir O'Moore Creagh VC, was said by his Military Secretary to be "very loathe (sic) to see an officer with such a confidential report appointed as professor at Staff College". Capper's reply stressed Vincent's experience and qualifications and Kitchener's personal knowledge of him, and went on to say that he believed Vincent was "one of those officers who, by reason of an excess of character are likely to give offence at a staff college and who do not, therefore, earn as good a report as they might." Creagh's Military Secretary wrote that the new C-in-C had not been consulted, but "had he been, would certainly have objected as he places complete reliance on Camberley reports .. [and].. cannot believe that no-one better could not have been found". Nevertheless the appointment was allowed to stand, although Creagh demanded "full details so as to inform CIGS and dissociate himself from ignoring Camberley report". Capper commented in his notebook, "Dear old Grannie. If he thought so ill of the appointment, why didn't he cancel it instead of allowing it to go on & and then growse (sic) like an old woman at a fair", but wrote asking the Military Secretary to "pass on my great regret that any action of mine should have put HE the C-in-C in a difficult position". The Military Secretary confirmed he had done so but

---

42   Ibid., p.12.
43   National Army Museum (NAM), 5201-33-17, Rawlinson Letter Book, Rawlinson to Capper, 22/10/14; Gary Sheffield and John Bourne (eds.) *Douglas Haig: War Diaries and Letters 1914-1918* (London: Weidenfeld & Nicolson, 2005) p.75 (26 October 1914); Brigadier-General J.E. Edmonds, *Military Operations: France and Belgium, 1914: Vol. II* (London: Macmillan, 1925), p.248.
44   Berkely Vincent, 'Artillery in the Manchurian Campaign', *Journal of the Royal United Services Institute,* 52(1), 1908, pp.28-52.
45   LHCMA, Capper Papers, 2/4/17.

added, "personally I cannot help feeling that what you have done must tend to weaken the value of Staff College reports, which is the result that must inevitably occur. I am not saying this officially but merely writing my own personal feelings on the matter". Capper was incensed. He commented in his notebook "Pretty hard cheek for a junior major of Hussars to express **his** displeasure at the official actions of a Brig. General. The man must be a mountebank and totally unfit for his position," adding later, "So he is. I ought to have 'downed' him. NEVER LET A MAN OFF. Stick to this maxim."[46]

Vincent's appointment aroused mixed reactions. Capper recorded that on 10 January 1910, "de Lisle[47] ... came up and warmly congratulated me on getting Vincent as professor at Staff College. He said we could not have picked a better man", describing him on the basis of their service together in South Africa as "excellent in the field and especially before the enemy".[48] Henry Wilson was less enthusiastic, writing to Capper from Camberley that Vincent's appointment

> leaves us all in a rather breathless condition. We cannot think who was responsible for his selection. I suppose my report on him was seen. We can scarcely believe it unless indeed, which seems likely, the opinion at Simla of a Camberley Staff College report is that it is not worth the paper it is written on. In this, as in every case, it represents the opinion, the unanimous opinion, of the whole of the staff here. Eleven of us. I feel inclined to ask for permission to be relieved from reporting on officers of the I[ndian] A[rmy] in future as it appears to be rather a waste of time. The personal part of this is a very small matter. What we all feel is that the selection and appointment of Vincent is by far the worst thing that has happened to the Quetta SC up to date. For this reason we are all most awfully upset about the business. And don't think I have any 'down' on Vincent. In some appointments he would do admirably but Quetta - Good Lord.[49]

That prompted Capper to comment that "one thing is now certain; it is everyone's business to run this college except TC's", but it is clear that Capper was influenced more by Vincent's pugnacious character than by his professional skills. In his later confidential report of 20 January 1911 on Vincent, Capper wrote that his "intellectual ability [was] not greatly marked", he did "not always sufficiently attend to detail", and needed "more practice in the minutiae of staffwork". Enumerating the various options, he added that Vincent was not suitable for intelligence, mobilisation and organisation, coastal defence, literary or headquarters posts, and had no particular aptitude for staff duties, military training, or administration. However he praised Vincent's practical skills;

> He is prompt and decided with troops in the field, and has a good judgement for seizing the right moment for action. He is bold and eager and is full of the offensive spirit. He

46   Ibid.
47   Colonel (later General Sir) Henry Beauvoir de Lisle, DSO.
48   LHCMA, Capper Papers, 2/4/17, note dated 10 January.
49   LHCMA, Capper Papers, 2/4/17, Wilson to Capper, 2 October 1909.

has plenty of character and self-reliance and is downright in his views ... He appears to me to be a leader, and suited best for outdoor work with troops.[50]

Some were beginning to think that Capper was himself beginning to exhibit an "excess of character". George Barrow, who had counted him as a close friend at Staff College in 1897, was taken aback to find in 1910 that "all that was bright and genial and human in him had disappeared and was replaced by a certain hard coldness, a repression, a conception of duty exaggerated to falsity". He concluded that Capper's genius was no longer balanced by judgement and that although "always commanding the greatest respect from those under him on account of his outstanding ability, his unyielding sense of duty, his gifts of speech and his professional knowledge .. he carried some of his principles to an extreme stage where they became unworkable".[51]

In fact, neither Vincent nor Capper was to stay much longer at Quetta. On 11 November 1910, Haig, then Chief of the General Staff in India, wrote to Capper congratulating him on being appointed to command the 13th Infantry Brigade in Dublin but adding that he was writing to Haldane, then Minister for War, and to Launcelot Kiggell, his successor as Director of Staff Duties to try to get Capper command of a Brigade at Aldershot instead, although nothing seems to have come of this. In the meantime, on 16 November 1910, just a few days after his letter to Capper, Haig wrote a scathing report on Vincent's technical knowledge and his appointment was terminated.[52] Capper was furious at the manner of Vincent's dismissal, and asked to be relieved immediately of his appointment as Commandant, leaving an interregnum pending the arrival of his designated successor, Colonel (later General Sir) Walter Braithwaite.[53]

On 19 February 1911, after a consequential brief period on half-pay, Capper took over the 13th Infantry Brigade in Dublin. Haig had his doubts about Capper's style, writing to Launcelot Kiggell, that "Capper did well [at Quetta] but was too full of nerves and too much of a crank to get the best out of his officers",[54] but he proved immensely successful as a trainer of troops, setting a standard to which others sought to aspire.[55] The 1913 Annual Report of the Inspector-General of the Home Forces was

50   LHCMA, Capper Papers, 2/4/17.
51   Barrow, *The Fire of Life*, p.123.
52   After Haig's departure from India, Vincent was given a staff appointment with the Indian Army and continued to serve on the staff in the Great War, initially with the Indian Army Corps and then as Chief Staff Officer of the 37th Division until 1917 when he was promoted to command the 35th Infantry Division. He ended his career as Officer Commanding British Forces in Iraq, during the suppression of the insurgency of Kurdish irregular forces (and some Turkish regular forces) in Northern Iraq in 1923 by combined operations of the Royal Air Force and the army, after which he retired with a knighthood and the rank of Brigadier General.
53   LHCMA, Capper Papers, II/4/17, Capper to Chief of General Staff, 4 December 1911.
54   LHCMA, Kiggell Papers, II/1/2, Haig to Kiggell, 22 October 1911
55   General Sir Aylmer Haldane, *A Soldier's Saga* (London: William Blackwood, 1948) p.269.

full of praise for Capper's brigade, describing various aspects of training as "excellent" and "thoroughly satisfactory" and the standard of efficiency of the brigade as "well above average", with "the spirit of the initiative" being "strongly marked" as a result of "the influence of the Brigade commander". The only hint of criticism was that "in the anxiety to press home an attack, there was a tendency to lose sight of the importance of endeavouring to gain superiority of fire..."[56] Capper's approach was exemplified by Appendix D of the Report, which describes how, in a field exercise, after the Divisional commander had erred in deploying his infantry in a position "which came under effective rifle fire from the enemy's position as soon as it was light", Capper "appeared to think he was justified in attempting to close with the enemy as quickly as possible", carrying out his attack "with great dash and spirit, but with ... no supporting fire of any kind".[57]

In April 1914 Capper was appointed Inspector of Infantry, but the outbreak of war only four months later meant that he had little time to make any significant impact, and no Annual Report was issued for 1914.

Capper was appointed to command the 7th Division on 27 August 1914. His division comprised virtually the last remaining regular troops in the United Kingdom, the 1st Grenadier Guards and the 2nd Scots Guards, two line battalions from Guernsey and Pembroke docks respectively, and artillery and engineers from Kent and Middlesex. These were augmented by troops summoned back to England from service in Gibraltar, Malta, Egypt, and South Africa. Whereas the home-based battalions which had made up the first six divisions of the British Expeditionary Force had included considerable numbers of reservists who might not have handled a rifle for several years and whose underlying fitness was very doubtful, the overseas-based battalions of the 7th Division had been kept up to strength by drafts from their linked battalions in the United Kingdom, and generally needed very few reservists, no more than 'about 100 or 130 men per battalion, a proportion easily assimilated', although two-thirds of each of the Guards battalions were reservists as a consequence of their having sent drafts to make up the numbers of other Guards battalions setting off for Belgium ahead of them.[58]

Although generally fitter than the men of the first six divisions, the 7th Division troops would not have been at peak physical fitness. Garrison duty in hot and enervating climates such as Malta and Egypt was not conducive to energetic training, certainly during the heat of the summer, and any lack of fitness would have been exacerbated by a sea passage in crowded troopships. The Divisional History records that "with characteristic energy and zeal General Capper started Brigade and even Divisional training directly units could be got together" and quotes an unidentified officer's comment that, even before orders to move had been received, the Division had

56   The National Archives (TNA), WO 27/508, Annual report of the Inspector-General of Home Forces for 1913, Appendix A.
57   Ibid., Appendix D.
58   C.T. Atkinson, *The Seventh Division 1914-1918* (London: John Murray, 1927) p.4.

"marched close on three hundred miles about the New Forest by way of hardening the men who had come off foreign service".[59]

On 2 October, the very day that its divisional artillery completed its mobilisation, the 7th Division was ordered to embark urgently for Belgium as part of IV Corps under the command of Rawlinson, in an attempt to relieve the besieged port of Antwerp. Within four hours of receiving their orders they were on the road to Southampton. Unfortunately, Antwerp's situation, already almost beyond redemption, was rendered impossible by the non-appearance of promised French troops, and IV Corps moved to Bruges and then on to Ghent to cover the retreat from Antwerp of the Belgian Field Army and the Royal Naval Division. The successful withdrawal of the Belgian Field Army from its besieged redoubt in Antwerp alleviated King Albert's fear that the loss of both his army and the small remnant of Belgian soil not occupied by the Germans could lead to the irrevocable extinction of his country, and gave time and opportunity to secure the Allies' northern flank by the inundation of the low-lying ground between Ypres and the sea. However that still left an open gap, guarded only by a thin screen of mainly cavalry units, through which the Germans, now consisting of four newly organised corps in addition to the troops released by the fall of Antwerp, could advance to the Channel ports. The BEF was hastening northwards, but the situation was critical in the extreme with an imminent risk, as the *Official History* puts it, that

the whole of Belgium must have been lost, and the Germans would have reached Dunkirk and Calais – which were indeed their objectives. If these ports had fallen to the enemy the effect on our sea communications and on operations generally might well have proved fatal not only to the British Empire, but to the whole of the civilised world.[60]

Capper's route marches in the New Forest proved their worth as the 7th Division, chivvied by Rawlinson in his brother's car,[61] covered up to 30 miles per day as it hastened to plug the gap. On 14th October, the Division reached a position five miles south east of Ypres where it joined Gough's and Allenby's cavalry to form an attenuated Allied line to the south of the Belgian Field Army's positions, much of it still largely devoid of infantry until the arrival of Haig's I Corps on 21st October. The British front line was of necessity over-extended, generally consisting of a fluctuating series of positions and stretches of shallow trenches that were far from continuous and held so thinly that at times the 7th Division, despite having sustained heavy losses, manned an eight mile frontage.[62]

The absence of a continuous and formalised trench system emphasised the need for leadership and initiative at all levels, while relentless German pressure and mounting British casualties necessitated constant restructuring of the line with units being reshuffled to plug gaps throughout the battle. The Divisional History describes the

59   Ibid., p.5.
60   Edmonds, *Military Operations*, p.126.
61   A. Rawlinson, *Adventures on the Western Front* (London: Andrew Melrose, 1925), p.171.
62   TNA WO 95/1627, 7th Division War Diary, 19 October 1914.

ubiquitous presence of Capper himself, "constantly up in the firing line to exhort and encourage the weary men, to instil into them something of his own unflinching determination to endure to the bitter end",[63] and the *Official History* relates one such episode on 31 October when

> the front line of the 20th Brigade, being now exposed to enfilade fire, began to give ground, like that of the 21st Brigade on its left. It was rallied by Major-General Capper and Br.-General Lawford and the Divisional and Brigade staffs, and led forward again; and at the same time Br.-General Ruggles-Brise brought up the last reserve, the eighty men of the 1/Grenadiers to help fill the gap.[64]

Faced with almost overwhelming odds, even Capper found few opportunities to take the offensive, but the effect, both moral and physical, of counter-attacks when they could be mounted, was immense. The IV Corps War Diary records that

> During the night of 25/26 October, the Germans attacked near Kruiseik and succeeded in breaking the line. General Capper promptly counter-attacked and, driving back the Germans, restored the original line and captured 7 officers and 189 other ranks besides several other small groups of prisoners.[65]

Similar counter-attacks by the Gordon Highlanders and Grenadier Guards on 29 October and, most notably, on 31 October, when the last eighty men of the Gordons regained half a mile from the nearly fresh German 39th Division, caused the Divisional History to comment;

> Once again the very audacity of the little force which presumed to hold a position out of all proportion to its actual strength had imposed on the Germans, who could not credit any troops with attempting to achieve impossibilities and therefore pictured the Seventh Division as having behind it vast reserves.[66]

However, such tenacious resistance came at a high price and 7th Division's losses were enormous. By 2 November, every battalion of the Division had lost its commanding officer[67] and "instead of the three infantry brigades ...each mustering 124 officers and 4,100 other ranks, they numbered respectively 18 officers and 900 men, 13 officers and 910 men, and 13 officers and 586 men – a fifth of their original strength".[68]

Captain (later Brigadier-General) Christopher Baker-Carr later wrote that

63   Atkinson, *Seventh Division*, p.80.
64   Edmonds, *Military Operations*, pp.334-5.
65   TNA WO 95/706, IV Corps War Diary, 26 October 1914.
66   Atkinson, *Seventh Division*, pp. 73, 98.
67   Ibid., p.96.
68   Edmonds, *Military Operations*, p.371.

Capper himself seemed to bear a charmed life. Day after day he exposed himself in the most reckless fashion. He wasn't brave; he simply did not know what fear meant. His steely blue eyes, beneath a thick crop of dark, wiry hair, stared at one with the look of a religious fanatic. One day, when I had spoken of the risk he was running, he turned on me almost fiercely. 'I consider it to be the duty of an officer in this war to be killed,' he said.[69]

Capper seems to have expected that same duty of his staff officers. In a lecture entitled 'Staff Duties' given to the Royal Military Society of Ireland on 29 February 1912, Capper had emphasised that the role of the staff officer as set out in *Field Service Regulations* was twofold, and included, as well as assisting the commander, the duty of giving every assistance to the troops in carrying out the instructions given to them.[70] He had also warned that the weak point of the army was "insularity between arms, between units, and, up to a certain point, between the staff and the troops themselves".[71] Smith-Dorrien wrote that "the advantage of sending staff officers ... to act as liaison officers ... has been has been proved to be very great",[72] but Capper went further, apparently regarding them as his personal representatives in the firing line, with a duty to encourage the men by showing the same disregard for danger as he himself always exhibited, as the diary of Brigadier-General John Charteris for 9 November 1914 illustrates:

The most active of the divisional GOCs, in the way of going forward and sending his Staff forward, is my old Staff College Commandant at Quetta, Tommy Capper. I saw him this week, and he said – and I think he meant it – "no good officer has a right to be alive during a fight like this." Certainly he takes as much – and more – risk as any of his own men, and his Staff follow his example. There is a story (probably quite untrue) that he came into the Staff Mess one day and said, "What! Nobody on the Staff wounded today; that won't do!" and forthwith sent everyone available up to the first-line trenches on some mission or other. It sounds rather brutal – but it's not unwise. It heartens the men and regimental officers enormously to see Staff officers, although the Staff officers can do very little to help them.[73]

There can be little doubt that the steadfastness of the 7th Division under Capper's inspirational leadership was absolutely critical to the avoidance of defeat and to ultimate success at Ypres, and his obituary in *The Times* quotes an eloquent appreciation provided by an anonymous "correspondent who served with him":

Those who went through the first battle of Ypres with the immortal 7th Division will know what the Army has lost by the death of General Capper. There were critics at the time who argued that General Capper must have sacrificed his men recklessly to incur

69   CD Baker-Carr, *From Chauffeur to Brigadier,* (London: Ernest Benn, 1930) p.49.
70   *Field Service Regulations 1909, Part II,* (London, H.M.S.O. 1909) pp.38-39.
71   LHCMA, Capper Papers, 2/4/4.
72   TNA WO 95/629, 'Memorandum relative to the experience gained by 2nd Corps'.
73   John Charteris, *At GHQ* (London: Cassell 1931) p.58.

such tremendous casualties; others who complained that the general was too often at the front piecing a broken line together, when he should, according to all regulations, have been in his office attending to the telephone. Those who know best remain convinced that the sacrifices were inseparable from the task, so successfully fulfilled, of foiling the German attempt to break through to Calais, and that no one but Capper himself could, night after night, by the sheer force of his personality, have reconstituted from the shattered fragments of decimated battalions a fighting line that would last through the morrow.[74]

Considering the risks he embraced, Capper's death had a certain inevitability. He survived until the Battle of Loos when, although about to assume command of a corps, he insisted on staying with his own 7th Division for the battle.[75] A recurrent legend that he was killed while riding his horse, "fully exposed between our own and the German lines" was recounted by George Barrow[76] and has since been repeated by modern historians such as Brian Bond[77] and Nikolas Gardner,[78] although his C.R.E., Colonel Boileau wrote unequivocally in 1920 that "General Capper was not killed riding his charger and waving his sword as rumoured at the time; he was shot in the back returning from visiting the front line while going down a shallow communications trench in the captured German front system". This was shortly after he had gone to organise an attack on the quarries at Hulluch where Captain E.P. Bennett VC MC of the 2nd Worcesters had seen him "running with our men...actually joining in the assault".[79]

The fact that such a story could gain currency, especially amongst those who knew him, is clear evidence that he was regarded as practising to the highest degree what he had always preached.

74   *The Times*, 1st October 1915.
75   LHCMA, Edmonds Papers, III/2/17.
76   Barrow, *The Fire of Life*, p.124.
77   Bond, *The Victorian Army and the Staff College*, p.208.
78   Nikolas Gardner, *Trial By Fire: Command and the British Expeditionary Force in 1914* (Westport, CT, USA: Praeger, 2003) p.16.
79   TNA CAB 45/120, quoted in Frank Davies and Graham Maddocks, *Bloody Red Tabs* (Barnsley: Pen & Sword, 1995), pp.53-4.

Brigade Command

10

"A Tower of Strength":
Brigadier-General Edward Bulfin

2nd Brigade

Michael Stephen LoCicero

Edward Stanislaus Bulfin KCB CVO (1862-1939) is not a name that readily comes to mind when contemplating British general officers of the First World War. Subsequent postings to the conflict's periphery theatres and the dearth of available personal papers[1] has somewhat obscured the courage and resolve displayed by this outstanding brigadier throughout the desperate first three months in France and Flanders. Indeed, his tactical acumen, aggressiveness and willingness to risk life and limb whilst providing personal leadership during periods of crisis were duly rewarded by field promotion to major-general and divisional command. This rapid rise, not unusual in a BEF reeling from a casualty-induced deficit of experienced officers, was particularly remarkable when one considers Bulfin's slow career progression from what were primarily unfashionable staff appointments to premier infantry brigade command – no small feat in the late Victorian and Edwardian army. It also provides some evidence of a pre-war meritocratic approach to promotion and the necessity, in the often dire circumstances of 1914, for middle-level commanders to rise to the occasion and display an appropriate professional blend of modern and traditional military ethos on the battlefield.

Early Life and Career

Bulfin was born on 6 November 1862, the second son of Patrick Bulfin Esq. JP of Woodtown Park, Rathfarnham, County Dublin and his wife Teresa *nee* Carroll of Dublin. Raised Roman Catholic, his education at Stoneyhurst College, a flourishing

---

1   A typescript extract facsimile of Bulfin's 1914 campaign diary can be found in The National Archives [Hereafter TNA] CAB 45/140: Ypres: Authors A-L. This chapter is based on this document. Surname and place names misspelled during the 1920s transcription have been corrected below.

Edward Bulfin. (Editor's collection)

Lancashire preparatory school based on the Jesuit tradition, and Kensington Catholic Public School were in keeping with the professed faith of and academic expectations for the prominent Victorian magistrate and subsequent Lord Mayor of Dublin's male offspring. Subsequent enrollment at Trinity College Dublin was terminated without taking a degree in pursuance of a military career.[2] Militia service, the traditional 'back door' to a Regular Army commission, with the 3rd Battalion Royal Irish Fusiliers was followed by commission into the Princess of Wales Own (Yorkshire) Regiment on 12 November 1884 at the age of 22.[3] Eight uneventful years with 2nd Battalion passed before Bulfin first saw active service in Upper Burma as a column commander during the Chin-Kachin Hills campaign of 1892-93.[4]

2   A *honoris causa* (LL.D) was bestowed by Trinity after the First World War.
3   John Bourne, 'Bulfin, Sir Edward Stanislaus (1862-1939)', Oxford Dictionary of National Biography, http://www.oxforddnb.com/view/article/32162, *Hart's Annual Army List 1899 Vol. 60*, p.256 and Byron Farwell, *Mr Kipling's Army: All the Queen's Men* (New York: Norton, 1981), p.147.
4   British occupation of the Burmese border town of Bhamo in December 1885 was followed by years of opposition from indigenous Kachin hill tribesmen. Successive punitive expeditions were carried out by the local military police until December 1892, when a small column in transit to Sima was ambushed and the town of Myitkyina raided simultaneously. A dispatched expeditionary force of 1,200 British and Indian troops suppressed all serious resistance by February 1893. See James Grant, *British Battles on*

Six more years of regimental duty would pass before Bulfin's relatively mundane career – promotion to captain occurred in January 1895 – reached a crucial juncture with the outbreak of the South African War in October 1899. A congenial and retrospectively fortuitous appointment as military secretary and aide-de-camp to fellow Irishman and Roman Catholic Lieutenant-General Sir William Butler (C-and-C South Africa) in November 1898 placed the 36-year-old captain in the cockpit of the approaching conflict. The now acclimatised Bulfin, having escaped his chief's summary recall by the British government in summer 1899, was appointed 'Special Service Officer' with authorisation to raise supplementary forces for the army on a local basis in September, and following the outbreak of war he became brigade major to Brigadier-General Reginald Pole-Carew (GOC 9th Infantry Brigade) in November.[5]

Participation in the opening Cape Colony battles of Belmont, Enslin, Modder River and Magersfontein generated opportunities for an ambitious officer to shine.[6] Sustained efforts by the fledgling brigade major to organise and direct the envelopment of the Boer right flank at Modder River demonstrated a keen tactical eye and earnest zeal that did not go unrecognised. General Lord Methuen (GOC 1st Division), in two campaign despatches chronicling operations from 23 to 28 November 1899, observed that Captain Bulfin, "on whose shoulders great responsibility rested, did admirable work" at Belmont and Modder River. Impressive service with 9th Brigade was rewarded by promotion to major and field command of one of the six mobile columns under Colonel Alexander Rochfort. Bulfin's small force of 458 effectives and two accompanying Maxim guns were, in turn, part of a concerted effort by 28 columns to sweep the Orange River Colony and Western Transvaal of Boer insurgents during the last 'guerilla' phase of the war. By the time of the peace settlement Bulfin had been mentioned in despatches three times and obtained the rank of brevet lieutenant-colonel. The acquisition of an excellent war record proved advantageous for a regimental officer seeking gainful employment in the post-war army. Subsequent secondment to staff duties and appointment as Deputy-Assistant Adjutant General [DAAG] 2nd Division placed the highly-regarded Bulfin on the staff path to further promotion.[7]

Land and Sea (London: Cassell, 1899), pp.635-38.

5   Bourne, 'Bulfin, Sir Edward Stanislaus (1862-1939)', ODNB, *London Gazette*, 26 February 1895, p.1149, Thomas Pakenham, *The Boer War* (New York: Random House, 1979), p.82 and Major M.L. Ferrar, *With the Green Howards in South Africa 1899-1902* (London: Eden, Fisher & Co., 1904), p.2.

6   *London Gazette*, 10 November 1899, p.6740 and 2 February 1900, p.694.

7   Sir Frederick Maurice, *History of the War in South Africa Vol. I*, pp.253-54, *History of the War in South Africa Vol. IV*, pp.429-34 and 478 (London: Hurst & Blackett, 1906 and 1910); Anon., *South African War Honours and Awards 1899-1902* (London: Greenhill, 1987); Lt. Col. Du Moulin, *Two Years on Trek: Being Some Account of the Royal Sussex Regiment in South Africa* (London: Murray & Co., 1907), p.315; and *London Gazette*, 19 April 1901, p.2705, 2 and 16 January 1903, pp.6 and 308.

Bulfin's tenure as DAAG lasted from 1902 to 1904. From 1906 until 1910 he held the post of Assistant-Adjutant and Quartermaster General, Cape Colony. Promoted substantive colonel in July 1908 and created a CVO in 1910, previously demonstrated efficiency with overseas postings begat steady advancement following his return to Great Britain. Command of the Essex Infantry Brigade, Territorial Force, "despite never having commanded a battalion" was confirmed in July 1911.[8] This was followed two years later by command of the Regular Army's premier 2nd Infantry Brigade, 1st Division, Aldershot Command.[9] This prestigious appointment emphasises Bulfin's unusual post-South African War progression from administrative staff officer to brigade command.[10] Lacking, as far as can be determined, membership to any sort of influential army clique or career-enhancing staff college certificate, he trod one of two less desirable ('Q' or Quartermaster branch and 'AG' or Adjutant-General branch) staff paths to field command before the First World War. That an officer with Bulfin's primarily AG staff experience was elevated to GOC 2nd Brigade attests to promotion based solely on perceived merit. The newly appointed brigadier's first important exercise of peacetime field command took place three months later during the large-scale Midlands army manoeuvres of September 1913 when 2nd Brigade, as part of Lieutenant-General Sir Douglas Haig's 'Brown Force' Army Corps (1st Division and 2nd Division), participated in the general pursuit of a numerically inferior 'White Army', comprised of Territorials, Yeomanry and elements of Regular cavalry, who engaged in a skilful 'fighting retreat' against almost overwhelming odds – a portent of things to come.[11]

Building a Reputation: Mobilisation to the Aisne

Bulfin and 2nd Brigade HQ were quartered at Blackdown Camp in the picturesque weald of West Sussex with two component (1st Northamptonshire and 2nd King's Royal Rifle Corps [KRRC]) battalions when mobilisation orders were received on 4 August 1914.[12] A brigade route march, "at full war strength", on 11 August exposed

---

8   Bourne, 'Bulfin, Sir Edward Stanislaus (1862-1939)', ODNB.
9   'Premier' in the context of 1st Division's component 1st Brigade Household regiment complement. Two of its four battalions were Foot Guards. Military tradition thus dictated that it could only be commanded by a Guardsman. Conversely, 2nd Brigade was highly rated on the basis of its line regiment composition. Bulfin assumed command of 2nd Brigade in June 1913.
10   Bourne, 'Bulfin, Sir Edward Stanislaus (1862-1939)', ODNB.
11   See Richard Holmes, *The Little Field Marshal: Sir John French* (London: Jonathan Cape, 1981), pp.149-50; Andrew Whitemarsh, 'British Army Manoeuvres and the Development of Military Aviation 1910-1913' in *War in History*, 14 (3), 2007, pp.325-46; and John Sunderland & Margaret Webb, *All the Business of War: The British Army Exercises of 1913* (Towcester: Towcester and District Local History Society, 2012).
12   2nd Brigade's remaining two (2nd Royal Sussex and 1st Loyal North Lancashire) battalions were quartered at Woking and Aldershot respectively.

the "soft" physical state of recently joined reservists: "[F]ours bad, many of the [1st] Loyal North Lancashire Regiment [LNL] fell out, not much time left to correct this." A royal visit, to "say goodbye to brigade HQ and the two battalions stationed there", by King George V and Queen Mary preceded entrainment at Farnborough for Southampton.[13] Embarkation of Brigade HQ, "half battalion of [2nd] Royal Sussex and whole of the Loyal North Lancashire Regt." on to the Holt cargo steamer *S. S. Agapenor* commenced on the afternoon of 12 August: "Ship very crowded, only standing room. Cast off at 11:30 p.m. when Colonel Knight[14] commanding L.N. Lancs read the King's message[15] and the men gave three cheers".[16]

The 2nd Brigade disembarked at Le Havre on 13 August as part of 1st Division (GOC Major-General Samuel Lomax), which, along with 2nd Division (GOC Major-General Charles Monro), was part of Sir Douglas Haig's I Corps. 1st Division's two remaining infantry brigades (1st Guards Brigade and 3rd Brigade) were commanded by Brigadier-General Ivor Maxse and Brigadier-General Herman Landon respectively. Bulfin's command spent the seven days (14-20 August) leading up to the BEF's concentration in the triangle Le Cateau – Hirson – Maubeuge unloading supplies and transport after which it entrained, via Rouen, Amiens and Arras, for Le Nouvion-en-Thiérache just beyond the southern fringe of the vast Mormal Forest. A short march the next day (16 August), brought it to the rustic commune of Esquéhéries. Heavy rainfall was succeeded by warm weather and clear skies. The next four days were spent carrying out lengthy morning route marches and afternoon outpost schemes. "Drums of the Northants played on the green … Men's billets crowded, all latrines dug".[17]

2nd Brigade marched from their congested billet to join the BEF, I Corps on the right, Lieutenant-General Sir Horace Smith-Dorrien's II Corps on the left, in the general advance with French forces on 21 August.[18] I Corps remained comparatively unengaged during II Corps' epic clash with General Alexander von Kluck's *First Army* at Mons on 23 August. As Bulfin recorded that day: "Orders arrived at 2:15 a.m. ordering us to march at 4 to ROUVEROY. Orders out at 3 a.m. moved off at 4 a.m. Raining. Very narrow winding streets. Heavy firing north of us about 12 noon. Ordered to move to GIVRY at 8 p.m. German aeroplanes hovering about during afternoon".[19] An innate combination of physical and moral courage coupled with a

---

13   Bulfin's elevation from substantive colonel to temporary brigadier-general, British
      Expeditionary Force was officially announced on 25 August 1914. See *London Gazette*,
      p.6689.
14   Lieutenant-Colonel G.C. Knight: Died of wounds 11 September 1914.
15   See Sir James Edmonds, *Military Operations: France and Belgium 1914 Vol. I, 3rd Edition*
      (London: Macmillan & Co., 1937), p.32.
16   TNA WO 95/1267: 2nd Brigade War Diary and CAB 45/140 Ypres: Authors A-L:
      Brigadier-General E.S. Bulfin Diary, 18 August 1914.
17   TNA CAB 45/140: Bulfin Diary 18 August 1914.
18   See Edmonds, *Military Operations 1914 Vol. I*, pp.64, 73 for 2nd Brigade's forward
      movements.
19   Ibid and TNA WO 95/1267: 2nd Brigade War Diary.

former regimental officer's paternal instincts – "Ordered to leave great coats behind in change of guard, protested but overruled. Men now have only waterproof sheets" – afforded Bulfin the steely resolve to overcome the unrelenting stress and strains of the retreat and keep his brigade intact: "Roads all blocked with crowds of country folk all fleeing the Germans – Ladies, gentlemen and poor people all racing along pell-mell in any sort of conveyance and on foot, children and women the largest proportion".[20] 2nd Brigade performed vital rearguard and flank duties throughout the retirement. A brief skirmish on 27 August inflicted heavy loss on pursuing lorry-transported German infantry and yielded a single *Uhlan* prisoner. The very real threat of encirclement and destruction was brought home when Bulfin observed the hard-pressed 2nd Royal Munster Fusiliers (1st Guards Brigade) repelling repeated attacks prior to being overwhelmed at Etreux: "1st Brigade on our right acting as rearguard heavily engaged. Saw one detachment, at least a mile away behind, fighting hard with the enemy pressing closely". The closing enemy juggernaut was barely evaded the following day: "Received orders at 2 a.m. to cover retirement of Corps … German cavalry in large numbers came up about 7 a.m. followed by two brigades of German infantry … At 10:30 Northants sent a message that German troops were attacking left rear, and reinforcements urgently needed. Sent message he [sic] must do without them …"[21]

Gruelling physical and mental fatigue will be forever associated with the Great Retreat. 2nd Brigade's ordeal was graphically summed up by Captain E.J. Needham of 1st LNL:

> This continued marching in the wrong direction was beginning to get on everybody's nerves. And it was getting increasingly difficult to keep the men cheerful. They could not understand it, and neither could we for that matter. But otherwise they were simply splendid. No one who did not go through that retreat can possibly imagine what it was like. Up and away at dawn every day, marching all day in a tropical sun and amidst clouds of dust, generally on the terrible rough pavé roads, or pushed down into the equally rough and very stony gutter by other columns of troops on the same road, or by staff cars rushing past and making the dust worse than ever. Never any proper meals, never a wash or a shave, never out of one's clothes, carrying a terrific weight of arms and equipment, and, as regards the 2nd Brigade, never getting a chance of a shot at the enemy except that one day [27 August] at Wassigny to cheer one up a bit.[22]

20   TNA CAB 45/140: Bulfin Diary 24 and 25 August 1914.
21   Ibid, 27 and 28 August 1914. See Edmonds, *Military Operations 1914 Vol. I*, pp.219-26 for 2nd Royal Munster Fusilier's stand at Etreux.
22   Captain E.J. Needham, 'The Ending Days: Red Reaping and Red Tape' in Sir John Hammerton (ed), *'The Great War … I Was There!' Undying Memories of 1914-1918 Vol. I* (London: Amalgamated Press, 1939), p.117.

The BEF's harrowing withdrawal of approximately 200 miles,[23] more or less maintained in conformity with French formations on either flank, continued south of the Marne River before Allied forces, "as much because of the failure of will on the part of Moltke, the German commander, as because of any Allied tactical success", turned the tide of the war with a climactic counter-offensive in early September.[24] Bulfin received orders to join the advance on 7 September:

> Ordered to march at 4 a.m., but this was cancelled. Sent for to [sic] Divisional Headquarters at 6 a.m. and told situation. Ordered to march at 9 a.m. Sent on Loyal North Lancs with section R.A. to secure AMILLIS and crossings over R[IVER] AUBETIN. Northamptons to ST ELOY. A German column moving north had passed through AMELLIS today, commencing at 5 a.m. and clear of the village at 6 a.m. From information, this is part of IV German Corps. Moved to JOUY SUR MORIN (19½ miles) Loyal North Lancs on high ground north of ST SIMOEN. German patrols hanging about our outposts. Constant shooting. Sussex captured a patrol of Imperial Guard and shot Guards officer. Moved up Northamptons to reinforce Loyal North Lancs.[25]

2nd Brigade performed advanced and rearguard duties during the painfully slow and cautious general pursuit to the Aisne River.[26] A sharp engagement near Priez on 10 September forced a strong German rearguard to retire from the field with some loss: "Our guns galloped up to the ridge all among our infantry and opened fire on Germans running away and fairly plastered them in columns of fours, crossing the MARNE [sic Orque] N[orth] of NEUILLY".[27] However, Bulfin's application of a textbook 'all arms' tactical scheme, utilising attached cavalry for reconnaissance and artillery to breakdown opposition to the infantry,[28] was somewhat marred when nearby batteries of other formations shelled the assaulting battalions (2nd Royal Sussex and 1st LNL) and forced them to retire in a tragic 'friendly fire' mishap that, according to Nikolas Gardner, stemmed "from the haphazard deployment of artillery detachments by divisional commanders".[29] The unfortunate incident was further

23   Richard Holmes, *Riding the Retreat: Mons to the Marne 1914 Revisited* (London: Pimlico, 2007), p.282.

24   Richard Holmes, *Army Battlefield Guide: Belgium and Northern France* (London: HMSO, 1995), p.97.

25   TNA CAB 45/140: Bulfin Diary 7 September 1914.

26   See Nikolas Gardner, *Trial by Fire: Command in the British Expeditionary Force in 1914* (Westport, Praeger, 2003) pp.73-86 and Jerry Murland, *The Battle of the Aisne 1914: The BEF and the Birth of the Western Front* (Barnsley: Pen & Sword, 2012), pp.22-35.

27   TNA CAB 45/140: Bulfin Diary 10 September 1914.

28   War Office, *Field Service Regulations Part I: Operations* (London, HMSO, 1909), pp.13-20, 91-94.

29   Gardner, *Trial by Fire*, pp.82-83. A private in 1st LNL later wrote of this incident: 'Unfortunately it was a wet morning, and the men had taken the advantage of putting their oil sheets round their shoulders to keep them dry, the oil sheets when wet being

compounded by poor communications between formations and, in Bulfin's eyes, resultant missed opportunities of the *arme blanche*. According to volunteer American chauffeur Frederic Coleman: "General Bulfin, commanding the 1st Brigade [sic], asked me to what I was attached. On learning I was with the cavalry he bemoaned the fact that the cavalry were not on his left, as the fast-disappearing transport of the enemy would have fallen an easy prey to one of our cavalry brigades on that flank".[30] The enemy was finally forced to withdraw in some haste from the Priez position after 1st Guards Brigade and 3rd Brigade came up on the right and left respectively.[31] The 'rough' post-engagement casualty estimate amounted to 182 killed, wounded and missing including Bulfin's brigade major – "He was close to me at the time" – seriously injured.[32]

Bulfin's brigade, acting once more as advanced guard for 1st Division, reached the Aisne at Bourg on 13 September: "Reached BOURG (crossing by canal bridge which was intact) about 2 p.m. Sent KRR[C] on to high plateau NW of BOURG. Sussex on spurs to the left of KRR. Rushed Loyal North Lancs Regt. on to spur N of same feature".[33] I Corps had, by this date, marched 70 miles in 7 days and captured approximately 1,000 prisoners.[34] The BEF's brief pause south of the Aisne was an ominous prelude to an unwelcome first encounter with stiffening enemy resistance and the beginnings of trench warfare. One Royal Flying Corps pilot, having observed the extent of German activity across the river, landed his aircraft near an approaching column to emphatically warn what lay ahead: "The flying-officer climbed slowly out of his machine and, coming stumbling toward us in his heavy kit, did not wait to find an officer, but shouted to us all: 'There they are, waiting for you up there, thousands of them'".[35]

The stalemate to come first manifested itself during extended operations (13-26 September) on the Aisne. Tired and dispirited formations of the German *First Army* and *Second Army*, having regrouped and reorganised north of the river, commenced the development of a system of entrenchments backed by massed artillery on and around the ridges and spurs of the dominant Chemins des Dames upland, assisted by the timely, morale boosting arrival of a fresh army corps.[36] Thus situated they planned

of a similar colour to the German uniform. In the distance our gunners bombarded us, mistaking us for the retiring enemy …' See F.A. Bolwell, *With a Reservist in France* (London: Routledge, 1917), p.38.

30   Frederic Coleman, *From Mons to Ypres with French: A Personal Narrative* (Toronto: William Briggs, 1916), p.111.

31   Edmonds, *Military Operations 1914 Vol. I*, p.360.

32   TNA CAB 45/140: Bulfin Diary 10 September 1914.

33   Ibid, 13 September 1914.

34   Andy Simpson, *The Evolution of Victory: British Battles on the Western Front 1914-1918* (London: Tom Donovan, 1995), p.16.

35   John Lucy, *There's a Devil in the Drum* (Dallington: Naval & Military Press, 1992 reprint of 1938 edition), p.166.

36   Edmonds, *Military Operations 1914 Vol. I*, pp.374-76, 392-94 and Murland, *Battle of the Aisne 1914*, pp.36-45.

to turn the tables on their pursuers at the earliest opportune moment by abandoning a perceived short-term defensive posture for a series of limited attacks with the objective of preventing the Allies from establishing bridgeheads on the northern bank of the Aisne. Field Marshal Sir John French, acting under the misapprehension that his advancing forces would encounter nothing more than enemy rearguards, issued optimistic orders to force the river obstacle and storm the heights beyond. Subsequent operations on a three-corps front between 13-15 September, during which the BEF sustained approximately 13,000 casualties killed, wounded and missing, failed to dislodge a determined defence before the deadlock set in.[37] It was during this nascent period of position warfare that superiors first took particular notice of the martial qualities displayed by Brigadier-General Bulfin.[38]

Bulfin received orders "to seize high ground around Cerny" opposite the BEF's right flank on the evening of 13 September. The attack objectives were relatively straightforward: 2nd Brigade, with two attached field batteries, was to spearhead the general advance of 1st Division by capturing the plateau from Cerny-en-Laonnois to Tilleul de Courtecon before daybreak on 14 September. Information regarding enemy defensive arrangements was scarce.[39] For the GOC 2nd Brigade, Jerry Murland notes: "a vigorous advance over potentially difficult ground without prior reconnaissance grated harshly on his professionalism." This concern was addressed by the immediate dispatch of two patrols. One of these subsequently reported that enemy piquets had been identified at a large 'Sugar Factory' complex NW of Troyon[40] and the adjacent Cerny – Chemin des Dames crossroads. Bulfin, following receipt of this intelligence, "ordered the Royal Sussex Regt. to support the K. R. Rifles" in an advance scheduled to start before dawn.[41]

The desperate uphill struggle that followed pitted high standards of British rifle marksmanship against fixed German machine-guns and superior artillery concentrations. The action fought "at close quarters, sometimes even hand-to-hand", rapidly degenerated into a hard-fought 'soldiers' battle'. "It was most difficult for divisional and brigade staffs, even battalion commanders, to follow all the vicissitudes of the combat and impossible to record them in detail", although available contemporary documentation[42] demonstrates that Bulfin did his best to make posterior sense of the confused fighting: "[O]rdered KRR and Sussex to push on at

37   Simpson, *The Evolution of Victory*, pp.17-19 and Edmonds, *Military Operations 1914 Vol. I*, Appendix 44.
38   See Edmonds, *Military Operations Vol. I*, pp.377-453 for the definitive account of what became officially known as 'The Battle of the Aisne'.
39   TNA CAB 45/140: Bulfin Diary 14 September 1914 and Paul Kendall, *Aisne 1914: The Dawn of Trench Warfare* (Stroud: The History Press, 2012), p.115.
40   The supposed sugar factory was actually a distillery. It provided 'commanding views of the Aisne valley and the Chemin des Dames'. See Kendall, *Aisne 1914*, p.113.
41   Murland, *Battle of the Aisne 1914*, p.121 and TNA WO 95/1267: 2nd Brigade after-action report, 2nd Brigade War Diary.
42   See 2nd Brigade after-action report in TNA WO 95/588: I Corps War Diary.

3 a.m. and seize ground N of TROYON".[43] 2nd KRRC led the way as it traversed the winding Vendresse – Troyon road through "drifting mist" toward the high ground; 2nd Royal Sussex, marching behind, would be in support. Bulfin departed shortly afterwards "with Northants in front, Loyal North Lancs following. Gunners following some way behind". Dawn was breaking when the leading company of 2nd KRRC clashed with a German outpost situated at a bend in the road. The battalion commander, his advance held up, ordered two companies to extend the firing line by deploying right and left of the road. This rough line was extended to approximately 800 yards when 2nd Royal Sussex took up positions on the right and left of the beleaguered 2nd KRRC. Bulfin's response was immediate and ultimately decisive: "Detached Northants to high ground S[outh] of TROYON, and moved round through VENDRESSE with Loyal North Lancs. Lot of shells and bullets flying about … Sent up two companies Loyal North Lancs and went on towards crossroads N of TROYON with remainder of battalion". From this vantage point he observed "Sussex on right of Sugar Factory KRR on left. [1] Guards [Brigade][44] started retiring on left, having got as far as CERNEY". Having ascertained the situation by direct observation, Bulfin ordered his only remaining reserve to carry the stalled line forward.[45] Private Frederick Bowell of 1st LNL recalled a steadfast Bulfin spurring his battalion on with the grim admonition: "That ridge has to be taken by nightfall – otherwise we shall be annihilated".[46] The latter subsequently wrote: "Big gap between Sussex and KRR. Sent in Loyal North Lancs … Captured 12 [field] guns on left of Sugar Factory, all personnel and teams having been knocked out by our machine-guns. Later captured 700 prisoners, but most killed by their own machine-gun fire". The victory proved short-lived: "All troops much mixed up. Germans made heavy counter-attack under heavy bombardment, recaptured Sugar Factory at 2 p.m. … Darkness came down with rain. Got tools from VENDRESSE and TROYON, and having pushed covering parties out, got men to dig in. Two heavy counter-attacks by Germans, but both beaten off. Our trenches ran along just under lip of crest, so we escaped full force of fire …"[47]

The costly fighting from 13-15 September put paid to GHQ's optimistic offensive strategy. A now wearied and somewhat depleted BEF, jammed tight between the Aisne and Chemins des Dames by an obstinate foe, hunkered down in embryonic trenches to engage in what was hoped to be interim static warfare. Bulfin's determined defence of captured ground against a series of enemy counter-attacks earned special praise from Major-General Lomax: "Genl. Bulfin commanding 2nd Brigade was a tower of strength – always cheerful and cool" and "From the 15th [September] the

43   Edmonds, *Military Operations 1914 Vol. I*, pp.395-96 and TNA CAB 45/140: Bulfin Diary 14 September 1914.
44   1st Guards Brigade came up on the left flank of 2nd Brigade between 8:00 and 9:00 a.m. See Edmonds, *Military Operations 1914 Vol. I*, p.398.
45   TNA CAB 45/140: Bulfin Diary 14 September 1914.
46   Bolwell, *With a Reservist in France*, p.48.
47   TNA CAB 45/140: Bulfin Diary 14 September 1914.

success of the Division in maintaining its ground is chiefly due to Brigadier-General Bulfin and his brigade ..."[48]

I Corps bore the brunt of numerous German counter-attacks from 15-19 September. 2nd Brigade, holding the line in one of the most contested sectors, readily adapted to the routines of trench warfare. An initial "poor attempt" to layout barbed wire obstacles was, in Bulfin's opinion, "better than nothing"; shallow fire trenches were deepened to 4 feet and various working parties instituted. Relief by 18th Brigade, 6th Division occurred on 19 September.[49] Brigadier-General John Charteris, Sir Douglas Haig's ADC and chief intelligence officer, subsequently claimed that "Bulfin was really almost peevish when he was told that his brigade was to be pulled out for a short rest and replied 'We never asked to be taken out – we can hang on here quite well'". Bulfin's true feelings were recorded in his campaign diary: "Cold and wet. Could not light fires. General Congreve VC [GOC 18th Brigade] came up with orders to relieve us tonight. Very glad as my splendid Brigade is worn out". 2nd Brigade's estimated casualties from 14 to 19 September amounted to 1,271 killed, wounded and missing.[50]

Bulfin's immediate superiors unexpectedly arrived the following morning to compliment the brigadier on the steadfastness and courage exhibited whilst conducting an enterprising offense and dogged defence: "General Lomax and Sir Douglas Haig came to visit us at 9:30. We were all very sleepy but Sir D said many nice things about my splendid Brigade".[51] A thoroughly impressed Haig, no doubt influenced by Lomax's effusive accolades, confided in his diary that evening:

> In spite of the wet, hunger & fatigue suffered, the troops seemed in excellent spirits. In fact I felt that a fine cheerful fighting spirit existed amongst the men: all I spoke to made light of their hardships and said 'Everything is all right Sir'. I attribute this splendid result to the fine soldierly qualities of the Brigadier (General Bulfin), who has been a tower of strength to the Divisional commander (Lomax) and myself during the retreat and subsequent fighting.[52]

2nd Brigade returned to the frontline on 25 September. Reinforcements consisting of 3 officers and 100 other ranks per battalion scarcely replaced previously

48   Haig Diary 14 September 1914, Field Marshal Sir Douglas Haig, drawn from 'The First World War Political, Social and Military Manuscript Sources: The Haig Papers from the National Library of Scotland (Brighton: Harvester Press Microfilm Publications LTD, 1987) and TNA WO 95/1267: Lomax cover letter for 2nd Brigade after-action report, 2nd Brigade War Diary.

49   TNA CAB 45/140: Bulfin Diary 15 and 19 September 1914 and TNA: WO 95/1267: 2nd Brigade War Diary.

50   John Charteris, At GHQ (London: Cassell, 1931), p.39 and TNA CAB 45/140: Bulfin Diary 19 September 1914.

51   TNA CAB 45/140: Bulfin Diary 20 September 1914.

52   Haig Diary, 20 September 1914.

sustained losses.[53] The lengthy tour, lasting through 15 October, of almost continuous trench work, active patrolling, fierce bombardments and several half-hearted German ripostes was highlighted by a successful raid on the Sugar Factory and the paternalistic bestowal of a "box of Three Castles Cigarettes" to 1st LNL for "bagging" a troublesome sniper.[54] It was during this time that Bulfin received a reply to an earlier enquiry about a device that would become a technological mainstay in the arsenal of the fast-developing 'new warfare': "About three weeks ago I wrote in asking for rifle grenades I had seen described in Army and Navy Gazette last year. GHQ promised to find out. Today two boxes turned up. I got about 50, gave half to the Loyal North Lancs and half to the Northants. Grenade is thrown out about 80 yards fired by a blank cartridge".[55] A close call was providentially avoided on 8 October when "the enemy suddenly opened [a] heavy bombardment in the sunken road on my headquarters, blew in my shelter, burning my bed valise, and smashing everything. Two clerks killed and several orderlies wounded. Fortunately I and Packenham [brigade major] were out going around the lines". Welcome decampment from the interminable Aisne impasse – "Orders received that we are to be relieved tomorrow by French 32nd Division. Thank God!" – was complete by the morning of 16 October.[56] 2nd Brigade entrained for Belgium the following day; the BEF was heading north.

Bulfin's capable handling of 2nd Brigade from the retreat to the Aisne deadlock identified him as one of the BEF's noteworthy infantry brigadiers. The esteem in which he and his command were held was freely acknowledged during a personal visit by Sir John French who "spoke to units and praised the Brigade" for its efforts.[57] Senior officers like French, Haig and Lomax, Gardner has observed, "showed a clear preference for individuals who displayed personal bravery under fire and a stoic acceptance of losses suffered by their formations … No British infantry commander in 1914 exhibited these qualities to a greater extent than Edward Bulfin". Combined losses killed, wounded and missing sustained by 2nd Brigade opposite Cerny-en-Laonnois, according to J.P. Harris, amounted to 1,581 or about one quarter of its fighting strength.[58]

53   TNA CAB 45/140: Bulfin Diary 20 September 1914.
54   Ibid, 26 and 10 October 1914.
55   Ibid, 29 September 1914 and John Terraine, *White Heat: The New Warfare 1914-18* (London: Sidgwick & Jackson, 1982), p.397. The rifle grenades in question were of the Hale's 1908 pattern. See TNA: WO 95/1270: 1st LNL War Diary entry (14 October 1914) for related commentary and illustrations.
56   TNA CAB 45/140: Bulfin Diary 14 October 1914.
57   Ibid, 22 September 1914. Additional praise was received before Bulfin's departure for Flanders: '10th October. Both General Haig and Field Marshal French sent messages saying how well the Brigade had done'.
58   Gardner, *Trial by Fire*, p.96 and J.P.Harris, *Douglas Haig and the First World War* (Cambridge: Cambridge University Press, 2008), p.91.

Fortitude at Ypres

The decision to transport – infantry by rail, cavalry by road – the BEF to French Flanders and Belgium proper had its immediate strategic roots in the frustrating Aisne stalemate and consequent effort by Allied and German armies to re-establish the war of manoeuvre by exploiting open flanks to the northeast during the so-called 'Race to the Sea'.[59] Subsequent protracted fighting around Ypres, where British, French and Belgian forces stood their ground against a succession of massive enemy onslaughts designed to breakthrough the Allied line and capture the vital channel ports, provided Brigadier-General Bulfin with fresh opportunities to demonstrate his previously lauded martial capabilities in circumstances of the utmost peril.

On 20 October, Haig's I Corps began to take up positions (Zonnebeke to Bixschoote) on the far left of a BEF front stretching approximately 36-miles, from La Bassée to the Yser Canal, in preparation for a general offensive aimed at exploiting erroneously perceived German weakness north of the Menin Road. Bulfin's brigade was placed in Corps reserve the following day: "Ordered to move on YPRES and halt to west of [YSER] canal. Halted all day. At 4 p.m. ordered to send on battalion to PILKEM (sent Northamptons at 5 p.m.). Headquarters and remainder of Brigade to BOESINGHE. Started at 5:30, roads very crowded. Loyal North Lancs on outpost round BOESINGHE".[60] Efforts to push ahead on a two (IV and I) corps front during 20-21 October came to a halt when confronted by the simultaneous advance by Duke Albrecht of Württemburg's *Fourth Army*. I Corps' part in the attack ended with a short advance by Lomax's 1st Division on to the general line Steenstraat – Koekuit – 1.24 miles east of Langemarck after which 1st Guards Brigade and 3rd Brigade entrenched for the evening. On the right, Monro's 2nd Division extended the Corps frontage SE to Zonnebeke station where it joined with the left of IV Corps. French, disillusioned by what appeared to be an enemy preponderance in men and guns, cancelled further offensive operations and ordered the BEF to adopt a defensive posture and dig-in.[61]

The now stationary I Corps preserved its prolonged front against repeated infantry assaults throughout 22 October.[62] Retiring French Territorials, survivors of a failed morning attack in the direction of Houthulst Forest, passed through 1st Division's frontline before dusk.[63] On their heels four battalions of *45th Reserve Division*, right-hand division of *XXIII Reserve Corps*,[64] pressed forward to storm

59   Holmes, *Army Battlefield Guide*, p.97.
60   TNA CAB 45/140: Bulfin Diary 22 October 1914.
61   Ian Beckett, *Ypres: The First Battle, 1914* (London: Pearson, 2006), pp.95-96.
62   These attacks were part of a large-scale general offensive (20-24 October) from La Bassée to Lombartzyde on the Belgian coast subsequently known in Germany as the *Kindermord bei Ypern*. See Beckett, *Ypres*, pp.98-101.
63   Ibid, pp.101-03
64   *XXIII Reserve Corps* (*45th Reserve Division* and *46th Reserve Division*) was one of six new army corps raised by the German Army following the outbreak of the war. Its general manpower composition consisted of a combination of older reservists, young

Haig's left flank, assisted by approaching darkness and a rising autumn mist.[65] This and other simultaneous assaults against I Corps' incipient defensive positions, the latest phase of persevering offensive operations by *Fourth Army* on a three (*XXIII*, *XXVI* and *XXVII*) corps front, were bloodily repulsed by rifle and machine-gun fire. One British officer observed German troops "with their arms and legs off trying to crawl away; others, who could not move gasping out their last moments with the cold night wind biting into their broken bodies and the lurid red glare of a farmhouse showing up some clumps of grey devils killed by the men on my left further down".[66] The grisly fiasco was partially compensated for by a small but significant breach of the British line. Enterprising companies of German infantry from *45th Reserve Division*, probing through the hazy gloom despite a punishing crossfire, managed to infiltrate gaps in a series of unconnected trenches defended by 1st Camerons (1st Guards Brigade) and seize the crossroads hamlet of Kortekeer.[67] Enemy occupation of this tiny rural community and its prominent 'cabaret' or wayside inn, situated "about a mile and a half north of Pilkem, where the road from that place leading to Houthulst Forest crosses the Bixschoote – Langemarck thoroughfare", created a dangerous rent in the centre of 1st Division's left flank. At 9:00 p.m. Haig, anxious to maintain the integrity of his thinly-held 4-mile frontage, "placed the operations for the recovery of the line in the hands of Br.-General Bulfin ... with orders to attack at dawn".[68]

Bulfin, his Brigade HQ still situated west of the Yser Canal at Boesinghe, spent most of 22 October reconnoitring the surrounding area. Orders "to send battalion to PILKEM as heavy attack on" were received after nightfall and 2nd KRRC promptly dispatched to support Guards Brigade. At 11:00 p.m. Haig's counter-attack order arrived:

> [R]eceived orders to move with the Loyal North Lancs and Sussex to PILKEM to not arrive there later than 5 a.m. The Cameron Highlanders have been driven from their trenches and I was to retake the trenches and capture the trenches [sic] round the inn at PILKEM [Kortekeer] crossroads. The [1st] Queens[69] were also placed under

men not conscripted during peacetime and wartime volunteers. See Intelligence Section of the General Staff, American Expeditionary Forces, *Histories of Two Hundred and Fifty-One Divisions of the German Army Which Participated in the War 1914-1918* (London: London Stamp Exchange, 1989 reprint of 1920 edition), pp.464-67, 469-72.

65   Anthony Farrar-Hockley, *Death of an Army* (New York: William Morrow & Co., 1967), pp.94-95 and Beckett, *Ypres*, pp.102-03.

66   Captain H. Dillon, 2nd Oxford & Buckinghamshire Light Infantry, quoted in Keith Simpson, *The Old Contemptibles: A Photographic History of the British Expeditionary Force August-December 1914* (London: Allen & Unwin, 1981), pp.94-96.

67   Edmonds, *Military Operations 1914 Vol. II*, pp.180-81.

68   Beatrix Brice, *The Battle Book of Ypres* (Stevenage: Spa Books 1987 reprint of 1927 edition), p.114 and Edmonds, *Military Operations 1914 Vol. II*, pp.181-82.

69   Detached from 3rd Brigade reserve.

my command and another [2nd South Staffordshire][70] was being sent up to assist. All guns with 1st and 2nd brigades are placed under my command and I was to be in command of the whole operation.[71]

A total of six battalions from three different units/formations were made available by Haig for the counter-thrust. Three (2nd KRRC, 1st Northamptons and 1st Queens) were positioned before sunrise to prevent the enemy from exploiting the Kortekeer inroad.[72] Exultant German infantrymen, Captain Needham recalled, could be heard "shouting, cheering and singing in front of us, which we gathered was the merry Hun disporting himself after his victory of the afternoon".[73] Bulfin's remaining three battalions (1st LNL, 2nd Royal Sussex and 2nd South Staffordshire) marched from Pilkem toward the ruptured front: "Loyal North Lancs under Major Carter and Sussex moved off at midnight. I met commanding officers at 4 a.m. at estaminet. S. Staffords arrived at 4 a.m. KRR and Northants to remain in trenches".[74]

The counter-attack scheme was, in Anthony Farrar-Hockley's words, prepared "deliberately but methodically" – diversion on the right; primary effort on the left: "Queens to make a converging attack on inn, timed by movement of Loyal North Lancs. S. Staffords in reserve midway between Queen's and Loyal North Lancs. North Lancs to get in touch with KRR, latter with Guards".[75] Bulfin, displaying a remarkably astute eye for terrain, discerned that his left battalion could advance "more or less under cover" to within 150 yards of the enemy's rudimentary trenches: "Approach of Loyal North Lancs concealed from inn by wood. Queen's in full view go right for inn. Loyal North Lancs to leave inn on right and go in with bayonets in works N and NW of inn. All guns to concentrate on inn and works west and north of inn. Units got into position by noon".[76] Thus 1st Queens, attacking across 1,000 yards of open country in the direction Kortekeer Cabaret, would draw attention away from 1st LNL's left-hand assault over the same kind of enclosed and undulating landscape that had impeded I Corps' progress during the foiled offensive of 20-21 October.[77]

All went according to plan: "Units got into position by noon. Heavy fire kept up. Germans in much greater strength than expected. Final advance delivered at 4 p.m. [;] very good timing, Queens and Loyal North Lancs almost simultaneous, latter carried farm buildings".[78] It was, Michael Flynn asserts, a prime example of seizure

70   Detached from 2nd Division reserve.
71   TNA CAB 45/140: Bulfin Diary 23 October 1914.
72   Edmonds, *Military Operations 1914 Vol. II*, pp.184-85.
73   Needham, 'Cabaret of Death! Shelled by Friend and Foe' in Hammerton (ed), *'The Great War ... I Was There!'Vol.1*, p.205.
74   TNA CAB 45/140: Bulfin Diary 23 October 1914.
75   Farrar-Hockley, *Death of an Army*, p.101 and TNA CAB 45/140: Bulfin Diary 23 October 1914.
76   Edmonds, *Military Operations 1914 Vol. II*, p.185 and TNA CAB 45/140: Bulfin Diary 23 October 1914.
77   Beckett, *Ypres*, p.93.
78   TNA CAB 45/140: Bulfin Diary 23 October 1914

of the initiative by an aggressive tactical defence. Exceptional leadership skills, advantageous terrain and the flexible tactics of the British Regular infantry combined to sweep the enemy from the field at bayonet point.[79] The attackers, undeterred by their general ignorance of the area, made good progress through an early morning mist supported by 30 guns. Private Bowell recollected: "We went up in short rushes, and a word of praise is due to the men who took part in it. I never even on the barrack square or drill-ground saw a better advance: the men went up absolutely in line, each man keeping his correct distance …"[80] 1st LNL, assisted by two companies of 2nd South Staffordshire, advanced to within a few hundred yards of the hostile trenches after negotiating an insubstantial barbed wire obstacle erected the previous evening. The *Official History* concisely conveys what happened next: "[S]o well was the movement timed that the whole front of the attack arrived almost simultaneously … Many of the enemy were already making off when the North Lancashire charged, but the sudden advance appears to have taken the others by surprise; and attention being for the moment taken off the Queen's, they were also able – the time being about noon – to cover the last hundred yards of open ground with astonishingly little loss". Following this, a LNL subaltern observed the "glorious sight of masses of grey-coated men standing up to surrender …"[81] Taking advantage of prevailing enemy demoralization and confusion, an extemporised advance by 1st Queens, 1st Camerons and 2nd KRRC reclaimed the lost Cameron trenches beyond.[82]

Kortekeer and its surroundings presented a somewhat incongruous scene in the immediate aftermath of the startlingly successful counter-attack. Buildings and trenches were hastily prepared for defence, whilst hilarity rooted in instinctive relief and sporadic souvenir hunting prevailed amongst disparate groups of assault infantry and 54 liberated Cameron prisoners "shaking hands and banging everyone on the back. Like a party everyone was laughing and talking. Some of the men were stripping badges off the Jerries. Others were smoking Jerry cigars …"[83] All around lay the tell-tale detritus – numerous *Feldgrau*-clad corpses, distinctive cloth-covered *Pickelhauben*, 'pork pie' soft caps, Mauser rifles with fixed 'quillback' bayonets, weighty leather equipment belts and peculiar calfskin field packs – of the German rout. Their total losses amounted to 490 killed and 791 captured, including 352 unwounded, many of which, Bulfin observed, "were mere boys".[84] Losses sustained by 2nd Brigade's component battalions amounted to 379 killed, wounded and missing.[85] The

79   Major Michael T. Flynn, 'Climax or Conclusion: Culmination in the Defence' (Fort Leavenworth, Kansas: School of Advanced Studies, 1993), pp.23-27 and Spencer Jones, *From Boer War to World War: Tactical Reform of the British Army, 1902-1914* (Norman, Oklahoma: University of Oklahoma Press, 2012), pp.73-88.

80   Bolwell, *With a Reservist in France*, p.75.

81   Lieutenant J.G.W. Hyndson 1st LNL quoted in Farrar-Hockley, *Death of an Army*, p.102.

82   Edmonds, *Military Operations 1914 Vol. II*, pp.185-86.

83   Hyndson quoted in Farrar-Hockley, *Death of an Army*, p.103.

84   Ibid, p.103 and TNA CAB 45/140: Bulfin Diary 23 October 1914.

85   This figure is based on estimates for the period 'Night of Oct. 22' and 'October 23'

latter were "nearly all killed but as the identity discs were not forthcoming they were shown as missing".[86]

Bulfin "sent a special order to the Brigade praising their good work done and especially the Loyal North Lancs".[87] Official approbation had previously been received from a satisfied Lomax: "Heartfelt congratulations on your skilfully conducted attack and on the use you made of 1st Queens". I Corps' message was equally effusive: "General Haig wire begins please congratulate Genl. Bulfin & all the troops concerned in the capture of the INN on the determination and pluck they have shown. Last night was indeed an anxious time for us all & I fully realise how hard everyone has worked to attain success". Ubiquitous gentleman chauffer Frederic Coleman subsequently related, in a strikingly triumphalist synopsis of events, the euphoria engendered by the Kortekeer counter-attack: "At Haig's headquarters Bulfin's 2nd Brigade success of the day previous was declared to have been splendid. Six-hundred German prisoners, a field strewn with 1,500 German dead,[88] and relief of the Cameronians [sic] from an isolated position were among the fruits of the victory". French, notwithstanding anxieties and innumerable distractions induced by the on-going Flanders battle, also took time to convey brief but sincere felicitations for the local success north of Ypres: "I congratulate General BULFIN and troops engaged in counter-attack. This is the third time I have had occasion to congratulate General BULFIN".[89]

Bulfin's elimination of the troublesome 'Kortekeer Salient' would have important short and long-term consequences for the remainder of what officially became known as the 'Battles of Ypres 1914'. The unsettling reverse was initially reported as an Allied breakthrough and "it is significant", according to Farrar-Hockley, "that there was neither a heavy bombardment of the Bixschoote – Langemarck line nor a counter-attack during the remainder of the day or the following night. A few

recorded in Bulfin's diary. Losses sustained by 1st Queens and 2nd South Staffordshire were not included in the total. 2nd Brigade returns (TNA WO 95/1267: 2nd Brigade War Diary) record a total of 328 killed, wounded and missing in the immediate aftermath of the Kortekeer counter-attack. Farrar-Hockley (p.103) estimates losses at 47 killed and 184 wounded, 'most of whom were hit during the approach', although it is difficult to ascertain what source these reduced figures originate from. The relevant volume of official history is silent on the subject.

86   TNA CAB 45/140: Bulfin Diary 23 October 1914.
87   Ibid 24 October 1914. See Bowell, *With a Reservist in France*, pp.83-84 for the congratulatory message text.
88   This exaggerated estimate of German losses appears to have been based on early reports: See TNA CAB 45/140: Bulfin Diary 23 October 1914 and Bowell, *With a Reservist in France*, p.83.
89   See sequence of 'C2123 Messages & Signal' forms in TNA WO 95/167: 2nd Brigade War Diary and Coleman, *From Mons to Ypres with French*, p.220. Haig, who never forgot the fighting around Kortekeer, remarked in his diary on the opening day of Third Ypres: 'Further to the west, our troops had established themselves beyond the Steenbeek and the French had taken Bixschoote and the Cabaret Kortekeer (which was so frequently attacked in October and November 1914)'. Haig Diary, 31 July 1917.

German patrols appeared, which were driven off, and it was evident that the enemy was uncertain as to what was happening".[90] Further offensives efforts by *Fourth Army* were, for the moment, shelved until the general situation became known with some degree of certainty. As the German official account of First Ypres dolefully observed: "With the failure ... to gain a decisive victory between Bixschoote and Langemarck on the 22nd and 23rd of October the fate of the XXVI and XXVII reserve corps [which attacked the British 2nd and 7th divisions respectively] was also settled. For the time being any further thought of a breakthrough was out of the question".[91]

For the British, the decidedly fruitful counter-attack was also a harbinger of the subsequent necessity to shift, irrespective of formal orders of battle attachments, improvised amalgams of infantry, cavalry, artillery and engineer units to critical spots in the line. "This ad hoc plugging of gaps with whatever troops were available", Ian Beckett has written, "was to become known as 'puttying up' or less prosaically to the French, *'boucher le trou'*".[92] Haig, by acute necessity, became the chief exponent of this novel 'Fire Brigade' defensive approach; Bulfin, the competent and cool-headed brigadier, its battle-proven practitioner.

An apparent "danger from every point of view" and offering no specific tactical advantage, the salient encompassing Kortekeer and its environs was abandoned to the enemy on 24 October. "Regrettably, no force was available to exploit the success", Farrar-Hockley notes, "but Brigadier-General Bulfin can hardly be blamed for that; he had simply been told to reclaim the Camerons' lost position and could not have expected such a triumph".[93] The French relieved I Corps that same day as a necessary preliminary to a projected attack in the direction of Passchendaele. 2nd Brigade's relief proved to be a long and laborious process: "French regiment arrived at 4 p.m. to relieve us ... Inn set on fire and burnt all night. After dark began relief by French, very slow work. Got last unit out by 11 p.m. and ordered to remain in reserve behind French till 4 a.m. ... All in [Ypres] billets by 8 a.m.". Bulfin was disturbed before he could turn in for well-earned rest: "Ordered to Divisional headquarters at 10. As I had no sleep for three nights, felt very stupid. Informed I was to be promoted Major-General tomorrow. Received cigarettes and matches from Sir D. Haig, wrote and thanked him. Sent cigarettes to Sussex on outpost."[94] 1st Division was now concentrated in corps reserve about Zillebeke whilst 2nd Division shifted right in order to take over the left of IV Corps' fragile line north of the Menin Road – "not a moment too soon", for the latter's component 7th Division "was stretched wafer-thin" after days of intense bombardment. On its left flank an enemy incursion into Polygon Wood was expelled by a timely counter-attack,[95] while to the right a

---

90   Otto Schwink, *Ypres 1914: An Official Account Published by Order of the German General Staff* (London: Constable & Co., 1919), p.39 and Farrar-Hockley, *Death of an Army*, p.104.

91   German official account (Schwink) quoted with bracketed annotation in Edmonds, *Military Operations 1914 Vol. II*, p.191.

92   Beckett, *Ypres*, p.152 and Edmonds, *Military Operations 1914 Vol. II*, p.279.

93   Brice, *The Battle Book of Ypres*, p.117 and Farrar-Hockley, *Death of an Army*, p.103.

94   TNA CAB 45/140: Bulfin Diary 24 and 25 October 1914.

95   Launched by 5th Brigade, 2nd Division.

ferocious assault on a key crossroad SE of Gheluvelt was contained with crippling losses. "By now 7th Division had lost 45% of its officers and 37% of its men."[96]

The bitter fighting around Ypres maintained its previously established course of thrust and counter-thrust with little or no advantage to either side throughout 25-28 October. Bulfin, retaining a brigadier's responsibilities despite the recent field promotion, remained with his command in corps reserve in the vicinity of the Menin Road at Hooge and, later, farther east at Veldhoek during this uncertain period. Anticipation of 2nd Brigade's projected role resulted in the immediate dispatch of "all mounted officers to reconnoiter roads south and north in case we are ordered to move at night".[97]

The storm broke on the 29th when a massed morning assault along the axis of the Menin Road obtained a brief breakthrough where the inner flanks of 1st Division and 7th Division conjoined, before it was hurled back by fierce counter-attacks.[98] This latest enemy drive was only the prelude to a mammoth general offensive from Bixschoote to Frelinghien spearheaded by *Armee Gruppe Fabeck*, a newly-interpolated shock formation of six divisions supported by 746 guns. Its principal task was to shatter the tenuous Allied defences east and south-east of Ypres once and for all.[99] The impending onrush would be confronted north and south of the Menin artery by a thoroughly reorganised I Corps on an extended frontage of approximately seven miles. All three of its component (7th, 1st and 2nd) divisions were in the line by 27 October. Haig, Gardner has observed, "nonetheless retained Bulfin's 2nd Brigade as a corps reserve, in addition to reserves held by each division". He was thus "relatively well-prepared to face the determined enemy attacks that commenced early on 29 October".[100] The deadliest phase of the Flanders campaign had begun. Clinging to discontinuous sections of primitive trenches, the small – by continental standards – British Expeditionary Force lacked sufficient ammunition for supporting field guns and was desperately short of trained reserves to replace skyrocketing casualties. Overwhelming German numerical superiority and crushing predominance in heavy and medium artillery would be primarily offset by lethally accurate rifle and machine-gun fire in an unceasing battle of attrition that imposed immense strains on the defenders' command and control infrastructure.

'Puttying up' proved an expedient measure during 29-30 October, as units of the various divisional reserves and two battalions (1st LNL and 2nd KRRC) from Bulfin's corps reserve were rushed forward to a variety of danger spots along the buckling front. Haig, troubled by enemy gains opposite his right flank in the vicinity of Zandvoorde – Hollebeke and the partial dissipation of his principal reserve, ordered three weak battalions (2nd Grenadier Guards, 1st Irish Guards and 2nd Oxfordshire

96   Holmes, *Army Battlefield Guide*, p.102.
97   TNA CAB 45/140: Bulfin Diary 27 October 1914.
98   The battle-weary 7th Division was placed under Haig's command on 27 October.
99   See Edmonds, *Military Operations 1914 Vol. II*, pp.259-60, 262-77.
100   Gardner, *Trial by Fire*, p.212.

& Buckinghamshire Light Infantry) under Brigadier-General Lord Cavan detached from 2nd Division and one (2nd Gordon Highlanders) from 7th Division to reinforce Bulfin's brigade on the evening of the 30th.[101] This reconstituted body of understrength units, together with 2nd Royal Sussex and 1st Northamptonshire, would henceforth be known as 'Bulfin Force'. Haig's plan was to commit this reformed reserve to a joint counter-attack with French General Moussy's detachment of five battalions at 6:30 a.m. on the 31st. Bulfin professed uneasiness about I Corps' plight, the forthcoming riposte and consequent absence of an available corps reserve as the second day of fighting drew to a close: "Found cavalry had retired early this morning leaving huge gaps which the Germans could have marched through. My men working like bees [;] went round first line (banks along margins of woods) with support trenches about 400 yards behind. Heavy shelling all day, a few casualties. Made a big dugout for self and staff. Don't feel a bit happy, no sort of reserve".[102]

The supreme crisis arose on 31 October when a chance enemy shell killed, wounded or temporarily incapacitated the combined headquarters staffs of 1st Division and 2nd Division in Hooge Chateau at the height of the German offensive.[103] I Corps HQ, its principal conduit to and from the various brigade HQs thus broken, remained more or less out of touch as on the spot mid-level commanders like Brigadier-General Charles FitzClarence V.C. (GOC 1st Guards Brigade)[104] and the newly-appointed Major-General Bulfin demonstrated enterprise, determination and flexibility to forestall defeat against fearful odds. The former's decisive counter-stroke at Gheluvelt remains one of the most celebrated episodes of the First Battle of Ypres; however, the latter's exploits in the defence of I Corps' endangered right flank, during which an audacious psychological ruse was employed to turn the tide of battle, are largely forgotten today.

Bulfin was awaiting the start of the provisional counter-attack at his makeshift headquarters within the mixed beech, oak and pine cover of Shrewsbury Forest when *Gruppe Fabeck's* massive artillery concentrations heralded a renewal of the offensive opposite the front Messines to Gheluvelt: "At about 6 a.m. a tremendous bombardment by the Germans began. The 7th Division on the left got it badly as they were on the ridge. My troops got it less being in low ground and out of sight".[105]

101 See TNA WO 95/588: 'Operation Order No. 28', 30 October 1914, I Corps War Diary and Edmonds, *Military Operations 1914 Vol. II*, pp.289 fn. 4, 293-94.
102 TNA CAB 45/140: Bulfin Diary 30 October 1914.
103 I Corps directed Bulfin to succeed the mortality wounded Lomax as GOC 1st Division. The former's absence near Hollebeke led to the appointment of Landon (GOC 3rd Brigade) in his place. See Edmonds, *Military Operations 1914 Vol. II*, p.324 and Beckett, *Ypres*, pp.173-74.
104 FitzClarence assumed command of 1st Brigade in September 1914. For full details of FitzClarence's career, see Spencer Jones's chapter elsewhere in this volume.
105 TNA CAB 45/140: Bulfin Diary 31 October 1914 and Patrick Butler, *A Galloper at Ypres* (London: Fisher & Unwin, 1920), p.159. Butler, the son of Bulfin's former South Africa chief Lieutenant-General Sir William Butler, noted the functional simplicity of the 'Bulfin Force' woodland HQ: 'I found some French and British orderlies in the wood,

Pre-empted by one-half hour, the forlorn Allied riposte had to be aborted under the intense shellfire. Masses of infantry from *XV Corps* and *II Bavarian Corps*, deployed "at first in waves and then in groups which gradually coalesced", began to advance at 12:25 p.m.[106] The shelling, Bulfin observed, "increased in intensity" at 1:00 p.m.: "Several shells a minute broke all along the line and men going down everywhere. No cover. Simply Hell". Bulfin Force maintained a solid front regardless of this galling enfilade fire from Zandvoorde Ridge until the arrival of ominous news from the left: "At 2:00 p.m. Brigade Major of 22nd Brigade dashed into my headquarters and told me the Germans had broken through, the 7th Division was retiring.[107] I saw them going from where I stood, also the Germans in long lines coming over the top of the ridge held by the 7th Division".[108] Unaware that a counter-attack had stabilised the situation on his immediate left, Bulfin assembled the commanding officers of 1st Northamptonshire, 2nd Royal Sussex and 2nd Gordon Highlanders to discuss arrangements for a conforming withdrawal: the looming threat of being outflanked and overwhelmed from the rear by closing bodies of enemy infantry brought about an instant change of plan: "I ordered the Northamptons to retire and the Sussex to cover the retirement. The Northamptons got about 700 yards back on to a road to swing their right round, pivoting on their left so as to keep touch with Cavan's brigade now on the left (as we were retiring). The Sussex to follow and come up on the outer flank of the Northamptons and from a line parallel to the road". The jeopardised left was thus curved back to the rear to form a refused flank.[109]

The stopgap manoeuvre commenced moments before Bulfin came within range of hostile small arms: "As I left my headquarters, Germans opened rifle and machine-gun fire on myself and my staff. My orderly carrying my coat was killed. I asked Colonel Jeudwine[110] to try and get reinforcements from GHQ and to tell them how hard we were being pressed. Streams of Germans in unending numbers kept pouring over the ridge. As far as I could see to the north, there were endless glinting of spikes of German helmets".[111] Bulfin Force's precipitate re-

holding officers' horses, and on reaching them I discovered that they were outside the Brigade Headquarters, which consisted of a large dugout or 'funk-hole'. In it were about seven officers, among them General Bulfin'. He also paid tribute to Bulfin's remarkable career progression: 'It was dramatic meeting him in this way. Years before, in 1899, just prior to the outbreak of the South African War, my father had chosen him, then a young regimental officer, to accompany him to the Cape as his Military Secretary. This was General Bulfin's chance, and from that moment he had never looked back'.

106 Edmonds, *Military Operations 1914 Vol. II*, p.334.
107 This unwelcome news was, according to the *Official History* (p.335), delivered by Lieutenant-Colonel H.F. de Montgomery (GSO 1 7th Division). I have, as almost all minor contradictions of this sort stem from slightly differing accounts of the Ypres fighting, generally adhered to Bulfin's typescript diary as the more immediate source.
108 TNA CAB 45/140: Bulfin Diary 31 October 1914.
109 Ibid and Edmonds, *Military Operations 1914 Vol. II*, p.335.
110 Lieutenant-Colonel Hugh Jeudwine (GSO 1 I Corps) had ridden forward to obtain information before proceeding to Lord Cavan's HQ.
111 TNA CAB 45/140: Bulfin Diary 31 October 1914.

deployment exposed the right of 22nd Brigade thus compelling a corresponding general retirement into the murky depths of Shrewsbury Forest, where the outwardly impassive Bulfin personally reorganised leaderless "groups of men whose company organisations had disappeared".[112] Circumstances were deemed serious enough for Major-General Thompson Capper (GOC 7th Division) to issue a warning order for a general withdrawal to the line Klein Zillebeke – Frezenberg. Captain Patrick Butler (Capper's ADC) recalled the endemic chaos with the antebellum conscription debate in mind: "I shall never forget the chill the sight gave me. It seemed at last our resisting power had been shattered; at last numbers had prevailed; at last nemesis had overtaken Great Britain for her sloth and unpreparedness; at last apathy of so many of her sons had met with their deserts. But oh! It did seem sad that *we* should have to suffer, and to admit defeat now, after our great stand!"[113] The situation, the *Official History* observed sans the pensive histrionics, appeared desperate "but the British commanders did not despair, and it soon became evident that the enemy's progress was slowing. The German units had been broken up by the advance under fire, and were obviously without much guidance from officers, most of whom had fallen".[114] Bulfin, sensing this weakness, began making arrangements for a counter-attack in a final attempt to save the crumbling front with whatever reinforcements could be assembled:

'Jeudwine rode back, coming along between our lines and the Germans, his hat and clothing hit in several places. He had given all my messages to Cavan and had got some reinforcements. Two dismounted squadrons of the 1st Royals[115] came up at 4 p.m. and I put them on the left of the Sussex. The wood here was pretty thick and the enemy could not see them coming up. The 26th Field Company R.E.[116] came up ... I put them in on the left of the Northamptons where there was a gap. I had sent Acland-Troyte,[117] my staff captain, back to ZILLIBEKE with the remainder of the Gordon Highlanders and all servants and cooks to prepare a second line. Jeudwine had found these and ordered them up to me; they arrived around 4:45 p.m.'[118]

The diverse scratch force was now in position. Bulfin issued the following terse order: "Big reinforcements are coming up behind you. When you hear the cheering, give the Germans a 'hellish minute' rapid rifle fire. Then boost them out, for the position on the other side of the road is better than this".[119] Tense, mud-covered

112   Beckett, *Ypres*, p.187 and Farrar-Hockley, *Death of an Army*, p.163.
113   Butler, *A Galloper at Ypres*, p.160.
114   Edmonds, *Military Operations 1914 Vol. II*, p.336.
115   1st Royal Dragoons detached from 3rd Cavalry Division.
116   One of 1st Division's two component Royal Engineer field companies.
117   Sir Gilbert Acland-Troyte (1876-1964).
118   TNA CAB 45/140: Bulfin Diary 31 October 1914.
119   Ibid, 'Information about the Counter-attack of the Second Infantry Brigade, 1st Division, British Expeditionary Force, at First Battle of Ypres on 31 October 1914, supplied by General E.S. Bulfin, KCB CVO – in 1914 Brigadier-General Commanding

men, many in torn and tattered uniforms, anxiously cocked their ears in anticipation of expected reinforcements; a paltry force of 84 men from 2nd Gordon Highlanders was all that was readily available. Bulfin shrewdly turned this parlous state of affairs to his advantage: "I told the Gordons to form line and advance through the wood cheering like mad. I ordered the first line to open a one minute rapid fire when they heard the cheering and told all first line to go for the Germans when the cheering proclaimed the arrival of reinforcements". The clever deception had the synchronal effect of fortifying the harried defenders whilst reducing the attackers to a state of alarm and confusion. Official historian James Edmonds later described the scene with vivid prose: "On the appointed signal being made, Captain Stansfield and his handful of Gordon Highlanders advanced, cheering loudly. The hellish minute broke out, a crescendo of rapid rifle fire – each man doing about eighteen rounds to the minute, for musketry as well as entrenching had been the great feature in the training of the 2nd Brigade.[120] Then, as the Gordons charged, to General Bulfin's surprise, every man in his exhausted, thin firing line sprang to his feet and went for the Germans with the bayonet".[121]

Charging down rides and plunging through thickets, the frenzied aggregate of half and quarter-reduced battalions, cavalry on foot and assorted ancillary details surged through the smoke-enmeshed forest to come to grips with their astonished foe: "No prisoners were taken but hundreds of Germans were lying bayonetted all through the wood or shot by our people … We had almost got back to our old line, but the Northamptons did not back up the Sussex, who got driven back but within 70 yards of their old line".[122] On the left, sorely-tried skeleton units of 7th Division "caught the spirit" and joined the advance. Almost all of the lost ground was back in British hands by 5:30 p.m. The headlong counter-attack was not, Farrar-Hockley observed, "one single glorious sweep; after the first 500 yards there were numbers of strongpoints, mostly in copses and farmhouses, to destroy".[123] Its singular success was, C.T. Atkinson surmised, "in part due to the Germans expecting it and believing that here at last the British were bringing into action their long and carefully concealed reserves".[124] The recaptured territory was in itself relatively unimportant except as a defensible "buffer zone" beneath the ridge, "but the drubbing given the Germans was exceptionally valuable" from a morale standpoint and ensured the enemy was largely

2nd Infantry Brigade'. This document, a preliminary chapter section draft compiled by Edmonds, also contains marginalia commentary provided by Bulfin.

120   This fusillade was yet another deadly application of the famous 'Mad Minute' of 15 aimed shots in 60 seconds, although the pre-determined rate of fire was often exceeded by the superlatively trained British Regulars. See Jones, *From Boer War to World War*, pp.9, 92-101

121   TNA CAB 45/140: 'Information about the Counter-attack of the Second Infantry Brigade … on 31st October'.

122   TNA CAB 45/140: Bulfin Diary 31 October 1914.

123   Farrar-Hockley, *Death of an Army*, pp.164-65

124   C.T. Atkinson, *The Seventh Division 1914-1918* (Uckfield: Naval & Military Press reprint of 1927 edition), p.98.

quiescent opposite the sealed right flank.[125] An autumnal afterlight cast long shadows on a ghastly wilderness carpeted with German bodies, all part of the burgeoning human cost of an enduring northern campaign collectively characterised by Holger Herwig as a military debacle.[126] Private David Shand of 2nd Gordon Highlanders remembered: "In the twilight we could see hundreds of dead Germans lying in front of us. Another man and I volunteered to go and collect some water bottles. I noticed my comrade collecting souvenirs. He asked me to help turn over a dead German officer who was lying face down on the ground. He was an enormous man. In turning the corpse over I put my hand where his stomach should have been. The sight made me sick. His mouth was wide open and he had a horrible expression on his face".[127]

The reclaimed frontage was, in conformity with the restored situation further north at Gheluvelt, realigned with some difficulty after dark. Losses had been severe for battalions not up to full strength prior to entrainment for Flanders. 2nd Royal Sussex alone suffered 405 killed, wounded and missing during 30-31 October and most units were down to quarter strength by the evening of the 31st.[128] It was against this precarious backdrop of indeterminate positions and threadbare orders of battle that Haig, misled by the appreciable success of Bulfin Force, ordered the attack resumed the next day. A disconcerted Bulfin – "[W]e were only clinging to the ground by our eyelids" – considered the order "mad" given that his men "were lying a yard apart with no supports or reserves, and if we lost, the whole line was gone". Determined to express these sombre tidings in the most direct manner possible, Bulfin galloped to I Corps HQ where he found Haig's chief of staff "Johnny Gough in bed in the chateau. I told him he must cancel the order, that if we were able to hold our line tomorrow it was as much as we could do, but to advance was madness and we would lose all the ground and YPRES into the bargain. He said all right, the order was cancelled, and I left falling off to sleep at 1:30 a.m." [129] Rest was a luxury the peripatetic Bulfin had to forgo: "I then went on to Brigadier-General Fanshawe, the gunner,[130] and got him to give me two howitzers which I put to and hid out some

---

125   Farrar-Hockley, *Death of an Army*, p.165.

126   Holger Herwig, *The First World War: Germany and Austria-Hungary, 1914-1918* (London: Arnold, 1997), p.116. The author of this chapter is, given the recent spate of Central Powers apologist campaign and operations literature, looking forward with anticipation to a coincident revisionist account of superior military effectiveness during the First Battle of Ypres.

127   Gordon Reid (ed), *Poor Bloody Murder: Personal Memoirs of the First World War* (Oakville, Ontario: Mosaic Press, 1980), pp.65-66. The First Battle of Ypres cost the Germans an estimated 134,300 men, 19,600 of which were recorded as fatalities. See Beckett, *Ypres*, pp.225-26.

128   Beckett, *Ypres*, p.188 and Edmonds, *Military Operations 1914 Vol. II*, p.339. Individual battalion strength of 1st Division averaged 934 officers and men on 19 October i.e., during the time of I Corps' concentration in Flanders.

129   TNA CAB 45/140: Bulfin Diary 31 October-1 November 1914 and Gary Sheffield, *The Chief: Douglas Haig and the British Army* (London: Aurum, 2011), p.95.

130   Brigadier-General E.A. Fanshawe BGRA 1st Division.

machine-guns from some scattered houses. I got back at 4, saw companies and laid down under a tree for an hour".[131]

Bulfin's successful appeal to remain on the defensive ensured there would be a brief period of respite for worn-down units to reorganise, cursory trenches strengthened and sparse reserves situated before the next German thrust. The anticipated assault opened in the south under the light of a full moon in the early hours of 1 November. *Gruppe Fabeck's* staggered efforts were, from right to left, now concentrated against Lieutenant-General Edmund Allenby's Cavalry Corps defences on Messines Ridge, Moussy's intervening French detachment and the right of I Corps. Its disposed manpower strength was daunting; the odds opposite Wytschaete in the Cavalry Corps' sector at least twelve to one in the attacker's favour. Messines Ridge was cleared of Allied forces by the evening of the 2nd. Elsewhere, stolid ranks of German infantry made limited progress in the face of furious resistance. It was during this phase of the long, drawn-out Ypres struggle that Bulfin was severely wounded and forced to relinquish command.[132]

1 November dawned fine and warm with an early morning mist. Any contemplated forward movement by Bulfin Force and 7th Division would be entirely dependent on a preliminary advance by Moussy's detachment. This was swiftly checked by shellfire before coming level with the British trenches; the German preparatory bombardment commenced almost immediately afterwards. It was shortly after 11:00 a.m. that a *Feldgrau* array of approximately three battalions were spotted closing with the eastern extremity of Shrewsbury Forest. The ensuing attack "passed right across the front of the 4th and 2nd infantry brigades.[133] Coming one after another, and being enfiladed at about 200 yards range, the battalions were all shot down, hardly any surviving".[134] Bulfin, having already committed his meagre (26th Field Company RE and 2nd Grenadier Guards) reserve to fill in gaps and bolster the firing line, was at his headquarters east of Zillebeke when tragedy struck: "I was walking with Frith and an orderly when a shell came and killed the orderly, smashed up Frith and I got hit in the head and so went down. I told Packenham to put the Brigade under Lord Cavan and got away into YPRES after I had been patched up".[135] The *Official History*

131 TNA CAB 45/140: Bulfin Diary 1 November 1914.

132 Holmes, *Army Battlefield Guide*, pp.109-10.

133 The two brigades comprising Bulfin Force.

134 TNA CAB 45/140: 'Information about the Counter-attack of the Second Infantry Brigade … on 31st October', Ypres Authors A-L. See Steven Jackman, 'Shoulder to Shoulder: Close Control and 'Old Prussian Drill' in German Offensive Infantry Tactics, 1871-1914', *The Journal of Military History* 68, January 2004, pp.73-104 for the origin and practice of the flawed tactical methodology so often employed by the German Army in 1914 with disastrous consequences.

135 Edmonds, *Military Operations 1914 Vol. II*, p.356, J.M. Craster (ed) *'Fifteen Rounds a Minute': The Grenadiers at War 1914* (London: Book Club Associates, 1976), pp.125-27; TNA WO 95/1267: 2nd Brigade War Diary, Bulfin Diary 1 November 1914 and Frank Davies & Graham Maddocks, *Bloody Red Tabs: General Officer Casualties of the Great War 1914-1918* (London: Leo Cooper, 1995), pp.120-21.

reflectively remarked with fulsome appreciation: "Towards noon, to the great loss of the BEF, that determined fighter, General Bulfin, was disabled by wounds; Major-General Capper (7th Division), who was on the spot, directed Br.-General Lord Cavan to take command in his place".[136]

Assessment

The 1914 campaign in France and Flanders compelled intermediate level British commanders to demonstrate acquired military skills and overt soldierly endurance during months of arduous fighting that all but destroyed the original BEF.[137] 1st Division had been particularly well-served by a noteworthy complement of professional and courageous brigadiers, FitzClarence (subsequently killed in action on 12 November 1914), Bulfin and Landon all garnering special praise in French's published despatches; conversely, Maxse, held responsible for the destruction of 2nd Royal Munster Fusiliers at Etreux and a costly 'smash-up' on the Chemin des Dames heights, appears, at least for the time being, to have been found wanting and sent home.[138]

Always immaculate in tailored uniform with "penetrating grey eyes' gazing from beneath his khaki and scarlet cap, Bulfin's general appearance exuded all the confidence and martial bearing of the Edwardian officer caste. This outwardly projected image was more than equalled by the quiet confidence and imperturbability of a thorough and exacting general officer who, nonetheless, managed to retain a regimental officer's paternalistic concern for the men under his command.[139] His individual path to wartime fame and advancement emerged following the markedly unprofitable series of offensive operations on the Aisne. The Kortekeer counter-stroke further enhanced a growing reputation and it is significant that Haig chose the newly-promoted major-general to command his principal reserve not long afterwards. Subsequent inspired leadership during the climax of the Ypres fighting attests to a judicious appointment based on a sound measure of the man and his previous accomplishments. The repute

136   Edmonds, *Military Operations 1914 Vol. II*, p.357.
137   BEF strength on mobilisation amounted to approximately 100,000 officers and men. Combined casualties for the period August-December 1914 (subsequent Regular Army reinforcements, Territorial Force and Indian Army losses inclusive) were 95,032 killed, wounded, missing and died of disease. See Gardner, *Trial by Fire*, p.34 and 'Table (iii). Approximate Casualties by Months in the Expeditionary Force, France (Since 22 August 1914)', War Office, *Statistics of the Military Effort of the British Empire During the Great War 1914-1920* (London: HMSO, 1922), p.253
138   Sir John French, *The Despatches of Sir John French Vol. I* (London: Chapman & Hall, 1914), pp.45-48, 68, 70, 138, 157, Gary Sheffield & John Bourne (eds), *Douglas Haig: War Diaries and Letters 1914-1918* (London: Weidenfeld & Nicolson, 2005), p.244 and John Baynes, *Far From a Donkey: The Life of General Sir Ivor Maxse KCB, CVO, DSO*, (London: Brassey's, 1995), pp.119-20.
139   J.M. Bourne, *Who's Who in World War I* (London: Routledge, 2001), p.44.

in which Bulfin was held did not, when one takes into account the heated exchange with Haig's chief of staff on the night of 31 October – 1 November, deter him from expressing uncomfortable truths to superiors when presumed necessary.[140]

Much has been made of the perceived disparity between the BEF's often maligned 'Donkey' executive leadership and the highly-trained and motivated 'Lions' that were deployed on the continent in August 1914. While there has been some measure of valid criticism concerning British GHQ and corps command during this anxious and uncertain period, it must be remembered that the majority of pre-war general officers devoted considerable time and thought to their chosen vocation and exhibited a consummate professionalism on active service that was, more often than credited, worthy of their elite soldier subordinates.[141] This was especially true for brigadiers operating within what was the smallest formation with a formal command structure.[142] An infantry brigadier's general responsibilities – as outlined by Peter Simkins in his seminal study of brigade command during 1916-18 – were training, administration and man management with a central focus on efficiency and maintenance of morale. In battle, he was expected to fulfil plans passed down by those above him by ensuring units were in the right place at the right time. His tasks, once battle was joined, were plan adjustment if judged necessary and a timely committal of reserves. The job description thus articulated, Simkins reminds us that "even the most dedicated, gifted or experienced of commanders were rarely able to meet all these criteria at the same time and the unremitting pressure inevitably undermined the physical or mental resilience of many".[143] It is evident, based on this taxing curriculum vitae and its potential career pitfalls, that Bulfin proved himself more than equal to the burdens commensurate with and, on occasions, beyond the scope of institutional expectations associated with achieved rank. Indeed, the "double edged traits" associated with historian Nikolas Gardner's "hybrid officer" are exemplified by Bulfin's performance in 1914. This ambiguous combination of modern military thinking and ingrained traditions of Victorian/Edwardian regimental soldiering, the former has speculated with penetrating hindsight, was at best a "mixed blessing" when considering the inherent value of personal leadership at the sharp end verses the loss of competent and experienced commanders.[144] Nevertheless, the prevalence

---

140   Ibid, p.44
141   For the most recent critical works concerning the BEF's command and control
      performance and pre-war transformation into a *corps d'elite* see Gardner, *Trial by Fire* and
      Jones, *From Boer War to World War* respectively.
142   Embodied by the trio of brigadier-general, brigade major and staff captain.
143   Peter Simkins, 'Building Blocks: Aspects of Command and Control at Brigade Level
      in the BEF's Offensive Operations, 1916-1918' in Gary Sheffield & Dan Todman
      (eds), *Command and Control on the Western Front: The British Army's Experience 1914-18*
      (Staplehurst: Spellmount, 2004), pp.145-47.
144   Gardner, *Trial by Fire*, pp.20-27, 238-39. Officer casualties (killed, died of wounds,
      died of disease, wounded and missing) during the period August to November
      1914 amounted to 3,642. See 'Table (iii) Approximate Casualties by Months in the
      Expeditionary Force, France (Since 22 August 1914)', War Office, *Statistics of the*

of this command and control conundrum was, given the often grave necessity for leaders to risk their lives by being well forward at critical moments, almost wholly unavoidable during the opening months of the western campaign.

Bulfin was still recuperating when Imperial Germany's bid to capture the strategically important channel ports ground to a final, bloody halt east of Ypres in mid-November. Surgery – "took a lot of metal from my head" – at Boulogne had been followed by swift evacuation to Great Britain on 3 November.[145] A rapid recovery in about six weeks' time enabled the promising major-general to assume command of 28th Division, a recently formed composite of Regular battalions culled from overseas garrisons, in December 1914.[146] This ostensibly propitious appointment belied the fact that absence resulting from Bulfin's injury precluded him from consideration for corps command during the succeeding "promotion race" of 1914-16.[147] Invalided home from France because of illness in December 1915, he was given command of the 60th (London) Division, a second-line Territorial formation, which he led with distinction in France, the Balkans and Palestine during 1916-17.[148] His seemingly immotile career was rescued from professional oblivion by Allenby, now C-and-C Egyptian Expeditionary Force, who, in recognition of his subordinate's acknowledged talents, promoted Bulfin to Lieutenant-General and GOC XXI Corps in August 1917. Grudgingly playing "the bludgeon to Sir Philip Chetwode's rapier", his considerable military attributes, plainly exhibited during the battles of Third Gaza (1-7 November 1917) and Meggido (19 September-31 October 1918), contributed to final victory in the Middle East.[149] A variety of assignments, including that of acting GOC Egypt in 1919, filled the remainder of his post-war army career until respectable retirement as a full general in January 1926. A substantial portion of Bulfin's latter years were devoted to his former regiment for which he, as designated Colonel-in-Chief, successfully campaigned to have 'Green Howards' adopted as its official title in 1920.[150] Interwar reflection, critical or otherwise, embodied in a published memoir was not to Bulfin's disposition or taste. Such publications that bear his name are confined to brief forwards for histories of specific formations and units once under his command.[151] Tangible personal testimony to 1914 and the critical

---

Military Effort of the British Empire During the Great War 1914-1920, p.253.

145   TNA CAB 45/140: Bulfin Diary 2-3 November 1914.

146   See Major A.F. Becke, *Order of Battle of Divisions, Part 1 – The Regular British Divisions* (London: HMSO, 1934), pp.105-11.

147   See Simon Robbins, *British Generalship on the Western Front 1914-1918: Defeat into Victory* (London: Frank Cass, 2005), p.53.

148   See Colonel P.H. Dalbiac, *History of the 60th Division (2nd/2nd London Division)* (London: Allen & Unwin, 1927), p.109.

149   Bourne, *Who's Who in World War I*, p.44.

150   See 'News in a Nutshell', *British Pathe*, http://www.britishpathe.com/programmes/news-in-a-nutshell/episode/asc/playlist/158, for a 1935 newsreel segment of a mufti-clad Bulfin at Portland to commemorate 'Alma Day' (20 September) as a guest of his old regiment.

151   See Dalbiac, *History of the 60th Division*, pp.9-10.

actions at First Ypres that made him are nonetheless commemorated on an ornate presentation mess gavel – currently on display at the Green Howards Museum – that bears the telling inscription: "Presented to the Officers Mess the Depot, The Green Howards by General Sir Edward Bulfin C.V.O. Colonel of the Green Howards in Memory of Ypres, October 1914".[152]

152 'Object of the Month: October 2009', *Green Howards Museum*, http://www. greenhowards. org.uk/newsdetails.php?ID=105. 'WON FAME AT YPRES: BRITISH GENERAL'S DEATH was the chosen heading for Bulfin's lengthy obituary (19 October 1939) in the antipodean *Cairns Post*.

11

"The Demon":
Brigadier-General Charles FitzClarence V.C.

1st (Guards) Brigade 1914

Spencer Jones

Charles FitzClarence is the most obscure of all the officers discussed in this volume.[1] He left no great mark on the pre-war army and his First World War career as commander of 1st (Guards) Brigade, of which he held command from 27 September until his death on 12 November 1914, was the shortest of the named officers surveyed in this work. However, the professionalism of his peacetime work makes him an interesting example of the pre-war officer class, and his vitally important combat actions in the First World War merit study.

FitzClarence had a well earned reputation as a fighter. He had won the Victoria Cross for his actions at the siege of Mafeking in 1899, and was described by a fellow officer in 1905 as "Most self reliant and gallant. One could not have a better man with me in a tight place."[2] These words were to prove prophetic. On 31 October 1914, FitzClarence was the ranking officer on the spot as the British Expeditionary Force found itself in the tightest place of the entire campaign. The Battle of Ypres was at its height and the Germans had broken through the front of 1st Division. There were virtually no British troops left to stem the German advance and the road to Ypres lay open. FitzClarence's decision to launch an immediate counter attack with the only reserves available proved, against all numerical odds, decisive. His action snatched victory from the jaws of defeat. However, FitzClarence's untimely death, killed by a stray bullet during the early hours of 12 November, obscured his achievement. His posthumous reputation was high in the immediate aftermath of the war and his achievements were featured in the 1925 film *Ypres*. However, his career has now largely

---

1   Contemporary papers variously render FitzClarence's name as FitzClarence, Fitzclarence and Fitz Clarence. For the sake of consistency, the former spelling will be used throughout this chapter.
2   The National Archives (Hereafter TNA), WO 138/25, Brigadier General Charles FitzClarence Personal File, Confidential Report, January 1905.

Charles FitzClarence. (Editor's collection)

been forgotten except by historians of the battle. This chapter aims to shed fresh light on this important officer.

Charles FitzClarence was born in Bishopscourt, County Kildare, Ireland on 8 May 1865. His paternal grandfather was George, First Earl of Munster, an illegitimate son of King William IV. The FitzClarences were a military family and Charles's father, George, had been a captain in the Royal Navy. Following education at Eton and Wellington College, Charles and his twin brother, Edward, chose to join the army. Like many of his contemporaries, FitzClarence began his career in the militia, transferring to the Royal Fusiliers in November 1886. A fit and lean figure standing 6'2 tall, FitzClarence certainly looked the part of the soldier.[3] However, his early career was blighted by several bouts of illness which limited his prospects for advancement.[4] This was a source of considerable frustration for the young officer, who was bitterly disappointed at missing out on the opportunity for active service in Sudan in the 1880s.[5] This frustration was magnified by the fact that twin brother Edward saw action in the theatre.[6]

Unable to secure a combat posting, FitzClarence's early career was taken up with the day to day duties of a lieutenant with some occasional work in administrative posts such as battalion paymaster.[7] Although he was competent in such peacetime roles,

---

3   G. Valentine Williams, 'First Ypres 1914: The Turning of the Tide' in John Buchan (ed.) *The Long Road to Victory* (London, Thomas Nelson & Sons, 1920), p.21.

4   TNA, WO 138/25, FitzClarence Personal File, Confidential Reports, February 1889 & April 1892.

5   'X', 'Gheluvelt 1914: The Man who Turned the Tide' in *Blackwood's Magazine,* Vol.CCII, 1917, p.217.

6   Marquis De Ruvigny, *De Ruvigny's Roll of Honour* (Uckfield, Naval & Military Press, 2003: Originally published in 1922), p.135. Sadly, Edward was killed at the Battle of Abu Hamed, 7 August 1897.

7   TNA, WO 138/25, FitzClarence Personal File, Record of Service 31 March 1914.

commanding officers were quick to note his desire for action and advancement.[8] He was picked out as a "promising young officer" and one who was "anxious to get on in his profession."[9] For his part, FitzClarence worked hard to improve his career prospects. He passed his exam for promotion from lieutenant to captain in 1890, although he had to wait until 1899 before formally assuming the rank.[10] In 1893, he passed a course of instruction at the School of Musketry at Hythe, taking particular interest in the use of the Maxim machine gun.[11] However, the catalyst for his career progression came in 1895 when he joined the mounted infantry.[12]

The mounted infantry were an unusual feature of the pre-1914 British Army. As the name suggests, they were a force composed of regular infantry soldiers who were given a ten week course in riding and mounted tactics. These soldiers remained part of their parent infantry battalions, but could now perform a role as mounted troops in the absence of cavalry. This was particularly useful for colonial expeditions, where small forces that lacked traditional cavalry still needed mounted troops for scouting and screening. The nature of mounted infantry work, which often involved operating independently to the front or flank of a force, required dynamic and free thinking officers. The mounted infantry could thus provide an outlet for adventurous soldiers who wished to escape the tedium of peacetime regimental life.[13]

FitzClarence was ideally suited to such a position. His work on the mounted infantry training course received lavish praise from commanding officer Lieutenant Colonel F.W. Stopford, who described FitzClarence as "A first rate M.I. officer."[14] FitzClarence's work continued to attract notice on his return to his regiment, and when the Royal Fusiliers were posted to Egypt he was given the local rank of captain commanding a company of mounted infantry. A confidential report for 1897 described FitzClarence as "A very smart, hard working and valuable officer. Shows great tact in the management of both officers and men. Is exceptionally self reliant and performs his duties as a company commander... in a very thorough manner."[15]

In July 1899, seeking further career advancement, FitzClarence volunteered to go to South Africa as a special service officer. Tensions between Britain and the Boer republics of Transvaal and Orange Free State had escalated to the point that a full

8   Ibid., FitzClarence's 'Professional Zeal' was consistently described as 'Great' in confidential reports of the 1890s.

9   Ibid., Confidential Reports, 6 December 1890, 6 July 1894.

10   Ibid., Record of Service 31 March 1914. FitzClarence served as a local captain of mounted infantry in Egypt from 1897 to 1899.

11   Ibid., Confidential Report, 6 July 1894. See also Mounted Infantry Course addendum, 24 November 1895.

12   Ibid., Mounted Infantry Course addendum, 24 November 1895.

13   Stephen Badsey, *Doctrine and Reform in the British Cavalry 1880 – 1918* (Aldershot, Ashgate, 2008), p.63.

14   TNA, WO 138/25, FitzClarence Personal File, Mounted Infantry Course addendum, 24 November 1895.

15   Ibid., Confidential Report, 1 February 1906.

scale war was expected before the end of the year. In anticipation of this conflict, special service officers were assigned to organise locally raised forces to supplement the regular army garrison of the country. FitzClarence joined Colonel [later Lieutenant-General Lord] Robert Baden-Powell in Rhodesia, where he assisted in raising two regiments of mounted rifles: the Rhodesia Regiment and the Bechuanaland Protectorate Regiment.[16] FitzClarence was given command of 'B' Squadron of the latter formation, stationed at the border town of Mafeking.

On paper, the unit was an unenviable command. The members of the squadron consisted primarily of colonial adventurers and frontier freebooters, and while such formations had proved useful in wars against poorly armed opposition such as the Zulu and the Matabele, it remained doubtful how well they would stand up against the modern weapons of the Boers.[17] There was little time to undertake anything except the most rudimentary exercises prior to the outbreak of war on 11 October 1899 and the unit was considered only partially trained when it was first committed to action.[18] However, in its commanding officer it possessed a leader of natural ability. After many years of waiting for the opportunity to see combat, FitzClarence finally had the chance to prove himself.

'B' Squadron was to receive its baptism of fire on 14 October, just three days after the outbreak of war. A British armoured train had sallied forth from Mafeking to attack a nearby Boer patrol, but had been surprised by the proximity and strength of advancing enemy forces and was in danger of being captured. FitzClarence led fifty men to the aid of the isolated train, but found himself seriously outnumbered and in danger of encirclement. His unit came under "furious fire" from front and both flanks.[19] However, FitzClarence's "bold and efficient handling" allowed his squadron to seize a key position and return the fire with great effect, inflicting stinging losses on the Boers and allowing the armoured train to escape.[20] FitzClarence's actions drew great praise, it being noted that "by his personal coolness and courage [he] inspired the greatest confidence in his men".[21] Writing after the war, Major-General Sir Frederick Maurice commented that FitzClarence had "manoeuvred brilliantly" during the engagement.[22]

Boer forces subsequently placed Mafeking under siege and the Protectorate Regiment served as part of the garrison. The British, under the leadership of the

---

16   In terms of combat role, mounted rifles and mounted infantry were essentially identical. The mounted infantry were distinguished by being drawn from regular British infantry units. Mounted rifles tended to be improvised formations that could consist of local troops or colonial volunteers. See Badsey, *Doctrine and Reform*, pp.14-15.

17   Max Arthur, *Symbol of Courage: the Men behind the Medal*, (Oxford, Pan MacMillan, 2005), p.160. Arthur claims the unit was known as "The Loafers" although the present author has been unable to find reference to the nickname in contemporary writing.

18   TNA WO 98/9, Victoria Cross Register, Captain Charles FitzClarence citation, p.8.

19   Ibid., p.8.

20   Ibid., p.8.

21   Ibid., p.8.

22   Frederick Maurice, *History of the War in South Africa* (London, Hurst & Blackett, 1906-1910), vol.III, p.147.

flamboyant Baden-Powell, sought to maintain an active defence so as to tie down Boer forces and prevent their transfer to the critical battlefront in Natal. On 26 October, FitzClarence led his squadron in a dismounted night raid against Boer line. Leading from the front, FitzClarence was the first man into the Boer trench and accounted for four of the enemy with his sword.[23] After fierce hand-to-hand combat the trench was cleared and the raiders withdrew under fire, with FitzClarence suffering a minor wound in the process. Baden-Powell was full of praise for FitzClarence in these two actions, stating "had this Officer not shown an extraordinary spirit and fearlessness the attacks would have been failures, and we should have suffered heavy loss both in men and prestige."[24]

However, on 26 December a British trench raid on the strong point of Game Tree Fort stumbled into a Boer ambush and was repulsed with heavy losses. FitzClarence, once again leading his men from the front, was shot through both legs and had to be carried to safety.[25] Recovery from these wounds kept him incapacitated for much of the remainder of the siege, which was finally lifted on 17 May 1900.[26] However, his dynamic leadership and courageous actions had not gone unnoticed. FitzClarence's courage in leading the Protectorate Regiment in the three separate actions earned him a Victoria Cross, which was presented to him by Lord Roberts in October 1900. Furthermore, FitzClarence's aggressive leadership and personal fighting prowess gave rise to his nickname of "The Demon", a moniker which endured for the remainder of his career.[27] FitzClarence remained in South Africa for several months, assuming the role of brigade major in the Rhodesian Brigade until February 1901, after which he returned to Britain to join the recently formed Irish Guards.[28] He was to remain associated with this regiment for the remainder of his peacetime career.

Having established a reputation in the Boer War, FitzClarence's career blossomed in the years that followed. He passed Staff College in 1902 and subsequently served from 1903 to 1906 as brigade major to 5th Brigade; from 1906 to 1908 he was the senior company commander in the 1st Irish Guards; and between 1908 and 1913

---

23   De Ruvigny, *Roll of Honour*, p.135.
24   TNA WO 98/9, FitzClarence citation, p.8. Interestingly, Leo Amery, *The Times History of the War in South Africa*, Vol.IV (London, William Clowes & Sons, 1906), p.583 presents a different account of the raid. Amery states that FitzClarence's attack was met with fierce Boer fire that scattered the raiders and prevented them reaching the trench. This account is contradicted by FitzClarence's medal citation and the account in Maurice, *War in South Africa*, Vol.III, p.153. Maurice described the action as a "brilliant affair."
25   Maurice, *War in South Africa*, Vol.III, p.163.
26   FitzClarence and his squadron played a role in repulsing the Boer assault on Mafeking, 12 May 1900. See Amery, *Times History*, vol.IV, p.595.
27   'X', 'Gheluvelt 1914', p.217.
28   The Irish Guards had been founded in April 1900 in recognition of the contribution of Irish soldiers in the Boer War.

he took full command of the battalion. By 1913, now a lieutenant colonel, he was promoted to command of the regiment and its district.[29]

FitzClarence's peacetime work drew virtually universal praise from his fellow officers. Although the Boer War had shown that he was a man of action, the years that followed showed that he was also an excellent instructor. A fellow officer noted that FitzClarence had "the great gift of being able to teach others."[30] Sir Horace Smith-Dorrien, an officer known for his own innovative training methods, commented "I formed a high opinion of Colonel FitzClarence as a commanding officer – the [1st Irish Guards] Battalion to my mind improved 50% under his command in the year [1910] at Aldershot."[31] In 1908 a confidential report praised FitzClarence's work: "An officer of a calibre that it would be hard to beat. His powers of command and leadership were proved many times in action in South Africa... He has been of the greatest assistance to the training of the battalion."[32]

FitzClarence took training very seriously and worked his troops hard. Indeed, the endurance of the moniker of "The Demon" may well have owed something to his disciplinary approach. In 1911 it was noted that he was "both loved and feared by his battalion which he has instructed with great ability", and his emphasis on unit discipline was highlighted in confidential reports for 1911 and 1912.[33] Nevertheless, the battalion's performance at manoeuvres proved the value of such stern measures. In 1910, the commanding officer of 1st (Guards) Brigade, Brigadier-General [later General Sir] Ivor Maxse, commented on the excellent handling of the 1st Irish Guards, identifying FitzClarence's emphasis on "thoroughness" as a key factor in its performance.[34] The battalion continued to draw praise for its work at manoeuvres in the years that followed.

The confidential reports of the era contain hints that FitzClarence was seen as a forward thinker. Several reports commented that he was well suited for promotion to the recently formed General Staff.[35] A 1912 report stated that "as a scientific and practical soldier he has few equals."[36] Yet, there is a certain dichotomy about assessments of FitzClarence's intellectual talents. Opinions were not unanimous. In December 1902, Lieutenant General H.G. Niles wrote a detailed confidential assessment of FitzClarence that concluded:

He is broad in his views rather than deep, and has perceptive faculties rather than reflective. He is not a man of high mental power or educational qualifications... He

29 TNA, WO 138/25, FitzClarence Personal File, Record of Service 31 March 1914.
30 Ibid., Confidential Report, 14 October 1908.
31 Ibid., Confidential Report, Smith-Dorrien comment, 22 December 1910.
32 Ibid., Confidential Report, 14 October 1908.
33 Ibid., Confidential Reports, 24 November 1911 & 7 December 1912.
34 Ibid, Confidential Report, Maxse comment, 15 September 1910.
35 Ibid., Confidential Reports in 1907, 1908, 1911, 1912 and 1913 all recommended FitzClarence for promotion to the General Staff.
36 Ibid., Confidential Report, 7 December 1912.

has plenty of common sense – is not a man of detail – and is not suited to heavy administrative office work.[37]

In a similar vein, a 1906 report commented "He is not at his best when he is behind a desk and is not an ideal staff officer."[38]

Regardless of the assessment of his intellectual ability, FitzClarence showed no particular inclination to pursue a staff career. Nor did he become involved in the theoretical, tactical and organisational debates that gripped the British Army during this era.[39] He did not write articles for any of the numerous military journals of the day, and although he attended a General Staff Conference in 1906, he did not participate in any of the discussions.[40] His interests appear to have been practical. He maintained his earlier interest in fire control and machine guns, passing the senior officer's course at the School of Musketry in 1907, but this was the only qualification that he added to his résumé prior to the First World War. Yet his practical approach achieved results. Although he failed to leave any great intellectual mark on the military of the era, the training and management of his company, and later his battalion, drew unanimous praise. A post-war assessment by an officer of the Irish Guards commented that FitzClarence was "the finest type of British officer" possessing "knowledge of his profession that would have commanded respect in any army in the world."[41]

From 1902 to 1914 FitzClarence had steadily advanced in rank and responsibility, and at the outbreak of war in August 1914 he was placed in command of the newly formed 29th Brigade, part of 10th Division, mustering at the Curragh in Ireland.[42] Thus, he was not present at the opening battles of the war and did not participate in the Great Retreat. However, he did not have to wait long for an opportunity to assume a combat command. On 22 September he was assigned to take charge of 1st (Guards) Brigade, replacing his former commanding officer, Ivor Maxse.[43]

37   Ibid., Recommendation by H.G. Niles, 19 December 1902.
38   Ibid., Confidential Report, 1 February 1906.
39   For differing interpretations of these debates see Timothy Bowman & Mark Connelly, *The Edwardian Army. Recruiting, Training and Deploying the British Army, 1902-1914* (Oxford, Oxford University Press, 2012) and Spencer Jones, *From Boer War to World War: Tactical Reform of the British Army, 1902-1914* (Norman, University of Oklahoma Press, 2012).
40   Joint Services Command and Staff College Library, Report on a Conference of General Staff Officers at the Staff College, 2-12 January, 1906.
41   Williams, 'Turning the Tide', p.21.
42   De Ruvigny, *Roll of Honour*, p.135.
43   Maxse was adjudged to have handled his brigade poorly during the engagements of August and September. He was removed from his position on the basis of being promoted to command the newly formed 18th Division, then mustering in England. Although ostensibly a promotion, to be removed from command of an elite front line brigade to take charge of a new, untried division at home was a clear punishment. It was only after his skilful handling of 18th Division at the Battle of the Somme in 1916 that his "misdeeds" of 1914 were considered forgotten. On this latter point, see Gary Sheffield & John Bourne (eds.), *Douglas Haig: War Diaries and Letters 1914 – 1918* (London,

Arriving in France on 27 September, FitzClarence inherited a battle-worn formation that consisted of the 1st Coldstream Guards, 1st Scots Guards, 1st Black Watch and 1st Cameron Highlanders. The brigade had taken heavy casualties in the opening weeks of the conflict. One of its original battalions, the 2nd Munster Fusiliers, had been cut off and wiped out during the rear guard action at Etreux on 27 August.[44] Subsequently, the brigade had been heavily engaged at the Battle of the Aisne on 14 September, suffering severe losses and enduring a "tremendous ordeal".[45] As well as losses amongst the front line soldiers, the staff of the brigade had been much disrupted by casualties and redeployments to new formations.[46] However, FitzClarence was fortunate to retain the services of the highly able Captain [later General Sir] Andrew Thorne as staff captain. The two officers forged an excellent working relationship that would serve the brigade well in the battles that were to come. Thorne commented on FitzClarence's arrival in a letter home, noting "Our new Brigadier is a great man. We are jolly lucky to have got him."[47]

FitzClarence arrived at 1st Brigade to find the formation dug in opposite the German trenches on the Aisne. Although major fighting had come to an end by the time FitzClarence took charge, the sector was characterised by fierce skirmishing and heavy bombardments. The 1st Brigade War Diary recorded that the troops endured "Heavy shell fire, constant sniping and half hearted attacks day and night".[48] Although the scale and intensity of fighting was very different from the earlier conflict, his experiences at the siege of Mafeking in the Boer War would have given FitzClarence familiarity with many features of trench warfare. Perhaps recalling his exploits at the siege, one of his initial actions as brigadier was to order the first British trench raid of the war. Surveying the front line, FitzClarence observed: "The [German] trenches are very close to our main line of trenches and are probably observation posts for the enemy's artillery. I considered it a necessary duty to attack them."[49]

On the night of the 4/5 October, a raiding party drawn from the 1st Coldstream Guards set out to seize a German position known as "Fish Hook Trench".[50] The raiders were followed by a party of Royal Engineers with orders to demolish the trench once it was in British hands. The Coldstreams were able to reach their target and wiped out the German defenders in hand to hand combat, but signs that the Germans were preparing a swift counter attack prompted the raiders to fall back before the Royal Engineers could complete their task. Nevertheless, FitzClarence felt that the raid

---

Weidenfeld & Nicolson, 2005), p.244.

44   The 2nd Munster Fusiliers were replaced by the 1st Cameron Highlanders on 5th September 1914.

45   Paul Kendall, *Aisne 1914: The Dawn of Trench Warfare*, (Stroud, Spellmount, 2012), p.153.

46   Imperial War Museum (hereafter IMW), Andrew Thorne papers, AT/1, Thorne to wife, 21 September 1914.

47   Ibid., Thorne to wife, 29 September 1914.

48   TNA, WO 95/1261, 1st (Guards) Brigade War Diary, 28 September 1914.

49   TNA, WO95/1263, 1st Coldstream Guards War Diary, FitzClarence to unknown recipient, October 5 1914.

50   Ibid., Appendix I, October 1914.

had been "entirely successful".[51] The Coldstreams lost two men missing and suffered eight wounded, including the officer in charge of the raid, 2nd Lieutenant Merton Beckwith-Smith, who won the Distinguished Service Order for his role in the action.[52] The Germans were believed to have suffered approximately 20 men killed.[53] In the aftermath of the raid, FitzClarence showed his grasp of trench warfare by submitting a written request for a variety of useful supplies for his brigade, including rifle grenades for clearing trenches, additional sand bags to resist shell fire and steel plates for securing loopholes against snipers. He also ordered 1st Coldstream to strengthen their forward sap with a view to using it as jumping off point for further raids, to "make the enemy's advanced trenches as uncomfortable as possible."[54]

However, 1st Brigade was not destined to remain on the Aisne. On 15 October, I Corps was transferred to the developing battlefront in Flanders, joining what would ultimately become known as the First Battle of Ypres. Although deployed to the front with the intention of extending the British line and advancing towards Antwerp and Brussels, I Corps was soon forced onto the defensive by a major German drive that aimed to expel the Allies from Belgium and break through to the Channel ports. Outnumbered, outgunned and under relentless pressure from German attacks, the British Expeditionary Force found itself fighting for its very life.[55] Ypres was the largest and most intense battle fought by the British Army in 1914. To understand the situation faced by FitzClarence and his fellow officers it is necessary to outline the general details of the fighting at Ypres and highlight some of the peculiarities of the battle. The conditions were unique in many ways and posed a particular set of command and control problems for the BEF.

The realities of modern industrial warfare, which had been somewhat obscured during the war of movement in August-September 1914, were starkly revealed at Ypres. Firepower dominated the battlefield. In this respect the Germans held a key advantage in the numerical strength and weight of their artillery. The British had already experienced some of the formidable power of German guns at the Battle of the Aisne, prompting a memorandum from I Corps to note that artillery "is the most formidable arm we have to encounter", but the intensity of the bombardments at Ypres was unprecedented.[56] The war diaries of the battalions of 1st Brigade recorded heavy

---

51   Ibid., FitzClarence to unknown recipient, October 5 1914.
52   Beckwith-Smith survived the First World War and commanded Guards Division during the Battle of France 1940. He later commanded 18th Division; he and his formation were captured at the fall of Singapore in February 1942. He died in a Japanese prisoner of war camp in November 1942.
53   TNA, WO95/1263, 1st Coldstream War Diary, Appendix I, October 1914.
54   Ibid., FitzClarence to unknown recipient, October 5 1914.
55   Good single volume accounts of this battle include Ian Beckett, *Ypres: The First Battle 1914* (Harlow, Longman, 2004) and A.H. Farrar-Hockley, *Death of an Army* (London, Arthur Baker, 1967).
56   TNA WO 95/588, I Corps War Diary, Memorandum on British and German Tactics, 28 September 1914.

shelling as an almost daily occurrence.[57] John Lucy, serving with the Royal Irish Rifles, described what this meant for front line infantry:

> ...the heavy shells came slowly down with thud and crash, their concussion alone shaking landslides from the back and front of our trenches, and making the earth rock as in an earth-quake. Field-guns and smaller howitzers joined in ... the enemy found our position, and we crouched wretchedly, shaken by the blastings, under a lasting hail of metal and displaced earth and sods, half-blinded and half-choked by poisonous vapours...[58]

Entrenchment was the only form of protection against such bombardment. Yet the pressures of battle, shortage of tools and exhaustion of the defenders meant that trenches were often crude, hastily dug affairs. Rain and snow filled the trenches with water and turned them into "absolute quagmires."[59] Official historian James Edmonds summed them up:

> The British defences around Ypres at this time were at best, short disconnected lengths of trenches, three feet deep. Hastily constructed during the few hours that the troops had been on the ground, they were without wire, dug-outs or communication trenches, and lacked anything in the nature of a second line.[60]

In terms of entrenchment methods, 1st Brigade had learned from its experience on the Aisne and had adapted, abandoning overhead covers which, although they protected troops from shrapnel, were liable to shatter into dangerous splinters if struck by high explosive.[61] Even so, their trenches only provided limited protection and the ferocity of bombardment often caused them to collapse. During severe shelling on 2 November, Captain Stracey of the 1st Scots Guards "...was buried for an hour and a half, hardly being able to breathe till he was dug out."[62]

The Royal Artillery could only offer sporadic counter-battery fire against German artillery concentrations. Severely outnumbered by the enemy's guns, the Royal Artillery was further hampered by a critical shortage of shells. The dearth of ammunition was so severe that shell supply was rationed, sometimes to as little as four rounds per gun, per day, although restrictions were lifted during emergencies.[63] Faced with such shortages, the Royal Artillery husbanded its resources and concentrated its fire against German

57   For example TNA WO 95/1263, 1st Black Watch War Diary, records heavy shellfire every day between 4 and 11 November 1914.
58   John Lucy, *There's a Devil in the Drum*, (London, Faber & Faber, 1938), p.220.
59   Everard Wyrall, *The History of the Somerset Light Infantry 1914 – 1919* (London, Methuen & Co., 1927), p.46.
60   James Edmonds, *Official History of the Great War: Military Operations France and Belgium 1914*, vol.II, (London, MacMillan, 1925), p.173.
61   IMW, Thorne Papers, AT/10/1, Undated diary entry.
62   F. Loraine Petre, Wilfrid Ewart & Cecil Lowther, *The Scots Guards in the Great War 1914 – 1918* (London, John Murray, 1925), p.52.
63   Edmonds, *Official History*, vol.II, p.13.

infantry attacks. Unfortunately, this meant that it could do little to disrupt the ferocious German shelling of the front line trenches.

However, German artillery superiority was somewhat offset by the superiority of British rifle and machine gun fire. The BEF benefitted from the quality of its pre-war training, which had emphasised rapid and accurate small arms fire. The culmination of British rifle training was the 'Mad Minute' exercise, where a soldier was required to fire fifteen aimed rounds in sixty seconds at a target 300 yards distant.[64] German infantry attacks consistently suffered severe casualties from British rifles and machine guns; losses were so great during the fighting in late October that some German divisional commanders argued the offensive should be abandoned.[65] One post-war German account recalled "[The] accuracy shown by the long service British soldiers with colonial experience who were deployed opposite the company, verged on the miraculous."[66] James Edmonds claimed in the British *Official History* that British small arms fire was so rapid that the Germans often mistook it for machine guns.[67] Historian Jack Sheldon has disputed this claim, but there remains anecdotal evidence in support of the idea.[68] Captain [later Brigadier General] James Jack recorded in his diary on 29 October 1914: "The 2/Cameronian machine guns are with this company. According to prisoners the Germans estimate their numbers about the farm to be six. This miscalculation is due... [to changes of] gun positions, and to the excellence of their crews; as well as to the volume of rifle fire which British infantry can produce."[69]

There was thus a degree of balance between the fire of the attacker and the defender. German bombardments forced the British to ground, exhausted the defenders, and inflicted a constant stream of casualties. Yet once the barrage had lifted to rear area targets, advancing German infantry faced a hail of bullets and suffered heavy losses, particularly amongst officers.[70] For hard pressed British troops, the relief from bombardment and the chance to vent frustration on the exposed German infantry was cathartic. John Lucy described the emotion:

> The guns stopped. Thank Christ. Thank Christ. We leaped to the trench front, and up came up our heads to see German infantry... We let them have it. We blasted and blew them to death... We had cancelled out our shell tortured day with a vengeance.[71]

Yet for all the BEF's skill with the rifle, the numerical strength and artillery superiority of the Germans inflicted remorseless, irreplaceable attrition on the defenders.

64   Jones, *Boer War to World War*, pp.93-95.
65   Beckett, *Ypres*, p.157.
66   Quoted in Jack Sheldon, *The German Army at Ypres 1914* (Barnsley, Pen & Sword, 2010), p.262.
67   Edmonds, *Official History*, vol.II, pp.462-63.
68   Sheldon, *German Army at Ypres*, p.xi-xii.
69   John Terraine (ed.), *General Jack's Diary* (London, Cassel, 2000), p.73. The position was actually defended by two machine guns.
70   Beckett, *Ypres*, p.100 states that some German units suffered 70% casualties.
71   Lucy, *Devil in the Drum*, p.224.

The British Expeditionary Force was small by the standards of European armies and had limited trained reserves with which to replace the spiralling casualties. However, the dwindling number of British soldiers fought on with grim determination. Their professional tenacity was matched by the bravery of their German opponents, who, in the words of historian Ian Beckett, "came on with considerable courage and died in large numbers."[72] Violence intensified as both sides struggled for victory. One German officer described combat amongst the villages of Flanders as "truly terrible", noting "We have to conquer the houses one by one, drag the enemy out of cellars and storage sheds, or kill them by throwing hand-grenades down at them. The casualties are always high."[73] A British officer summed up the nature of the battle: "It was not a case of 'Hands Up!' or any nonsense of that sort; it was a fight to the finish."[74] The regimental historian of the Somerset Light Infantry recorded the attitude towards the enemy:

> There was even joy – unholy joy – as the mangled bodies of Germans were flung into the air, as so much refuse tossed on to a rubbish heap. For war had become a ferocious and terrible business, shorn of its one-time chivalry; 'to kill the enemy' was the intention of both sides.[75]

The fighting around Ypres was virtually constant from the beginning of the German offensive on 19 October to the last great attack on 11 November. Edmonds offered a striking description of the conditions:

> ...it must be remembered that the fighting was almost continuous, hardly interrupted at night, and that the troops had no rest. Many successful repulses by fire of German attacks receive no mention whatever in the diaries – they were regarded as a matter of course...To give a true picture of the long hours of patient and stubborn resistance there should be some mention on almost every page of bursting shells, blown-in trenches, hunger, fatigue and death and wounds... the troops must be imagined as fighting in small groups, scattered along the front in shallow trenches, often separated by gaps amounting to two, three or even four hundred yards...many an officer fell in attempting to get from one group to another.[76]

The maelstrom of First Ypres posed unique problems for command, control and organisation. The absence of significant lulls in the fighting prior to November placed immense pressure on all levels of command. As one officer recalled "The strain on the commanders, staffs and the troops themselves was terrible, and can hardly be realised by those who have not been placed in similar circumstances."[77] The fluid situation,

72   Beckett, *Ypres*, p.100.
73   Quoted in Ibid., p.100.
74   Quoted in Williams, 'The Turning of the Tide', p.19.
75   Wyrall, *History of the Somerset Light Infantry*, pp.40-41.
76   Edmonds, *Official History*, vol.II, pp.175-176.
77   Mercian Regiment Archive, 'Gheluvelt 31 October 1914', recollections of Major B.C.

rudimentary communications, absence of contiguous trench lines and the inability to assemble significant reserves in the face of constant German pressure meant that brigadiers such as FitzClarence had to show flexibility and initiative when organising the British defence.

An initial command problem was where to locate headquarters. The brigade headquarters needed to be close enough to the front line to enable control of the battalions, but if placed too close it was in danger of being overrun by German breakthroughs. Indeed, during a relative lull in the fighting in early November, FitzClarence fortified his headquarters position with hasty trenches and obstacles, ordering his battalions to do the same for their command posts.[78] These improvised positions were to prove of great value during the attack of the Prussian Guard on 11 November.

A more immediate problem when forming headquarters was the risk of being hit by German artillery. German guns actively targeted buildings behind the lines, seeking to wipe out gatherings of officers and disrupt command and control. Lieutenant Colonel C.B. Morland, commander of the 2nd Welch Regiment, had two buildings blown down over his head and believed it was safer in the front line than in buildings to the rear.[79] James Jack was involved in two hasty relocations of headquarters due to German shelling.[80] Mindful of the danger, during the critical days of the battle FitzClarence placed his headquarters at a farm building that would become known as FitzClarence Farm. Andrew Thorne related:

> The moment we arrived, the Germans started shelling us. They landed about 6 within 100 yds. of the house. After that we got to work and had a large 'dug out' made with a lot of earth piled up all around it and a few shutters & doors overhead to keep some of the rain out.[81]

This dug out served as FitzClarence's command post during the day, and he and his staff only returned to the house at night.[82] The position gave the headquarters relatively safety from German shelling at the expense of comfort. A fellow brigadier, Count Edward Gleichen, related his experiences of commanding from a dug out at Ypres:

> It was frightfully cramped, and we were always getting half-empty sardine-tins oozing over official documents, and knives and forks lost in the mud and straw at the bottom, and bread-crumbs and fragments of bully beef and jam mixed up with our orders and papers.[83]

Senhouse-Clarke.
78   Edmonds, *Official History*, vol.II, pp.377-78.
79   Beckett, *Ypres*, p.102.
80   Terranine (ed.), *General Jack*, pp.73-74.
81   IMW, Thorne Papers, AT/1, Thorne to wife, 30 October 1914.
82   TNA, CAB 45/182, Hugh Jeudwine to James Edmonds, 22 April 1923.
83   Edward Gleichen, *The Doings of Fifteenth Infantry Brigade, August 1914 – March 1915*, (London, Blackwood, 1917), p.215.

A second problem was the difficulty of communications. One staff officer recalled: "Telephone equipment of all kinds was very scarce and lines bad. My recollection is that messages forward of Divisional HQ were almost exclusively sent by runners. Lines were not as well laid as they were later, and were frequently cut by traffic as well as by fire."[84] Attempts to lay new telephone lines at night were difficult and at risk from German shelling and stray small arms fire. Frank Richards of the Royal Welch Fusiliers even recalled a 'friendly fire' incident when a sentry opened fire on a party running a telephone line to a forward trench in the darkness.[85] The only alternative to telephones was to employ runners, but this was a dangerous duty to undertake on a fire swept battlefield. There was also an inevitable, but potentially serious, time delay between the despatch of a runner with orders or information and the reaction of the intended recipient.

Further hampering brigade to battalion communications was the attrition rate amongst front line officers. The fragmented British lines and the pressure of continuous combat placed a great burden of leadership upon junior officers. They rose admirably to the challenge, but frequently paid for their courage with their life. 1st Brigade suffered severely in this regard. For example, during intense fighting on 29 October the 1st Coldstream Guards lost all their officers, leaving the survivors under the command of the quartermaster.[86] Two replacement officers who arrived to take charge of the remnants of the unit were both lost on the 2 November.[87] Indeed, by the time 1st Brigade went into reserve on 12 November, the formation had been reduced from its paper strength of approximately 4000 troops to just 4 officers and around 300 men.[88] Shortage of officers weakened the strength of the defenders and required brigadiers to spend much time organising the front line, even down to positioning sub-units such as platoons, a job usually handled at company level.

Unreliable communications, fragmented positions, and the heavy attrition suffered by junior officers created a leadership vacuum that inevitably drew higher ranking officers, especially brigadiers, closer to the front. As a result FitzClarence frequently left his dugout to visit his forward battalions and organise the defence in person. Historian Nikolas Gardner has been critical of this aspect of British command, arguing that the personal leadership of officers such as FitzClarence was risky and, ultimately, wasteful of life.[89] Yet this assessment ignores the nature of the fighting at Ypres. Commanding the disorganised and much depleted battalions of 1st Brigade in the midst of combat was no easy task. The limitations of available technology meant that FitzClarence could not rely on telephones and in any case, German breakthroughs frequently rendered telephone communication irrelevant as the front line suddenly shifted. The chaotic and fluid nature of the battle required quick decisions that could only be provided by

84   TNA, CAB 45/182, Jeudwine to Edmonds, 22 April 1923.
85   Frank Richards, *Old Soldiers Never Die*, (London, Faber & Faber, 1933), p.46.
86   TNA, CAB 45/140, Major Boyd to Edmonds, 18 May 1922.
87   TNA, WO 95/1263, 1st Coldstream Guards War Diary, 2 November 1914.
88   Petre, Ewart & Lowther, *Scots Guards in the Great War*, p.54.
89   Nikolas Gardner, *Trial by Fire: Command and the British Expeditionary Force 1914* (Westpoint, Praeger, 2003), pp.227, 229.

officers on the spot. This was a role that FitzClarence performed admirably. During the battle, he was nicknamed "G.O.C. Menin Road" for his energetic leadership.[90] John Terraine considered FitzClarence to have been "the soul of the defence" and Anthony Farrar-Hockley has argued that he set "a superb example as a commander in battle."[91] His proximity to the front meant that at critical moments he was able to react quickly, sealing breaches in the line and organising counter attacks.

The ability to make quick decisions was to play a critical role during the fighting for Gheluvelt on the 29 and 31 October. Gheluvelt was a small village with a pre-war population of just over one thousand people. However, its location astride the Menin to Ypres road gave it great strategic value in 1914. The Menin road cut through surrounding woodland and provided the quickest and most direct route to Ypres. The German offensive towards Ypres sought to drive along this road, but Gheluvelt served as an obstacle to the advance. Outflanking and avoiding the village was impractical due to the dense woodland that lay on either side of the road. Furthermore, British control of Gheluvelt and the high ground immediately behind it gave them observation of German attacks on Messines Ridge to the south, allowing the British to call down accurate artillery fire into the rear of German forces advancing against the ridgeline. Faced with these problems, the capture of Gheluvelt became a key German objective, and a formidable force of infantry, cavalry and artillery was assembled for the task. German forces comprised 30th Division, 54th Reserve Division, and 3rd Cavalry Division, plus various attached regiments and considerable artillery support.[92] Recognising the strategic value of the hamlet, the British were determined to defend the village at all costs.[93]

1st Brigade was given the task of covering the eastern approaches to Gheluvelt. By 29 October it was holding a position that ran from Polderhoek Wood in the north to the Menin road in the south.[94] All four battalions were committed to this overstretched line, leaving no significant reserves. To offset this weakness, FitzClarence was given temporary command of the 1st Gloucestershire Regiment, detached from 3rd Brigade.[95] Despite this reinforcement, the Guards Brigade was in a vulnerable position. After undertaking personal reconnaissance of the front, FitzClarence became

90   Edmonds, *Official History*, vol.II, p.369.
91   John Terraine, *The Ordeal of Victory* (Philadelphia, Lippincott, 1963), p.121; Farrar-Hockley, *Death of an Army*, p.165.
92   Intelligence Section of the General Staff, American Expeditionary Forces, *Histories of Two Hundred and Fifty-One Divisions of the German Army Which Participated in the War 1914-1918* (London: London Stamp Exchange, 1920).
93   For a detailed discussion of German forces arrayed against Gheluvelt, see A.F.A.N. Thorne, 'Gheluvelt Cross Roads, October 29th, 1914' in *Household Brigade Magazine*, Summer 1932, pp.175–179.
94   Ibid., p.174. Thorne's article is the best single account of the action on 29 October. As well as being a participant, Thorne had an emotional connection as his brother-in-law had been killed in the battle.
95   Ibid., p.174.

particularly concerned about the brigade's right flank.[96] This position was held by the battered 1st Coldstream Guards, reduced to approximately 350 men in earlier fighting but required to defend some 1500 yards of ground.[97] Attempting to bolster this weak flank, FitzClarence detached individual companies from his battalions to cover vulnerable points.[98] Unfortunately, this meant there was considerable intermixture of troops, with companies from separate battalions of the brigade mingled amongst one another. Thorne noted that this "was unsound but almost unavoidable."[99] Furthermore, much work needed to be done to improve existing trenches in the brigade area but, as Thorne recalled after the war, "reiteration of G.H.Q. orders for I Corps to attack, although the arrival of superior enemy forces rendered a successful attack very unlikely, unhappily prevented the concentration of all available minds and means on the defence of this vital sector."[100] Conscious of the vulnerability of his formation FitzClarence persuaded Major-General Samuel Lomax, commanding 1st Division, to assign the machine gun sections of 1st Gloucestershires and 1st South Wales Borderers to the brigade. FitzClarence personally positioned these four additional machine guns to cover expected avenues of attack.[101]

On 29 October the Germans launched a major offensive against Gheluvelt. Despite fierce resistance, the inherent weakness of 1st Brigade's position meant that they could not prevent a German break in. During the confused fighting, the 1st Coldstream Guards were surrounded and practically wiped out. The battle emphasised the difficulty of brigade command at Ypres. Telephone communications collapsed under the preparatory German bombardment and several runners were killed whilst attempting to carry messages from the front line.[102] Although the German attack had begun at 5.30am, the first reports emphasising the severity of the situation only reached FitzClarence's headquarters at approximately 7.00am. He immediately ordered the 1st Gloucestershires to make a counterattack to relieve the pressure on the Coldstream Guards.[103] Unfortunately, in the heat of battle, the commander of the Gloucesters, Colonel A.C. Lovett, decided it would be quicker to launch his four companies forward individually rather than organising a battalion level counterattack.[104] This diluted the impact as the companies advanced piecemeal, becoming embroiled in local actions and quickly losing impetus. An afternoon counterattack launched by 3rd Brigade was unable to make progress in the face of heavy German artillery and machine gun fire.

96   TNA WO 95/1261, 1st Brigade War Diary, Report on Operations October 27 – Nov 2.
97   Edmonds, *Official History*, vol.II, p.264.
98   The 1st Coldstreams were reinforced with a company of 1st Black Watch and 70 men of the 1st Gloucesters. See Thorne, 'Gheluvelt Cross Roads', p.175.
99   Ibid., p.175.
100   Ibid., p.175.
101   Ibid., p.175. Edmonds, *Official History*, vol.II, p.264 claims that the Borderers' machine guns were ordered forward but subsequently disappeared. However, this is not borne out by the later, more detailed account given by Thorne.
102   TNA, WO 95/1261, 1st Brigade War Diary, Report on Operations October 27 – Nov 2.
103   Ibid. FitzClarence stated he had ordered the counterattack at 6.55am.
104   Thorne, 'Gheluvelt Cross Roads', p.179.

However, the Germans had been forced to fight for every yard gained and had suffered severe casualties. One officer of the 1st Scots Guards, which resisted several German attacks over the day, commented "God knows how many we killed."[105] In the confused fighting, some parties of German infantry pushed forward to the outskirts of Gheluvelt, but were held off by defenders occupying the village chateau, which was serving as the headquarters of the 1st Scots Guards. This improvised defence was organised by the battalion's adjutant Captain Stephenson, who responded to a suggestion that it might be prudent to retreat with a shout of "No b_____r retires as long as I am alive!"[106] This ad hoc position repelled the German advance and prevented a breakthrough. Although the line had been driven in, it had not been broken. Gheluvelt remained in British hands.

Nevertheless, the fighting of the 29 October, sometimes known as the Battle of Gheluvelt Crossroads, did not seem like a victory to the British. At 4.45pm there was a crisis meeting of the 1st Division's brigade commanders FitzClarence, Edward Bulfin and Herman Landon, plus various battalion and artillery officers, where it was agreed to form a new defensive line on the outskirts of Gheluvelt village.[107] 1st Brigade retreated in the evening and took up a hastily entrenched position. The remnants of the 1st Coldstream Guards were withdrawn from the line during the night, leaving the brigade with just three much reduced battalions. Fortunately for the British, the German attackers, primarily drawn from the 54th Reserve Division and 3rd Cavalry Division, were equally exhausted after the day's fighting. A relative lull settled over the battlefield on the 30 October as the Germans reorganised and prepared for a major attack on the 31 October.

The British line covering Gheluvelt was perilously thin and there was concern that any German breakthrough here would be able to drive on Ypres virtually unimpeded. Edmonds commented of the defences "The line that stood between the British Empire and ruin was composed of tired, haggard and unshaven men, unwashed, plastered with mud, many in little more than rags."[108] The much reduced 1st Brigade held a shorter line than on 29 October, once again covering the eastern approaches, with its right flank anchored on 3rd Brigade. There were virtually no reserves behind the defenders. Hastily made contingency plans stated that in the event of a German breakthrough, 2nd Division, to the north, would counter attack to seal the breach. Yet with fighting raging along the entire line the practicalities of this operation were in doubt. The only immediate aid that 2nd Division could provide was to send the 2nd Worcestershire Regiment, consisting of 12 officers and 480 men, to act as an emergency reserve.[109]

105   Quoted in Petre, Ewart & Lowther, *Scots Guards in the Great War*, p.50.
106   Quoted in Thorne, 'Gheluvelt Cross Roads', p.180
107   Edmonds, *Official History*, vol.II, p.272; Thorne, 'Gheluvelt Cross Roads', p.181. Bulfin commanded 2nd Brigade and Landon led 3rd Brigade.
108   Edmonds, *Official History*, vol.II, p.304.
109   Mercian Regimental Archive, 'Gheluvelt': Transcript of Notes by Major E.B. Hankey.

At dawn on 31 October the Germans began "a murderous attack from their big guns" producing "a more terrible storm of shells than ever".[110] An infantry attack followed at 6.00am but was repulsed by British rifle fire. This victory was short lived, for the German artillery renewed the bombardment at 9.30am. The shelling was of exceptional intensity and accuracy. Gheluvelt was set ablaze and there were "many direct hits on the trenches."[111] Hammered by this bombardment and with trenches reduced to "a broken and bloody shambles", the British line could not resist a second German infantry assault.[112] The attackers crashed through a weak point in 3rd Brigade's defences and then proceeded to roll up the British line to both north and south, taking 1st Brigade in the flank. The British position crumbled under the pressure. A great gap was torn in the line, opening up the Menin – Ypres road, and allowing the Germans to surge forward. Gheluvelt fell into German hands at approximately 1.00pm.[113] Although individual battalions continued the fight, including the three units of 1st Brigade, 1st Division as an organised body had effectively been broken and the road to Ypres lay open.

The scale of this crisis should not be underestimated. BEF commander Sir John French considered the situation the "worst" moment of his entire life, recalling; "Personally I felt as if the last barrier between the Germans and the Channel seaboard was broken down, and I viewed the situation with the utmost gravity."[114] Casualties amongst the front line defenders were horrendous and the survivors were severely shaken. Edmonds commented "the area behind Gheluvelt presented a scene that to the onlooker seemed to exhibit every element of disaster", being marked by wrecked artillery pieces, abandoned equipment and a steady stream of retreating soldiers.[115]

At this critical moment there was a further blow for the British. At approximately 1.15pm a crisis conference between 1st and 2nd Division staff was hit by German shell fire. Lomax, commanding 1st Division was mortally wounded, while Major-General Charles Monro, commanding 2nd Division was knocked unconscious and did not fully recover for several hours.[116] The loss of both divisional commanders ruptured the chain of command and threatened to paralyse the organisation of the defence. Sir Douglas Haig, commanding I Corps, ordered Bulfin to take command of 1st Division. However, Bulfin could not afford to leave his heavily engaged brigade and in his absence, Landon was instructed to take charge of the division. Unfortunately Landon could not be located in the chaos of battle.[117] Therefore, during the critical hours of the

110   Quoted in Beckett, *Ypres*, p.167; Petre, Ewart & Lowther, *Scots Guards in the Great War*, p.51

111   Edmonds, *Official History*, vol.II, p.312.

112   Williams, 'Turning of the Tide', p.18.

113   The timings for the fighting around Gheluvelt are approximations at best. In the heat of the battle officers did not take note of the exact time, and subsequent reports offer inconsistent and contradictory information.

114   John French, *1914* (London, Constable & Co., 1919). pp.252-253.

115   Edmonds, *Official History*, vol.II, p.318.

116   Farrar-Hockley, *Death of an Army*, p.165.

117   Beckett, *Ypres*, p.174.

battle for Gheluvelt, 1st Division had no commander. This dislocation of the chain of command was a key factor in prompting Haig's famous ride towards the front line.[118]

With no orders forthcoming from divisional or corps level, it was up to officers on the spot to organise the defence and stave off a decisive defeat. FitzClarence was the ranking officer on the scene and thus assumed a huge degree of responsibility. Fortunately, he was able to maintain intermittent telephone contact with 1st Scots Guards, stationed at Gheluvelt chateau, and was thus in closer control of the situation than on the 29 October.[119] Nevertheless, the sound of intense fighting at the front and the numerous stragglers retreating past his headquarters made FitzClarence anxious, and he ultimately abandoned his dugout and commanded from horseback.[120] Throughout the morning he and Thorne visited units of the embattled 1st Brigade and organised the resistance.[121] His three battalions fought hard and fortunately avoided the scale of disaster that had befallen 3rd Brigade on their right flank, but the breaking of the British line meant that they were forced to give ground to avoid becoming surrounded. By 12.30pm, all that was left of the defenders of Gheluvelt were a handful of troops from the 1st Scots Guards and 1st South Wales Borderers, clinging on in the grounds of the chateau. After reconnoitring the front line, FitzClarence briefly considered withdrawing these survivors to Polderhoek Wood and abandoning Gheluvelt entirely but, recognising that such a retreat would remove the last barrier to the German advance, he swiftly rejected the idea.[122] Instead, as Thorne recalled, FitzClarence "decided that an immediate counter-attack was to be made."[123]

The only troops available for this attack were the 2nd Worcesters. Strictly speaking FitzClarence did not have authority over this formation, which was detached from 2nd Division, although he had been informed by Lomax early on the 31 October that it was available as an emergency reserve.[124] However, this information had not reached the commander of the Worcesters, Major [later Brigadier General] Edward Hankey, who confessed he "knew nothing of the general situation."[125] Hankey was only informed at 10am that his battalion "could be used as a last resource", adding "I didn't know by whom!"[126] Indeed, Hankey was initially reluctant to accept orders from FitzClarence,

118   Gary Sheffield, *The Chief: Douglas Haig and the British Army*, (London, Aurum, 2011), pp.94-95. See Professor Sheffield's chapter elsewhere in this volume for a full discussion of Haig's decision.
119   Edmonds, *Official History*, p.320.
120   'X', 'Gheluvelt 1914', p.216.
121   Farrar-Hockley, *Death of an Army*, p.164.
122   TNA, WO 95/1261, 1st Brigade War Diary, Report on Operations October 27 – Nov 2.
123   TNA, WO 138/25, FitzClarence Personal File, letter from Andrew Thorne, 11 August 1915.
124   There had been prior arrangement between the divisional commanders, Lomax and Monro, about the deployment of the Worcesters, but this had not been made clear at front line level.
125   Mercian Regimental Archive, 'Gheluvelt': Transcript of Notes by Major E.B. Hankey.
126   Ibid.

who as a brigadier from a separate division had no formal authority over the battalion, although he relented once the gravity of the situation had been explained.[127]

Recognising that the Worcesters were new to the area, FitzClarence took the time to thoroughly brief Hankey on the ground around Gheluvelt, a process that lasted approximately 20 minutes.[128] FitzClarence then gave the order "To advance without delay and deliver a counter-attack with the utmost vigour against the enemy, who were in possession of Gheluvelt, and to re-establish our line there."[129] Thorne guided the Worcesters to a clump of woodland approximately 200 yards from the village whilst FitzClarence observed the attack from a nearby vantage point. As the Worcesters were preparing for their attack they were disrupted by retreating troops:

> Parties from various regiments in the 1st Division (majority of whom were severely wounded men, and all of whom were completely exhausted by the constant bombardments and massed attacks on their line) having been driven in by overwhelming odds retired actually through the ranks of the Battalion, even warning them that it was impossible to go on, and that it was murder etc. to attempt it.[130]

Nevertheless, three companies of the Worcesters, consisting of 8 officers and 370 men, began their advance at approximately 2pm.[131] Hankey's terse impressions of the attack were "deafening noise – retreating men – shouting commands".[132] The battalion advanced in two lines at a brisk jog, trying to cover the shell swept ground as quickly as possible without losing cohesion. One officer recalled:

> The advancing lines were immediately spotted and exceedingly heavy artillery fire was opened upon them from the left front. The shrapnel fire was terrific and over 100 casualties were left on that space alone. The space had to be crossed in one long rush, any other plan was quite impossible.[133]

However, although the battalion suffered at the hands of artillery fire, the German infantry in Gheluvelt did not see the attack until it was upon them. Farrar-Hockley described German forces as being in "that dangerous state of relaxation to be found

127   TNA, WO 138/25, FitzClarence Personal File, letter from Charles Corkran, 15 August 1915.
128   Mercian Regimental Archive, 'Gheluvelt': Transcript of Notes by Major E.B. Hankey. FitzClarence initially briefed the Worcesters' adjutant, Captain Clarke, and subsequently briefed Hankey in person.
129   TNA, CAB 45/140, 'A Short Account of the Action of Gheluvelt 31st October 1914' by Major B.C.S. Clarke, 6 June 1922.
130   Ibid.
131   Mercian Regimental Archive, 'Gheluvelt': Transcript of Notes by Major E.B. Hankey. One company had been detached earlier in the day for defensive duties.
132   Ibid.
133   TNA, CAB 45/140, 'A Short Account of the Action of Gheluvelt 31st October 1914' by Major B.C.S. Clarke, 6 June 1922.

when inexperienced troops have taken a first objective under unseasoned leaders."[134] The Germans appear to have been concentrating on searching remaining buildings and engaging the surviving defenders in the chateau.[135] As a result they were taken by surprise and "quickly dealt with both by the bayonet and point blank rifle fire."[136] A German account from the 247th Reserve Infantry Regiment, which lost virtually all its officers in the day's fighting, revealed something of the confusion at the moment of the counter attack:

> The village itself was in an utterly indescribable, chaotic state. The thunder of the guns and the chattering of the rifles was continuous, then amidst it all, came the shout, "The British have forced their way back in!".... Formations were hopelessly intermingled, so the officers did not have a firm grip on their own men... the exhaustion of the men was too great.[137]

The Germans were routed from the village and contact was established with the defenders of the chateau. Hankey met with Colonel H.E. Burleigh Leach, commanding officer of the 1st South Wales Borderers, greeting him with "My God, fancy meeting you here" to which Leach is said to have replied "Thank God you have come."[138]

The position was still dangerous. Hankey recalled that at this point Gheluvelt was a "No man's land [of] burning & shells!"[139] German artillery began a fresh bombardment of the village, making physical occupation largely impossible. Although there was no organised body of Germans left in the ruins, small groups and individuals remained and needed to be rooted out before the hamlet was secure. Hankey sent back for reinforcements for this work, unaware that none were available.[140] In the early evening, conscious that they could not hold the position indefinitely, FitzClarence ordered his troops to abandon the devastated village and withdraw to a new defensive line at Veldhoek.

However, the counter attack had been decisive. The German advance had been thrown back, the gap in the British line on the Menin – Ypres road had been closed, and a disastrous defeat had been averted. Although the battle continued for several weeks, the Germans never had such an opportunity again. Future attacks buckled the British line but never came so close to breaking it. FitzClarence and 1st Brigade remained at the front and continued to fight throughout the Battle of Ypres, being involved in particularly fierce combat on 2 November and when resisting the assault of the Prussian Guard on 11 November. In the early hours of 12 November, FitzClarence was organising a night attack at the head of his old regiment, the 1st Irish Guards,

134   Farrar-Hockley, *Death of an Army*, p.167.
135   Harry Fitzmaurice Stacke, *The Worcestershire Regiment in the Great War* (Kidderminster, G.T. Cheshire & Son, 1928), p.34.
136   TNA, CAB 45/140, 'A Short Account of the Action of Gheluvelt 31st October 1914' by Major B.C.S. Clarke, 6 June 1922.
137   Quoted in Sheldon, *German Army at Ypres 1914*, pp.173-174.
138   Quoted in Stacke, *Worcestershire Regiment*, p.34.
139   Mercian Regimental Archive, 'Gheluvelt': Transcript of Notes by Major E.B. Hankey.
140   Ibid.

when he was hit and killed by a stray bullet.[141] It was a tragic end to a short but critically important career.

FitzClarence's role in organising the Gheluvelt counter attack was not immediately recognised. His untimely death further delayed recognition, and it was not until 1915 that he was finally identified as the key officer.[142] Haig was so impressed by FitzClarence's actions that he ordered documents testifying to his role to be retrospectively placed in the I Corps War Diary.[143] FitzClarence was posthumously judged as "the man who saved Calais" and "the man who turned the tide."[144] The plaudits were well earned. FitzClarence's "soldierly instinct" and quick decision-making had undoubtedly saved the British line from collapse.[145] Indeed, FitzClarence's conduct throughout his time in command of 1st (Guards) Brigade was exemplary. He took command of a tired and bloodied formation and led it through some of the fiercest fighting in British military history. At the Battle of Ypres he proved himself a natural leader. His ability to act on his own initiative and to respond quickly to events at the front was demonstrated most clearly at Gheluvelt, but he also proved his skills on 2 November when he organised a scratch force of stragglers for a counter attack. His tireless energy in managing the defence was shown throughout the battle, but was perhaps most clearly in evidence during the repulse of the Prussian Guards Corps after a day of intense fighting on 11 November.

FitzClarence's leadership was matched by the courage and professionalism of the soldiers he commanded. The British Expeditionary Force owed much of its tactical success to the process of reform that had been undertaken in the years after the Boer War, and in many ways FitzClarence embodied the best aspects of the post-Boer War officer class. He seems to have steered clear of cliques or army politics, and whilst he left no intellectual mark on the force, his attitude towards training was that of a consummate professional. Reformers of the era had often spoken of their desire to create a spirit of initiative within the British Army; FitzClarence's conduct at the Battle of Ypres proved that such ideas had not been lost on him.

His leadership drew admiration from friend and foe alike. Prince Eitel Friedrich, second son of the Kaiser and commanding officer of the 1st [Prussian] Footguards Regiment which had battled 1st Brigade on 11 November, wrote of FitzClarence "He was an opponent before whom we dip our swords in respectful salute."[146] Captain Valentine Williams of the Irish Guards wrote "In the roll of honour of the British Empire no name will stand higher than that of Charles FitzClarence, V.C."[147] The regimental history of the Coldstream Guards stated "The untimely death of this

---

141 The most detailed account of FitzClarence's death can be found in Michael Craster (ed.), *Fifteen Rounds a Minute: The Grenadiers at War 1914* (Barnsley, Pen & Sword, 2012), pp.134-138.
142 'X', 'Gheluvelt 1914', p.214.
143 Sheffield, *The Chief*, p.420, endnote 112.
144 Williams, 'Turning of the Tide', p.12.
145 Ibid., p.22.
146 Quoted in Sheldon, *German Army at Ypres*, p.349.
147 Williams, 'Turning of the Tide', p.32.

gallant and distinguished Guardsman was felt and deplored far beyond his immediate command; his was a loss to the whole Army."[148] Perhaps the most touching tribute came from Andrew Thorne, who wrote a poignant letter to his wife the day after FitzClarence's death: "Charles and I are nearly heartbroken. He was such a splendid man to serve and a glorious one to follow. I hadn't known him intimately for long but he was one who you would follow directly he came along and gave you the order. He was so splendid."[149]

148   John Ross-of-Bladensburg, *The Coldstream Guards 1914 – 1918*, Vol.I, (London, Oxford University Press, 1926), p.244.
149   IMW, Thorne Papers, AT/1, Thorne to wife, 12 November 1914. The Charles referred to is Charles Corkran, brigade major of 1st Brigade.

12

David Henderson and Command of the Royal Flying Corps

James Pugh[1]

For an officer whom Prime Minister H. H. Asquith referred to as "a long way the best instructed & most level headed of our Generals," David Henderson remains one of the British Army's least known figures of the Victorian / Edwardian era.[2] His somewhat surprising absence from the literature is the result of a number of challenges. Henderson's papers, held by the Royal Air Force Museum (RAFM), have been characterised by Cooper as "fragmentary," and his description is apt.[3] This reflects a more general point that affects the wider study of air power in 1914. As captured by the memoirs of Baring, Henderson's personal assistant between August and December 1914, the fluid nature of warfare during the opening campaigns of the First World War prevented the Royal Flying Corps (RFC) from establishing a rhythm and routine to their activities.[4] This was reflected in the frequent shifts of the RFC's Headquarters (HQ) during the move into Belgium, and the subsequent retreat.[5] As with the wider British Expeditionary Force (BEF), it was not until the front stabilised that the RFC were able to operate in a more considered and routine fashion.[6] As such, orders, letters, memorandum, and papers were sent in a hap-hazard fashion between the Directorate of Military Aeronautics (DMA) at the War Office (WO), RFC HQ, and the RFC's

1   The author is extremely grateful to Dr Spencer Jones for offering assistance and support above and beyond the call of editorial duty. In addition, the author would like to thank the archive and library staffs at the University of Glasgow, Brasenose College, Oxford, and the Joint Services Command and Staff College, Shrivenham.

2   M. Brock & E. Brock, eds., *H. H. Asquith, letters to Venetia Stanley* (Oxford, Oxford University Press, 1985) [1982], pp.390-391. Letter, Asquith to Stanley, 22 Jan 1915.

3   M. Cooper, *The Birth of Independent Air Power: British Air Policy in the First World War* (London, Allen & Unwin, 1986), pp.25-26, fn.40.

4   M. Baring, *R.F.C. H.Q.* (London, Bell & Sons, 1920), chapters two to five.

5   F. H. Sykes, *Aviation in War and Peace* (London, Edward Arnold & Co., 1922), p.55.

6   F. H. Sykes, *From Many Angles: An Autobiography* (London, G. G. Harrap & Co., 1942), p.139; Baring, *R.F.C.*, p.56.

David Henderson. (Bain collection, Library of Congress)

squadrons in the field.[7] This was exacerbated by the prevalence of the short-war myth; a belief that influenced RFC doctrine (as did the practical experience of military aviation during the pre-war period).[8] By 1916, the business of aerial warfare had become institutionalised in the BEF, and the relevant and densely packed Air Ministry files, held at the National Archives, Kew, demonstrate this reality.[9] Important primary source material is available but, for much of the opening campaigns of the conflict, the RFC, like the BEF, was forced to give full attention to stopping the German onslaught. Thus, RFC personnel are perhaps to be forgiven if their first priority was not filing paperwork with the WO.

A major source of material on Henderson, particularly between August and December 1914, comes from autobiographical material written by senior RFC officers. Important sources are provided by Henderson's Chief of Staff (CoS), Frederick Sykes, who, after a varied career during the First World War, would rise to become the RAF's second Chief of the Air Staff (CAS); and Hugh Trenchard, who would command the RFC's First Wing before eventually succeeding Henderson as commander of the RFC in France.[10] These have formed the foundations upon which researchers have built.[11] These sources provide a plethora of detail on Henderson and his command of

7   For example, see The National Archives (TNA), Air Ministry File (AIR) 1/118/15/40/36-Précis of remarks, Henderson to Brancker, 9 Sep 1914.

8   General Staff, AP 144, *Training Manual, RFC (Military Wing), Part II* (Jun 1914), p.49. See also Sykes, *War and Peace*, p.45; Sykes, *Angles*, pp.123-124.

9   Examples are found in the TNA, AIR 1 series. This vast collection was established to aid the official historians, Raleigh and later Jones, in writing *The War in the Air* series.

10   Sykes, *Angles*, especially chapters four to six; Trenchard Papers (TP), RAFM, MFC 76/1/61-Autobiographical Notes, especially pp.61-74.

11   A. Boyle, *Trenchard* (London, Collins, 1962); E. Ash, *Sir Frederick Sykes and the Air*

the RFC, and they form a significant aspect of the referential basis of this chapter.[12] However, troubling personal relations have come to characterise the leadership of the RFC and RAF, particularly with the arrival of Trenchard to the front in November 1914.[13] The Sykes-Trenchard rivalry, given significant prominence in these memoirs and biographies, has done much to prevent an objective understanding of command within the RFC.[14] This presents another limitation when exploring Henderson's command of the RFC during 1914.

More generally, there is a dearth of academic scholarship on Henderson, in both his pre-RFC career and his time as commander of the RFC.[15] H. A. Jones, who completed five of the six volumes of *The War in the Air* series, wrote a privately published memoir of Henderson in 1931 and, later, a brief biographical article in the *Journal of the Royal Air Force College* (1936).[16] Henderson is most often encountered in studies that explore British air power during the First World War, but his role tends to be eclipsed by that of Trenchard.[17] Outside of specialist air power studies, Henderson's role with the RFC is relatively unknown and, even within specialist works, some reference is inevitably made to his "shadowy" presence in the literature.[18] Recent articles by Prins are useful for narrative details, but they are not written for a scholarly audience.[19]

In the wider, non-air power literature on the campaigns of 1914, the RFC does not feature heavily.[20] This is perhaps understandable, given the extent of the RFC

Revolution, 1912-1918 (London, Frank Cass, 1999).

12   Other important autobiographical sources include N. Macmillan, *Sir Sefton Brancker* (London, William Heinemann, 1935) and M. Baring, *R.F.C.*

13   M. Cooper, 'A House Divided: Policy, Rivalry and Administration in Britain's Military Air Command 1914–1918,' *Journal of Strategic Studies*, Vol.3, No.2 (Summer, 1980): pp.178-201.

14   It was a rivalry that grew in bitterness, particularly after the conflict. For example, see Henderson Papers (HP), RAFM, AC71/12/195, letter, Trenchard to Lady Henderson, 7 Oct 1954. See also *The Times*, 2 Oct 1954.

15   A notable exception is T. G. Fergusson, *British Military Intelligence, 1870-1914: The development of a modern intelligence organization* (London, Arms & Armour, 1984), chapters eight and nine.

16   H. A. Jones, *Per Ardua ad Astra*: *Sir David Henderson KCB, KCVO, DSO, A Memoir* (London, Hatchard, Privately Published, 1931). A draft of this rare book is found in HP, RAFM, AC71/4/2. See also HP, RAFM, AC71/12/12-H. A. Jones, 'Sir David Henderson, Father of the Royal Air Force,' *The Journal of the Royal Air Force College*, Vol. XI, No. 1 (Spring, 1931): pp.6-12.

17   Notable exceptions include Cooper's *Air Power* and Ash's *Sykes*.

18   R. Higham, *The Military Intellectuals in Britain, 1918-1939* (New Brunswick, NJ., Rutgers University Press, 1966), p.123, n.

19   F Prins, 'Forgotten Founder [Part I],' *Aeroplane*, Vol. 40, No.4 (Apr 2012): pp.60-63; F. Prins, 'Forgotten Founder [Part II],' *Aeroplane*, Vol. 40, No.5 (May 2012): pp.36-38.

20   For typical examples, see J. E. Edmonds, *Military Operations: France and Belgium* (*OH*), *1914, Vol. II,* (London, Macmillan & Co., 1925), p.342; N. Gardner, *Trial by Fire: Command and the British Expeditionary Force in 1914* (Westport, CT., Praeger, 2003), p.77.

contribution to these campaigns, reflected in its very limited strength and capabilities.[21] Buckley's conclusion, that air power gained more from the First World War than the conflict gained from air power, does much to indicate wider historiographical attitudes to British military aviation during this period.[22] Nonetheless, the RFC was an integral component of the BEF, and the Corps reflected the doctrine, practices, and wider cultural identity of the British Army.[23] As Terraine suggests, "the RFC was part of the Army and did not pretend to be anything else."[24] It is a grave error to divorce the experience of the RFC from that of the wider BEF, and this chapter embeds the Corps in the wider historiography of the British Army of the era.

This chapter attempts to follow the advice of Michael Howard, exploring Henderson and his command of the RFC in "width," "depth," and "context."[25] The chapter is divided into four sections, the first of which examines Henderson's military career up to 1911; the point at which he took his first tentative steps into the world of aviation. It establishes the significance of his educational experiences in civilian and military life, and of his growing expertise in the field of tactical reconnaissance. It was his personal reputation, hard earned, that did much to garner support in the British Army for the development of an aviation arm. The second section explores Henderson's role at the WO as he oversaw the development of aviation policy between 1912 and 1914. He continued to use his considerable reputation to good effect, generating significant interest in military aviation during this period. The final sections focus upon his command of the RFC from August to December 1914, including his almost month-long appointment as General Officer Commanding (GOC), 1st Division. Whilst Henderson was an air power commander, he was also a career soldier in the British Army. The analysis that follows illuminates some of the wider issues that faced the Edwardian Army as it went to war in 1914.

Henderson is deserving of the title "Father of the Royal Flying Corps," but the picture that emerges of the RFC's first GOC is challenging.[26] Henderson was an intelligent and well respected officer within the British Army who, by 1914, had earned himself significant patronage from military and political elites. His role in the development of British military aviation was crucial, yet his performance during the opening campaigns of the First World War was more ambiguous. He emerged from 1914 with his reputation enhanced, but his command of the RFC was not without its problems.

---

21   W. Raleigh, *The War in the Air: Being the Story of the part played in the Great War by the Royal Air Force (WIA), Vol.I* (Oxford, Clarendon Press, 1922), p.411.

22   J. Buckley, *Air Power in the Age of Total War* (London, Routledge, 1999), p.68.

23   J. Pugh, 'The Conceptual Origins of the Control of the Air: British Military and Naval Aviation, 1911-1918' (PhD Thesis, University of Birmingham, 2012), chapters two, four, and five.

24   J. Terraine, 'World War I and the Royal Air Force,' *Journal of the Royal Air Force Historical Society*, No.12 (1994), p.13.

25   M. Howard, 'The Use and Abuse of Military History,' *Journal of the Royal United Services Institute (JRUSI)*, Vol.107, No.2 (Feb 1962), pp.7-8.

26   See HP, RAFM, AC71/12/195, letter, Trenchard to Lady Henderson, 7 Oct 1954.

Early Career, 1883 – 1911

Given that relatively little about Henderson's early life and career has been published, it is worth drawing certain parallels with his contemporary, Douglas Haig. Terraine called Haig the "Educated Soldier," and the evidence suggests that Henderson was an unusually well-educated soldier who earned a reputation as an "extremely bright and hard-working professional."[27] Individuals such as Haig and Henderson, who came from a professional background, reflected the changing sociological make-up of officer recruits of the British Army.[28] As with Haig, Henderson joined the British Army from university without completing his studies.[29] However, unlike Haig, who read for a generalist "Pass degree" at Brasenose College, Oxford, Henderson undertook specialist engineering studies at the University of Glasgow. He worked under Professor James Thompson and matriculated at the age of just fifteen.[30] The origins of his decision to forgo his degree and join the British Army are unclear.[31] Nonetheless, his decision to join the British Army highlights two interesting factors: first, he entered Sandhurst with an unusual educational background based on an inherently technical subject rather than the more general educational background of officers such as Haig; and second, Henderson opted to join an infantry regiment, the Argyll and Sutherland Highlanders, rather than a more fashionable cavalry regiment (possibly reflecting his dislike of riding) or the Royal Engineers (RE).[32] Given his background in engineering, it is interesting that he did not join the RE. However, the range of factors affecting an individual's decision with regard to enlistment and choice of regiment were extremely varied.[33]

There is some suggestion that senior officers were resistant to the introduction of air power because they were concerned that it would undermine the value of cavalry, but the flaws of this interpretation have been demonstrated by Whitmarsh.[34] Badsey

---

27   Fergusson, *Military Intelligence*, p.158. Cooper also makes this comparison. Cooper, 'House Divided,' p.180.

28   S. Robbins, *British Generalship on the Western Front, 1914-1918: Defeat into Victory* (London, Frank Cass, 2005), p.39. Henderson's family ran a successful ship building firm on the Clyde, D. and W. Henderson and Co. For example, see *The Engineer*, 6 Jan 1988, p.6.

29   Royal Military College Sandhurst, Student Register, 1882-1883.

30   University of Glasgow Archives, R8/1/6 and R8/1/7: Matriculation Records, 1877-1880 / 1881. The archives of Brasenose College, Oxford hold records on Haig's matriculation. See also G. Sheffield, *The Chief: Douglas Haig and the British Army* (London, Aurum, 2011), pp.15-17.

31   H. A. Jones, 'Sir David Henderson,' p.6.

32   Henderson noted he "hated" cross country riding whilst at the Staff College. See F. H. Sykes, 'Military Aviation,' *The Aeronautical Journal*, Vol.17, No.67 (Jul 1913), p.137.

33   D. French, *Military Identities: The Regimental System, the British Army, and the British People, c.1870-2000* (Oxford, Oxford University Press, 2005), pp.50-55.

34   D. Divine, *The Broken Wing: A Study in the British Exercise of Air Power* (London, Hutchinson, 1966), pp.37-39; A. Whitmarsh, 'British Army Manoeuvres and the Development of British Military Aviation, 1910-1913,' *War in History*, Vol.14, No.3

notes that "cavalrymen [such as Sykes] played a willing role in the establishment of the fledgling airpower of the British Army," yet the RFC's most senior officer was an infantryman.[35] Coming from an infantry background, Henderson was particularly well equipped to take a positive interest in aviation as he had no regimental affiliation to protect, and, given his education in engineering, he was also able to grasp the inherently technical foundations of flight.

Henderson's service between 1883 and 1892 took in the typically varied imperial postings of the period, and H. A. Jones characterises him as a popular and active regimental officer.[36] He spent time attached to the RE, further strengthening his experience and knowledge of engineering.[37] Offering further evidence of his intellectual ability, Henderson sat the Staff College entrance examinations of May 1893, coming third in the "Order of Merit."[38] Henderson took up his place at Camberley in 1894 and graduated in 1896. The particulars of his time at the College are not well-preserved.[39] However, College records indicate that, in July 1894, Henderson was elected President of the Mess Committee.[40] This was less glamorous than the much coveted post of Master of the Drag Hunt, but it was an important organisational role that would have brought Henderson to the attention of his colleagues and the directing staff.

Henderson's attendance at Camberley coincided with a greater emphasis at the College on the intellectual aspects of the course.[41] Yet, an increasingly important function of the College was to "create a sense of uniformity and harmony in the Army as a whole."[42] As Corbett was to write, "words must have the same meaning for all," and the education provided at Camberley went some way to providing the British Army and its Staff College graduates with a shared language that reflected the corporate image of the organisation and the values and beliefs to which it gave precedence.[43] These included the importance of offensive action, moral superiority, flexibility, and the traits of effective leadership.[44] Thus, by the time he was sent to serve in Africa, Henderson

(Autumn 2007): pp.325-346.

35   S. Badsey, *Doctrine and Reform in the British Cavalry, 1880-1918* (Aldershot, Ashgate, 2008), p.237.

36   These postings included southern Africa, Ceylon, and Hong Kong. H. A. Jones, 'Sir David Henderson,' p.7.

37   Ibid, p.7.

38   *Report on the Examination for Admission to the Staff College Held in May, 1893; With Copies of the Examination Papers* (London, HMSO, 1893), p.6.

39   HP, RAFM, AC71/4/2-H. A. Jones, Draft, *Per Ardua*, chapter two.

40   Joint Services Command and Staff College Library, Shrivenham, SC-M1, Officers Mess, Staff College Minute Book. Proceedings of a General Mess Meeting Held 9 Jul 1894.

41   B. Bond, *The Victorian Army and the Staff College, 1854-1914* (London, Eyre Methuen, 1972), p.155; French, *Military Identities*, p.161.

42   Bond, *Staff College*, pp.258-259.

43   J. Corbett, *Some Principles of Maritime Strategy* (London, Longmans, 1911), p.3; P. Gray, *The Leadership, Direction and Legitimacy of the RAF Bomber Offensive from Inception to 1945* (London, Continuum, 2012), p.19.

44   Values and beliefs eventually captured in *Field Service Regulations*. For example, see General Staff, War Office, *Field Service Regulations, Part One: Operations*. Reprinted with

was a product of an increasingly professional organisation and was equipped with the intellectual and practical tools necessary to undertake imperial service for the British Army.

Imperial service, particularly during the Boer War, allowed Henderson to create significant personal connections with some of the most influential officers in the British Army.[45] Henderson's Boer War experience is discussed by Fergusson and, from a range of sources, it is possible to draw some important conclusions.[46] First, Henderson demonstrated his abilities as an organiser and as a staff officer. Serving as Kitchener's Director of Military Intelligence, Henderson oversaw the rapid expansion of the Field Intelligence Department.[47] As *The Times* history of the conflict noted, Henderson's appointment to Kitchener's staff saw a significant improvement in the British Army's centralised intelligence service, based on the creation of a responsive intelligence function.[48] As Atwood records, Kitchener would start his working day in conference with his intelligence director before seeing Henderson again in the early evening.[49] Henderson became a vital member of Kitchener's "inner circle," securing an important and influential patron in the process.[50] Whilst debate exists on the importance of patronage, Kitchener proved to be one of two powerful backers who supported Henderson's career.[51]

Henderson proved to be a highly competent staff officer and developed a reputation as an effective tactical leader. During the siege of Ladysmith, Henderson came to prominence when he provided successful reconnaissance support and leadership during a raid against Boer guns, and both the official history and *The Times* history highlight his role in the success of the operation.[52] The Boer War was a trying ordeal for the British Army, with personal reputations won and lost, and bitter post-war disputes regarding strategy, tactics, training, and technology.[53] However, Henderson

amendments, 1912 (London, HMSO, 1912), p.126.

45   A summary of Henderson's post-1898 service (up to the end of 1917) can be found in War Office, *The Army List: War Services of Officers* (London, HMSO, Dec 1917), p.2776.

46   Fergusson, *Military Intelligence*, chapters eight and nine.

47   Fergusson, *Military Intelligence*, pp.158-159; Marquis of Anglesey, *A History of British Cavalry, Vol. IV: 1899-1913* (London, Leo Cooper, 1986), pp.254-255, n.

48   L. S. Amery, ed., *The Times History of the War in South Africa, Vol.V* (London, Samson Low, Marston & Co., 1907), p.108 and pp.268-269; Fergusson, *Military Intelligence*, p.159.

49   R. Atwood, *Roberts & Kitchener in South Africa, 1900-1902* (Barnsley, Pen & Sword, 2011), pp.231-232 and p.242.

50   Amery, *Times History, Vol.V*, pp.274-275

51   T. Bowman & M. Connelly, *The Edwardian Army: Recruiting, Training, and Deploying the British Army, 1902-1914* (Oxford, Oxford University Press, 2012), pp.35-36; Travers, *The Killing Ground: The British Army, the Western Front and the Emergence of Modern War, 1900-1918* (Barnsley, Pen & Sword, 2003) [1987], pp.3-6.

52   J. F. Maurice, [Official] *History of the War in South Africa, 1899-1902, Volume II* (London, Hurst & Blackett, 1907), pp.546-547; L. S. Amery, ed., *The Times History of the War in South Africa, Vol.III* (London, Samson Low, Marston & Co., 1905), pp.167-169.

53   S. Jones, *Boer War to World War: Tactical Reform of the British Army*, 1902-1914 (Norman,

emerged from the conflict with an enhanced reputation.[54] In October 1902, he was awarded the Distinguished Service Order, his name appearing in the *London Gazette* alongside such notable figures as Sir John French, Sir Ian Hamilton, Douglas Haig, and Edmund Allenby.[55] As at Staff College, the Boer War provided further opportunities for relationship building and officers came to know colleagues with whom they would serve as General Officers during the First World War.[56] The Boer War also secured Henderson's reputation as an authority on tactical intelligence, and as a thoughtful and reflective officer. His subsequent writings were presented in a practical and non-threatening fashion, and he avoided the label and stigma associated with the term "intellectual."[57]

Three important developments took place in the aftermath of the Boer War: Henderson wrote two influential texts on intelligence and reconnaissance; he established an excellent working relationship with Sir John French, the second of his patrons; and, finally, he took his first tentative steps into the field of aviation. This last decision was handled with great skill and tact, and Henderson played a significant role in creating a positive impression of aviation to senior officers within the British Army.

Henderson's writings on intelligence and reconnaissance demonstrated his cautious approach to progress and reform. In his 1904 manual, *Field Intelligence: Its Principles and Practices*, and his later offering, *The Art of Reconnaissance* (three editions between 1907 and 1914), Henderson recognised the growing importance of technological solutions to the challenges facing military professionals.[58] For Henderson, the bicycle and motorcar would become important methods of transport for intelligence gathering, but he was careful never to question the value of existing systems, particularly cavalry.[59] This was the type of cautious and deferential progressiveness that Henderson utilised to further the cause of aviation within the British Army. Henderson was not of the Herbert Richmond or J. F. C. Fuller school of reform and innovation.[60] He couched his writings in careful language and made sure he noted the importance of new technologies in supporting and supplementing existing ideas and systems.[61] In this

OK., University of Oklahoma Press, 2012), *passim*.

54   His rakish portrait, published as part of *The Times History*, would have drawn further attention to Henderson. L. S. Amery, ed., *The Times History of the War in South Africa, Vol. VI* (London, Samson Low, Marston & Co., 1909), opposite p.528.

55   *London Gazette*, 31 Oct 1902.

56   J. James, *The Paladins: A Social History of the RAF up to the outbreak of World War II* (London, Macdonald, 1990), pp.24-25.

57   The same could be said for Haig.

58   D. Henderson, *Field Intelligence: Its Principles and Practices* (London, HMSO, 1904); D. Henderson, *The Art of Reconnaissance* (London, John Murray, Third Edition, 1914) [1907].

59   Henderson, *Field Intelligence*, p.13.

60   For relevant examples, see J. F. C. Fuller, 'The Tactics of Penetration: A Counterblast to German Numerical Superiority,' *JRUSI*, Vol.59, No.2 (Jul-Nov, 1914): pp.378-389; B. D. Hunt, *Sailor-Scholar: Admiral Sir Herbert Richmond, 1871-1946* (Ontario, Wilfrid Laurier University Press, 1982), pp.32-38.

61   See Henderson's cautious preface to the third edition of *The Art of Reconnaissance*. Pages

manner, Henderson's progressive ideas did not threaten to undermine his professional relationship with Sir John French, who was notoriously protective in his attitudes towards the British Army's cavalry arm.[62] Henderson served in various capacities on the staffs of French, rising to CoS during the latter's time as Inspector-General, and accompanied Sir John on tours of India and Canada.[63]

Henderson became French's expert on aviation and, during 1908, when the British Government undertook investigations into the "question of aerial navigation," Sir John consulted with Henderson.[64] French presented Henderson's opinions as part of his submission to the Sub-Committee, and these were crafted with Henderson's characteristically cautious language.[65] From 1909, Britain began to take a growing interest in aviation.[66] When the British Army decided to send a small delegation to the Great Aviation Week held at Reims in August 1909, Henderson accompanied French and another senior officer, Sir James Grierson.[67] Both Hallion and Wohl demonstrate the significance of this event, as aviation came to be viewed as an increasingly practical and important pursuit.[68] During the meeting, Henderson, French, and Grierson were provided with access to senior military and political figures in France; a country that took a leading role in the development of military aviation during this period.[69]

There were a variety of reasons that individuals became interested in aviation, and a study conducted by a naval air service medical officer provides illuminating statistics.[70] Of Henderson, Divine states that his interest was not for personal gain, as he was already "strongly placed on the ladder of promotion."[71] However, both Ash and Cooper argue to the contrary, suggesting that Henderson took every opportunity to further his own

---

174 to 175 demonstrate Henderson's sensitive brand of iconoclasm.

62   See Badsey, *British Cavalry*, chapters four and five. French publicly acknowledged this attitude in 1913. See Sykes, 'Military Aviation,' pp.138-139.

63   War Office, *The Army List* (London, HMSO, Dec 1914), p.37; H. A. Jones, 'Sir David Henderson,' p.8.

64   TNA, Cabinet (CAB) Paper 16/7-Report and Proceedings of the Sub-Committee of the Committee of Imperial Defence on Aerial Navigation, 28 Jan 1909, pp.86-87.

65   Ibid, pp.86-87.

66   N. Jones, *The Origins of Strategic Bombing: A Study of the Development of British Air Strategic Thought and Practice up to 1918* (London, William Kimber, 1973), pp.26-27.

67   *Flight*, 4 Sep 1909, p.541. Others in attendance included David Lloyd George and Richard Haldane.

68   R. P. Hallion, *Taking Flight: Inventing the Aerial Age from Antiquity to the First World War* (Oxford, Oxford University Press, 2003), pp.257-265; R. Wohl, *A Passion for Wings: Aviation and the Western Imagination, 1908-1918* (London, Yale University Press, 1994), pp.100-110.

69   *Flight*, 4 Sep 1909, p.535. French can be seen sat close to the President of France. On French aviation, see C. Christienne & P. Lissarague, *A History of French Military Aviation*. Translated by F. Kianka. (Washington, D.C., Smithsonian Institution, 1986), pp.32-53.

70   H. G. Anderson, *The Medical and Surgical Aspects of Aviation* (London, Hodder & Stoughton, 1919), pp.71-72.

71   Divine, *Broken Wing*, p.33.

career, frequently displaying a "selfish character."[72] The reasoning behind Henderson's decision likely embraced both a genuine operational interest in air power and an opportunity to further his career, and these motivations were not mutually exclusive. Henderson's decision to take his aviation certificate resulted in some notable publicity in the specialist aviation journals of the day, bringing Henderson to prominence in Britain's small, if growing, aeronautical community.[73] For this decision, he would also garner public praise from French in 1913.[74] For an officer of the reputation and standing of Henderson to take an interest in flight was a vital first step in the process of legitimising aviation as an acceptable and necessary pursuit in the British Army. Henderson was not a "crank" or an "intellectual," and his career path to this point was largely conventional.

Henderson and the RFC, 1912 – 1914

Henderson became an increasingly important member of Britain's aeronautical community, and was present during some of the most significant discussions that took place in various forums during 1911.[75] His finger was on the pulse of contemporary thought relating to the development of military aviation, and he was ideally suited to represent the British Army in government committees on aviation. Henderson was a senior member of a small technical sub-committee, tasked by the Committee of Imperial Defence to provide recommendations for the establishment of a "National Corps of Aviators."[76] This was to be an inter-service organisation, and representatives of both the Army and Navy were involved in developing tentative policy to create a flying corps.[77] However, the conclusions and proceedings of the committee came to be dominated by the view of the Army, with Henderson's influence and seniority playing an important part in this process.[78]

The actual report, whilst signed by representatives of the WO and Admiralty, was produced by a small team headed by Henderson, with Sykes acting as unofficial secretary and scribe.[79] Henderson's views on air power, shaped via the prism of his reconnaissance expertise, focused on the use of aircraft in the reconnaissance role. The report, backed by enthusiastic support from Churchill (as First Lord of the Admiralty) and Seely (as Secretary of State for War), was approved, and the RFC, with Military

---

72   Ash, *Sykes*, p.195; Cooper, *Air Power*, p.22.
73   *Flight*, 26 Aug and 2 Sep 1911, p.745 and p.759 respectively.
74   Sykes, 'Military Aviation,' p.138.
75   For example, see P. Radcliffe, 'The Military Aeroplane II,' *Aeronautical Journal*, Vol.16, No.2 (Jan 1912): pp.13-23.
76   TNA, CAB 16/16-Report of Committee of Imperial Defence Sub-Committee on Aerial Navigation, 29 Feb 1912.
77   Ibid.
78   N. Jones, *Strategic Bombing,* p.36.
79   TNA, CAB 16/16, Report, 29 Feb 1912; Ash, *Sykes*, pp.25-26.

and Naval Wings, was created in April 1912.[80] Given Henderson's expertise and role in the creation of early aviation policy, it was fitting that he was given responsibility for overseeing the Army's contribution to the RFC project. As a result, Henderson was posted from French's staff and appointed as the Director of Military Training (DMT). He established an aviation branch within the Directorate and, in September 1913, he established the DMA, becoming its first Director-General (DGMA).

Smith suggests that Henderson became a "passionate advocate for air power," but in practice he approached his task cautiously and, rather than trying to make sweeping organisational changes, he attempted to integrate the DMA into the existing structure of the WO and the Army Council.[81] Outside the administrative and organisational responsibilities of the DGMA, Henderson grasped the significance of proving the value of aviation to the British Army. In his 1904 manual, Henderson had stressed the importance of winning the trust of one's Commander-in-Chief (C-in-C) and inspiring confidence in one's colleagues.[82] From his military career up to this point, it is apparent that Henderson recognised that relationship building was an essential foundation upon which efficient and effective services were constructed. In many respects, Henderson's time as DGMA demonstrates some of the traits of successful strategic leadership.[83] In particular, Henderson played an important role in managing and facilitating the "interfaces" that existed between his Directorate and other organisations. As Gray suggests, these "interfaces exhibit friction during times of stress or competition for resources," and the birth of the RFC was characterised by such friction.[84] Sefton Brancker, who would serve as Henderson's deputy in the Directorate, has left a valuable overview of this period.[85] Given his technical expertise, reputation, and seniority, Henderson played a vital role at the WO, managing the interfaces to secure resources and generate positive interest in the RFC.[86] In managing these interfaces, particularly those that existed internally within the Army and the WO, Henderson undertook a multi-faceted approach to the development of the RFC: first, establishing and raising the profile of the Corps; second, seizing opportunities to provide the Army with practical examples of the value of aviation; and, finally, creating coherent doctrine.

His first step was to appoint a commander for the Military Wing (MW) of the RFC, and Henderson selected Frederick Sykes, a young captain with an avid interest in aviation, a background in reconnaissance and intelligence, and a graduate of the

---

80   Brancker records the close working relationship of Seely and Churchill. Macmillan, *Brancker*, pp.44-45.

81   R. A. Smith, 'Henderson, Sir David (1862–1921),' in *Oxford Dictionary of National Biography, Online Edition*, ed., L. Goldman (Oxford, OUP, 2008). http://www.oxforddnb.com/view/article/33808 (accessed 31 Oct 2012); Macmillan, *Brancker*, pp.34-35.

82   Henderson, *Field Intelligence*, p.1.

83   Gray, *Leadership*, p.3. The concept of interfaces is explored throughout Gray's study.

84   Gray, *Leadership*, p.79.

85   Macmillan, *Brancker*, chapters three and four. Brancker died before he had completed his memoirs, and Macmillan completed the project.

86   Macmillan, *Brancker*, pp.34-35.

Staff College at Quetta.[87] Influenced by Trenchard, the official histories have largely airbrushed Sykes from the history of the RFC. However, the scholarship of Higham and Ash has returned Sykes to the prominent place he deserves.[88] As Ash records, the decision to appoint Sykes, and the reaction of the wider RFC, have been corrupted by the recollections of Trenchard.[89] There is no evidence from the time to demonstrate that Sykes was given anything but the fullest support by his colleagues and superiors, and his appointment was an excellent decision by Henderson.[90] Sykes was fully seized of the Henderson agenda, and strove hard to build relationships, raise the profile of the Wing, and improve the operational effectiveness of his unit. In 1913, Sykes spoke of creating a "partnership" between the Corps, the Army and Navy, and the general public.[91] As Ash notes, Sykes was "a salesman to the receptive and a gadfly to the sceptical."[92] As part of these efforts, Sykes spoke publicly on developments in military aviation, delivering annual lectures in 1913 and 1914.[93] Henderson himself had set the precedent, and gave a talk to the Aeronautical Society of Great Britain in July 1912.[94]

Sir John French was scheduled to chair the lecture, and his involvement was the result of his personal interest in aviation, and of his close connection with Henderson. By this stage, French occupied the post of Chief of the Imperial General Staff (CIGS), the professional head of the British Army. He was also effectively the C-in-C designate of the BEF. Ill-health prevented French's attendance, but his place was taken by Sir James Grierson.[95] This level of interest was a crucial aspect of consolidating the position of the RFC within the Army, and, in a period of parsimony, a lack of institutional support could have strangled the RFC project at birth.[96] Henderson's cautious rhetoric was important, but the DGMA needed to provide tangible evidence of the capabilities

87   Ash, *Sykes*, chapters one and two.
88   Higham, *Military Intellectuals*, pp.122-126; Ash, *Sykes, passim*. On *The War in the Air* series, see J. J. Abbatiello, *Anti-Submarine Warfare in World War I: British Naval Aviation and the Defeat of the U-Boats* (London, Routledge, 2005), chapter six; C. Goulter, 'British Official Histories of the Air War,' in *The Last Word? Essays on Official History in the United States and the British Commonwealth*, ed. J. Grey (Westport, CT., Praeger, 2003), pp. 133-146.
89   Ash, *Sykes*, p.26.
90   Ibid, p.26.
91   Sykes, 'Military Aviation,' p.135.
92   E. Ash, 'Air Power Leadership: A Study of Sykes and Trenchard,' in *Air Power Leadership: Theory and Practice*, eds. P. W. Gray & S. Cox (London, HMSO, 2002), pp.162-163.
93   *Flight*, 7 Dec 1912, pp.1127-1132; Sykes, 'Military Aviation;' *Flight*, 14 Feb 1914, pp.170-173.
94   D. Henderson, 'The Design of a Military Scouting Aeroplane,' *Aeronautical Journal*, Vol.16, No.62 (Jul 1912): pp.167-175.
95   Henderson, 'Scouting Aeroplane,' p.167.
96   M. Paris, *Winged Warfare: The literature and theory of aerial warfare in Britain, 1859-1917* (Manchester, Manchester University Press, 1992), pp.251-252.

of air power. This opportunity came during the manoeuvres of 1912, and, as a result, the British Army had an increasingly positive attitude toward aviation.[97]

Grierson's growing interest in aviation is well documented in the literature, and he is famous for his use of aircraft during the manoeuvres of 1912.[98] As a result, Grierson addressed a meeting of the Aeronautical Society in November 1912. It was during this meeting that he made his oft-quoted remark regarding the "mastery of the air."[99] In tangible terms, this was the culmination of a very successful period for Henderson and the RFC. Influential figures in the Army were taking notice of aviation and the RFC's budget continued to rise. In 1911 – 1912, the military aviation budget stood at £131,000. In 1912 – 1913, the Army Estimates allocated £501,000 to the RFC.[100] Henderson's own personal link to Asquith should not be underestimated, and the former was successful at cultivating support from Britain's political and military elite.[101] In practical terms, this support resulted in pilot strength rising from 21 trained pilots in March 1912 to 134 by the following year. In the Army Estimates of 1914 – 1915, provision was made for an establishment of 200 pilots.[102] This was minuscule compared to wider defence spending, particularly that of the Navy, but the efforts of Henderson and Sykes were beginning to pay dividends.

The talks delivered to the Aeronautical society continued into 1913, and French did not allow ill-health to again prevent his participation in the ongoing discussion of military aviation. The lecture delivered by Sykes, whilst generally cautious in nature, was not quite as reserved in tone as Henderson's effort of the previous year.[103] It is telling that Henderson was present for the event, and, in participating in the post-lecture discussion, he gently reined in his subordinate by noting that he "agreed generally" with Sykes.[104] Henderson was playing a delicate balancing act; he did not want to discourage his imaginative and creative subordinates, nor did he want the RFC to appear as an iconoclastic force that would alienate the growing support of senior officers within the British Army. In a similar vein, Henderson's contribution to Sykes's lecture of the following year adopted an encouraging but cautious tone.[105] It is evident that such an approach had a positive impact on French, and, in providing his thoughts on the "excellent lecture" of 1913, Sir John noted that aviation was "one of

97   Whitmarsh, 'Army Manoeuvres,' pp.335-344.
98   Ibid. pp.335-344.
99   *Flight*, 7 Dec 1912, p.1127.
100   War Office, *Cd 6064: Memorandum of the Secretary of State for War relating to the Army Estimates for 1912-13* (London, HMSO, 1912), p.7; War Office, *Cd 6888: Memorandum of the Secretary of State for War relating to the Army Estimates for 1913-14* (London, HMSO, 1913), pp.3-4.
101   Brock & Brock, *Asquith*, p.122. Letter, Asquith to Stanley, 24 Jul 1914.
102   War Office, *Cd 6888*, pp.3-4; War Office, *Cd 7253: Memorandum of the Secretary of State for War relating to the Army Estimates for 1914-15* (London, HMSO, 1914), pp.3-4.
103   Sykes, 'Military Aviation,' *passim*.
104   Sykes, 'Military Aviation,' p.137.
105   *Flight*, 14 Feb 1914, p.173.

the most important questions for modern soldiers to study."[106] French's thoughtful and progressive contribution to proceedings, in which he grasped the significance of aviation in terms of reconnaissance and the control of the air, supports Badsey's portrait of Sir John elsewhere in this volume. The significance of his relationship with Henderson should not be understated, and, as Holmes was to write of French, the latter's "well-developed" understanding of air power "owed much to his long-standing relationship with ... Henderson."[107] In more "selfish" terms, by continuing to draw positive attention to military aviation, Henderson also continued to attract positive personal attention. For example, in November 1912, a full page portrait of Henderson appeared in *Flight* as he was named by the publication as one of their "Men of the Moment in the World of Flight."[108]

Another aspect of Henderson's strategy for raising the profile of the RFC involved the use of the press. The RFC undertook a proactive campaign to "market" their vision of air power to a range of audiences, including their patrons in the Army and Government, the public, who would foot the political and economic bill, and even young schoolboys, who would ultimately become the recruits of the next war. This process included talks at public schools by serving officers and even a well publicised visit by King George V and Queen Mary, which left "Their Majesties ... [impressed with the] capacity and efficiency of the Royal Flying Corps."[109] Perhaps the most successful public relations endeavour came with the Wing's summer training program at their camp in Netherton, timed to garner maximum attention from the press.[110] An article in *Flight* recorded that it was down to the courtesy of Henderson that the publication had been allowed to spend time at the camp.[111] The result was a glowing tribute, and *Flight* commented that "so high is the standard of efficiency attained that it is most difficult to believe that it is only a little more than two years since this Corps was first formed."[112]

Henderson's relations with the press were not always so successful, and the Wing came in for almost constant criticism from C. G. Grey, the caustic editor of the *Aeroplane*. In his dealings with Grey, Henderson displayed another side of his personality, rarely seen and rarely recorded. Henderson was protective of the RFC, and was not afraid to drop his usually measured and cautious tone: "I think the *Aeroplane* is useful and your criticisms are of much value ... But with regard to your correspondents ... [I am] rather tired of being spoon fed with advice which is so obviously based on ignorance and

---

106   Sykes, 'Military Aviation,' pp.137-138.
107   Holmes, *Field Marshal*, p.317.
108   *Flight*, 9 Nov 1912, p.1015.
109   J. C. Slessor, *The Central Blue: Recollections and Reflections* (London, Cassell, 1956), p.2; Sykes, *Angles*, p.109.
110   P. Joubert de la Ferté, *The Third Service: The Story Behind the Royal Air Force* (London, Thames and Hudson, 1955), p.20; TNA, AIR 1/772/204/4/304-Concentration Camp, Training Scheme, Jun 1914.
111   *Flight*, 3 July 1914, p.670.
112   Ibid, p.670.

lack of advisory care in reading official publications."[113] Henderson's defensive attitude could be explained as an attempt to protect his own reputation as much as that of the RFC.

Lectures to forums such as the Aeronautical Society or articles in the press were a viable method to spread the informal doctrine of the RFC. However, as an experienced staff officer and manual writer, Henderson understood the importance of producing an official manual for consumption by an internal audience. This would help to establish the corporate identity of the RFC, setting out the Corps' vision for the use of air power and its war fighting functions.[114] The result was the production of the MW's *Training Manual, Part II* (1914).[115] Henderson's hand is absent from the archival record relating to the production of the *Manual*, but two of his staff officers, Edward Ellington and Sefton Brancker, were issuing instructions on Henderson's behalf, and it is clear that approval for the *Manual* came from Henderson during his time as DMT.[116]

The *Manual* was to be widely disseminated, and Henderson's Directorate made frantic efforts to provide copies to interested parties. These included copies for Major-General Monro and his staff in time for the manoeuvres of 1913, and additional copies for the annual General Staff conference of January 1914.[117] Of central importance was ensuring that the content of the *Manual* was in keeping with the wider organisational beliefs and values of the Army, as espoused in their clearest form in *Field Service Regulations*. The *Manual* embraced the core themes of moral superiority and the importance of the offensive, and put forward its ideas based on a language and philosophy that would be reassuringly familiar to the Army as a whole.[118]

The *Manual* also contained specific ideas about the use of air power and the organisational structure and role of the RFC.[119] In his role as an intelligence expert, Henderson had emphasised the importance of developing a responsive intelligence function providing direct support to the C-in-C.[120] This was a central theme of his development of the RFC, and he pushed hard to ensure that military aviators reported directly to the most senior officers in need of information, rather than reporting via an intelligence staff.[121] During the General Staff conference of January 1914, Henderson

---

113   National Aerospace Library (NAL), Farnborough, Papers of C. G. Grey (CGG), File 1, Henderson to Grey, 9 May 1912.

114   TNA, AIR 1/785/204/4/558-Sykes to unknown, very probably the DMA, 29 Apr 1913.

115   N. Parton, 'The Evolution and Impact of Royal Air Force Doctrine, 1919-1939' (PhD Thesis, University of Cambridge, 2009), chapter two.

116   TNA, AIR 1/762/204/4/175-Ellington to Sykes, 28 May 1913; TNA, AIR 1/785/204/4/558-Brancker to Sykes, 11 Oct 1913.

117   TNA, AIR 1/785/204/4/558-Sykes to GSO, 'White Force,' HQ 2nd London Division, 9 Sep 1913; Brancker to Sykes, 11 Oct 1913.

118   For example, see War Office, *Training Manual, Part II*, p.47.

119   War Office, *Training Manual, Part II*, p.24.

120   Henderson, *Field Intelligence*, pp.31-32.

121   Ultimately, the RFC would not get its way in this regard. J. Beach, 'British Intelligence and the German Army, 1914-1918' (PhD Thesis, University College London, 2004), p.76.

clashed with John Gough over this very question.[122] Moreover, Henderson felt that the squadrons of the RFC should be controlled centrally, rather than being attached to specific divisions.[123] This was an issue that would reappear during the opening campaigns of the First World War, and Henderson would fight hard for his vision, abandoning his cautious approach when he deemed it necessary.

Of course, the *Manual* was almost completely focused on aerial reconnaissance and, in striving to create coherent doctrine, the MW have been criticised for their narrow focus.[124] For Neville Jones, this narrow doctrinal focus left the MW lacking any offensive capability in 1914.[125] Indeed, for Henderson's focus on rhetoric and relationship building to be successful, it needed to be built upon the foundation of an operationally effective and efficient air service. He took a close interest in the material preparations of the Wing, for which he was ultimately responsible, and he was involved in the issuing of aircraft and aero-engine specifications, weapons testing, and the creation of deployment plans. However, in attempting to create an operationally effective unit, Henderson and Sykes were forced to resort to a relatively ad-hoc series of measures and arrangements. The historiography characterises these efforts, particularly the development of an offensive capability for the Wing, as lacking in both urgency and effective long-term planning.[126]

However, there was relatively little infrastructure upon which to build the MW, and Sykes was frequently bogged down in a range of administrative and organisational matters.[127] Nonetheless, because of the MW's narrow focus on reconnaissance, a direct result of Henderson's influence and expertise, the Wing developed in something of a one dimensional fashion.[128] Henderson's involvement in the design of aircraft and aero-engines is a case in point. The MW relied too heavily on aircraft designs produced by the government-owned Royal Aircraft Factory.[129] A focus on stable aircraft and reliable low powered engines had some merit if aircraft were to be used solely for unopposed and flexible reconnaissance.[130] However, as Henderson's letters during the opening of the First World War make clear, the RFC desperately needed high-performance fighting aircraft to secure control of the air.[131] In many respects, Henderson was placed in a very difficult position, given the nature of aeronautical technology during this period and

122   I. Beckett, *Johnnie Gough, V.C.* (London, Tom Donovan, 1989), pp.148-149.

123   *Flight*, 14 Feb 1914, p.173.

124   Paris, *Winged Warfare*, pp.157-158.

125   N. Jones, *Strategic Bombing*, p.48.

126   For example, see Paris, *Winged Warfare*, pp.216-217.

127   Ash, *Sykes*, p.26. For examples of the administrative and organisational work undertaken by Sykes, see TNA, AIR 1/118/15/40/52.

128   N. Jones, *Strategic Bombing*, p.16.

129   C. Goulter, *A Forgotten Offensive: Royal Air Force Coastal Command's Anti-Shipping Campaign, 1940-1945* (London, Frank Cass, 1995), pp.8-9.

130   For an example of Henderson's involvement in the development of aircraft and their engines, see War Office, *Cd 6286: Military Aeroplane Competition, Judges Report* (London, HMSO, 1912).

131   TNA, AIR 1/118/15/40/36-Précis of remarks, Henderson to Brancker, 9 Sep 1914.

the lack of reliable data and experience upon which to base long-term planning. It was a significant achievement that the British Army was supported by even a small number of aviation units on the outbreak of war. Criticisms relating to the narrow focus and lack of long-term planning are persuasive, but the team of Henderson and Sykes must be given credit for the progress made between 1912 and 1914.

Henderson and the RFC in 1914

Henderson was intimately involved in the two controversies that continue to characterise the RFC's deployment to France on the outbreak of war: first, his decision to leave his post at the WO and take up the role of operational commander of the RFC; and second, the mobilisation of the Corps in which almost all serviceable aircraft were sent to the Continent, leaving no nucleus upon which to create additional squadrons.

Sykes is most often criticised for the decision to deploy almost the entire strength of the RFC at the outbreak of war, and both his supporters and detractors note his adherence to the short-war myth.[132] As Morrow records, "the RFC's chief planner ... [Sykes] ... was convinced ... of a short and glorious war. He threw nearly every man and machine into the fray, believing that neither could stand more than three months in the field."[133] From at least mid-1913, the mobilisation plans of the RFC had been the subject of discussion, scrutiny, and modification by a planning *team* that included Sykes.[134] The latter had a long exchange of letters with the DMA regarding this process, and, as late as May 1914, Sykes was asking pertinent and penetrating questions of Henderson with regards to future planning, reserves, and the creation of new squadrons.[135] Trenchard's biographer suggests that Sykes took a childish view with regards to the mobilisation of the RFC, yet this does not acknowledge the role of Henderson and his staff.[136] It was Henderson's decision to take every available aircraft to accompany the BEF.[137] It was also Henderson's decision not to provide Trenchard with experienced pilots around which to create new squadrons until November 1914.[138]

Of course, Sykes agreed with Henderson, and in his memoirs he made some effort to justify the decision.[139] For Sykes, the nature of the crisis facing Britain demanded the highest effort to ensure that the BEF was provided with maximum support from its aviation branch. Sykes was willing to concede that, in putting together schemes for mobilisation, military aviators fell under the spell of the short-war myth, itself in

132   For example, see Ash, *Sykes*, pp.41-42.
133   J. Morrow, *The Great War in the Air: Military Aviation from 1909-1921* (Washington, Smithsonian Institution Press, 1993), p.75. For other figures relating to RFC strength, see TNA, AIR 1/118/15/40/39-Brancker to CIGS, 7 and 8 Aug 1914.
134   TNA, AIR 1/118/15/40/56-Mobilisation planning file, 1913-1914.
135   TNA, AIR 1/761/204/4/156-Sykes to Henderson, 9 May 1914.
136   Boyle, *Trenchard*, pp.116-117.
137   Divine, *Broken Wing*, p.49.
138   Cooper, 'House Divided,' p.181.
139   Sykes, *Angles*, pp.123-124; Sykes, *War and Peace*, pp.45-46.

keeping with a wider trend in the BEF.[140] RFC policy in August 1914 was driven by the immediate demands of the BEF, with little regard to long-term planning.[141] However, the RFC were seriously concerned about the reliability of the aircraft they possessed, and pre-war experimentation indicated that serviceability rates would severely limit the capabilities of the Corps.[142] Between 12 August and 5 October 1914, the RFC lost 49 aircraft (destroyed, struck off or missing), including four in the UK.[143] Given that the RFC possessed less than 100 useable aircraft at the outbreak of war, this figure was considerable.[144] If Henderson had not taken sufficient numbers of aircraft to the continent in 1914, the RFC may have lacked the ability to provide any assistance to the BEF.

The second controversy surrounds Henderson's decision to assume operational control of the RFC at the outbreak of war. As Sykes noted in his memoirs, Henderson had made him a verbal promise that he would be given command of the RFC in the field when war came.[145] That this promise was made has been questioned, although Higham suggests that, given the proposed size and importance of the RFC, the existence of such a promise did "not seem so improbable."[146] RFC mobilisation plans noted that the Commander of the MW (Sykes's role) was to possess operational command of the RFC's squadrons during war time, yet it was perfectly in the remit of Henderson to modify these orders.[147] As Mead records, given that Henderson had occupied staff posts since 1897, his decision to take operational control of the RFC would be a "challenge."[148] This supports Slessor's criticism of the WO, in which he notes that good staff officers were often held back from operational roles, becoming "a sort of goldfish swimming round in a bowl without ever getting out to the open sea."[149]

With Henderson assuming operational command of the unit, the RFC's leadership went through a process of reorganisation, and Sykes was appointed as Henderson's CoS.[150] There is some suggestion that the Sykes-Henderson relationship was already under strain by late 1913, and, with the creation of the DMA, Henderson had reduced the organisational and administrative responsibilities of Sykes's post.[151] In a paper of September 1913, Sykes had stated that it was "insufficient ... merely to carve some niche

140   Sykes, *Angles*, pp.123-124; Sykes, *War and Peace*, pp.45-46.
141   Cooper, *Air Power*, p.21.
142   Morrow, *Great War*, p.75-76.
143   TNA, AIR 1/812/204/4/1253-RFC aircraft destroyed or struck off, 12 Aug to 5 Oct 1914.
144   TNA, AIR 1/2314/223/10/1-Extracts from Statistical Abstract No.23, Growth of the RFC.
145   Sykes, *War and Peace*, p.27; Sykes, *Angles*, p.122.
146   Cooper, 'House Divided,' p.181; Higham, *Military Intellectuals*, p.124.
147   Ash, *Sykes*, pp.39-40 and pp.50-51.
148   P. Mead, *The Eye in the Air: History of Air Observation and Reconnaissance for the Army, 1785-1945* (London, HMSO, 1983), p.48.
149   Slessor, *Central Blue*, p.39.
150   TNA, AIR 1/118/15/40/56-DMA Staff to Sykes, 5 Aug 1914.
151   TNA, AIR 1/118/15/40/56-Brancker to Sykes, 10 Nov 1913 and Sykes to Brancker, 16 Dec 1913; Cooper, *Air Power*, p.8; Ash, *Sykes*, pp.33-35.

in the military organization into which inventions fit."[152] The somewhat iconoclastic quality of this paper was not in keeping with Henderson's cautious approach to organisational development, and Henderson may have concluded that he needed to reign in his CoS. Ash goes as far to suggest that, even before the war, Henderson had started to feel animosity toward Sykes, resenting his "youthful enthusiasm and higher commitment to [air power]."[153]

However, no trace of bitterness can be found in the memoirs of Sykes. He was clearly disappointed not to command the RFC in wartime, but he was magnanimous and pragmatic about the incident. In the first instance, Sykes accepted that he lacked seniority, and second, he noted that Sir John French had a very close working relationship with Henderson: "French wanted Henderson near him, and no other position was available. If a more senior officer was needed Henderson was the best choice, and he was certainly a charming man to work under."[154] Given the importance Henderson ascribed to building a relationship with the C-in-C, his close personal relationship with French, and the importance he attached to making sure the RFC served senior commanders directly, it is small wonder that Henderson believed his correct place was serving with the BEF at the front. Henderson was doing for French what he had done for Kitchener in South Africa, and for Sir George White at Ladysmith.[155] Of course, Henderson's decision also reflected a widespread phenomenon in the BEF, and, fuelled by the prevalence of the short-war myth, many staff officers scrambled for a place at the front.[156]

Divine argues that the decision was not "in the best interests of the Corps," and both Cooper and Neville Jones have criticised Henderson, noting that this left the RFC without experienced officers in the WO.[157] Brancker, Henderson's deputy, was left to manage the DMA, but his memoirs are not specifically critical of Henderson's decision.[158] In a more general sense, Brancker was highly critical of the exodus of staff officers from the WO, recording that it was the "only amateurish feature in the whole original plan of campaign – it was illogical and unpardonable, and had bad results later on."[159] However, with Kitchener's appointment as Secretary of State for War at the beginning of August 1914, another of Henderson's patrons had returned to the WO. Given Henderson's excellent working relationship with Kitchener, the former may have felt happy leaving the DMA in the hands of a relatively junior officer. As Brancker records, his lack of seniority did not affect his relationship with Kitchener,

152   TNA, AIR 1/757/204/4/100-Sykes, 'Notes on Questions of Policy in Military Aviation,' 8 Sep 1913.
153   Ash, *Sykes*, p.194.
154   Sykes, *Angles*, p.122.
155   HP, RAFM, AC71/4/2-H. A. Jones, Draft, *Per Ardua*, chapter four, p.2.
156   J. Gooch, *The Plans of War: The General Staff and British Military Strategy*, c.1900-1916 (London, Routledge & Kegan Paul, 1974), p.302.
157   Divine, *Broken Wing*, p.77; Cooper, *Air Power*, pp.16-17; N. Jones, *Strategic Bombing*, p.51.
158   Macmillan, *Brancker*, pp.58-59.
159   Macmillan, *Brancker*, p.62.

who "was an enormous asset to the R.F.C. He instinctively understood aviation, and realized fully its vast possibilities; he saw me [Brancker] constantly, perhaps four of five days a week at least, and often twice a day ..."[160] Henderson may have been a more experienced administrator and staff officer than his deputy, but Brancker performed admirably in his absence.

In order to evaluate Henderson's decision to lead the Corps and its controversial deployment, they must be viewed through the prism of the operational performance of the RFC between August and November 1914. This is the subject of some discussion in the literature, and no clear consensus exists as to the value of the RFC's contribution in 1914. The first volume of *The War in the Air* (1922) provides a generally positive appraisal of the RFC's performance, particularly during the retreat of late August 1914.[161] Raleigh notes the significant role played by the RFC in providing French with the "first intimation" of the German First Army's wheeling manoeuvre, providing Franco-British forces with the opportunity to stem the tide facing them.[162] Such conclusions are supported by the Canadian official history and Mead's *Eye in the Air* (1983).[163]

In contrast, both Cooper and Divine emphasise the very limited contribution made by the RFC during August and September 1914.[164] Cooper stressed that the RFC lacked aircraft in both quality and quantity, and that senior officers within the BEF were not willing to rely solely on intelligence provided by the RFC.[165] For Divine, even though the RFC provided the BEF with excellent intelligence, particularly during mid to late August, this was limited by a lack of experience in both acquiring and interpreting data from aerial reconnaissance.[166] In turn, this was aggravated by the general friction of utilising "a new and wholly untried development in war."[167] Jordan offers a more positive appraisal, suggesting that, in spite of significant practical and logistical difficulties, air power helped shape the intelligence picture available to the BEF's General Headquarters (GHQ).[168] Edmonds provides a balanced analysis of the RFC's contribution to the BEF. He observes that, whilst aircraft were able to supply GHQ with a range of data, staff officers had very limited experience interpreting such information.[169] Moreover, factors such as the weather and enemy night marches limited

160   Macmillan, *Brancker*, pp.66-67.
161   Raleigh, *WIA, Vol.I*, pp.316-322.
162   Raleigh, *WIA, Vol.I*, pp.298-303 and p.316.
163   S. F. Wise, *Canadian Airmen in the First World War: The Official History of the Royal Canadian Air Force, Volume I* (Toronto, CA., University of Toronto Press, 1980), pp.336-338; Mead, *Eye in the Air*, pp.51-58, esp. pp.56-58.
164   Cooper, *Air Power*, pp.18-19; Divine, *Broken Wing*, pp.50-52.
165   Cooper, *Air Power*, pp.18-19.
166   Divine, *Broken Wing*, pp.50-52.
167   Divine, *Broken Wing*, p.52
168   D. Jordan, 'The Army Co-operation Missions of the Royal Flying Corps / Royal Air Force, 1914-1918' (PhD Thesis, University of Birmingham, 1997), p.85.
169   Edmonds, *OH, 1914, Vol. II*, p.419.

the effectiveness of the Corps.[170] Nonetheless, Edmonds singles out the role played by the RFC on 22 August, in which aerial reconnaissance indicated the change of direction of the German First Army.[171] As Edmonds records, Henderson brought the aerial reconnaissance report personally to GHQ, and this helped inform the intelligence picture available to French.[172]

Hallion offers some perceptive analysis of the RFC contribution, particularly in relation to the battle of the Marne.[173] The coalition context of the First World War is well established in the literature, and, during this period, the RFC began to create important links with their French colleagues.[174] In the first instance, the RFC won approval from General Joffre, commanding French forces during this period.[175] As Spears noted, Joffre praised the RFC when in conversation with French, and noted that the aerial intelligence he received had greatly added his decision-making abilities.[176] The RFC's performance, based upon Henderson's model of a responsive intelligence gathering asset, helped to smooth difficult Franco-British relations.[177]

Ash presents an excellent overview of the RFC contribution to the campaign of 1914.[178] In general, he accepts the original interpretation of Raleigh, but suggests that the performance of the RFC was "at times chaotic."[179] Problems existed with the BEF's intelligence system, but the inexperience of aerial observers served to undermine the reputation of the RFC.[180] Ash also makes two very important distinctions: first, that the manner in which GHQ used aerial intelligence was in a "confirmatory role rather than as … [a] primary information source;" and second, that the evidence cited to demonstrate the important role played by the RFC is "indirect."[181] The despatches of Sir John French praise the RFC and Henderson specifically, but they do not provide direct evidence of the impact of aerial intelligence on the decision making process of GHQ.[182] It was the subsequent expansion of the RFC that demonstrated the positive impression that had been made by Henderson and the Corps.[183] If aircraft had not

170   Edmonds, *OH, 1914, Vol. II*, p.276, p.281, p.296, and p.450.
171   J. E. Edmonds, *Military Operations: France and Belgium (OH), 1914, Vol. I*, (London, Macmillan & Co., 1937) [1923], pp.67-68.
172   Ibid, pp.67-68.
173   Hallion, *Inventing Flight*, pp.346-347.
174   E. Greenhalgh, *Victory through Coalition: Britain and France during the First World War* (Cambridge, Cambridge University Press, 2005); Pugh, 'Conceptual Origins,' chapter five.
175   Sykes, *Angles*, p.138.
176   E. Spears, *Liaison 1914* (London, Cassell, Second Edition, 1999) [1930], p.414.
177   R. A. Prete, *Strategy and Command: The Anglo-French Coalition on the Western Front, 1914* (Montreal, McGill-Queen's University Press, 2009).
178   Ash, *Sykes*, pp.54-57.
179   Ash, *Sykes*, p.54.
180   Ash, *Sykes*, p.57.
181   Ash, *Sykes*, p.54 and p.57.
182   J. French, *The Despatches of Sir John French, Vol. I* (London, Chapman & Hall, 1914), p.16, p.58, pp.60-61, and pp.158-159. See also Ash, *Sykes*, pp.56-57.
183   Ash, *Sykes*, p.57.

provided at least some useful service during 1914, French (and later Haig) would not have devoted significant resources to increasing the aerial capability of the BEF.

In his account of 1914, French offered some more direct evidence of the value of aviation. With reference to 23 August 1914, French noted that he had decided to "await aircraft reports from Henderson before making any decided plan."[184] French clearly believed that the RFC would form an integral part of the BEF and its intelligence gathering capabilities. Such thinking is evidenced by French's decision to visit squadrons shortly after their deployment to France, holding "important" discussions with Henderson.[185] In addition, both of French's Corps commanders felt they were being provided with important support from the air. Sir Horace Smith-Dorrien, commander of II Corps, noted in his diary that he was receiving "splendid information" from an aeroplane squadron attached to his command.[186] Such feelings extended into the BEF's other Corps, and Haig had staff officers positioned at RFC airfields so as to receive intelligence reports in the most rapid fashion.[187] Haig also made reference in his diary to the assistance he received from the RFC in locating German batteries and directing the fire of his artillery.[188]

Henderson's daily routine and activities throughout this period are difficult to establish, but he was playing an important role in operating at the interfaces that existed between the RFC and the BEF.[189] Given that there is little consensus in the historiography, it is impossible to say how seriously RFC reports would have been taken in 1914 had an officer of the reputation and seniority of Henderson not been available to liaise directly with GHQ.[190] As noted, Henderson was following his own advice of 1904, and he continued to invest heavily in providing a responsive and personal service to his C-in-C. In turn, French felt able to rely on the RFC to undertake a variety communicative and reconnaissance related missions.[191]

In executing these duties, Henderson spent this period in frenetic activity, and this began to affect his health and his ability to command the RFC.[192] The fluid operations of 1914 were a great strain on all the BEF's personnel, particularly its senior officers. Perhaps the most famous example is the death of Grierson on the way to the front, although a range of officers suffered health problems that were attributed to the pace

184   J. French, *1914* (London, Constable & Co., 1919), p.61.
185   G. French, ed., *Some War Diaries, Addresses and Correspondence of Field Marshal the Right Honourable, Earl of Ypres* (London, Herbert Jenkins, 1937), pp.144-145. Extract from War Diary, 14 Aug 1914. See also, French, *1914*, p.33.
186   Imperial War Museum, 87/47/10, Smith-Dorrien Papers, Diary 6 Sep 1914; A. Corbett-Smith, *The Marne-and After* (London, Cassell & Co., 1917), p.80. The author wishes to thank Dr Spencer Jones for these references. See also Sykes, *Angles*, p.140.
187   Beckett, *Johnnie Gough*, p.188.
188   G. Sheffield & J. Bourne, eds., *Douglas Haig, War Diaries and Letters, 1914-1918* (London, Weidenfeld & Nicolson, 2005), Haig Diary, 16 Sep 1914, p.71.
189   Baring, *R.F.C.*, chapters two to five.
190   Jordan, 'Army Co-operation,' p.19.
191   G. French, *War Diaries*, pp.155-157; Sykes, *Angles*, pp.137-138, p.141, and p.151.
192   Ash, *Sykes*, pp.50-51 and p.65.

of operations and strain of command.[193] Although the specifics of Henderson's health problems in 1914 are unclear, Henderson had been wounded during the Boer War, and this continued to bother him.[194] By late 1914, Joubert noted that Henderson was sick with "overwork and severe winter weather."[195] Baring concurs, noting that Henderson was frequently so busy with work that he arrived late for meals and "never had enough to eat."[196] Nonetheless, by late October 1914, Henderson's efforts had obviously impressed French, and he was promoted to Major-General for "distinguished conduct in the field."[197]

With 1st Division, November to December 1914

By November 1914, the RFC appeared to be in good shape and enjoyed the confidence of the three most senior commanders within the BEF, as well as Kitchener and senior figures in the French Army. This does not disguise the fact that, during this month, the RFC faced leadership difficulties that reflected deep divisions concerning the organisational direction of the Corps, and troubled personal relations amongst Henderson's senior commanders. The nature of this period is complicated by confused, contradictory, and overtly seditious statements in the relevant memoirs.

In the first instance, the organisational development of the RFC was affected by the general expansion of the BEF during late 1914. French was particularly impressed with the tactical reconnaissance that the RFC had been able to provide to the BEF.[198] In turn, he sought to decentralise aspects of the RFC, providing the new Armies with autonomous air power assets.[199] The response of the RFC to this suggestion revealed the divided nature of the Corps' senior command team. For Henderson and Sykes, this decentralising process did not remove the need for a centralised RFC HQ to retain control of RFC units in the field. As the size of the RFC grew, an additional level of command was to be created and squadrons were to be grouped into Wings. Wings were to provide flexible support to the Armies to which they were attached, but Henderson and Sykes believed that an RFC HQ was vital as Army, Corps, and Divisional commanders lacked the specialist and technical knowledge necessary to make the most efficient use of air power.[200] In contrast, Trenchard and Brancker argued for total decentralisation; Wing commanders should report solely to their respective Army commanders and RFC HQ should be replaced with an RFC representative

---

193   Robbins, *British Generalship*, p.38 and p.56.
194   Jones, 'Sir David Henderson,' p.8.
195   Joubert, *Third Service*, p.32.
196   Baring, *R.F.C.*, p.39; HP, RAFM, AC71/4/2-H. A. Jones, Draft, *Per Ardua*, chapter four, p.5.
197   *London Gazette*, 3 Nov 1914.
198   Hallion, *Inventing Flight*, p.347.
199   Raleigh, *WIA, Vol.I*, p.331.
200   Sykes, *Angles*, pp.143-146; HP, RAFM, AC71/4/2-H. A. Jones, Draft, *Per Ardua*, chapter four, p.6.

serving on the staff at the BEF's GHQ.[201] Henderson used his considerable influence and standing with French and Kitchener to squash the Trenchard-Brancker scheme, and his own plan was approved during late 1914 and published in January 1915.[202]

Henderson's plan was viewed favourably by French, and, before final approval was granted, the creation of Wings was already underway in the RFC.[203] As such, Henderson sought to find officers to appoint as Wing Commanders. It was in these circumstances that Trenchard was placed in command of First Wing. Boyle's account of this process is tainted by Trenchard's vindictive attitude toward Sykes.[204] There is some suggestion that the Henderson-Sykes relationship was under further strain at this stage, particularly in light of the increasingly critical attitude Sykes adopted in relation to Henderson's decision to continue to occupy two roles: as DGMA and as the operational commander of the RFC.[205] However, there is no evidence to suggest that Henderson made promises to Trenchard that would have effectively undermined the ability of Sykes to undertake his duties as CoS.[206] Moreover, given Trenchard's obvious frustration at being left in the UK, it seems highly probable that he would have rushed to accept command of the First Wing rather than issuing a series of demands to Henderson.[207] By this stage, Trenchard was well liked by Kitchener and received the backing of Brancker as Henderson's deputy.[208] However, Henderson's decision to appoint Trenchard reflected that he lacked officers with sufficient seniority to take up command at the Wing level.

Whilst this process was ongoing, developments at the front would take a hand in precipitating leadership difficulties in the RFC. Samuel Lomax, GOC, 1st Division, was mortally wounded at the end of October 1914.[209] Lomax's replacement, Herman Landon, was in charge of the Division for less than a month, and, although Haig's diary offers little in relation to 1914, by 1915, Landon did not enjoy the confidence of Haig or his staff.[210] The origins of Henderson's appointment as GOC, 1st Division are unclear, and the posting is not recorded in the *Army List* or in his RAF Service record.[211] For H. A. Jones, Henderson was an ambitious officer who desired a return to the infantry.[212] Given the planned reorganisation of the RFC, Henderson may also

---

201   Ash, *Sykes*, pp.60-61.
202   Cooper, 'House Divided,' p.182; HP, RAFM, AC71/4/2-H. A. Jones, Draft, *Per Ardua*, chapter four, p.6. A copy of the approved plan is found in Sykes, *Angles*, pp.525-526. See also *Flight,* 22 Jan 1915, p.57.
203   HP, RAFM, AC71/4/2-H. A. Jones, Draft, *Per Ardua*, chapter four, p.6.
204   Macmillan, *Brancker*, p.70; Boyle, *Trenchard*, p.123.
205   Sykes, *Angles*, pp.146-147; Ash, *Sykes*, p.62.
206   Divine, *Broken Wing*, pp.68-69.
207   Boyle, *Trenchard*, p.123.
208   Macmillan, *Brancker*, p.80.
209   Edmonds, *OH, 1914, Vol. II,* pp.323-324.
210   Sheffield & Bourne, *Douglas Haig*, Haig Diary, 29 Aug and 2 Sep 1915, pp.139-141.
211   TNA, AIR 76/221/33-Sir David Henderson, Record of Service; War Office, *The Army List* (London, HMSO, Sep 1915), p.33. The Division is also without its own history.
212   H. A. Jones, *The War in the Air: Being the Story of the part played in the Great War by the Royal Air Force (WIA),* Vol.II (Oxford, Clarendon Press, 1928), p.79; HP, RAFM,

have felt that there was no place for a Major-General within such a structure.[213] For James, Henderson had been "pleading" to leave the RFC, whilst Ash notes that his "reluctance to leave was an act. He had pushed hard for the transfer and was excited to go."[214] However, for Boyle, Henderson's appointment was the result of two factors: first, Haig's desire to replace Landon; and second, the influence of French in recommending Henderson for the role.[215] In many respects, Henderson's appointment illustrates the analysis of Robbins, who noted that,

> "[f]or many, the war represented a new impetus for careers providing opportunities for advancement ... Those officers, who were in the right place and rank in 1914 and 1915 and had good reputations, were able to move furthest up the ladder at a time when the Army needed commanders to step into the vacuum created by expansion."[216]

Henderson was not abandoning the RFC, and, with Sykes taking command of the Corps, he clearly felt that his "baby" was in good hands.[217] Holmes suggests that Henderson's appointment to 1st Division was temporary, but letters to and from Henderson during this period suggest the move was to be permanent.[218] As James records, the goal of many officers was to command their own regiment. If this was not possible, a divisional command was highly desirable.[219] Henderson had some connection with the division, and had served as the Assistant Adjutant General to the formation between 1905 and 1906.

Henderson was with the division for less than a month, and Baring, whom Henderson took along as an intelligence officer, provided one of the few first hand accounts of this period.[220] It appears that Henderson was a popular commander, and his division enjoyed visits from French and the King during his short tenure in charge.[221] If this was to be the apex of Henderson's career, he was not given long to enjoy the experience. As Edmonds and Wynne recorded, "Henderson, at the urgent request of the Secretary of State for War, had on 19th December been recalled to resume command of the [RFC]."[222] Baring notes that it was as early as 30 November that Henderson had

AC71/4/2-H. A. Jones, Draft, *Per Ardua*, chapter four, p.5.

213 HP, RAFM, AC71/4/2-H. A. Jones, Draft, *Per Ardua*, chapter four, pp.6-7.
214 James, *The Paladins*, p.54; Ash, *Sykes*, p.62 and p.72, fn.97.
215 Boyle, *Trenchard*, pp.124-126.
216 Robbins, *British Generalship*, pp.53-54.
217 Sykes's appointment does not show up in the *Army List* or in his RAF Service Record. War Office, *The Army List* (London, HMSO, June 1915), p.290; TNA, AIR 76/493/67-Frederick Sykes, Record of Service.
218 Holmes, *Field Marshal*, p.401, n.17. HP, RAFM, AC71/4/5 and AC71/4/398-Letters, David Henderson to Lady Henderson and Ian Henderson to David Henderson.
219 James, *The Paladins*, p.54.
220 Baring, *R.F.C.*, pp.69-76.
221 Baring, *R.F.C.*, pp.72-73 and p.76.
222 J. E. Edmonds & G. C. Wynne, *Military Operations: France and Belgium (OH), 1915, Vol. I* (London, Macmillan & Co., 1927), p.21, fn.

indicated that he may have to return to the RFC.[223] As Ash records, with Henderson removed, Sykes and Trenchard clashed over the organisation of the Corps.[224] Given that the RFC was such a small community during this period, tensions and personality clashes were difficult to disguise. As an instructor at the RFC's Central Flying School (CFS) noted, "The Lord only knows who is commanding – I don't. Trenchard is clearly the man it ought to be. Henderson is said to be commanding 1st Division, and to be away from RFC HQs overseas. Sykes is presumably commanding."[225] However, there is no evidence to suggest that Henderson's return was an attempt to regain control over warring factions within the RFC.

In many respects, Henderson's month long foray with 1st Division reflected the high regard in which he was held by both French and Kitchener. French had obviously highlighted Henderson as one of the most promising Major-Generals now serving at the front. French's promotion of Henderson, and his 7 September despatch, provide clear evidence in this regard. Given the long established and effective working relationship that existed between Henderson and French, this is unsurprising. However, Kitchener also saw Henderson as a highly valuable asset and, in conversation with Brancker, noted that he required an officer of Henderson's seniority and standing to command the expanding RFC.[226] Again, to quote from Robbins, "[t]o be effective, the British Army had to promote rapidly those officers with outstanding managerial skills and technical expertise."[227] Henderson possessed both these qualities, although, like many other officers of his generation, he lacked experience of command at the higher levels.

Divine records that French "resented Kitchener's interference," which hints at the wider problems that characterised the relationship between the BEF's C-in-C and the Secretary of State for War.[228] Henderson could be viewed as a pawn in the wider power struggle between French and Kitchener, but it was the latter that ultimately made the correct decision. Kitchener was right to highlight that there was still no-one in the British Army, in terms of technical expertise, seniority, and reputation, who could replace Henderson. Whether the result of genuine concerns, or as part of Trenchard's efforts to undermine his character, Sykes was not viewed as the man to lead the RFC at this stage.[229]

In addition, as Henderson's difficulties with ill-health demonstrate, he was simply not up to the task of commanding a division on the Western Front. His disappointment at losing his command was profound, and this may have affected his already fragile health.[230] Nonetheless, he lacked the attributes of robustness and

223   Baring, *R.F.C.*, p.73.
224   Ash, *Sykes*, p.62.
225   NAL, CGG, File 3. Letter, J. Fulton to C. G. Grey, 19 Dec 1914 (emphasis in original). Fulton had served with Trenchard at the CFS, and so his evidence must be treated with care.
226   Macmillan, *Brancker*, pp.81-82.
227   Robbins, *British Generalship*, p.56.
228   Divine, *Broken Wing*, p.71; Holmes, *Field Marshal*, pp.231-235.
229   Sykes's links to Henry Wilson may have also affected such perceptions. Ash, *Sykes*, pp.22-23.
230   Baring, *R.F.C.*, p.76.

stamina; characteristics that do much to explain the performance and longevity of commanders such as Haig and Trenchard.[231] Of course, by continuing to occupy two roles with the RFC – as the DGMA and as its GOC – Henderson continued to put significant strain on his health.[232] Upon his return to the RFC, Henderson did not lighten his work load, and divided his time between London, Paris, BEF, GHQ, RFC HQ, and the constantly shifting locations of his Wings and Squadrons.[233] By March 1915, Henderson was "laid up, and had to stay in bed," followed by an enforced period of leave in the south of France.[234] The result saw Sykes running the RFC for large periods during early to mid 1915, and Brancker running the DMA with only intermittent support from Henderson.[235] Henderson's return to the RFC was characterised by a curious vendetta against Sykes, and it is difficult to resist Cooper's conclusion that "Britain's senior air officers could not get on with each other."[236]

Conclusion

In evaluating Henderson's command of the RFC during 1914, it is important to remember that his most noteworthy contributions of the war were still to come: his part in fighting for resources on behalf of the RFC, and his vital role in the creation of the RAF.[237] Air power played a relatively minor role in the campaigns of 1914, and would continue to do so until at least 1916. Nonetheless, Henderson's contribution to the campaign of 1914 was significant. Without his guiding hand in the years 1911 to 1914, it is difficult to imagine the British Army being as receptive to aviation. That he was in a position to assert such an influence reflected his hard won reputation within the Army, based upon his obvious and carefully utilised intellectual gifts, and his strengths as a staff officer and intelligence expert. His ability to work at the interfaces was facilitated by the important professional and social connections that he had cultivated in his career to 1911 (and beyond). His cautious approach to reorganisation and reform greatly increased the Army's receptivity to aviation, and, importantly, the RFC was seen as an integral component of the BEF. Countering the critical interpretations of scholars such as Travers, the growth, development, and integration of aviation were, in many respects, driven by seemingly "conservative" senior officers.[238]

Henderson's involvement in aviation during this period was not without some difficulties, particularly in relation to the focus of the RFC, but Henderson's effect on

231   I. F. Marcosson, *A Visit to Sir Douglas Haig* (London, The Avenue Press, 1917), p.31; Sykes, *Angles*, p.134.
232   TNA, AIR 76/221/33-Sir David Henderson, Record of Service; Ash, *Sykes*, p.65.
233   Baring, *R.F.C.*, pp.79-85.
234   Baring, *R.F.C.*, pp.85-86.
235   TNA, AIR 1176/204/1/2595-Sykes to GHQ, 2 Feb 1915.
236   Cooper, 'House Divided,' pp. 183-184 and p.198; Ash, *Sykes*, pp.62-63, pp.66-67, pp.92-93, and pp.194-196; Higham, *Military Intellectuals*, pp.137-138.
237   Cooper, *Air Power*, chapters six to eight.
238   Travers, *Killing Ground*, p.76-78.

the development of the Corps was generally positive. He understood the importance of building relationships, and did much to ensure that the rhetoric of the RFC matched the reality of its operational capabilities. These capabilities were well understood by the BEF, and Henderson (and Sykes) must be given much credit for crafting air power doctrine in a language that would ensure the smooth assimilation of aviation into the Army. His time at Staff College, and his close links to political and military elites, helped facilitate this process.

His command of the RFC in 1914 was successful because, even with problems, the BEF was accompanied by an air power asset that was, in the first instance, present in something close to sufficient strength, and, in the second instance, able to provide a responsive and flexible service to the BEF and its senior commanders. An examination of the most contentious aspect of his performance – his decision to assume operational control of the RFC – reveals a complex picture. In many respects, his foray into France in 1914 was an attempt to relive the old glories of his days as a field intelligence officer. Nonetheless, his absence from the WO was offset to a significant degree by the outstanding performance of Brancker, and the very meaningful support offered by Kitchener. The personal service Henderson provided to French and the BEF was extremely important, and, without his work at the interfaces in France, the intelligence provided by the RFC may have been given less prominence by GHQ. Thus, the intelligence picture available to French and his command team may have been less complete, undermining the ability of the Franco-British forces, possibly to a significant extent, to stem the German advance

The health problems experienced by Henderson during this period indicate that he lacked the stamina and robustness necessary to hold an operational command for an extended duration. Of course, after 1914, the front stabilised and the fluid and chaotic warfare of the opening campaigns were replaced by a hard, grinding struggle. This change did not place any less strain on commanders, and it was under such conditions that leaders like Trenchard and Haig came to prominence. However, through training and experience, Henderson was a staff officer of the highest quality, and his return to the UK in mid-1915 saw his skill-set put to the most efficient use for the RFC, the BEF, and Britain's war effort.

Command at the Sharp End

13

The Infantry Battalion Commanding Officers of the BEF

Peter Hodgkinson

In this chapter the origins, experience and qualities of the infantry battalion commanding officers of the British Expeditionary Force of 1914 will be examined. The discussion will focus in the most part on the regular army which bore the brunt of virtually all the fighting in France and Flanders in 1914.

As David French has observed: "Whether on the battlefield or in barracks, the most important person in any unit was its CO. His knowledge could make or break his unit".[1] The quality of the British officer on the outbreak of the First World War has, however, been the subject of considerable debate. A principal excoriator of the British officer corps has been Tim Travers.[2] His thesis is that the British officer corps on the eve of war was still largely Victorian and public school in many of its attitudes (although how it could have been otherwise is difficult to imagine), with "an overwhelming emphasis on individual personalities, and on social and regimental hierarchies"; a system operating through "the influence of dominant personalities, of social traditions, and of personal friendships and rivalries". Travers' arguments are, however, only set out for the highest levels of army command and he states, without elucidation, that "this does not mean that at the lower levels the army was not well trained and well led in 1914".[3] What levels exactly are deemed competent are not clear.

In his study of "war managers", Simon Robbins acknowledges many of Travers' observations concerning the senior officer corps, yet points out that "the interpretation that the social background of the officer corps was responsible for the failings of the Army … while providing a possible answer for the shortcomings of some officers remains dubious and conveys the impression of monolithic stupidity among the officer

---

1   D. French, *Military Identities: The Regimental System, The British Army and the British People c. 1870-2000* (Oxford: Oxford University Press, 2005), p.147.
2   T. Travers, *The Killing Ground: The British Army, the Western Front, and the Emergence of Modern Warfare 1900-1918* (Barnsley: Pen & Sword, 2003), pp.3-36.
3   Travers, *Killing Ground*, p.6.

The educated soldier. Lieutenant-Colonel Adrian Grant-Duff, Military Assistant Secretary in the Committee of Imperial Defence, killed commanding 1st Black Watch on the Aisne. (Editor's collection)

corps which is not convincing". He concludes: "Enjoying the social activities of their class and era did not preclude soldiers from being professional once on the battlefield".[4]

Travers' sole comment concerning battalion COs in fact refers to 1914, and is a reference to General Sir Aylmer Haldane's diary, claiming an attempt to:

> get rid of a certain Colonel Churcher before the war. Subsequently Churcher's conduct at Mons was such that he was sent home .... Overall, Haldane recalled that three out of four Battalion commanding officers were not fit for command, and all had been sent home by the end of September 1914. Haldane may have been over-critical, but the ratio of incompetent officers in the 10th Infantry Brigade was probably not unique.[5]

For the sake of accuracy, 10th Brigade was not actually at Mons, first seeing action when in reserve at Le Cateau on 26 August. Haldane had, however, long been unhappy with the performance of Lieutenant-Colonel D.W. Churcher, 1st Royal Irish Fusiliers, who was indeed replaced on 10 September 1914, four days before the expiry of his four year term of command. Churcher nevertheless served as a GSO2 from 15 December 1914 and a GSO1 from 1 July 1916 until the end of the war. The other two COs 'sent home' were Lieutenant-Colonels J.F. Elkington, 1st Warwickshire, and A.E. Mainwaring, 2nd Royal Dublin Fusiliers, who were both court-martialled for

4   S. Robbins, *British Generalship on the Western Front 1914-18: Defeat Into Victory* (Abingdon: Frank Cass, 2005) p.17.

5   Travers, *Killing Ground*, p.14.

surrendering St Quentin on 27 August 1914. Travers therefore chooses one of the most atypical occurrences of the war at the level of battalion command by which to judge commanding officers. If Travers intended to imply that 75 per cent of the 1914 BEF's battalion COs were incompetent, then the data presented in this chapter will show him to be wrong.

The officer corps certainly had its contemporary critics during this period, some of whom were prepared to speculate about even more damning percentages than Travers. Viscount Esher, a member of the Elgin South African War Commission, declared in 1904 that "only two out of every forty regimental officers were any good at all. The rest were 'loafers".[6] He was clear that only an educated soldier, and by this he meant those who had passed staff college, had the truest worth. He was, of course, expressing a growing perception of the value of the educated soldier.[7]

Whatever the inadequacies of pre-Boer War officer education and the relevance of the British officer's war experience, the period 1902-14 was one of significant change following review of the army's performance in the Second Boer War. Passing over the well documented organisational reforms, much less well recognised are the considerable changes wrought in the actual way of fighting, which affected every regimental officer and soldier, changes largely ignored or downplayed by Travers.

By the end of the Boer War, the British Army had undergone a revolution in its practice of war.[8] As a result of its learning at the hands of the Boers, the infantry had mastered the problem of crossing the fire-swept zone by changing from attack in formation to advancing in extended order, in rushes using cover. Further, there had been considerable advances in artillery-infantry cooperation, and artillery was regularly using a form of direct suppressive fire until the infantry was within 50 yards of the enemy. Thirdly, British eyes had opened to sophisticated use of entrenchment, and entrenchment to repel counterattack became standard practice. Lastly, the army came to appreciate the value of individual marksmanship in addition to the power of volley fire, leading to a major focus on this area in the inter-war years. These profound changes were encapsulated in *Combined Training 1902*.[9]

At a battalion level there were further changes, with an emphasis, stemming directly from open order assault, on junior leadership. To this end, battalion organisation changed from eight to four companies in 1913, giving more officers per company. *Field Service Regulations 1909*, often referred to by modern historians, were therefore something more distant and less than revolutionary for the regimental officer, the major changes that affected the battalion on the battlefield having been enacted before its

---

6   Quoted in B. Bond, *The Victorian Army and the Staff College* (London: Eyre Methuen, 1972) p.183.

7   Bond, *Victorian Army*, p.183.

8   S. Jones, *From Boer War to World War* (Norman: University of Oklahoma Press, 2012); A.J Risio, *Building the Old Contemptibles: British Military Transformation and Tactical Development from the Boer War to the Great War 1899-1914*; Master of Military Art & Science thesis, Georgia Institute of Technology and Fort Leavenworth, 2005.

9   War Office, *Combined Training* (London: HMSO, 1902).

publication.[10] One author described the comparison as from "baseline new doctrine in *Combined Training 1902* to the capstone doctrine in *Field Service Regulations, 1909*".[11]

The significance for battalion command in the opening months of the First World War is that many of the infantry COs had either been lieutenants or captains during the Boer War, and had either learnt on the spot or experienced the profound changes of the ensuing 12 years. The years of their earlier professional development had therefore been redolent with change - they were used to it. Not all, clearly, could or would adapt and evolve either in peacetime or war, but those that could and would apply learning, and foster it in others, would likely be those that proved successful in battalion command.

The Regular Battalion COs of August 1914

In August 1914 there were 157 infantry COs of regular infantry battalions - nine for the four Guards and 148 for the 69 other infantry regiments.

Social Background

The social origins of senior officers during this period are well documented. Edward Spiers' analysis of colonels of 1914 reveals 7 per cent from the peerage and baronetage; 26 per cent from the gentry; 23 per cent from an armed services background (a significant proportion being "either sons of serving officers or had relatives in the services");[12] 14 per cent from the clergy; and 12 per cent professional.[13] A lieutenant-colonelcy was largely the province of the landed gentry and upper middle classes.

In comparison with cavalry regiments, only four of the 157 COs were titled, namely: Lieutenant-Colonels Lord R. Le N. Ardee (1st Grenadier Guards); The Hon. G. H. Morris (1st Irish Guards); The Hon. C.J Sackville-West (4th Kings Royal Rifle Corps); and Sir E. R. Bradford Bt. (2nd Seaforth Highlanders).

To illustrate the variety of backgrounds, Lieutenant-Colonel A. Grant-Duff, 1st Black Watch, did not have a military father. He was the son of Sir Mountstuart Grant-Duff, Liberal MP and Privy Counsellor, and had been educated at Wellington College before going to the Royal Military College (Sandhurst). Of others with a non-military background, Lieutenant-Colonel L.J. Bols, 1st Dorsetshire, (and a future Lieutenant-General) was the son of a Belgian diplomat, born in Cape Town and educated at Lancing College.

---

10   War Office, *Field Service Regulations, Parts One & Two* (London: HMSO, 1909). For example, G. Sheffield & D. Todman, *Command and Control on the Western Front – The British Army's Experience 1914-18* (Staplehurst: Spellmount, 2004), in which there are references on 12 pages. FSR dealt primarily with operations.
11   Risio, *Building*, p.9.
12   Robbins, *Generalship*, p.6.
13   E. M. Spiers, *The Late Victorian Army 1868-1902* (Manchester: University Press, 1992), p.94. The remaining 18 per cent were "other" or "don't know."

Conversely, Lieutenant-Colonel A.D. Geddes, 2nd Buffs, was a model of military lineage. He was the son of Colonel J.G. Geddes and was educated at Cheltenham College. His brothers J.G. and G.H. Geddes were respectively a Brigadier-General and Lieutenant-Colonel of Royal Artillery. Of others who had military siblings, Lieutenant-Colonel W.L. Loring, 2nd Royal Warwickshire, was one of three serving brothers (Major C.B. Loring of the 37th Lancers, Indian Army, and Captain W. Loring of the Scottish Horse were the others), all of whom were dead by November 1915. On a more illustrious level, Lieutenant-Colonel C.L. Nicholson, 2nd East Lancashire, was one of three brothers who became Major-Generals, another brother being an Admiral. The father of this remarkable quartet was General Sir L. Nicholson, Royal Engineers.

Lieutenant-Colonel O.G. Godfrey-Faussett, 1st Essex, was also the son of a Colonel. Lieutenant-Colonel G.B. Laurie, 1st Royal Irish Rifles, was the son of Lieutenant-General J.W Laurie, but had been educated in Canada and attended the Royal Military College there. Mirroring Bols' foreign ancestry, but with more humble military connections, Lieutenant-Colonel V.W. de Falbe, 1st North Staffordshire, was the son of a Danish Navy captain. In contrast, Lieutenant-Colonel C.E.A Jourdain, 2nd Loyal North Lancashire, was the son of the Rector of Mapleton, (Lieutenant-Colonel G.M. Gloster, 1st Devonshire, also had a clerical father); the father of Lieutenant Colonel L.I. Wood, 2nd Border, was a Suffolk solicitor; whilst the father of Lieutenant-Colonel A.W. Abercrombie, 2nd Connaught Rangers, was a Bengal civil servant.

Routes to Commission

The COs of August 1914 had entered the army over a twelve year period. In terms of the routes that they had taken to becoming a commissioned officer, in contrast with the figures for overall commissions 1885-1906,[14] an 'educated' soldier, i.e. a Sandhurst graduate was more likely to achieve battalion command (71 per cent against 55 per cent of officers overall), and a Militia entrant (28 per cent against 41 per cent) or a man who had been commissioned from the ranks (one per cent against three per cent) less likely.[15] For those who had been to Royal Military College (RMC), the years spent there collectively cover the period 1880-92. The bulk attended in the period following the War Office assumption of responsibility, when it was made compulsory that all commissioned officers (excluding Militia officers and promoted NCOs) should be graduates of the RMC, and educational standards required for admission were tightened.

In respect of the Militia, from 1872, each regiment had been allowed to nominate one 2nd lieutenant for commission each year. To give an example of one of the 28 per cent who became CO, Lieutenant-Colonel H.O.S Cadogan, 1st Royal Welsh Fusiliers, commanding at the outbreak of war, was schooled at the Royal Academy, Gosport, where he failed the exam for both Woolwich and Sandhurst. He was commissioned in the 4th Royal Welsh Fusiliers, and came under the patronage of Colonel Hon.

14   HMSO, *Return as to the Number of Commissions granted during each of the years 1885 to 1906 inclusive* Parliamentary Paper (1907) 111
15   Figures from Quarterly Army List, June 1914.

Savage Mostyn, late CO of the 1st Battalion. He attended a 'crammer' in Camberley run by Lieutenant-Colonel T.G.R. Mallock and after 11 months passed the Militia Comprehensive Exam and acquired a commission in his patron's late battalion.[16]

From Second Lieutenant to Lieutenant-Colonel

Infantry battalion COs took nearly 25 years to reach the rank of lieutenant-colonel,[17] and had an average age of 47 years 11.5 months, having been in post on average for 23 months when the First World War broke out. In August 1914, three were brevet colonels, namely S.C.F Jackson, 1st Hampshire; W.C.G Heneker, 2nd North Staffordshire; and W.R. Marshall, 1st Sherwood Foresters. Sixteen per cent of the group had achieved the rank of lieutenant-colonel in a different regiment from the one in which they had spent their years as major, indicating that the regimental system was not sufficiently rigid to prevent the able moving for promotion.

Since the abolition of purchase, promotion beyond the rank of lieutenant had been governed by seniority within the regimental list balanced by both the positive recommendation of the CO and confirmatory success in qualifying examinations.[18] This was not a system designed to allow officers of equal ability the same opportunity to rise to battalion command, as the official historian, Sir James Edmonds, noted: "Military talent is rare and is not immediately evident. Seniority rules bar its ascent".[19] The seniority principal was not necessarily paramount, for example Lieutenant-Colonel H.O.S Cadogan, 1st Royal Welsh Fusiliers, wrote to his mother from India in May 1912: "Lloyd, who is senior to me, (has) been passed over and ... I [have] got command of this Battalion".[20] In the three years prior to August 1914, fifteen per cent of CO appointments involved passing over a more senior major.

The examination for promotion to lieutenant-colonel was a test of "Tactical Fitness for Command". The candidate would firstly be examined in a three hour theoretical paper. This consisted of a tactical problem involving the operations of a force "not exceeding a brigade of infantry with a brigade of artillery and a regiment of cavalry, and a proportion of mounted infantry, RE, ASC, and RAMC ..." The candidate then had

---

16   H. Cadogan, *The Road to Armageddon* (Wrexham: Bridge Books, 2009), pp.23-6.

17   On average two years and five months as 2nd Lieutenant; seven years and six months as Lieutenant; nine years and three months as Captain; and seven years and nine months as Major. Forty (25 per cent) had achieved brevet Major appointments, such appointments recognising achievement and ability. Sixteen (10 per cent) had achieved brevet Lieutenant-Colonel status.

18   HMSO, Parliamentary Paper C.1569 *Report of the Royal Commission on Army Promotion and Retirement* (1876).

19   J.E. Edmonds & & R. Maxwell-Hyslop, Military Operations Fance and Belgium 1918 Vol V (London: Imperial War Museum, original date 1947) p.593.

20   Cadogan, *Armageddon*, p.157.

to write "(i) a general appreciation of the situation, (ii) the action which he proposes to take, and (iii) the orders necessary for the execution of his plan". [21]

The second part of the examination took place in the field with troops, judged by a board of three officers, the president of which was a General. The task was to command in "any minor tactical operations which may be ordered, a mixed force, of which the strength must not be less than one battalion of infantry, a battery of artillery, and one squadron of cavalry, to which may be added ... a proportion of mounted infantry and RE." COs were thus being examined in what constituted at that time 'all arms' operations. In the practical exam, which was against a real 'enemy', the candidate was given the "general idea" the night before and a "special idea" on the ground, to which he had half an hour to respond and hand in his written orders. Credit was to be given for "intelligence, judgment, common sense, and readiness of resource in making the best of any situation". The balance of marks was 300 for the written exam, 100 for the practical test. [22] Success was not a formality – in 1912, 38 per cent of candidates failed "Fitness to Command". [23]

War Service

Twelve per cent of the 157 regular COs had had no previous war service. The remaining 138 had served in an average 1.7 campaigns each over a period of nearly 25 years, stretching from the First Sudan War 1884-5 to the Northwest-Frontier campaign of 1908.

Lieutenant-Colonel F.G. Anley, 2nd Essex, (who would ultimately be promoted major-general) had served in six campaigns, namely Sudan 1884-5; Dongola 1896; Nile 1897, 1898 and 1899; and South Africa 1899-1902. Three had served in five campaigns each. E.P Strickland, 1st Manchester, (also ultimately promoted major-general) had served in Burma 1887-9, Dongola 1896, and Nile 1897, 1898, and 1899; Lieutenant-Colonel C.R Ballard, 1st Norfolk, had served in Burma 1891-2, Chitral 1895, North-West Frontier 1897-8, South Africa 1899-1902, and East Africa 1902-4; and Lieutenant-Colonel H.R Davies, 2nd Oxfordshire and Buckinghamshire, had served in Burma 1887-8, North-West Frontier 1897-8, Tirah 1897-8, China 1900, and South Africa 1901-2. [24]

Six COs had served in four campaigns; 19 had served in three; and 32 had served in two. Of the remaining 77 who had served in only one campaign, all except 16 had served in the Second Boer War. Sixteen and a half per cent of the collective war

---

21   HMSO, *The King's Regulations and Orders for the Army, 1912. Reprinted with Amendments Published in Army Orders up to 1 August 1914.* Appendices XII & XIII pp.452-456.

22   HMSO, *King's Regulations*, pp.452-456.

23   TNA WO 279/57. *Report on the Staff Conference held at the Staff College, Camberley*, 17-20.

24   War Services of Officers of the Army, *Quarterly Army List*, January 1914.

experience had been gained against African tribes; 37 per cent had been gained in Asia, primarily India and Burma, and 46.5 per cent against the Boers.

Thirteen had previous experience of command in the field. Lieutenant-Colonel W.C.G. Heneker, 2nd North Staffordshire, had been in command in Southern Nigeria 1902, and twice again in 1903.[25] Eight had commanded mounted infantry columns/battalions in South Africa. Others had commanded colonial or native troops. For instance, Lieutenant-Colonel J. Ponsonby, 1st Coldstream Guards, had commanded the 5th New Zealand Regiment in South Africa, where Lieutenant-Colonel G.C. Knight, 1st Loyal North Lancashire, had both raised and commanded the 1st New South Wales Mounted Infantry Regiment; and Lieutenant-Colonel W.M. Watson, 1st Duke of Wellington's, had commanded a Chinese Regiment at the relief of Tientsin and Peking in 1900.

Staff Service in Peace and War

Some form of staff service was both the mark of an ambitious officer and one perceived as having the qualities to rise in the regiment or army. To what extent it might also have been the result of patronage is unclear. It was not, however, necessary to have such service to rise to the rank of lieutenant-colonel as 12 per cent of the regular COs had not served in any staff post.

At the most basic level of staff experience, that of battalion administration, 36 per cent of the regular COs had been adjutants to a regular battalion as a lieutenant or captain and thirty-eight per cent had been adjutants in their regiment's militia or Volunteers. Overall, 59 per cent had served as adjutant.

Outside the regiment an extraordinary range of staff positions were to be had, which might lead to or result from attendance at the Staff College, Camberley. Twenty-two per cent of the regular COs were *psc*, having passed the two year course at the Staff College. Eight (26 per cent) of this group had attended in the period immediately prior to the Second Boer War when a "new progressive spirit" was apparent.[26] The remaining 74 per cent had attended in the aftermath of the Boer War, an era when under new Commandant, Sir Henry Rawlinson,[27] the course became "more practical and up to date",[28] incorporating the lessons of that conflict.

Forty-six per cent had achieved extra-regimental staff posts. Lieutenant-Colonel C.L. Nicholson, 2nd East Lancashire, who, as already noted, would rise to the rank of major-general in 1916, had perhaps the most richly experienced staff career. A pre-1899 *psc*, he had served as ADC to the Governor and Commander in Chief, Gibraltar

---

25   Heneker wrote a book of tactical guidance for Bush Warfare in 1907 based on his experiences, indicating, as does the Journal of the Royal United Services Institution for the period, that British regimental officers of this period had questing minds, unrecognised by Travers.

26   B. Bond, *The Victorian Army and the Staff College* (London: Eyre Methuen, 1972), p.148.

27   Appointed 1903.

28   Bond, *Victorian Army*, p.197.

(1891-3), as Staff Captain then DAQMG for Mobilisation, India (1901), and had then been DAQMG at the headquarters of Bengal East Command for four years, returning as DAQMG for Mobilisation, India, before returning home and serving successively as Brigade-Major for 15th and 16th Brigades, Irish Command (1905-9), and finally serving as a GSO2 in South Africa (1911-12).

Lieutenant-Colonel S.C.F. Jackson, 1st Hampshire had no *psc* qualification, but had served as ADC to a Major-General, Bengal (1889-93), as ADC to the Commander-in-Chief, East Indies, (1893-4), and as a Station Staff Officer, India (1897) before moving to be DAAG at Army HQ in Bombay (1897-1902). He had then served as DAAQMG to both the 8th and 6th Divisions, Irish Command (1906-10).

If Viscount Esher's vision had been for Staff College graduates to provide a professionally trained General Staff, then indeed some of the regular COs of 1914 had scaled these heights. Lieutenant-Colonel A. Grant-Duff *psc*, 1st Black Watch, had been Assistant Military Secretary to the Committee of Imperial Defence from October 1910 to September 1913, where he had been responsible for the production of the mobilisation 'War Book'.[29] Sadly, for a man of such obvious ability, Grant-Duff was killed at the Battle of the Aisne, 14 September 1914. Lieutenant-Colonel A.D. Geddes *psc*, 2nd Buffs, had been a GSO3, then GSO2 at Army Headquarters (1904-8) and then had spent two years as GSO2 at the War Office. Geddes was also killed early on in 1915 at the Second Battle of Ypres by a shell that struck his battalion HQ.

Lieutenant-Colonels A.R.S. Martin *psc*, 1st Royal Lancaster, and D.C. Boger, (without *psc*), 1st Cheshire, had both been attached to the General Staff at the War Office, as had Lieutenant-Colonel H.P. Hancox *psc,* 2nd Royal Inniskilling Fusiliers. Three (perhaps silver-tongued) officers had served as military attachés. Lieutenant-Colonel H.C. Lowther (without *psc*), 1st Scots Guards, had served in Madrid, Lisbon and Paris and Lieutenant-Colonel J.D. McLachlan *psc,* 1st Cameron Highlanders, in Washington and Mexico. Lieutenant-Colonel C. Wanliss (without *psc*), 2nd South Lancashire, had likely had his patience tried at the notoriously protracted Seistan Arbitration Commission 1903-5.[30] The main difference between those who were *psc* and those who were not lay in home appointments. An officer did not become a GSO2 or 3, a brigade major (or, more obviously, gain a Staff College post) in the UK, without having the qualification. This challenges Martin Samuels' assertion that the army was in the grip of a 'cult of rank' where battalion officers were practically excluded from the work of the General Staff.[31]

29   The "War Book", as it was known, was instigated by the Committee of Imperial Defence. Covering 12 Government departments in 12 chapters it charted the incremental steps from "precautionary" to "strained relations" to "war stage", full mobilisation to meet any threat. Grant-Duff devised a column format which allowed easy reference to what each department might do at each stage. http://pw20c.mcmaster.ca/case-study/adrian-grant-duff-preparing-first-world-war, accessed 20 June 2012.

30   The commission laid down the boundaries between Persia and Afghanistan.

31   M. Samuels, *Command or Control?* (London: Frank Cass, 1995) pp.34-60.

Forty-four per cent of the 139 COs who had war service had performed extra-regimental staff service in war. Seventeen per cent had served as adjutants to their battalions in the field, eleven proceeding to extra-regimental service.

Of the eight who were *psc* by the time of the Second Boer War, four had actually had no staff experience in war by 1914; only Lieutenant-Colonel C.R. Ballard, 1st Norfolk, had a rich war staff service experience. Ballard had been Transport Officer in Tirah, 1898, and in South Africa 1899-1902 was variously Adjutant of Roberts' Light Horse, Staff Captain to a Station Commandant, and Staff Officer to a Mounted Infantry Corps Mobile Column. Lastly, in 1903 he had been Transport Officer to the Somaliland Field Forces. Six of the 23 who acquired their *psc* status after the Boer War had no wartime staff experience by 1914.

If the officer was of the group identified as suitable for staff progression, not having the *psc* initials was no bar to war staff experience. Lieutenant-Colonel T.O. Marden, 1st Welsh, and a future major-general, had served in South Africa as variously Commandant Worcester; Railway Staff Officer; Staff Officer to the Commandant, Colesberg; Staff Officer to the Assistant Inspector General; on Lines of Communication work; and as Commandant Colesburg. More prestigiously, Lieutenant-Colonel N.R. McMahon, 4th Royal Fusiliers, had served in South Africa as the ADC to a major-general commanding an infantry brigade, as a brigade-major and as DAAG. He was killed in action at Ypres on 11 November 1914, prior to taking command of 10th Brigade.

Prestigious staff jobs could however go to men, some perhaps favourites, some undoubtedly talented, who did not have a *psc* and who were never going to obtain one. Thus, Lieutenant-Colonel C.S. Davidson, 2nd South Staffordshire, was ADC to the major-general of an infantry brigade in South Africa, and later brigade-major.

The Quality of the Regular Battalion Commanders of August 1914

Age

At an average of just under 48 years old, were they too old for combat? Age is not a simple issue – there are also the linked issues of physical fitness and stamina. The official historian suggested that "age is biological and should not be reckoned by the calendar. Each case should be judged for itself". He continued:

> … activity is the criterion; in 1914 some lieutenant-colonels could be seen running forward with the best of athletes; others collapsed because they were worn out by marching a few miles; not being able to ride their horses in battle, and two were tried by court martial for dereliction of duty, when bodily fatigue with consequent mental break-down was their offence.[32]

32   Brigadier-General J.E. Edmonds & Lieutenant-Colonel R. Maxwell-Hyslop, *Military Operations France and Belgium 1918, Vol. 5* (London: Imperial War Museum, 1993), p.613.

David French notes the War Office conclusion that "in the closing stages of both World Wars the average age of unit commanders in the teeth arms was between 28 and 36", and that it was regarded as "conclusively proved" that this was the best age.[33]

Although the age of an infantry CO on 29 September 1918 was a month under 35,[34] youth was not the rule. The oldest 'combat' CO appointed in 1918 was a Territorial, Lieutenant-Colonel F.J. Popham, 2/5th Royal Lancaster, who was nearly 48; the oldest Territorial CO on 29 September being Lieutenant-Colonel W. Oddie of the 1/5th West Yorkshire, who was 51. The oldest appointee to a regular battalion in 1918 was Lieutenant-Colonel A.E. Gallagher of 2nd Royal Inniskilling Fusiliers, who was nearly 47, making him the oldest regular CO on 29 September 1918. The oldest 'combat' Service battalion CO on 29 September 1918 was Lieutenant-Colonel C.E. Hudson of the 11th Sherwood Foresters, who was 48. Therefore it cannot be concluded that being 48 was 'too old'.

Education

The education of the regular lieutenant-colonels of August 1914 was better than that of their predecessors, but it was somewhat patchy. Their basic military education was almost certainly inferior to that of most of the captains who in 1914 might have aspired to succeed to battalion command. Twenty two per cent were, however, *psc*, and three-quarters of these had attended Camberley after 1902, an era during which one instructor claimed that "some of very best soldiers in the army were to be met at Camberley."[35]

Not all knowledge was acquired via formal education. In terms of 'on the job' development 88 per cent had served in some form of staff post. The regimental system has been criticised for keeping officers' "mental horizons ... confined to their own regiments",[36] yet in peace and war, 64 per cent had performed extra-regimental staff service. Fifty-nine per cent had been regimental adjutants. The adjutant's job was "to organize the daily routine, run an office, cope with correspondence, write orders, answer queries from brigade, anticipate company needs, stave off troubles and ensure the proper deportment of ORs and junior officers. A quick mind helped."[37] Given that the latter post was within the gift of the CO, it may be presumed that the most able served as adjutants, not least as any CO would have wished it so to ensure that their own work load was as light as possible. The regular COs were, therefore, largely administratively able.

---

33   D. French, *Military Identities* (Oxford: University Press, 2005), p.275, based on TNA WO 32/13253. Memo, by Military Secretary, 25 November 1946.

34   29 September 1918 is the day all five of the British armies in France and Flanders were in action at the same time.

35   Lieutenant-Colonel E.S May, quoted in Bond, *Victorian Army*, p.195.

36   French, *Military Identities*, p.3.

37   K. Radley, *First Canadian Division, CEF 1914-1918* PhD Thesis, Carleton University, Ottawa (2000), p.85.

Experience of war

The war experience of battalion officers was rich, but what was its true value? David French has asserted that "between 1870 and 1970 the British army fought only four wars in which it found itself fighting against an enemy that was equipped to the same modern standard as itself, and was organized into large combined arms formations". Prior to the First World War, the only conflict that met this criterion was "the opening months of the Second Anglo-Boer War".[38]

Forty-seven per cent of the regular COs had accumulated war service in South Africa in 1899.[39] This experience had been at the highest rank of captain, and only ten had command experience in war. However, it was not simply the experience of 1899, but the processed lessons of these months which became established practice in 1900, which were important; and seventy-one per cent saw service 1900-02. Their key learning, as we have noted, was as lieutenants and captains, and likely achieved before they were too set in their ways of command.

Much of their war experience, both before and after the Second Boer War, had been in the "policeman of the empire" role. G.F. Ellison, *psc*, a keen military observer who ended the First World War as a major-general having served in staff posts, writing in the immediate aftermath of the Boer War, had deep reservations about the value of this "small war" military service.[40] Ellison's main complaint, mirroring Lord Esher, was the lack of an intellectual approach to a science of soldiering. He thought that the small war experience could lead to "a dangerous narrowing of the intellectual vision" through the view that "war could only be learnt from war," and, moreover, that only the British way in war was worth learning from.[41] In short, the army had learnt the wrong thing by concentrating on the wrong experiences.

Whilst not suggesting complete inapplicability, Ellison believed that "The qualities of both body and mind that make for success in the leadership of small expeditions and for the conquest of savage tribes" did not enable a commander to develop the mental facility "to deal with administrative questions of the most complex nature or to solve strategical problems on which the fate of nations may depend ... something more is required than mere physical bravery, a strong will, nerves of iron and a body impervious to fatigue".[42]

It is true that the campaigns of conquest, suppression of insurrection, or punitive expeditions bore little resemblance to continental European warfare. The British army of 1914, however, had experience of a great deal of tactical diversity, and in its campaigns conducted amidst hostile geography and nature, its commanders had become masters of small-force logistics. Far from necessarily suffering from narrowed vision, the battalion CO of 1914 had the potential for a broad vision provided by varied empire experience

38   French, *Military Identities*, p.265.
39   HMSO, *Quarterly Army List*, January 1914.
40   G. F. Ellison, *Considerations Influencing the Selection of Officers for Command and the Staff*, NAM 8704-35 Ellison Mss. No. 30.
41   Ellison, *Considerations*.
42   Ellison, *Considerations*.

balanced against nearly 12 years of training suitable to continental war with the revised tactics and developments of the post-1902 period. In comparison, his German counterpart had never been on active service, and there is no evidence that the German army looked down on Britain's colonial war experience.

Of course, not all of the August 1914 COs can be cast in a progressive light. Lieutenant-Colonel W.M. Bliss 2nd Scottish Rifles, aged 48, had become CO on 10 October 1913. His had not been a popular appointment as he had come from the 1st Battalion. He had no war experience, but had served as a regular adjutant 1894-98. One of his officer's described him as "Crimean in many ways – steeped in outmoded tradition and not prone to delegation of duties." Reviewing his officers' opinions of him, John Baynes summarises him as not "very clever … [but] … he was genuine and sincere, and within his limitations a sound, practical officer."[43] Bliss died in front of uncut wire at Neuve Chapelle on 10 March 1915, his leadership, however flawed, being from the front.

Whilst the COs of August 1914 had passed through some sort of intellectual quality-control for promotion, it was the rich patina of experience that marked this group as exceptional in terms of its varied nature, both in staff and war service. Their war experience suited them to managing battalions in the encounter battles of 1914, and may even have been particularly important in managing the retreat from Mons. Once trenches were dug for more than momentary inhabitation, their store of experience, as for all commanders, irrespective of nationality, no longer served them as well.

The Campaign of 1914

The campaign of 1914 was brutally hard on the regimental officer. By the end of 1914 the BEF had, outside of the debilitating retreat of August/September, passed through the battles of Mons, Le Cateau, the Marne and the Aisne, and had been violently mauled at First Ypres. On 31 December 1914 there were 123 regular battalions in France. After First Ypres it has been claimed that "in most cases, there were barely one officer and 30 men left" from the battalions "who had arrived in France in 1914".[44] Officially, by 30 November 1914, 842 officers were dead and 688 missing, with 2097 wounded, a quarter of the pre-war officer class.[45] Keith Simpson notes that of the 1st Queen's, of 26 officers 24 were casualties by this date; from the 1st Norfolk, 15 of 26; from the 3rd Worcestershire, 15 of 28; and of the 1st Northamptonshire, 26 of 26.[46]

The era lacked a science of leadership, yet John Bourne remarks that "'Leadership' was a concept which the Army was confident it understood", namely "Courage, Duty and

43   J. Baynes, *Morale: A Study of Men and Courage*, (London: Cassell, 1967) p.113.
44   I.F.W. Beckett, *Ypres – The First Battle 1914*, (Harlow: Pearson, 2004), p.177.
45   Brigadier-General J.E. Edmonds, *Military Operations France and Belgium 1914, Vol II*, (London: Macmillan 1925) p.467.
46   K. Simpson, 'The Officers', in *A Nation in Arms: A Social Study of the British Army in the First World War*, I.F.W. Beckett & K. Simpson, Eds (Manchester: Manchester University Press, 1986) p.69.

Discipline".[47] With the traditional emphasis on the "moral" effect of "vigorous offensive"[48] the battalion commander led from the front to demonstrate these virtues. This style of leadership came at a price, for by the end of 1914, 18 of the regular COs of August 1914 were dead, and of those who replaced them as lieutenant-colonel, a further seven had been killed in action. The Aisne and First Ypres were particularly bloody, claiming six and eleven lieutenant-colonels respectively. Deaths per month of lieutenant-colonels ran at 5.6 in 1914, and 11 per month in France in 1918. The 1914 casualties were, however, from only 146 battalions, in comparison with the 507 of 29 September 1918. Multiplying the 1914 monthly total by a factor of three and a half gives a projected monthly comparison figure of nearly 20, indicative of the lethal nature of the fighting of that year.

Of the two commanding officers who died when II Corps stood and fought at Le Cateau, both fell leading from the front. Lieutenant-Colonel C.A.H. Brett, 2nd Suffolk,[49] found his battalion in a poor position. Brett gathered his officers and told them "they were committed to it, and everyone must do the best he could ... there was to be no retirement."[50] Brett placed himself with his forward companies and was killed early on by a shell. In the same battle, 2nd Royal Lancaster, commanded by Lieutenant-Colonel A. McN. Dykes, found themselves on top of a hill at Haucourt under heavy shellfire. Fighting in the front line, Dykes fell early on, shouting encouragement: "Men, if you want your lives for God's sakes extend" and, finally "Good bye, boys."[51]

Twenty-five lieutenant-colonels were wounded, and of the COs of August 1914, fourteen were so severely wounded that they never returned to command. Not all wounds were physical in nature. Lieutenant-Colonel Henry Delme-Radcliffe,[52] CO 2nd Royal Welsh Fusiliers, did not lack courage; 2nd Lieutenant P. Davies wrote of him and his second-in-command at the Battle of the Aisne under fire "walking along the top of a scratchy trench and telling me that my men should always remember the value of cover ... They, in the open!"[53] He was invalided on 26 October 1914 with a "nervous breakdown" according to Private Frank Richards, and being "a bit of a nervous wreck" according to the Medical Officer of 19th Field Ambulance.[54]

---

47   J.M. Bourne, 'British Generals in the First World War' in Sheffield, G.D. ed. *Leadership and Command – The Anglo-American Military Experience Since 1861* (London: Brassey's, 2002) pp.94-6.

48   General Staff, War Office, *Field Service Regulations, Part 1* (London: Harrison, 192) p.126.

49   A 49 year-old veteran of Hazara (1888) and South Africa (1899-1902).

50   C.C.R. Murphy, *The History of the Suffolk Regiment 1914-1927* (London: Hutchinson, 1928) p.32.

51   www.dnw.co.uk/medals/auctionarchive/viewspecialcollections/itemdetail. lasso?itemid=3809 (accessed 16 May 2012).

52   A 48 year-old veteran of Burma (1886-7) and South Africa (1899-1902).

53   D. Langley, 'Personalities of the 2nd Bn Royal Welch Fusiliers', Stand To!, April 2007, 79, pp.26-7.

54   F. Richards, *Old Soldiers Never Die* (London: Faber, 1965), p.55. T. Hampson, *A Medical Officer's Diary and Narrative of the First World War,* http://myweb.tiscali.co.uk/ philsnet/T%20Hampson%20WW1%20Diary%20100.htm accessed 20/09/2011.

Five lieutenant-colonels of August 1914 (and eleven in all) were prisoners of war by the end of December 1914. The first to be taken was Lieutenant-Colonel D.C. Boger, 1st Cheshire, in the withdrawal from Mons on 24 August, when the battalion found itself isolated and enveloped during rear guard fighting at Audregnies. Ordering withdrawal, Boger was shot in the foot and right side. He crawled away but was finally located by the Germans. With Company Sergeant-Major Frank Meachin he was taken to a temporary hospital in a convent at Wiheries, but escaped. A Roman Catholic priest took them to the home of a woman called Libiez, the mother of a local lawyer, who hid them for several weeks in the loft of an outbuilding. Their hiding place was revealed and two nuns took them to the convent in Wasmes, and Libiez's son provided false civilian identification cards, and they were taken on to the Berkendael Medical Insitute, to the matron Edith Cavell. The now bearded Boger was wearing the floppy tie and black hat of a peasant. After a number of weeks, still lame, Boger attempted the journey to the Dutch border, down the canals on a coal barge. Stopping in a café for a drink, Boger, alone, as the more mobile Meachin had already crossed the border, was recaptured, and spent the rest of the war as a prisoner of war.[55]

Competence

As noted earlier, two COs of the original BEF, Lieutenant-Colonels J.F. Elkington, 1st Warwickshire, and A.E. Mainwaring, 2nd Royal Dublin Fusiliers, were both court-martialled for surrendering St Quentin on 27 August 1914. Two parties of these battalions, led by their exhausted COs, arrived at St Quentin on 27 August 1914 fresh from the Battle of Le Cateau the previous day. The mayor implored them to sign a surrender document to save the townspeople from any fighting with the pursuing German army. The colonels complied, but an element of 2nd Cavalry Brigade, led by Major G.T.M. Bridges intervened, recovered the document, and galvanised the two COs and their battalion remnants.[56] Both lieutenant-colonels were subsequently court-martialled and cashiered. Mainwaring, not a well man, was one of the very few who should probably never have gone on active service. He was "subject to bouts of debilitating illness. During manoeuvres in September 1913 he suffered so severely from colitis that he was forced to return to Gravesend ahead of his battalion".[57] After his being cashiered he returned to civilian life. By contrast, Elkington joined the French Foreign Legion as a private, serving with distinction on the Western Front until wounded. His courage exonerated him in the eyes of the British Army; he was reinstated to his original rank and awarded the DSO.

In addition, five infantry lieutenant-colonels were relieved of command before 31 December 1914.[58] The fact that some were relieved of command does not necessarily

55   http://grandadswar.mrallsophistory.com/boger.html, accessed 20 June 2012.
56   See P.T. Scott, *Dishonoured* (London: Tom Donovan, 1994).
57   Scott, *Dishonoured*, p.9.
58   D/APC/HD/ABLW/187116 Army Personnel Centre – War Office letter dated 17

mean they were incompetent. Of these, Lieutenant-Colonel N.A.L Corry, 2nd Grenadier Guards, had been sent home for withdrawing without orders, being out of contact with his Brigade Commander, from Bois la Haut on 23 August 1914 at Mons.

> Colonel Corry determined to take upon himself the responsibility of ordering the retirement of the two battalions. His impression was that in the case like this, when local conditions could not be known to the Divisional Staff, it was for the man on the spot to make his own decision. Superior authority, however, afterwards held that while under exceptional circumstances such powers might well be delegated to the man in *mediis rebus*, in a case like this it could not be admitted that an officer in actual touch with the enemy was the best judge of how long a position should be held. It was felt that there were many considerations in the decision of the sort, of which the officer in the front line could know very little. Colonel Corry was therefore severely blamed to his action, and was a fortnight later relieved of his command.

Corry had simply fallen foul of the vagaries of being the 'man on the spot',[59] and the War Office noted him as "not an inefficiency case".[60] Corry subsequently assumed command of 3rd Grenadier Guards on 29 November 1914, and took them to France.

The remaining four were a different matter. Lieutenant-Colonel C. Wanliss, 2nd South Lancashire, was sent home on 29 August 1914, judged "totally unfit to command in the field" by his divisional commander Major-General H. Hamilton.[61] This decision was approved by General Sir Horace Smith-Dorrien, Field Marshal Sir John French and F. W. N. McCracken, his brigadier. Wanliss was put on the sick list, ordered to take complete rest and sent back to England. Wanliss saw the report on him prepared by McCracken, and endorsed by Major General F.D.V. Wing and Smith-Dorrien, and submitted a detailed rebuttal, but the Army Council felt they had "no alternative but to accept the opinion formed" by the reporting officers.[62] The removal of Wanliss did not cure the problems with his battalion, who continued to perform poorly in the view of brigade staff.[63]

Lieutenant-Colonel D.W. Churcher, 1st Royal Irish Fusiliers, who as we saw earlier, clearly had an unhappy pre-war relationship with his brigade commander, was replaced on 10 September 1914. Similarly, Lieutenant-Colonels H.P. Hancox of the 2nd Royal Inniskilling Fusiliers and O'Meagher of the 2nd Munster Fusiliers were sent home.

It is possible to assess viability in the whole group of 1914 COs in terms of endurance and promotability. If the number of COs who were either killed in action (40), wounded unable to return to command (14), prisoners of war (8), or who remained in India (5),

---

January 1915 in the file of Lieutenant-Colonel C. Wanliss.

59   Sir F. Ponsonby, *The Grenadier Guards in the Great War, 1914-1918, Volume One* (London: Macmillan, 1920) p.27.

60   D/APC/HD/ABLW/187116 Army Personnel Centre.

61   D/APC/HD/ABLW/187116 Army Personnel Centre.

62   D/APC/HD/ABLW/187116 Army Personnel Centre.

63   T. Astill, *The Great War Diaries of Brigadier-General Alexander Johnston 1914-1917* (Barnsley: Pen & Sword, 2007) pp.38-9 & 53.

is subtracted, 90 COs remain whose progress can be followed through the war. Of these, 15 were invalided, 15 were retired or sidelined into inactive administrative posts; and two court-martialled. One took up a series of senior staff posts. Twenty-eight were promoted to Brigade command, 25 to Divisional command, and three to Corps command, giving a viability, or 'endurance and promotability' rate of 64 per cent. The indication is that nearly two thirds of COs were leaders of stamina and quality.

The question 'How good were these men?', is impossible to answer directly. The 64 per cent competence rate, however, is in stark contrast to Travers' implied 75 per cent incompetence rate. It is clear that at the level of battalion command, regimental officers were much more rigorously chosen, educated and experienced than Travers gives them credit for, with less evidence of the dominance of seniority principles and regimental particularism than has been presumed.

The Territorial Force COs of August 1914

Given that the Territorial Force (TF) was called upon to reinforce the BEF to the extent that 31 December 1914 there were 23 TF battalions in France, their COs need also to be examined. The Territorial Force had been created out of the Volunteer Force by the 1907 reforms of R. B. Haldane, Secretary of State for War, with the express purpose of providing home defence.[64] After the outbreak of war battalions were, however, invited to volunteer for Imperial Service.

In August 1914 there were 207 Territorial Force COs in post. Thirty-three of the TF COs (16 per cent) were ex-regulars. They had an average age of 45 years 4 months, and were therefore approximately 2.5 years younger than their counterparts who had remained in the regular army. Ten per cent had retired as lieutenant, 45 per cent as captain, and 45 per cent as major, and they had been retired for an average of 8 years 3 months. It is probable that they retired because they were unlikely to be promoted beyond the rank of major in the regular army. Three, however, were recently retired lieutenant-colonels from the Indian army.

The remaining 174 TF COs had all been Volunteers, and their average age was 47 years 8 months. There was, however, considerable variation in their ages. Lieutenant-Colonel Sir M. Sykes, 5th Green Howards, was the youngest at 35 years 5 months, whilst 32 per cent were over the age of 50, the oldest being Lieutenant-Colonel A. R. Meggy, 4th Essex, who was 59 years and 3 months old.

Officers commanding TF units were "appointed for 4 years, but extensions (not more than two) for 4 years" could be granted. Officers other than those holding commands or staff appointments were to retire at 60, but again might be "allowed an extension of service, which will not be granted for more than two years at a time, or beyond 65".[65] The 207 TF COs had been in post for an average of three years one month. Forty-six (22 per cent) had been in post over four years, 15 being COs of Volunteer battalions,

---

64   The Territorial and Reserve Forces Act, 1907.
65   *The Territorial Year Book* (London: Hodder & Stoughton, 1909), p.22.

and two had been in post before the turn of the century. Overall, 95 per cent of TF CO appointments were from within the regiment.

Staff and war service

In comparison with the regular COs, the ex-regular TF COs had a lower rate of occupancy of peacetime staff positions, (30 per cent against 82 per cent) with a somewhat higher rate of occupancy of wartime staff positions (55 per cent against 91 per cent). The Territorial officers had no access to staff positions.

Of the 34 ex-regular TF COs, seven (20 per cent) had no war service. Of the remaining 26, three had served in three campaigns, seven in two, and the remainder in one campaign, spanning the period of the Third Burma War (1885-9) to the North-West Frontier (1908). They had half as much war experience as their counterparts who had remained in the regular army. Of the 173 'pure' TF COs, 138 (80 per cent) had no previous war service. The remainder had service in the Second Boer War, only sixteen of them having seen service there in 1899 and 37 between 1900 and 1902. TF COs, apart from those who were ex-regulars, were, therefore, deficient in both education and staff experience, and their war experience was limited.

The Campaign of 1914

The first Territorial battalion to go into action was, famously, the 1/14th Battalion, London Regiment, the London Scottish, on the Messines Ridge on 31 October. Having landed in France on 16 September it had been put to lines of communication duties. Sent to Ypres on 29 October, it was commanded by 42 year-old Lieutenant-Colonel G.A. Malcolm, an East India Merchant and 'pure' TF CO, who on 10 October was "greatly indignant" about being "too late to have a look in".[66] Malcolm's 'look in' lasted until 15 February 1915, when he was invalided home.

As of 31 December 1914 all of the TF battalions were still commanded by the men who had brought them to France, except for two COs who had swiftly been invalided. Lieutenant-Colonel G.A. Blair (1/10th Liverpool), a Major in the TF Reserve in August 1914, was invalided on 25 November 1914, after 23 days in France. He had replaced the CO of August 1914, Lieutenant-W. Nicholl, who had been transferred to command the newly raised 2/10th. Lieutenant-Colonel G.B. Heywood (1/6th Cheshire) a TF Captain in August 1914 was invalided on 18 December 1914 after 38 days in France. He had replaced the CO of August 1914, Lieutenant-Colonel A.J. Sykes, who had not only been replaced but retired.

---

66   J.C. Dunn, *The War the Infantry Knew* (London: Jane's, 1987) p.69.

Competence

As with the regular COs, no objective competence rating can be calculated for the TF COs of August 1914. The first test of suitability for command was, of course, whether they took their battalions into active service. Whilst it might be argued that they were never primarily intended to see service abroad, TF COs definitely faced the potential of commanding their battalions in action on home soil.[67]

Of the 206 battalions,[68] 26 CO, did not see active service because their battalions remained in England or were posted to a non-combat zone. Of the 180 remaining, 71 did not, being removed from the command of their battalions before they went abroad, as with Lieutenant-Colonels Nicholls and Sykes referred to above. (Lieutenant-Colonel D.C. Campbell, CO 1/6th Black Watch, was removed from command by death, in the Autumn of 1914, and hence never had the chance to lead his battalion). The remaining 109 give an "appropriate to command in war" rate of 61 per cent.

The reasons for 39 per cent not proceeding on foreign service are probably twofold. (It was not connected with previous experience as 56 per cent of 'Territorial only' COs went abroad in comparison with 60 per cent of ex-regular COs). Firstly, regimental histories sometimes refer to age and health. Whilst health remains an unknown factor, the TF COs who did not take their battalions abroad were only two years older than those who did (48 years three months versus 46 years 3 months, on average.) It is, of course, possible that in these part-time soldiers, who would most likely be less fit than regulars of the same age, two years made a difference. It is more likely that 'age and health' was to a great extent euphemistic and that foremost was perceived appropriateness and competence. Lieutenant-Colonel Sir M. Sykes, CO 1/5th Green Howards, was pressed into service by Lord Kitchener onto the de Bunsen Committee, advising on Middle Eastern affairs; and Lieutenant-Colonel B.A. Firth, CO 1/4th Yorks & Lancs, who was a member of the prominent Sheffield steel family, resigned to pursue a career the munitions industry. The point is the same – these last two men were inappropriately positioned for battalion command if, in the event of war, they could not lead their battalions.

Lord Derby[69] described Lieutenant-Colonel H.L. Beckwith of the 4th Loyal North Lancashire as "absolutely useless ... to show you what sort of man he is he says he cannot go out now to the Front but he would be ready to go out later when the weather gets warmer".[70] The best perspective that might be put on Lieutenant-Colonel

---

67   Haldane "expressed the hope that between one-sixth and one-quarter" of the TF would "actually opt to undertake a foreign service obligation." [*Hansard* 4th Series Vol. 169, 1301, 25 Feb. 1907 cited in Mitchinson, *Defending Albion*, p.6].

68   There were technically 207 battalions, but one, 7th King's Liverpool, the one remaining Volunteer battalion, was not commanded by a lieutenant-colonel.

69   The 17th Earl of Derby, MP, appointed Director-General of Recruitment in 1915, was one of the originators of the local recruitment ('Pal's Battalions') movement.

70   Derby papers LRO 920 DER(17)33 13 February 1915 [quoted in P. Simkins, *Kitchener's Army: The Raising of the New Armies 1914-1916* (Barnsley: Pen & Sword, 2007) p.221]. Beckwith resigned in October 1914, but later served as a major in the Labour Corps.

R.G. Hayes' (15th London) refusal of Imperial Service was that he recognised his limitations.[71] His leadership example seems to have led to a good deal of refusal of imperial service in his battalion, and degraded morale. Garth Pratten's observation on Australian Militia COs on the outbreak of the Second World War is absolutely applicable to these auxiliary COs - "senior command was perhaps beyond all but the most committed part-time officer".[72] As William Mitchinson summarises, "although usually keen and proud of their unit, many … were, in the opinion of the professionals, not up to the task of commanding a battalion".[73] The TF County Associations had clearly had difficulty in completely asserting authority over the local interests involved in battalion command that had historically been marked.[74]

Of the 109 TF COs of 1914 who eventually proceeded to command battalions on active service thirty seven per cent were lost to command through being killed (15), seriously wounded (5), or invalided (20). Nineteen (17 per cent) were relieved and retired, and 18 (16 per cent) were relieved but employed further in third-line battalion commands or administrative jobs. Fifteen were longevitous in battalion command, into late 1917/1918, and four were promoted temporary brigadier generals.

In an attempt to review the overall viability as COs of those who took their battalions to war, a cut-off of six months will be taken as likely to reveal the effects of age, health and ability. Removing those who could not have furthered their careers due to suffering death or serious wounds, there remains a group of 89 men and of these 63 (71 per cent) were promoted or served over six months, and hence were "viable commanders".

If the group who did not take their battalions overseas are included, the overall viability rate for the TF COs in a sustained continental war falls to 31 per cent. This may not have been what they were primarily intended to do, but it was what they were required to do. The majority were not up to the challenge.

Attrition of command in the BEF in 1914

On 31 December 1914, 52 (42 per cent) original regular lieutenant-colonels were still in command of their battalions. The high levels of dead and wounded may be seen as either profligacy with a crucial resource, or a reflection of the ferocity of the fighting. Fifty-four battalions (44 per cent) were commanded by men who were majors at the outbreak of war; 16 (13 per cent) were commanded by men who had been captains, and one by a 2nd lieutenant, G.C.B Clark, 2nd Royal Scots who had, however, been promoted to major.

---

71   J. Knight, *The Civil Service Rifles in the Great War* (Barnsley: Pen & Sword, 2004), p.33.

72   G. Pratten, *Australian Battalion Commanders in the Second World War* (Melbourne: Cambridge University Press, 2009) p.31.

73   K.W.Mitchinson, *England's Last Hope – The Territorial Force, 1908-14* (Basingstoke: Palgrave Macmillan, 2008), p.159.

74   Volunteer battalions had been very much the personal fiefdoms of their COs – indeed, they had a major personal interest, being personally responsible for any debts incurred.

Despite the terrible depredations of First Ypres, this snapshot suggests that notwithstanding a 58 per cent attrition in original COs, the state of battalion command in the BEF would not at first glance appear to have been fatally 'deskilled' with such a high proportion of lieutenant-colonels and pre-war majors in command. At times, however, the situation had been desperate.

To take two examples, the 1st Coldstream Guards had landed in France on 13 August 1914 under Lieutenant-Colonel J. Ponsonby. When he was wounded on 15 September 1914, the second-in-command, Major the Hon. L. d'H Hamilton took over only to be killed on 29 October 1914. Depletion of officers of the battalion meant that Lieutenant J. Boyd took over for two days, being replaced on 1 November by Captain E.G. Christie-Miller, who was taken prisoner the following day. Command devolved on Lieutenant Boyd again for another two days, before he was replaced by Captain G.J. Edwards, who was superseded by the return of Lieutenant-Colonel Ponsonby on 21 November.

The 1st Cheshire found themselves in similar straits. After the disaster at Audregnies on 24 August 1914, where the battalion was shattered and Lieutenant-Colonel D.C. Boger was taken prisoner, there were no majors present to assume command, and Captain J.L. Shore became CO until 16 September. His replacement by Major F.B Young, a major from the Reserve of Officers, was part of a succession of 7 COs during the month of October. Young was replaced by Major C.B. Vandeleur (second-in-command 1st Scottish Rifles), who was succeeded by three captains of the 1st Cheshire, F.H. Mahony, J.L Shore (again) and B.E. Massy and one of the 2nd Munster Fusiliers, G.A. Woods. Lieutenant T.L. Frost of the 1st Cheshire was in command as October came to a close. He was replaced after 5 days by a major from the Reserve of Officers, J.A. Busfeild, who gave way to Major H.S. Hodgkin, a regular captain in August 1914, who was in command at the year's end.

These two examples show that the most alarming reality for the BEF was that attrition was taking place not just at senior level but also extensively at the level of middle-ranking battalion officers.

Conclusion

If, as James Edmonds states, "In every respect the Expeditionary Force of 1914 was incomparably the best trained, best organized, and best equipped British Army which ever went forth to war",[75] then certainly the regular COs of 1914, contrary to the views of Tim Travers, were the most educated, experienced and probably competent group of COs that the British army had ever required to take its battalions on active service. Despite the fact that their appointments did not take place within a meritocracy, two thirds of them demonstrated endurance or promotability. In comparison, only a third of the Territorial Force COs (who had not, in their defence, been intended to embark on continental campaigning) proved viable COs. However, the ferocity of the fighting of 1914 (and the requirement to provide brigade commanders to the expanding army) began to erode not only the stock of experienced senior regular officers, but the stock of middle ranking battalion officers who would increasingly be required to step up to the mark of battalion command across the whole army.

75   J. E Edmonds, *Military Operations, France and Belgium 1914, Vol 1* (Nashville: Battery Press, 1996) p.10.

14

The Company Commander

John Mason Sneddon [1]

> *A new school of officers has risen since the South African War, a thinking school*
> *of officers who desire to see the full efficiency which comes from a new*
> *organisation and no surplus of energy running to waste.*

Richard Haldane, Secretary of State for War, 1906. [2]

This chapter is concerned with the training and role of "middle management" in an infantry battalion of the Regular army in 1914 – the company commander – a stratum in the military hierarchy that seems to have been neglected and marginalised in writings about the period, but whose training, and leadership abilities, were one of the most important determinants of how the soldier fared on the battlefield. This chapter will attempt to narrow this gap in the historiography of 1914, but company commanders remain an under researched field and it would be unwise to assume that the opinions expressed in this chapter are the last word, and will not be subject to modification resulting from further research.

Between 1903 and 1914, absorbing the bitter lessons of the Boer War, the British army underwent one of the most revolutionary changes in its history. The administration of the War Office was restructured; the position of Commander-in-Chief was replaced by the General Staff; [3] the home-based army became the basis of the

---

1 The author would like to thank Aimée Fox-Godden and Spencer Jones for much useful comment and support.
2 R B Haldane, House of Commons, Army Debates 1906, p.42. See also John K. Dunlop, *The Development of the British Army 1899-1914* (London: Methuen 1938), p.248.
3 The General Staff was established in 1904. It became the Imperial General Staff in 1909 after co-opting military representatives of the self-governing Dominions such as Canada and Australia.

Maj. R.G. Cooper-King, West Yorkshire Regt.

Capt. R.G. Featherstone, 1st Devons.

Capt. R.N. King, 1st Lincolns.

Capt. O. Steele, 1st Royal Berkshire.

Capt. C.L. Price, 2nd The Royal Scots.

Capt. W.M. Kington, DSO, 1st Royal Welsh Fusiliers.

Six Company Commanders Killed in Action 1914

Expeditionary Force; the reserves were reorganised into the Territorial Army; and there was a complete rethinking of tactics to address the problems arising from the increased firepower resulting from magazine rifles, machine guns and quick-firing artillery.

It was within this period of turmoil that the career of a company commander developed, progressing from a 2nd lieutenant, sometime around 1900, to a senior captain or a major by 1914.

ooooo

Making an Army Officer

A snapshot of company commanders is shown in the table below, constructed from information gleaned from the obituaries of all captains and majors who were serving in infantry battalions and killed in action between August and December 1914, although not all were acting as company commanders at the time of their death.[4] This gives a sample of 466 officers, 385 of them captains and 81 majors. These obituaries are short, and many omit information that would have been of interest to this study, such as school and early military career, so we are looking at a snapshot, rather than a portrait.

Rank		Education		Family		Army Entrance		Combat	
Capt.	385	Public School	319	Military	162	Militia	254	Boer War	254
Major	81	Other	64	Married	211	RMC	161	Other	101
		Graduates	51			Other	52		
		psc	19						

In confirmation of previous studies on the social composition of the Edwardian army, these officers came from a privileged background that represented the upper 'professional' middle class of Edwardian society. About one third came from families where their father, or a grandfather, had served, the others from families following various occupations, but with the law and church over represented and many had, in their ancestry, upwards connections to the traditional landed aristocracy.[5] Public school education was almost obligatory but a small number were educated privately, or abroad. The traditions of their social class, combined with their upbringing at home and education at school, would instil in these boys a concept of "gentleman manliness".[6]

4   The source for this information is L.A. Clutterbrook & W.T. Dooner (eds.), *The Bond of Sacrifice. Vol 1: August to December 1914* (London, Cranford Press, 1917).

5   The sons of the landed aristocracy were over-represented in the Cavalry and Guards, which are not discussed explicitly in this chapter but which would make an interesting study in their own right.

6   See Christopher Moore-Bick, *Playing the Game. The British Junior Infantry Officer on the Western Front 1914-18* (Solihull. Helion & Company Ltd. 2011), pp.30-31 for a useful discussion of this concept.

This combined with the suppression of any indulgence, or weakness, that could distract from the attainment this "muscular Christian" ideal, would have given these boys a common background that was almost designed to instil military discipline in their souls.

On leaving school most eschewed Sandhurst to volunteer for the Militia as the quickest way of turning themselves into junior officers and participating in the then ongoing Boer War. The contribution of the Militia to this war was significant, with almost twice as many officer entrants coming through the Militia than through Sandhurst, which was unable to meet the increased demand for junior officers. Major-General H.C. Borrett, Assistant Adjutant-General for Recruitment, in his evidence to the post-war Elgin Commission, stated that the shortage of junior officers was resolved by recruiting "suitable young gentlemen and sending them out without any training at all".[7]

The transformation from public schoolboy to army officer began when the gentleman joined his battalion, for it was here that the young officer began to hone his conformity to the army's unique sense of honour and acquired the powerful *espirit de corps* that derived from being a member of the battalion.[8] As Edward Spiers has noted an officer had to be born, bred and educated as a gentlemen, or be prepared to act and behave like a "natural" gentleman within the confines of regimental society.[9] Embodied in these norms were requirements of dress and deportment, an emphasis on honour and integrity, and conformity with the manners and etiquette of polite society.

One consequence of this image of 'an officer and a gentleman' was conformity in attitude and outlook across the army. Existing military officers assumed that only young men, with the right type of breeding and education, would be able to uphold these standards, and consequently selected subalterns that would turn out to be like themselves. This was done by a process of vetting which determined, to their satisfaction, that the young officer was "the right sort"' Interestingly, elite regiments in the pre-1914 German army had very similar methods of identifying the "right sort of officer".[10]

Thus boys from the right background were selected and subsequently made into officers. The bulk of this moulding was undertaken within the social "cocoon" that was their battalion and which knew, unto itself, what "right" looked like when it came to the behaviour and deportment of its officers. It was this ability to conform, combined with the necessity of a private income, that ensured that the army always drew its officers from the same narrow stratum of society and reinforced the public perception,

7   *Report of the Royal commission Appointed to Inquire into the Military Preparations and Other Matters Connected with the War in South Africa* (London, H.M.S.O. 1903) (hereafter The Elgin Report) Vol.1, Evidence given by Major-General H.C. Borret, pp.220-1.

8   Officers, like other ranks, normally served their entire military career in the battalion to which they were first posted. Before the war it was a relatively rare occurrence for either to be transferred to another battalion within the Regiment.

9   Edward. M. Spiers, *The Army and Society, 1815-1914* (London, Longman 1980), p.30.

10   Mark R Stoneman. *Particularistic Traditions in a National Profession: Reflections on the Wilhelmine Army Officer Corps.* http://homepage.mac.com/markstoneman/newsletter11.pdf (last access April 2012).

accurately expressed in literature and theatre of the period, of army officers as a socially conservative body of rather limited horizons.

In his study of the 2nd Scottish Rifles John Baynes gives an excellent account of the officers' mess when the battalion was stationed in Malta in 1914.[11] All unmarried officers lived in the officer's mess furnished, and operated, as much as possible like a comfortable country house of the period.[12] It had two principal rooms. The first was a large ante-room containing comfortable furniture, newspapers (even the odd book), games and other items of recreation such as a piano, as well as regimental trophies and photographs. The other 'space' was a smaller, but an equally well-appointed dining room. Officers always wore formal dress for dinner.

In this world of their own making most battalions had their idiosyncratic rules and rituals. For example, in the mess of the 2nd Scottish Rifles, only Turkish cigarettes were smoked in the ante-room, and newly joined subalterns, in their first six months, could not address a senior officer unless spoken to first. They also had to wait three years before they could stand on the hearth rug in front of the fire! Two rules that were common across most battalions were that a woman's name might never be mentioned, nor could 'shop', or work, be discussed in the mess. This later rule is often cited as evidence for lack of professionalism and intellectualism, but Baynes, himself a serving officer when he wrote his book, suggests that it was an important corrective to the fact that for most of each day officers were immersed in their duties and banning 'shop' in the mess made them discuss something else and thus ensured the area was reserved for relaxation.[13] There was also the ever present danger of mess servants overhearing snippets of conversation, or even the name of an individual soldier, all of which they then could feed into the insatiable battalion rumour machine.

Within a battalion the morale, happiness, and military effectiveness depended upon many factors with the relationship between officers, and the soldiers they commanded recognised as one of the most important.[14] There was a general expectation that a successful commander would be fearless, but there was a clear distinction between courage and competence. A company commander could be strict in enforcing military

11   John Baynes, *Morale. A Study of Men and Courage. The Second Scottish Rifles at the Battle of Neuve Chapelle 1915* (London: Cassell 1967).

12   Only two officers were married on the Malta station. In the table the proportion of married majors and captains is probably on the high side, inflated by the influx of officers from the Reserve. Prior to mobilization these officers were, to all intents and purposes, civilians following their chosen career and a higher proportion of them were married when compared with Regular officers.

13   On alleged anti-intellectualism, see Martin Samuels, *'Command or Control?' Combined Training and Tactics in the British and German Armies 1888-1918* (London: Frank Cass 1995), pp.34-60; for the refutation, see Baynes, *Morale*, p.29.

14   For a detailed discussion of this issue in the First World War, see Gary Sheffield, *Leadership in the Trenches: Officer Man Relations, Morale and Discipline in the British Army in the Era of the First World War* (London, Palgrave Macmillan, 2000). For a modern study see Sergio Catignani, *Motivating Soldiers: The Example of the Israeli Defense Forces.* (The U.S. Army Professional Writing Collection Autumn 2004) http://carlisle-www. army.mil/usawc/Parameters/04sutumn/catignan.htm (last accessed April 2012).

discipline, but as long as he was never capricious or unfair, and in the discharge of all his duties was perceived to behave as a gentleman, he would usually gain the support and admiration of his men. It was this trust that their officer will do 'the right thing' that had the greatest influence of the behaviour of soldiers on and off the battlefield.

In the twelve years between the Boer War and the First World War the more adventurous young officers would apply to be seconded to colonial forces, mainly in Africa, where there was the possibility of adventure, or even a 'police' action against recalcitrant natives. If they were fortunate enough to be in a battalion serving in India there was the possibility of action along the Afghan border or they could demonstrate their thirst for risk and adventure by gathering information, often in disguise, in the more hostile regions of the North-West Frontier, or indulge in a passion for game hunting, from tigers in lowland jungles to antelope on Himalayan heights.

Most officers carried their schoolboy enthusiasm for games, both individual and team, into the army and participated, with their men, in inter-company sports.[15] Many would play in inter-regimental competitions, and a significant number played their chosen sport at a standard high enough to represent the Army, or play for one of the high-class civilian clubs. These sporting activities were not only to encourage, and sustain, physical fitness among officers and men. Officers consciously used inter-company, and inter-regimental, competitions, to inoculate in their men a competitive spirit, and a fierce pride in their unit, for it was widely recognised that the morale of infantry soldiers was intimately tied to strong regimental loyalties. Sport was fiercely competitive and physical fitness was taken very seriously. Baynes notes that company officers took pride in being genuinely fit and tough, and records a young officer of the 2nd Scottish Rifles who made a bet that he could ride a mile, run a mile, swim a mile and row a mile all within the space of one hour. He won his bet with seven minutes to spare.[16]

In this modern age, when successive reorganisations and reductions in the British Army have seen the disappearance of many famous regiments, it is difficult to perceive the intense loyalty officers, men, and their civilian supporters, gave to their regiment. Company officers, along with the senior NCOs, used a mixture of encouragement and punishment to ensure that their men maintained the standards that the battalion expected, even under the most extreme conditions. For example the Northumberland Fusiliers, one of the oldest regiments in the British army, had a formidable reputation for discipline and smartness. This reputation was so important that officers and NCOs sometimes resorted to physical violence during the retreat from Mons to prevent their exhausted men dropping out or straggling, as to do so would be to the great detriment of the battalion's reputation for discipline.[17]

---

15   In their obituaries families took great pride in recording the deceased's athletic prowess for to 'play the game', fairly, honestly, and to do the best according to one's ability, both in sport and society, was the mark of a sportsman and gentleman.

16   Baynes, *Morale,* p.120.

17   John Sneddon, *The Devil's Carnival. The 1st Battalion Northumberland Fusiliers. The First Hundred Days of Armageddon August-December 1914* (Brighton, Reveille Press 2012), pp.108-109.

ooooo

Military Training and Development.

In discussion with a senior General: "Never forget Robertson that we have two armies – the War Office Army and the Aldershot Army. The first is always up to strength and is organised, reorganised and disorganised almost daily. The second is never up to strength, knows nothing whatever about the first and remains unaffected by any of these organising activities. It just cleans its rifle and falls in on parade".

Field Marshal Sir William Robertson.[18]

Many studies on the Victorian army emphasise a culture of anti-intellectualism, anti-professionalism and an almost religious belief in improvisation and "can-do" when on active service, attitudes that contributed to the glaring deficiencies across the military establishment exposed by the Boer War.[19] The many committees and commissions of enquiry that carried out the post-mortem on the army's performance all had something to say about officer education, and their fitness for promotion and command. In the fullness of time a consensus developed as to what an officer's education, as preparation for modern war, should look like, and this was articulated in the various army regulations and training manuals introduced from 1902 onwards.

What the army expected can be found in *King's Regulations 1912* (Reprinted with amendments 1 August 1914); *Infantry Training (4-Company Organisation 1914)*; *Field Service Regulations. Part I. Operations 1909* (Reprinted with amendments 1914) and the various training manuals for each branch of the service. The brief summary below is only intended to give a flavour of that training and education. *King's Regulations* stated:

A Commanding Officer is responsible to the King for the maintenance of discipline, efficiency and proper system in a unit under his command.

In a battalion the commanding officer, assisted by the senior major, is responsible for the systematic and efficient instruction of officers under his command in all their professional duties and for their due preparation for examinations for promotion.[20]

To ensure that the above instructions were carried out a Staff Officer from Area Command was appointed by the General Officer Commanding to assist and advise

---

18   William Robertson, *From Private to Field Marshal* (London, Constable & Co. 1921), p.159.

19   For example see: Byron Farwell, *For Queen and Country. A Social History of the Victorian and Edwardian Army* (London, Allan Lane 1981) and Anthony Cayton, *The British Officer. Leading the Army from 1660 to the Present* (Harlow, Pearson Educational 2007).

20   *King's Regulations 1912* (London, H.M.S.O, 1912), pp.20-21.

battalion commanders in these educational tasks, and the General, who carried out the unit's annual inspection, was required to report specifically on the methods of instruction used and the results achieved. Battalion officers were expected to train their juniors to discharge the tasks of their seniors - for example a lieutenant taking a company or battalion parade - and after two years in the service junior officers were expected to be able to discharge all the duties of the company commander and be competent in every respect to undertake the duties of a field officer. Failure could mean discharge from the army. This emphasis on professionalism, and the training of junior officers to undertake the duties of senior positions, was a direct result of the experience of the Boer War.

Within their companies junior officers mastered the details of company and battalion administration and acquired the skills of their men, such musketry, drill and fieldcraft, as well as stripping and assembling personal weapons, and undergoing instruction in the armourer's workshop so they could carry out minor repairs in the field. This training was focussed on the development of the young officer as a trainer of men during peace and a leader in time of war. Its success can be seen in many regimental histories which recount the confidence with which junior officers assumed command when their seniors had been killed or wounded.

In addition there were opportunities outside the battalion to go on courses, or attend schools of instruction, to become certificated instructors. These were much more numerous in the technical branches, such as the engineers or artillery, but many infantry officers would become approved instructors in musketry, signalling, map reading and survey, physical education or language specialists, all of which assisted greatly in the promotion stakes. Furthermore, many carried an increment in salary, an important motivator for officers who did not possess substantial personal wealth.

To monitor and improve this huge educational effort the War Office put in place a system of annual inspections and confidential reports.[21] The inspection of a battalion was directed at testing the efficiency and capacity of the unit commander to command his unit and to assess its state of preparedness for war. The inspection was comprehensive and tested the battalion and its individual components. For example, when examining the rifle companies, the formations were assessed on drill work; fire discipline; physical training; bayonet fighting; revolver practice; machine gun practice; signalling; range finding; musket efficiency; field firing; field manoeuvres; internal administration and all other items prescribed for the annual course of training. At company level it would be directed towards testing the capacity of individual officers, NCOs, and section leaders to act as instructors and leaders of their men, and the general efficiency of the soldiers in their command.[22]

As to be expected any passable commander, with a pride in his battalion, would have them drilled to perfection to pass this inspection. However, there is a danger in placing too much faith in these examinations as indicators of military efficiency. To be trained to pass the inspection was not the same as being trained for the test of war. As one artillery

---

21   There was also a comprehensive educational programme available for men and NCOs.
22   *King's Regulations 1912*, pp.20-29.

inspector complained in 1905; "Nothing in my experience is more conducive to failure [in war] than a contentment with being word perfect in the Drill Book."[23]

More important from an individual perspective was the annual confidential report made to the Army Council on every officer. His immediate superior drew up this appraisal and the officer was allowed to see, and comment on it, before it was forwarded to the War Office. There was also a section where the officer could enumerate his own achievements during the year including courses attended, professional reading, and any special skills. They were critical to his career for they impacted directly upon his ability to discharge his present duties and his fitness for promotion by making one of three recommendations: (i) accelerated promotion (very rare) (ii) promotion in the ordinary course of time and (iii) promotion delayed. Should two successive reports recommend that an officer's promotion be delayed a special report, by three senior officers, was prepared to consider whether the army should retain that officer's services. Such special reports were automatic during the first three years service of a newly commissioned subaltern to assess his development and suitability to be a useful army officer.

The combined effects of these two processes allowed the officer corps to develop a self-regulating process that defined what was expected of an army officer and encouraged standardisation of the army's unwritten norms for leadership and professionalism. In other words the army believed it understood what "right looked like" when it came to leadership, professionalism and competency.

The Examination of Officers for Command

In addition to the twin processes of inspection and annual reports officers had to pass an examination to demonstrate their fitness for command and eligibility for promotion. The policy, procedures and curriculum relating to these examinations were laid out in *King's Regulations*.[24] The curriculum was identical at all levels of command from 2nd lieutenant to major, with candidates required to demonstrate more knowledge, and experience, as they progressed up the promotion ladder. To ensure uniformity across the army a staff officer from the War Office attended random examination boards to evaluate standards.

At each level the examination was divided into two parts. Firstly, a written and oral examination in subjects such as military law, organisation, administration, equipment and military history. In the step up from 2nd lieutenant to lieutenant candidates had, in addition, to complete written papers relating to the roles of artillery, engineers, Army Service Corps, Royal Army Medical Corps, Army Veterinary Corps and sanitation. The second part was a practical and oral examination in relationship to the candidate's *Tactical Fitness for Command*. [25]

---

23   Quoted in Spencer Jones, *From Boer War to World War: Tactical Reform of the British Army 1902 - 1914* (Norman, University of Oklahoma Press, 2012), p.45.

24   *King's Regulations 1912*, pp.197-204.

25   My emphasis.

For the factual part of the examination many officers would resort to the services of one of the many 'crammers' and when he felt he was prepared, apply to his commanding officer for permission to sit the appropriate examination.

For infantry officers the core curriculum comprised:

A. (i) Regimental duties.
    (ii) Drill and field training.

B. Small unit tactics, including knowledge of map reading, field sketching and field engineering (practical, theory and problem solving). This section was professionally the most importantly and the minimum pass mark was 60 out of 100 marks.

In the examination for captains and majors candidates were required to resolve theoretical tactical problems with a force not exceeding a brigade of infantry, with a brigade of artillery, a regiment of cavalry and appropriate support units attached. The candidate had to write a general appreciation of the situation, the action he proposed to take and formulate the orders necessary to execute his plan.

In the practical examination candidates were provided with a battalion of infantry, a battery of artillery and a squadron of cavalry and were then presented with a variety of tactical situations that they had to resolve. These examinations were usually organised during annual training when 'enemy' troops would be available to disrupt even the best-laid plans. The examiners awarded marks for intelligence, judgement, common sense and readiness to make the best of any situation that arose. The examination regulations stipulated that there were many ways of solving a tactical problem and the candidate should not be penalised for coming up with solutions different from those held by the examiners.

If an officer failed one part of a subject he was required to sit the whole examination again. If he failed the tactical examination (section B) twice, he was required to leave the army.

These regulations represented the Army Council's ideal and it was hoped standards of examination would rise as the army trained for a European war. It was as good as anything conducted by the much lauded German army but, unlike the latter, there was no central authority that ensured the training was uniform across the army and conformed to an approved tactical doctrine. As discussed elsewhere in this volume, diversity of method was encouraged at a tactical and operational level, and neither the Army Council or the Imperial General Staff showed any real inclination to develop a unified military doctrine for the army. The Army Council occasionally used its authority to enforce compliance with training manuals to ensure that the army was trained to the same standards, but it generally avoided intervention. In the absence of such central control and direction there was the potential for dangerous 'slack' in the system, which sometimes led to outmoded and idiosyncratic training.[26] Such

26   For example, as late as 1910 there was concern that some units were still using old

individualistic behaviour may have been more common at battalion level where the commander had great influence and power, particularly overseas where battalions could be scattered in single garrisons, and the control exercised by higher levels of command were correspondingly light.

An example is given by Baynes in relationship to Lieutenant-Colonel W.M. Bliss, the commander of the 2nd Scottish Rifles in Malta in 1914. He is described as not very clever but within his limitations a sound and practical officer who was a stickler for detail. In his solid traditional way he got results in terms of the smartness of his battalion and his men's proficiency in basic military skills such as marching and shooting, but little up to date tactical training was carried out by the battalion Described by one of his officers as 'Crimean in many ways, steeped in outmoded tradition and not prone to the delegation of duties' Bliss was clearly in breach of the spirit of *King's Regulations* but regimental loyalty and pride ensured that his subordinate officers kept their thoughts about his competence to themselves.[27] Under his command the battalion was almost wiped out in the Battle of Neuve Chapelle in March 1915.

Training For War

The regulations did not specify in detail how a company commander trained his unit but issued general guidance and outlined the scope and depth of the curriculum to be covered in the annual training cycle. The first statement in *Training and Manoeuvre Regulations 1914* laid out the objective: "The sole object of military training is to prepare the forces for war, success in battle being constantly held in view as the ultimate aim".[28] Responsibility in achieving this objective was spelt out in *Infantry Training (4-Company Organisation) 1914*. Section 2.1: "All commanders, from platoon commanders upwards are responsible for the training of their commands".[29]

Infantry Training 1914 has much to say about the responsibilities of company officers in the training of their men for war which are worth repeating:

- The company is the principle training unit in the battalion, and it is essential that it should be regarded as a self-contained unit.
- The company commander will arrange for the continuous training of his company throughout the year. He is responsible, not only that his platoon and section commanders are well trained, but also that there is a capable subordinate to take the place of each leader if necessity should arise.
- The development of initiative in all subordinate commanders is of vital importance, and anything likely to tend to its suppression must be avoided.

fashioned volley fire, prompting a rare instance of Army Council intervention. See Jones, *From Boer War to World War*, p.98.

27   See Baynes. *Morale*, p.113.
28   *Training and Manoeuvre Regulations*, (London, H.M.S.O., 1912), p.9.
29   *Infantry Training (4-Company Organisation) 1914* (London, H.M.S.O., 1914), p.3.

- In view of the importance of decentralization of command it is essential that superior officers should never trespass on the proper sphere of action of their subordinates.
- Company officers will take post where they can best exercise supervision over their commands, watch the enemy and receive and transmit orders.
- The soldier will be taught the importance of the relationship between fire and movement and the wise employment of every feature of the ground is of great importance in promoting fire effect and reducing casualties.

Such ideas were not new in 1914 and this current statement was only the latest distillation of ideas from combat experience on the North West Frontier and Boer War and the debates on tactics that were prominent in the professional press in the decade before the First World War.[30] As fate would have it the new training manual, *Infantry Training (4-Company Organisation) 1914*, was issued just before mobilisation leaving no opportunity for the principles to be adopted across the army or any training carried out using the manual. However, as stated above, many of the principles were already incorporated into tactical training at a company level and their application would serve the infantry well in the bitter battles of 1914.

Constraints to Efficiency

At the outbreak of war, company commanders faced a number of barriers to achieving the peak of combat readiness envisaged in *Field Regulations*. The army was still in the midst of transition from a colonial gendarmerie to a modern army and the whole system was under enormous strain as it wrestled with financial stringency, the innate conservatism of many senior officers ensconced in the administrative branches of the service, and the demanding duties of policing the British Empire.

Then there was that relic of Victorian imperialism, the Cardwell System, designed to provide troops for the expansion of British influence in the world or deal with native unrest within the empire. In this system two linked battalions formed a regiment which rotated between a home and overseas posting, the home-based battalion acting in the defence of the mother country, and as a 'feeder' of trained troops to its sister battalion. The survival of this system into the twentieth century, in which most of the army's trained men languished in overseas barracks, was financial. The Treasury could keep the cost of the army to a minimum by charging the colonial administrations, especially India, for the privilege of having British troops based on their soil.

In addition to robbing the Expeditionary Force of many experienced soldiers, the Cardwell system had an insidious impact upon the training of home-based battalions. These were tasked with two conflicting objectives; to provide trained reinforcements for the battalion overseas and train itself for war. As an economy measure these battalions were maintained at about 60% of their war strength, but within this total were the

30   Jones, *Boer War to World War*, pp.40-49.

new recruits, who would often be posted overseas once fully trained, and the older soldiers who were waiting to leave the army. The consequence was that no company commander had the opportunity to train his command at full strength with the men who would actually fight in time of war. Expediencies such as attempting to train officers by giving them theoretical exercises to work out, or amalgamating companies for training, which brought together officers and men who did not know one another and had no experience of working together, proved to be unsatisfactory substitutes. As William Robertson noted in his autobiography, training of the army before 1914 was largely a case of trying to make bricks without straw.[31]

Another consequence was seen following the declaration of war when the battalions were brought up to strength by mobilizing their reserves who, contrary to popular belief, were not the highly trained soldiers visualised in *Field Regulations*. There were men who had left the army anytime between 1905 and 1914, the older group over-represented as it consisted of men who, after serving their statutory period in the reserve had elected to extended this by a further four years (Section D Reservists) in order to retain their army pay of three shillings and sixpence a week, paid over and above any earnings as a civilian.[32] Reservists were expected to attend twelve training days a year, including the annual camp where they received a refresher course in shooting and musketry, although the opportunity to train them in small unit 'fire and movement' tactics was obviously limited. In order to retain a residue of *espirit de corps* many battalions, during the training period, allocated reservists to their old companies so that they were with comrades they knew and commanded by familiar officers and NCOs.

On mobilization the influx of reservists presented company commanders with a number of organisational and tactical challenges. For example, the 1st Battalion, The Gloucestershire Regiment, required 600 NCOs and men, two captains and seven subalterns to bring it up to war strength. The impact of this huge influx of reservists on the fighting efficiency of the battalion has never been analysed but can well be imagined. "A" company was commanded by Captain R.E. Rising, a regular battalion officer, his second in command, Captain A. St. J. Blunt, was also a regular officer but he had been transferred in from another regiment, the York and Lancaster so would not know any of the officers, NCOs or men in the company, nor the culture and ethos of the battalion.[33] No.1 Platoon was commanded by its platoon sergeant, platoons 2 and 4 were commanded by Special Reserve 2nd lieutenants of less than two years standing, and No.3 platoon by 2nd Lieutenant Baxter who was commissioned into the battalion in January 1913. The other companies in the battalion also had a significant number of reserve officers, which

31   William Robertson, *From Private to Field Marshal* (London, Constable & Co. Ltd. 1921), p.159.
32   The structure of the reserve was complex. For a concise, accessible explanation, see http://www.1914-1918 net/reserves.htm (last access April 2012).
33   *Hart's Army List* of December 1914 shows that large numbers of officers from the Gloucestershire Regiment were on extra-regimental appointments.

must have had consequences for control and command within the company by putting additional strain and responsibility of its commander.[34]

Although rarely mentioned in regimental histories the 'sorting out' of the reservists, to identify those fit for service, was the major task of company officers. The 1st Battalion Northumberland Fusiliers received 641 reservists on 6 August but many had been out of the army for between seven and nine years and over 200 had to be returned to the Depot for further training. Fortunately this still left enough men to maintain the battalion at war strength.

While waiting for embarkation company commanders undertook what training they could but, as they were confined to their mobilisation depots, this was limited to drill and route marching to toughen the reservists with some work on the ranges directed at improving fire control. However Captain St. John, of the 1st Northumberland Fusiliers, does makes passing reference to introducing the men to the principles of scientific warfare that had been introduced into infantry tactics since they left the army.[35]

The Four-Company Structure

The British army was the last great military power to organise its infantry battalions into four large rifle companies of 200-240 men rather than its traditional 8 small companies of about 100 men. This organisational change had been debated within the army, with various degrees of passion, ever since the Crimean War. The change had been resisted throughout the nineteenth century as the smaller company organisation proved to be an effective mechanism for troops fighting the 'small wars' of empire.[36] The Boer War changed everything and the issue of controlling troops on the battlefield so that they could deliver effective fire, and advance in the face of the enemy's fire, became an important item of debate.

On the traditional battlefield, where the infantry fought in lines, squares or columns a company commander could exercise effective direct control of his hundred or so men, but the experience of infantry combat in the Boer War reinforced the view that the volume of fire delivered by modern weapons forced the attacking infantry to move forward as a loose line of skirmishers, taking advantage of any natural cover that was available. This change in small unit tactics had serious consequences for the company commander's ability to exercise effective command and control over his men when they were widely dispersed and 'gone to ground' to shield themselves from enemy fire. The solution, as advocated by 'modernizers' such as Ivor Maxse, was to adopt the four-company structure used by the German and French armies. This was intended to simplify the process of control and command by pushing authority, and responsibility,

---

34   R.M. Grazebrook, *The Gloucestershire Regiment War Narratives 1914-1915* (Reprinted by The Naval and Military Press Ltd, no date [original 1927]), pp.9-10.

35   Sneddon, *The Devil's Carnival*, p.42, footnote.

36   R J Kentish, 'The Case for the Eight Company Battalion' in the *Journal of the Royal United Services Institute*, Vol 56(2), 1912, pp.891-928.

down the chain of command. Under this new scheme the company was divided into four platoons, a structure new to a British battalion, commanded by a subaltern, with a sergeant as second in command. The company commander now only controlled, and directed, four men in battle, his platoon leaders, which left him with more time to watch the enemy, and deal with local tactical situations as they developed. In turn the platoon was divided into 4 sections, each of 10-12 men commanded by a NCO, and these formed the fire-sections of the company. The platoon leader was responsible for the training and development of these NCOs, whom he commanded in battle and they in turn were responsible for the training of their section.[37]

Thus company commanders had been presented with an entirely new system of command and control shortly before mobilization and had only one training cycle to practice it.[38] The extent by which the combat efficiency of companies was affected by the introduction of this new organisation has been over-looked in studies of the BEF in 1914. It is not alluded to in most regimental histories, even though it was completely unknown to many of the officers and men of the reserve who returned to the colours.[39] This may imply that all went well, and that there were no problems, but it is the nature of reorganizations in complex structures is that it takes time for new structures to 'bed-in' and with this one there was no time. Most probably, as most regimental histories were written several years after the war, it is not discussed as the issues of 1914 appeared of small account when compared with the greater events to come.

The Test of Combat

John Bourne has described the fighting of 1914 as epitomising 'soldier's battles' where the key decisions were made at the sharp end, among formations at company level, or even below.[40] This statement encapsulates one of the challenges when discussing the BEF, namely the need to cut through the myriads of myth, and 'received' history, that has grown up around the events of 1914. It has become almost *de rigour* to praise the Old Contemptibles, who are portrayed, even by modern historians, as paragons of military valour and prowess. As other chapters in this volume show, history has not been so kind to their commanders, particularly Sir John French.

That being said the performance of the BEF in 1914 does permit us to be confident that, at a company level, it was at least as well trained as its German counterpart. The long serving Regulars, who made up about 40% of the BEF, were more experienced

---

37   F. I. Maxse, 'Battalion Organisation' in *Journal of the Royal United Services Institute*, Vol.56(1), 1912, pp.53-86; Hereward Wake, 'The Four-Company Battalion in Battle' in *Journal of the Royal United Services Institute*, Vol.59(2), 1914, pp.362-377.
38   It came into effect in early 1913.
39   Aldershot Command had been using the four company system for some years prior, having adopted the system for training under the aegis of John French, but this was a method of making up for shortage of troops and did not represent a true tactical change.
40   J.M. Bourne, *Britain and the Great War 1914-1918* (London: Edward Arnold, 1989), p.160.

than most continental soldiers; the young soldiers, who had at least two years service, were a match for the German conscript; while the reserves, perhaps not up to standard in physical fitness, musketry and infantry tactics, retained sufficient knowledge and experience from their days as a regular to give a good account of themselves when put alongside familiar, experienced, company officers and NCOs.[41]

Currently the most damning criticism of the training and combat effectiveness of the BEF comes from those historians who see the Prussian/German army between 1812 and 1945 as a paragon of military efficiency. Martin Samuels and Terence Zuber, attack the performance of the BEF on the grounds that it lacked a unified doctrine and had an inflexible system of command which stifled innovation and creativity. Both claim that junior officers learnt little of war, and were, in any case, too interested in their social life, and sports, to take their military education seriously,[42] seeing the training and education of British officers as inferior in every way to that of his German counterpart who, in contrast, was well trained, self-disciplined, and the master of minor tactics.[43]

These authors support their arguments with extensive reference to German training manuals, yet in truth British and German regulations of the period are almost identical in their expectations of how their armies trained for war. In both armies responsibility was pushed right down the chain of command to the individual officers or NCO who would lead the men in battle. Special attention was paid to the training of officers, through the use of tactical exercises and manoeuvres designed to appreciate the importance of flexibility of response to the ever-changing tactical situation on the battlefield. In this respect British company commanders were better equipped than German officers at the same level for many had participated in the Boer War, and a significant minority had seen action in subsequent imperial conflicts.

If the German army had an advantage in training it was their Major Training Areas, large tracts of land put aside for realistic combat training, whereas the British were limited to Salisbury Plain and a smaller training area close to Aldershot. However, these constraints did not apply to India where vigorous trainers could give free reign to inventive combat exercises. For example, during autumn manoeuvres in 1906 the

---

41   It is often forgotten when comparing British and German troops that many German
       soldiers were reservists as well. During the Battle of Ypres, many were recent volunteers
       whose military training had been limited to a hasty and attenuated version of the basic
       training given to the pre-war conscript. On this point, see I.F.W. Beckett, *Ypres: The First
       Battle* (Harlow, Longman, 2004), pp.46-47.

42   Martin Samuels, *Command and Control? Training and Tactics in the British and German
       Armies 1888-1918* (London: Frank Cass 1995); Terence Zuber, *The Mons Myth* (Stroud:
       The History Press 2010).

43   Although controversial, the present author recommends these books as a thought
       provoking counterpoint to Anglo-centric books on the Great War. However, it should
       be noted that the praise heaped upon the German army by Samuels and Zuber is
       contradicted by the work of others. See in particular, Eric Dorn Brose, *The Kaiser's Army:
       The Politics of Military Technology in Germany During the Machine Age 1870 - 1918* (New
       York, University of Oxford Press, 2001) and Stephen Jackman, 'Shoulder to Shoulder:
       Close Control and "Old Prussian Drill" in German Offensive Infantry Tactics, 1871-
       1914' in *Journal of Military History*, 68(1), 2004, pp.73-104.

innovative trainer Horace Smith-Dorrien devised a scheme, based upon the Russio-Japanese War, which visualised a fortified position of great length whose flanks could not be turned. Along the middle 2,000 yards of this supposed line he had his command spend the summer learning how to build a strongly fortified position, three trench lines deep with bunkers, machine gun nests, command and communication centres and ammunition dumps, all protected by defensive artillery. Once the construction was complete, his units practiced assaulting this position using co-ordinated infantry-artillery tactics, with the infantry employing non-standard weapons such as hand grenades and trench mortars. At the end of the exercise each company commander had to take his men over the defences and explain to them every point of the exercise.[44] With more limited resources Smith-Dorrien continued his vigorous regimen of training when he was appointed GOC Aldershot, a post he held from 1907 to 1911. Smith-Dorrien's exercises show that the British Army was, when given time and resources, capable of realistic and highly effective training.

When we come to evaluate the training of infantry companies and the performance of their commanders during combat in 1914 we are hampered by the fact that only a small number of detailed reports have survived. One of the best is that of Captain G.D. Lister, commanding "A" Company, Royal West Kents.

At 8.00am on 23 August he was ordered to take his company across the Mons canal to cover the retirement of a reconnaissance party of cavalry and cyclists. Having no idea of the nature of the enemy in front he reconnoitred the area around the village Tetre and placed three of his platoons in the best position to cover a retreat back to the canal. They strengthened their positions by loop-holing gardens walls and deepening ditches. Meanwhile No.3 platoon, in reserve, cleared barbed wire fences from the fields along their line of retreat, a route carefully chosen so not to block supporting fire from the troops on the canal.

The first sign of action was when four cyclists hurtled down the road and reported that their detachment had been wiped out by enemy artillery. They were followed almost immediately by what appeared to be hundreds of enemy infantry debouching from Terte. These Germans were instantly engaged and an intense firefight developed. With no information as to the fate of the reconnaissance party he was meant to be covering, Captain Lister held on throughout the morning but his position was soon becoming untenable. The number of enemy infantry was increasing by the minute; an enemy battery had come into action; and a German machine gun company was now supporting the attack on his platoons. It was time to go. He moved half his reserve up to support the withdrawal of No.1 platoon, which was most exposed and taking heavy casualties. However, at the same moment, No.4 platoon abruptly disengaged and, unable to stop this movement, Lister ordered his remaining reserve half platoon to occupy a shallow ditch and cover the ground vacated by No.4 platoon. A very contrite platoon sergeant later reported that the platoon's commander, Lieutenant Anderson, had been killed and

44   A full discussion of this remarkable exercise is found in Horace Smith-Dorrien, *Memories of Forty-Eight Years Service*, (London, John Murray, 1925), pp.337-338.

when someone reported that the rest of the company had gone the sergeant withdrew the platoon, something he realised should not have been done without a direct order.

Captain Lister had established a small reporting post between his HQ and forward platoons and as soon as this reported that No.1 platoon was clear, he left his HQ to move across the road to supervise the withdrawal of No.2 platoon. As he did so he saw a file of British troops moving down the road and, realising that they would be annihilated if they did not take cover, ran into the field to attract their attention, but fell wounded. The next thing he remembered was being roused by a German, who gave him a drink and bandaged his wound. About 90 of his 200 men made it back to the main position on the canal, the others killed or prisoners.[45]

Several points stand out. Captain Lister was lucky in that he was wounded and survived. As a group, officers suffered a higher ratio of killed to wounded than did their men and, as most were shot, it suggests that they were indulging in activities that attracted the attention of enemy marksmen. A number of reasons for this spring to mind. Captain Lister was a Boer War veteran but he, along with the rest of the BEF, appear to have forgotten an important lesson, namely that in action officers should not be conspicuous by their uniforms, or identifiable by wearing swords or carrying a walking stick.[46] Secondly, *Infantry Training 1914* suggested the company commander take a position where he is best placed to manage and support his troops in action. This is behind the firing line, in a position where he can send and receive messages, ideally see his own positions, and those of the enemy, and crucially be in command of his reserve. This Captain Lister appears to have done for most of the action but during the later stages he moved into the firing zone to supervise the withdrawal of No.2 platoon, perhaps overanxious after the confusion in the withdrawal of No.4 platoon. In this he behaved no differently from many of his contemporaries. From a reading of regimental histories one gains the impression that for many company commanders this important command function was superseded by a desire to lead from the front and inspire and instil confidence in their men by displays of personal courage. As a result many fell while carrying out duties that could have been delegated to a subordinate, such as reconnoitring and evaluating the enemy's position and strength, or moving among widely scattered sections of men to gain information and give instructions.

Finally how effective were the pre-war company commanders in preparing their men for war? With the publication of extracts of German regimental histories by authors such as Jack Sheldon we can now appreciate that their German adversary rated their military qualities and skills very highly.[47] Despite the high attrition rate of officers and NCOs in most British battalions, the rifle companies and platoons, often reduced to a fraction of their establish strength, continued to function and fight according to the principles of their pre-war training, clearly demonstrating the effectiveness of their company commanders as trainers of soldiers for war.

45   C.V. Molony, *Invicta: With the First Battalion the Queen's Own Royal West Kent Regiment in the Great War* (London, Nisbet & Co. 1923), pp.7-11

46   In the aftermath of the Boer War officers had been forbidden from carrying swords into battle and were expected to carry rifles instead. However, this regulation had been abandoned in 1908. See Jones, *From Boer War to World War*, p.80, 84.

47   Jack Sheldon, *The German Army at Ypres 1914* (Barnsley: Pen & Sword 2010), p.262.

15

"Amateurs at a professional game": The Despatch Rider Corps in 1914

Michael Carragher

Less than two weeks after Franz Ferdinand's assassination the weekly British motorcycle press carried the following appeal: "Several motor cyclists are required by the War Office to act as despatch riders on 28th July to 8th August next, and also on 3rd August to 8th August...."[1] Here, it would seem, is hard evidence that when European statesmen were yachting in the fjords or taking the waters, those reviled British generals were ahead of all the politicians in appreciating the gravity of the Sarajevo assassination and planning for the consequences. Such a case, however, cannot be sustained: despatch riders were required merely for annual manoeuvres. Yet the appeal for civilians to play a military role, the very need for them to do so, says much about the problems that the British High Command had to contend with a century ago—and also about how they engaged with these problems and "muddled through" to overcome them.

"Muddled through" is a term whose connotations have metamorphosed down the decades. For long, John French, Douglas Haig and fellow senior officers have been portrayed as bumbling incompetents who won the Great War only because the sort of special providence that Bismarck claimed looks out for children, idiots and Americans had been temporarily extended to cover the British High Command.[2] That the British Expeditionary Force, initially a small band of professionals, later a citizen army of a country traditionally distrustful of soldiers, indeed muddled through against the superb *millionenheer* forces of the martial Second Reich, was once considered a great source of pride. Muddling through called for a creative approach to working around potentially catastrophic problems; for making the most of limited resources; for thinking outside

---

1   *The Motor Cycle*, July 9th, 1914, p.56.
2   Particularly egregious examples of such portrayal include Alan Clarke's *The Donkeys* (London, Hutchinson, 1963), John Laffin's *Butchers and Bunglers of World War One* (Gloucester, A.Sutton, 1988), and Denis Winter's *Haig's Command* (London, Viking, 1991).

BRAVO! TOMMY.

Despatch riders from a contemporary patriotic postcard. (Editor's collection)

the box—and the barracks square. The appointment of Sir Eric Geddes in 1916 exemplifies such thinking, but it was evident long before; Geddes was far from the first civilian whose skills had been deployed, perforce, toward military ends.

In 1914 the British high command was in an exacting position. It recently had been demoralised and remained in a state of confusion after the Curragh Incident; and although events of recent years had enforced recognition that direct military support for France would be necessary to contain Germany in any European war, since 1910 government had been by what effectively was a coalition of the Liberal and Irish Parliamentary Parties, many of whose MPs, Irish and Little Englander, were suspicious of, if not downright hostile to, the British Army. The Liberals' programme of social reform demanded the *quid pro quo* of Home Rule for Ireland, the prospect of which provoked the Curragh Incident; this did little to dissuade its detractors that the Army was potentially as great a threat to liberty as it had been in Cromwell's or James II's time. Furthermore, delivering all political promises called for time, energy, parliamentary imagination—and money. Meanwhile the expensive naval race that the Liberals had inherited in 1905 kept running, for no island empire, indeed no country that valued its sovereign independence, could afford to ignore the German threat. The Royal Navy remained the Senior Service; the British Army, figuratively speaking, was still "The Absent-Minded Beggar" of Kipling's poem and had to do the best it could with what it had.

The army had, however, benefited from the wish to avoid repetition of the sort of international embarrassment Britain had suffered in the South African War. Reforms, notably those of R.B. Haldane, had wrought great improvement, and officers like Douglas Haig and Michael Rimington had written exemplary manuals on modern campaigning.[3] The 18-pounder and the SMLE rifle gave the Army field guns and small arms to rank with the best, and the British volunteer spirit responded to the begging bowl with eleemosynary gusto when war broke out.[4] Thus, in 1914 the British Army was aware of its limited strengths and had gone some way to remedy its significant weaknesses.

The critical weakness for high command through the war years was the hiatus in communications. This accounts for many of the problems experienced by commanders on both sides: for the first and only time in history the gap between the scale of the battlefield and forces deployed, and the limitations of contemporary communications technology, left the battlefield commander with little control after battle had been joined. Commanders were forced to fight a twentieth-century war with nineteenth century communications, and if "Victorian campaigns were waged as much against nature as against indigenous opponents",[5] the Victorian generals of the Great War were fighting as much against technology—or rather, the lack of it—as against the Germans.

Problems with communications were particularly acute in 1914, a phase of the war marked by movement and "battles of encounter", factors that called for communications systems suited to fluid conditions. In an age of instant communication it is all too easy to forget the limitations imposed by the technology of a century ago, and so overlook and dismiss the virtues and the triumphs implicit in muddling through problems that frequently devolved onto the despatch rider. By dint of speed, autonomy and adaptability, and — not least — courage and dedication to duty, the Despatch Rider Corps delivered what no other mode of communications could have done.

When the War Office advertised for civilian motorcyclists to act as despatch riders it was muddling through in the way that proved necessary to defeat the Second Reich: mobilising all resources, military *and* civilian. On taking office as Secretary of State for War, Lord Kitchener sourly remarked that the British government comprised the bravest men in the world, for they had just taken on to fight the most powerful army in existence without an army of their own—which he then of course set out to raise.[6] In the meantime, it was down to the Old Contemptibles to help prevent German victory.

But how to command and control those Old Contemptibles? Small though the BEF was by Continental standards in 1914, it comprised four — quickly six —divisions

3   Douglas Haig, *Field Service Regulations* (London, HMSO, 1909); MF Rimington, *Our Cavalry*, (London, Macmillan, 1912).

4   Not merely by Kitchener's volunteers; for example, because British motor- and aero-industries had used German magnetos, these essential components became almost unavailable after war broke out. A national appeal saw civilians stripping magnetos from their vehicles and sending them to the War Office.

5   Ian FW Beckett, "Command in the Late Victorian Army", in *Leadership and Command: The Anglo-American Military Experience Since 1861*, ed. GD Sheffield (London, Brassey's, 2002), p.38. Beckett is citing General Charles Callwell.

6   An inversion of the German situation, where the powerful military dictated the direction of the war from the very beginning, before spuriously claiming civilian betrayal had somehow been the cause of their defeat in 1918.

deployed, along with cavalry; already far too large a force to control by voice command and gallopers. The BEF did have what then was state-of-the-art communications in the form of radio and telegraph; but it didn't have enough of either, and the peculiar nature of the first weeks of campaigning compromised the usefulness of both. The Great War was marked by problems in communications; the Great Retreat was to create a particular crisis for C[3] (Command, Control and Communication).

Aware of its shortages — though hardly of the impending shortcomings of radio and telegraph — the army early on had looked to the new-fangled motor bicycle. In 1901 cars and motor tricycles had been used on French Army manoeuvres; two years later they were to be found on British manoeuvres, "supplied by members of the Motor Volunteer Corps", reflecting the partly-amateur nature of the British Army, and the volunteer spirit that was to become so important in 1914. On these manoeuvres the motorcycles, approximately thirty in total, "behaved on the whole splendidly",[7] and some authorities speculated that the motorcycle would replace the galloper completely, "especially in a European conflict, where the roads are plentiful" (indeed, in 1914 gallopers played no significant role, horses quickly being debilitated).[8] One officer reported in 1909 that despatch riders were "most useful" on manoeuvres; he acknowledged that in a lecture on "The Use of Motor Vehicles in War" he had "not dealt with motor cycles because they were so important as to demand a Paper to themselves".[9] Yet despite the demonstrated value of motorcycles to command and control, the BEF had a mere fifteen on the outbreak of war, "even though a shortage had been identified early in 1914".[10] This number was increased perhaps tenfold within a few days of war's outbreak, thanks to civilian volunteers.[11]

Who were these "most useful" despatch riders? What exactly did they do? How were they organized to optimise their potential? And how useful did they really prove in 1914?

Despatch Riders

The ideal despatch rider (DR) had "native ability ... keenness ... initiative ... readiness to meet an emergency", and was physically robust.[12]

---

7   Horace G. Wyatt, *Motor Transport in War* (London, Hoddard & Stoughton, 1914/1915), pp.41, 44-45.
8   *Motor Cycling*, 11 August 1914, p.453.
9   *The Royal Automobile Club Journal*, 9 December 1909, p.410-12.
10   Charles Messenger, *Call-to-Arms: The British Army 1914-18* (London, Cassell, 2005), p.497.
11   Corelli Barnett gives the figure of fifteen in *Britain and Her Army 1509-1970* (London, Penguin, 1974), p.391. For further discussion of numbers see Michael Carragher, *San Fairy Ann? Motorcycles and British Victory 1914-1918* (Eastbourne, FireStep, 2013).
12   AP Corcoran, *The Daredevil of the Army: Experiences as a "Buzzer" and Despatch Rider* (New York, Dutton & Co, 1919), pp.17-18.

He should in the first place be fit and in hard training, ready at a moment's notice to undertake any mission that may be given him. He should be a good horseman, a cyclist, and something of a mechanic; be able to find his way by day or night, with the aid of the sun, stars or compass; know the names and ranks of all generals, staff officers and commanders of units; possess a good knowledge of scouting, to enable him to pass safely through hostile territory; and — perhaps most difficult of all — be qualified to deliver a verbal message word for word as he receives it.[13]

A good deal to ask, but a good deal was delivered:

To ensure good service in this important branch during mobile warfare, men of exceptional intelligence, endurance and courage, and, especially, men possessing initiative of a high order, were required [and] the University Officers' Training Corps came to the rescue with a particularly good type of men for the purpose.[14]

An officer described DRs as being, "for the most part, University students and young schoolmasters, with a sprinkling of young businessmen".[15] Competition riders, whose skill and daring were limpidly of value in DR work, also featured.[16] Not all were young: a middle-aged doctor sacrificed practice and security — soon his life — to duty.[17]

All these men were well off. Some stepped in off the street and bought new motorcycles almost as casually as proletarians might buy a packet of cigarettes.[18] Knowledge of French and German was looked for in the aspirant DR, especially so in the Intelligence Corps, whose "Scout Officers" were more privileged than the Signals Service's DRs, being appointed as subalterns rather than as corporals, but "were never under any circumstances to consider ourselves officers", rather "despatch riders pure and simple".[19] Their background was an important factor in what DRs did in 1914 and beyond. Lord Blackwood, later killed at the Yser Canal, was a Scout Officer, but his commoner colleagues had no less sense of assurance in the rightness of Britain's cause or their place in it. Their worldview seems alien when viewed through the lens

13   Herbert Strang, *The British Army in War* (London, Humphrey, 1915), unpaginated.
14   RE Priestley, *The Signals Service in the European War of 1914 to 1918 (France)* (Chatham, Mackay & Co, 1921), p.16.
15   JC Dunn, *The War the Infantry Knew, 1914-1919: A Chronicle of Service in France and Belgium* (London, Abacus, 1994), p.15.
16   *The Motor Cycle*, 24 June 1915, p.619; AJ Sproston, "Four Months Under Fire: Despatch-Rider's Adventures", in *The Daily Mail* (London), 14-19 December 1914.
17   Sidney Nelson Crowther, a former international rugby player, was killed at First Ypres. Frederic Coleman, *From Mons to Ypres with French* (Toronto, William Briggs, 1916), p.201.
18   WHL Watson, *Adventures of a Despatch Rider* (Edinburgh, Blackwood, 1915), p.5; Paul Maze, *A Frenchman in Khaki* (London, Heineman, 1934), p.60.
19   Roger West, "Diary of the War: Retreat from Mons to the Battle of the Aisne" (Imperial War Museum document 67/122/1), pp.14-15, 46.

of cynicism that surfaced out of the muddy war they helped to win. They volunteered because they could have done no less: "Physical coward or no physical coward" — young Willie Watson had no illusions of personal courage — "it obviously had to be done".[20]

Their background, their enormous class confidence and consequent sense of assurance were to affect the despatch rider's performance. Their initial suspicion of soldiery[21] could not be entirely dispelled in their brief training, which barely lasted a fortnight.[22] Instead these men discharged their duty out of their *sense* of duty, not because they were following orders. Indeed, when Roger West volunteered to destroy a bridge in the face of advancing Germans he did so against the advice of his commanding officer.[23] These social and psychological factors were to render DRs eminently suitable for command in later years; all DRs of 1914, whose careers are traceable to date, became "temporary gentlemen".

In August 1914, however, all that lay in the future. The bulk of volunteer despatch riders had no real notion of what lay in store for them. Some might have partaken in annual manoeuvres in previous years, but even these, and the few "Old Sweats" among them, could never have anticipated what they would have to accomplish when they went to war.

Despatch Riding

The central duty of the DR was to maintain communications, acknowledged from the beginning as "most difficult" by Horace Smith-Dorrien and other commanders.[24] "Information is the evidence upon which judgments are made…. Information of the enemy and our own troops comprises the most important conditions under which war is waged".[25] But given the scale of twentieth-century armies, communicating all this information, so that it might be collated and distilled into judgment, and then communicating judgment and coordinating the activities that judgment mandates, was far from easy. Nowhere was this more critical — and the potential consequences for failure more dangerous — than during the retreat from Mons to the Marne, a movement that "would have seemed incredible and impossible to military experts, who know … the frightful difficulty of keeping an army together in such circumstances".[26]

---

20   Watson, *Adventures*, p.4.
21   Ibid, p.6.
22   Ibid, pp.6-12; some had no training at all. See West, "Diary", pp.3-6.
23   West, "Diary", p.57.
24   Quoted in Robin Neillands, *The Old Contemptibles: The British Expeditionary Force, 1914* (London, John Murray, 2004), p.156.
25   Col. JFC Fuller, "The Application of Recent Developments in Mechanics and other Scientific Knowledge to Preparation and Training for Future War on Land" in *Journal of the Royal United Services Institute*, LXV, May 1920, p.241.
26   Philip Gibbs, *The Soul of the War* (New York, Robert McBride, 1915), p.82.

That the BEF did hold together was thanks to despatch riders. In theory there were superior forms of communication. Cable had been used since the Crimean War, and would become the mainstay of the Signals Service during positional warfare; wireless had been deployed in South Africa (although without much success), and would grow in usefulness. One signaler claimed that a lorry-mounted 1.5kW Marconi wireless set "did excellent work" in 1914;[27] yet its contribution must have been limited, as most, if not all, of the field sets were with the cavalry. This was the right place for them, for the cavalry, "the distant eyes of the commander-in-chief",[28] ranged far and had the onerous task of screening the open left flank, unaided after Sordet's French force was redeployed to the Sixth Army,[29] and providing the rearguard against a vastly superior pursuing force. Wireless, however, did not obviate the need for DR communication with cavalry as well as with infantry, artillery and air arm units.[30] Wireless was primitive, and its fragility, together with the dangers of *en clair* communications or, alternatively, unacceptable delays in ciphering and deciphering, made wireless unsuited to the needs of an army in full-tilt retreat. Eventually "tactical radio capable of transmitting voice" became available,[31] but one signalman described wireless as being "in little more than its infancy" as late as 1918.[32]

Telephone was little better during the Great Retreat. At Mons telephone communication could be listened into by anyone within miles.[33] Sometimes Signals could use civilian telephone infrastructure, but this was rudimentary in places, notably in agricultural districts. There was almost none at Le Cateau for this reason, although the one in the railway station was used to link II Corps with GHQ.[34] Often the French husbanded civilian networks for their own use,[35] and in some places they had sabotaged telegraphic and telephonic systems in their retreat. British attempts to lay fresh lines were hampered by lack of time and shortage of cable. Manpower was also in short supply, as men of the Signals Corps had to bolster the fighting line as early as Mons,[36] imposing a further load on despatch riders. Cable was so scanty —like all of the BEF's

27   AP Corcoran, "Wireless in the Trenches" in *Popular Science Monthly*, May 1917, p 795,

28   Barnett, *Britain and Her Army*, p.367.

29   Apart from d'Amade's Territorials, "scattered ... hastily organised and ... lacking in equipment": F Maurice, *Forty Days in 1914* (New York, Doran, 1919), p.89; Robin Neillands, *The Old Contemptibles*, p.153; James Edmonds, *History of the Great War: Military Operations, France and Belgium, 1914* (London, Macmillan, 1933), p.245.

30   Watson, *Adventures*, p.54; Corcoran, *Daredevil*, p.19; WH Tait, IWM document PP/MCR/161, 26 August and 6 September 1914.

31   Douglas J Orsi, "The Effectiveness of the US Army Signal Corps in Support of the American Expeditionary Force Division and Below Manoeuvre Units During World War I" (Fort Leavenworth, KS: Master's Dissertation, 2001), p.11.

32   John Jackson, *Private 12768* (Stroud, Tempus, 2005), p.205.

33   Priestley, *Signals Service*, p.58. However, the telephone at Mons railway station helped establish the position of advancing Germans, an improvised intelligence section of the cavalry simply making calls across Belgium and collating the information—excellent intelligence that was dismissed by GHQ: Messenger, *Call-to-Arms*, p.52.

34   Walter Reid, *Douglas Haig: Architect of Victory* (Edinburgh, Birlin, 2009), p.185.

35   Priestley, *Signals Service*, pp.17-19; Neillands, *Old Contemptibles*, p.145.

36   Neillands, *Old Contemptibles*, p.116.

materiel — that before retreating farther precious time had to be given to reeling in for re-use as much as possible.[37] Even at Mons some brigades were running short and near Le Cateau the Germans captured "a complete cable detachment", a serious loss to add to cable already abandoned.[38] Although Signals were able to lay enough cable to provide a connection between GHQ and I Corps, communications with II Corps, 35 miles distant, and bearing the brunt of the fighting, had to be by DR and staff car, for the single telephone line from the railway station could only handle so much.

One DR reported being attached to a "flying telegraph company — the kind of people who venture as far as possible forward, and, in the case of retreat, wait until the very last to cut the wires".[39] Despatch riders were also used by these units for "spying out the routes and indicating the best way in which labour could be saved and a reliable circuit obtained in the shortest possible time".[40] After the Marne cable shortages persisted; the retreating Germans had destroyed local infrastructures, so one DR reported elatedly: "in Chouy the Germans had overlooked a telephone — great news for the cable detachment".[41]

Fortunately the BEF was not entirely dependent on electronic communication: "Cable communications were out of the question for the present, with the Huns close on our heels. It was up to the Despatch Corps now to keep ... the British Army articulate."[42] These are the words of a despatch rider; but his superiors were in unanimous agreement. Major Priestley, of the Royal Engineers, engaged personally in the Great Retreat and professionally in communications, acknowledged:

> It is evident that the mainstay of the intercommunication system in a rapid retreat must be the despatch rider and the orderly, assisted to a small extent only by the occasional use of permanent lines ... but [through the retreat] units reached their destinations so late, and had in many cases to leave so early, that it was not worth while to make the practice [of laying cable] general. As a general rule, reliance was placed entirely on despatch riders.[43]

It is easy to imagine the fatal chaos that might have resulted without DRs, given the paucity and unsuitability of wireless sets and a pace too fast to lay cable effectively. Besides the frantic pace, divisions were broken up along parallel roads, something that often made cable communication impossible.[44] Riding these roads was a challenge in itself. Surfaces ranged from *pavé*, huge cobbles that resisted wear but made for an uncomfortable and even dangerous ride, to unsurfaced tracks; sometimes DRs had to deliver messages on foot.[45] In addition, they had to find their way, particularly

37   Corcoran, *Daredevil*, p.32.
38   Priestley, *Signals Service*, pp.30, 18-19.
39   Tait, PP/MCR/161, 28 August 1914.
40   Priestley, *Signals Service*, p.28.
41   Watson, *Adventures*, p.100.
42   Corcoran, *Daredevil*, p.37.
43   Priestley, *Signals Service*, pp.18, 21-22.
44   Corcoran, *Daredevil*, p.32; West, "Diary", p.102.
45   West, "Diary", p.32.

problematical when riding transverse to the line of movement, especially when "off the map". A division, comprising three brigades — as well as divisional troops, artillery, and other attachments such as Army Service Corps and field ambulances — had to be broken up along as many roads as feasible if progress was to be made. It was the despatch rider's job "to take messages up and down the column or across country to brigades and divisions that were advancing along roads parallel to ours".[46] The task of one DR, attached to the 5th Division,

> was to keep touch with the 14th Brigade which was advancing along a parallel road to the west. That meant riding four or five miles across rough country roads, endeavouring to time myself so as to reach the 14th column just when the SO [Signals Officer] was passing, then back again to the Division, riding up and down the column until I found our captain.[47]

Senior officers appreciated the difficulties that effective communication meant:

> Fresh orders had then hurriedly to be written, and despatched by the orderly of each unit (who was attached to our headquarters) to his respective unit, giving the time at which the head of the unit was to pass a given point on the road so as to dovetail into its place in the column in the dark, and all with reference to what we were going to do, whether the artillery or part of it was to be in front or in rear, what rations were to be carried, arrangements for supply, position of the transport in the column, compositions of the advanced or rear-guard, &c., &c. It sounds very complicated, and still more so when you have to fit in not only your own brigade but all the miscellaneous troops of your "Brigade Area."[48]

Challenging as this was even in the advance to Mons, it became far more difficult afterward. Through the retreat DRs often rode for more than a full day at a stretch. Corporal Corcoran averaged two messages an hour, riding "day and night", over roads that might be "no more than … paths".[49] In best British muddling tradition, the departing BEF had been supplied with maps only of those "regions adjacent to the Franco-Belgian border where it proposed to operate". After the retreat began "a wire arrived [at the War Office] demanding the instant despatch of maps of the country as far to the rear as the Seine and the Marne".[50] New maps were supposed to have been supplied within 24 hours, but if they were they didn't reach the men who most needed them.[51] It was impossible to deliver maps to an army on the move, and then to get them to despatch riders who were never at rest. Those maps that were available were "useless",

46   Watson, *Adventures*, p.153.
47   Ibid. p.23.
48   Lord Edward Gleichen, *The Doings of the Fifteenth Infantry Brigade, August 1914 to March 1915* (London, Blackwood, 1917), pp.93-94.
49   Corcoran, *Daredevil*, pp.39-40.
50   Charles Edward Callwell, *Experiences of a Dug-Out* (London, Constable, 1920), p.21.
51   Messenger, *Call-to-Arms*, p.49.

according to Willie Watson. One of his colleagues became lost because he was "mapless (maps were very scarce in those days)", and sometimes "it was by pure accident I found my way". Such French maps as could be found were "extremely unsuited to a despatch-rider's work";[52] indeed, they were unsuited to any serious military endeavour.[53]

Lack of maps created particular problems in transverse communication among the various units that, because of their size, had to be split up along parallel roads. If longitudinal cable communication was difficult for an army on the move, transverse to the line of march it was impossible. The five divisions of the BEF travelled along five different *major* routes, over-spilling onto any minor roads that ran in the right direction.[54] Apart from the obvious problems for control and resupply this fragmentation caused, separation from one's companions, and uncertainty as to whether one was moving in the right direction, could sap morale, so the appearance of a despatch rider, to correct or confirm one's route, could be a terrific boost. Indeed, this could save men from death or capture, a constant threat in the fluid, confusing conditions, particularly in the early stages of the retreat, with "the Germans all down our left flank for miles".[55] It was less fraught on the right wing, but Douglas Haig himself once drove into enemy outposts.[56] To aggravate the problems of transverse communications, after Haig's uncharacteristic flutter when attacked at Landrecies, his I Corps set off on a line of retreat east of the Oise, so that for seven days the two corps of the BEF were separated by that river.[57] Inter-corps communication therefore demanded that despatch riders had to hunt for bridges. The limitations and locations of these might hugely increase the distance travelled, especially for men without maps. In such circumstances DRs were often riding round the clock, sometimes up to three hundred miles a day.[58]

At other times the distances were shorter, but they were never easy. Plotting out the details he provides using modern maps reveals that Roger West's reported movements on a very busy day total well under 100 miles.[59] This seems surprising after reading his account, for he was hardly out of the saddle on this and most other days. A straight line from his point of departure to that of arrival measures about a quarter of the mileage that he covered. But West was attached to the independent 19th Brigade, which covered the left flank of the BEF and was partly outflanked and infiltrated by German cavalry. On this day alone West encountered Germans several times — sometimes crossing their path, sometimes being pursued — and repeatedly had to retrace his journey and find other routes.[60] In addition, it was always difficult to find the

52   Watson, *Adventures*, pp.26, 55, 61, 203; West, "Diary", p.32.
53   Philip Warner, "Le Cateau", in *Purnell's History of the First World War*, I, Number 8, ed. Barrie Pitt, (London: BPC Publishing, 1969), p.210.
54   James Edmonds, *History of the Great War*, endplate maps.
55   West, "Diary", p.33.
56   Reid, *Douglas Haig*, p.186.
57   Barbara Tuchmann, *The Guns of August* (New York, Bantam, 1976), pp.396-97.
58   Corcoran, *Daredevil*, p.39. Corcoran can be reluctant to let unembellished truth stand in the way of a good story, but this figure cannot be discounted.
59   West, "Diary", pp.18-28.
60   See also account of Tait, PP/MCR/161, for this day, 24 August.

recipients for his despatches amidst the confusion. Officers could be hard to locate and groups of troops could be isolated from the main body of the retreat. In such a crisis of command and control, DRs played a vital role. Having gained knowledge of German movements during the course of their own travels, West, and doubtless many others, were frequently able to save men from walking into German captivity.[61] If journeys measured in miles seem short, when measured in hours, on a primitive motorcycle, they were exhausting. "To ride four miles or so along country lanes ... does not sound particularly strenuous. It was."[62]

Column riding was more predictable than sustaining transverse communication, but hardly easy: "half a mile or so, and then a halt", leapfrogging from junction to junction, "heart-breaking work"[63] — though another DR found it "slow but pleasant".[64] The fact that movement was more settled and routine may account for the latter's contentment, especially as it contrasted with dangerous days in close contact with the enemy. The column rider was essential to maintaining contact among battalions, brigades and divisions, and maintaining movement along the route, especially during the retreat, when roads became choked with troops and refugees. French troops sometimes retired along roads that obliquely crossed the British line of retreat, producing congestion so bad that even a motorcycle, with its primitive transmission, might have to be pushed.[65] Northeast France was so crammed that traffic management constituted a critical problem.[66]

> An extraordinary state of affairs. Hardly a single formed body of troops and every field full of wagons and transport ready to turn into the column which was already miles long. The inevitable block and I thought we should probably be cut off by the Germans... We would go on for 100 yards and halt for a minute then on again only to halt 50 yards further.[67]

Clearing such traffic jams and keeping columns on the move was vital if the BEF was to survive. It was not the DR's job to act as traffic policeman but rather to advise column officers of difficulties and obstructions, when junctions could be "a mess of mixed transport standing wheel to wheel and facing in all directions".[68]

In addition to being kept on the move the BEF also needed to be held together and avoid becoming so strung out that it could be broken up by pursuing Germans. "After Le Cateau there were practically no battalions, just a crowd of men and transport

---

61   West, "Diary", p.43.
62   Watson, *Adventures*, p.193.
63   Ibid, p.38.
64   Tait, PP/MCR/161, 30 August 1914.
65   West, "Diary", pp.31, 33.
66   Niall Ferguson argues that Moltke's stripping of the German right wing made no difference to the outcome of Schlieffen's plan: the road network was so congested that a single division could not have made a fighting difference. Though a controversial claim, this helps convey the problems a despatch rider had to contend with.
67   Jolyon Jackson, *Family at War: The Foljambe Family and the Great War* (Yeovil, Haynes, 2010), p.68.
68   West, "Diary", p.31.

pouring along the road ... no organized unit larger than a platoon" — a subjective perception but not a misrepresentative view.[69] West described one straggler who was captured by Uhlans but allowed to go, his captors explaining that "hundreds more were coming along behind so they could not be bothered with him" — clearly confident of victory and greedy for richer spoils.[70] The DR not only had to round up and direct bewildered stragglers, but sometimes bring worn out men along on his carrier, constant work that exhausted the rider.[71]

Positional warfare led to the establishment of sophisticated "Motor Traffic Circuits" incorporating one-way systems for heavy Mechanical Transport vehicles; this made the DR's work easier but roads remained hazardous, far more so than German shells or bullets (until mobile warfare was restored in 1918), and he remained essential to command and control. The column rider was needed to maintain contact between units, men on the march from railheads or long lines of waggons or lorries, and ensure smooth uninterrupted movement along the route, and as the war of materiel and the ASC grew in importance, the DR remained part of the network of command and control; less critical than he had in 1914, but essential to the end.

DRs also performed a myriad of other duties. They were expected to fetch and carry almost anything an officer might think of, some trivial indulgences but others, such as munitions when these were running short in the middle of battle, vital.[72] In part because of the class to which most of them — in the early days at least — belonged, their regard for duty, and sterling discharge of it, helped save the Old Contemptibles to fight another day, and seed the New Armies.

Organisation

Organisation was to evolve through the war. Movement, which characterised the early weeks of the war, required particular flexibility. Most DRs belonged to the Motor Cycle Despatch Corps, part of the Signals Section of the Royal Engineers, a section that one DR called the "nerves of the modern army".[73] This metaphor was invoked by many. The Signals Office was "the nerve centre of the Army in the field, for into it radiate the tentacles along which flash messages from every part of the field of operations, from the base and from England".[74] It was these messages that warranted command and control. "[O]ne liaison officer described the army as: 'A giant with a quick and brilliant brain, but whose nervous system is slow, lethargic and inadequate'",[75] and when wires, wireless or radio were "dis" — disabled — the fastest means of communication, and the most

69   Watson, *Adventures*, pp.203-04.
70   West, "Diary", p.42.
71   Ibid., pp.15-16, 46, 57, 65; Watson, *Adventures*, p.34.
72   West, "Diary", p.43.
73   Corcoran, *Daredevil*, p.x.
74   *The Times History of the War*, XVIII (London, *The Times*, 1915), p.119.
75   Brigadier Peter Young, "The Great Retreat" in *Purnell's History of the First World War*, I, No 8, ed. Barrie Pitt (London, BPC Publishing, 1969), p.201.

consistently reliable, was the despatch rider. Reflecting recognition of the importance of DRs to command and control in every endeavour, the air arms maintained their own — providing different motorcycles than the Army did — and the artillery, the cavalry, the RAMC, and the ASC eventually all had dedicated despatch riders.[76] Though nominally attached to divisions-based Signals Companies — they came to form the same loyalty to their division as other soldiers felt toward their regiments[77] — DRs also were attached to corps and army HQs, as well as to GHQ, and might be seconded to brigades. West was attached to 19th Brigade, which had independent command until it was incorporated into 6th Division in October. Corporal Grice seems to have been attached to II Corps HQ. Eventually,

> A Divisional Signals Company, to which despatch riders were attached, comprised "five sections, headquarters [and] Nos 1, 2, 3, and 4. Headquarters and No 1 are attached to the headquarters staff of the division; 2, 3, and 4 being attached to the first, second and third brigades respectively."[78]

Much of this lay in the future in 1914, however. Organisation of the Despatch Rider Corps evolved through the Great Retreat, "and of these [improvements] the most important was the allotment of certain despatch riders to different portions of the formation. This made possible a more rapid and efficient interchange of messages".[79] Theoretically four DRs were allocated to each brigade, and indeed exactly four Scout Officers were seconded as DRs to the (independent) 19th Brigade;[80] but details varied. Some divisions allocated only two DRs to each brigade; others developed a system suited to a hard-pressed army in retreat, with two riders each to the flank-, rear- and advance-guards, and two more to the billeting officers. Some divisions did not have even ten DRs left by the time the BEF turned on the Marne, far less the stipulated sixteen, so clearly flexibility was called for if commanders were to muddle through. In the Great Retreat the DRs of the 1st and 2nd Divisions were under less pressure than those of II Corps and 19th Brigade, who not only had to manage an orderly retreat but had to do so against German flanking attacks, which placed them in greater danger of death or capture. Furthermore, at Aldershot Haig had trained his men in retreat manoeuvres,[81] and the flank of I Corps was covered, if partially and intermittently, by Lanrezac's Fifth Army, so under less danger from the Germans. It seems reasonable to suppose that in recognition of this relative lack of pressure DRs of I Corps took upon themselves greater responsibility to maintain communication across the Oise between the two corps.

---

76   In 1916 DRs of the artillery came under control of the Royal Engineers. Even as cable was reducing the relative importance of DRs in front line duty, the need to sustain larger and larger forces in the field was increasing the importance of the ASC, and DRs were essential in column riding and traffic management.

77   Watson, *Adventures*, pp.129, 266-70.

78   *Motor Cycling*, 6 July 1915, p.220.

79   Priestley, *Signals Service*, p.24.

80   West, "Diary", p.13.

81   Reid, *Douglas Haig*, p.188.

Certainly flexibility was essential as DR strength became depleted. As late as First Ypres, "Three quarters of us [divisional DRs] rode between the divisional and the brigade headquarters, the rest attached to brigades, and either used for miscellaneous work or held in reserve so that communication might not be broken if the wires were cut or smashed by shells";[82] "the rest" would equate to 1.333 DRs per brigade, assuming a full complement of sixteen DRs, but even by then, after reinforcement, a full complement was hard to maintain. The pressures of the retreat caused rapid wastage of motorcycles and loss of personnel,[83] and after the 4th Division arrived on the eve of Le Cateau it imposed further strain on communications for it came without any Signals.[84] By the time the BEF turned on the Marne some divisions were down to one-third of their despatch riders;[85] "There are fifteen motor-cyclists now", one DR reported in early October, "and all telegraph lines are laid out, so that things are different from the absolute inferno of the retreat, when we were only six".[86]

Positional warfare allowed time for rest, reinforcement and more formal organisation. Through the winter of 1914-15 the 5th Division's DRs "averaged fourteen in number",[87] two short of the stipulated requirement but almost twice the number available when truly needed in the retreat. With the advance toward the Aisne cable-laying began in a systematic and effective way,[88] but both that battle and First Ypres were dangerous for DRs,[89] who still had to sustain communications as an effective cable network, proof against shellfire, had yet to be laid. "We as dispatch riders had rather a bad time as the enemy kept the three towns, Ypres, Zonnebec and Zillebec humming with shells, and there was no way of getting past them, without going through [the shellfire]".[90] Many were killed and more injured, for although cable reduced the workload of DRs, it never removed the need for them.

Evaluation

Until recently no study has been made of despatch riders,[91] so conclusions on their effectiveness must be tentative until further study provokes debate. Of his nature the DR never could have been a war winner, but in servicing communications, in serving command and control, he was critical; and if he never could have won the war he could,

82   Watson, *Adventures*, p.158.
83   At least two motorcycles were lost as early as Mons—ibid, pp.34, 61, 85.
84   Chris Baker, *The Long, Long Trail*, http://www.1914-1918.net/4div.htm, accessed 8 August 2012.
85   Corcoran, *Daredevil*, pp.22-24.
86   OH Best, IWM document 87/56/1, 5 October, 15 October 1914.
87   Watson, *Adventures*, p.239.
88   Tait, PP/MCR/161, 7 September 1914.
89   Watson, *Adventures*, p.111.
90   Best, 87/56/1, 20 November 1914.
91   Michael Carragher, "The Value of Motorcycles to the British War Effort, 1914-1918" (Dissertation, University of Birmingham, 2007).

like Jellicoe, have lost it — not in an afternoon, but in the course of the retreat from Mons when he held the BEF together. He was to reprise this role after Ludendorff's breakout restored mobility in 1918 and to earn his keep all through the war; but 1914 was his hour of glory. In the course of the retreat all armies suffered from failure of "modern" communication systems, but unlike the Germans, and ironically in part because it had had to make do and muddle through, the BEF was not entirely dependent on these; thus it was able to sustain coherence and avoid being overwhelmed by vastly superior numbers. In 1918 the citizen army of a nation suspicious of soldiery played a great part in defeating the most martial power on earth, the meritocracy fostered by democracy eventually overcoming the immediate advantages militarism and dictatorship may confer; but the first citizen soldiers had put on uniform, with the blue-and-white brassard of the Signals Service on their arms, as early as 4 August 1914.

Testaments from popular accounts of the time need to be treated with caution, declaiming as they were to a nation demoralised by its army's humiliating retreat, shocking casualty lists, and growing acceptance of Haig's and Kitchener's gloomy prognosis of a long war. Yet they bear examination. "Every General Staff Officer to whom I have spoken is enthusiastic about the work [the 'motor cyclist corps'] is doing, and as a corps, it certainly has not its equal in any army in the field".[92] "When the full history of the European war is written there will be many tales of valour and devotion to duty by 'the Signals', as despatch riders are called in the army";[93] "No men are braver, and very few render more important service, than the motor cycle scouts."[94] "After this war the learned in such things will have to write a treatise on the psychology of the motor cyclist, for indeed he does things entirely without parallel, as will be confirmed by those whose lot it has been to control any number of these enthusiasts".[95]

While acknowledging the caution that must be brought to such testimonies, they cannot be discounted. The initiative and sense of duty which early DRs brought to their work ensured that they attracted official as well as popular attention.[96] Roger West blew up an important bridge in the teeth of the German advance, an action for which he volunteered. This action, for which his colonel considered him "a fool", involved his climbing the pier in order to lay explosives while wearing a carpet slipper over a swollen, badly infected foot, an affliction he had endured from the start of the retreat and was to suffer to the end of it.[97] That West was "the man who saved Paris" may have been "a gross if enthusiastic overstatement", yet his demolition of the Pontoise Bridge not only gave respite to the BEF, it also may have impeded a flank attack on Lanrezac's army while this was disengaging from the Battle of Guise.[98] Thus one British DR subtly affected French

---

92   *The Motor Cycle*, 22 October 1914, p.408.
93   Strang, *The British Army in War* (unpaginated).
94   William E Sellers, *With Our Fighting Men: The Story of their Faith, Courage, Endurance in the Great War* (London, The Religious Tract Society, 1915), p.76.
95   *The Motor Cycle*, 27 January 1916, p.71.
96   For example, Eric Goodheart gained the DCM, WN Gurdon the DCM, Watson the DCM and West the DSO. See Carragher, *San Fairy Ann*, Appendix 2.
97   West, "Diary", 57-60.
98   Ibid, p.7.

as well as British morale, and fostered Allied solidarity, when both badly needed boosting, as well as making a direct and perhaps important contribution to the actual fight.[99]

All that said, though, the DR remained a cog in a huge machine; and if in 1914 he bore a disproportionate part of the load imposed on that engine of war he never did so alone. In the retreat he owed his own survival to the cavalry, a force that since has been almost as denigrated as the DR's role has been forgotten.[100] By its scouting and screening, and dismounted marksmanship, the cavalry gave invaluable cover, under which, and with the heroic endurance of the PBI, the DR held the BEF together, to fight another day, and another, up to that last eleventh hour.

Its fighting retreat proved that the BEF was no Contemptible Little Army, and in gritting the cogs of Schlieffen's — or Moltke's — plan, and in securing Ypres, the BEF made a critical contribution to preventing defeat in 1914. The "Donkey School" of cynicism would discount the role of the generals in this, but an army without command and control is a mob. Yet it is no less true that command and control cannot be effected without communications, and failure of the Schlieffen Plan illustrates Colonel Fuller's point on the importance of information — and the value of the British DR in reflection of that: "German failure at the Marne in 1914 can be traced in a large part to the failure of their signal net". Moltke sent his armies into the field dependant on "radio and telephone exclusively; and with no provisions for alternate means of communication".[101] Over-reliance on wireless and cable contributed to the Germans' communications problems through August 1914 and highlights the importance of the British despatch rider.

That importance may be measured in other ways. On 1 September 1918, in preparation for the assault on the Drocourt-Queant line, the Canadian Corps handled 7,811 messages, of which 2,440 were carried by DR, "the balance by land wires or wireless".[102] The BEF now were rampant, rather than on the run; cable was ubiquitous, and with the Germans in retreat it was less prone to disruption by shellfire; and wireless had improved. Yet close to the end of the war the DR still transmitted almost a third of all messages. This measure of his importance to command and control, as late as then, highlights how vital was his role in 1914, when wireless and cable were scarce and, at best, compromised in their efficiency.[103]

Despatch riders' importance in 1914 also may be gauged by the consequences of communications failure. On 24 August three separate instructions to disengage and

99   "[I]f von Kluck's masses could be brought down upon the [Fifth Army's] flank, the whole French line would be rolled up"—Maurice, *Forty Days*, p.136.

100 Stephen Badsey, Gervase Phillips and David Kenyon in recent years have published important revisionary work on the role of cavalry.

101 Fuller, "The Application of Recent Developments", p.241; Samuel G Myer, "The Fourth Arm" in *Military Affairs*, VIII, No 3, Autumn 1944, pp.169-70. See also Ferris, *The British Army and Signals Intelligence*, p.5.

102 JFB Livesay, *Canada's Hundred Days* (Toronto, Thomas Allen, 1919), p.346.

103 As late as 1953 the DR remained marginally more effective than the telephone in relaying information at divisional level; see BD Hankin, "Communication and Control of Military Forces" in *OR* IV, No 4 (Birmingham, Operational Research Society, 1953), p.68.

fall back failed to reach the 1st Cheshires; all but two officers and 200 men were killed or captured (some 80 percent).[104] Two days later, after Landrecies, a DR, detailed to instruct several units to fall back, was unable to locate one of his targets, the 2nd Munster Fusiliers;[105] the entire battalion was lost. That same day most of two companies of the 2nd Connaught Rangers also were lost at Le Grand Fayt, cut off after contact was lost with Brigade HQ: "at that juncture nobody knew where anyone else was, or what was happening".[106] If such was the case at brigade and even battalion level, imagine the task of the despatch rider, trying to hold entire divisions together, and sustain communications with others, across unmapped miles?

Imagine, too, if Haig *had* been captured at Landrecies. The blow to the chain of command would have been severe, possibly fatal given the demands of the retreat. Although no DR can take credit for his escape, how many men *were* saved from capture or death by being warned by some peripatetic DR, seeking the recipient of his despatch, that they had gone astray? For "many exhausted stragglers, who had lost their way in the withdrawal, had fallen into the enemy's hands".[107] How many were saved such a fate, and how many more felt their morale buoyed by mere sight of a DR, confirming that the BEF was still coherent, or were grateful for a lift on his carrier when at the end of their rope? Evidence suggests that morale among the rank and file was higher than it was at GHQ; but there were suicides, and some men died of exhaustion,[108] reservists often being in bad shape.[109] For how long could morale be sustained without cohesion, and orders to keep it so? And who was to transmit those orders but the despatch rider. Besides, demoralisation could trickle down, as it did at St Quentin (until dispelled by Tom Bridges and his toy drum). How many more "St Quentin incidents" might there have been had demoralisation become widespread?

Contemporary testimony even from officers needs to be filtered through the exigencies of the time. The commander-in-chief remarked on

---

104   Neillands, *The Old Contemptibles*, p.149.
105   This despatch rider was captured according to *The War Illustrated*, Vol. VII, p.2494; possibly he was cut off from the Munsters by enemy forces — see Niall Barr, "Command in the Transition From Mobile to Static Warfare, August 1914 to March 1915) in Gary Sheffield and Dan Todman (eds), *Command and Control on the Western Front: The British Army's experience 1914-18*, p.26.
106   HFN Jourdain, *The Connaught Rangers, Volume II* (London, RUSI, 1926), p.412. Some of the Rangers and Fusiliers escaped, and constituted the bulk of the "Iron Twelve", who operated behind the German lines until captured and killed in February 1915.
107   Maurice, *Forty Days*, p.123.
108   Bernard John Denore, "The Retreat from Mons", in CP Purdom (ed), *On the Front Line: True World War I Stories* (London, Constable, 2009), p.18; Lyn Macdonald, *Ordeal By Fire: Witnesses to the Great War* (London, Folio, 2001), pp.16-17; West, "Diary", p.49.
109   Many had fallen on hard times since leaving the colours, and were too malnourished for the long retreat — George Coward, *Coward's War: An Old Contemptible's View of the Great War*, ed. Tim Machin (Leicester, Matador, 2006), p.17. Others were bad soldiers. See Gerald Achilles Burgoyne, *The Burgoyne Diaries* (London, Harmsworth, 1985).

the splendid work which has been done throughout the campaign by the [motor] cyclists of the Signal Corps [who] have been conspicuously successful in maintaining an extraordinary degree of efficiency in the service of communications. Many casualties have occurred in their ranks, but no amount of difficulty or danger has ever checked the energy or ardour which has distinguished their Corps throughout the operations.[110]

Johnnie French was a soldiers' general, volatile in mood and expression, and relieved to still be in the fight; but "Wully" Robertson was famously unimpressionable, and had been an instructor in signalling, so spoke with authority; besides, his testimony was made after the war, when there was no need to gild any lilies:

The despatch riders ... performed invaluable service.... Most of [them] were boys under twenty years of age who had joined on the outbreak of war ... and the manner in which they carried out their duties in the face of great hardships and dangers confirmed me in the opinion that the English boy has no superior.[111]

A brigade commander was in no doubt: "what we should have done without them passes my imagination, for they were quite invaluable".[112] "In our case the motor cyclist was so necessary that without him, several of him, we were lost."[113]

They weren't all boys, and they weren't all English,[114] but Wully's point is taken, by another professional, long after war had ended: "the service given by the despatch riders was superb, and though casualties to men and machines were fairly frequent [in 1914], and the strength of many units was down to a minimum, touch was kept and messages cleared with exemplary promptitude".[115] Yet another professional, with more than seven decades of perspective, is even more forthright: "At no time in this century has signals intelligence affected campaigns more significantly than at the very hour of its birth, in 1914"[116] — when the linchpin of Signals was the despatch rider.

That the DR has been forgotten may be ironic tribute to his very success: because "[he] is likely to become conspicuous only when he fails in the task assigned him",[117] he came to be overlooked by history because he *didn't* fail. Had he failed, the history of the Great Retreat would have been very different. Their service is all the more remarkable given that DRs were, for the most part, very young men with no more than a couple of weeks' army training, if any at all, "amateurs at [a] professional game".[118] That these amateurs muddled through proved essential to eventual victory.

110   Priestley, *Signal Service*, p.42 — citing Sir John French's despatch of 20 November 1914.
111   Sir William Robertson, *From Private to Field Marshall* (London, Constable, 1921), pp.211-12.
112   Gleichen, *Doings*, p.93.
113   *The Motor Cycle*, 27 January 1916, p.71.
114   Corcoran, for instance, was Irish.
115   Priestley, *Signals Service*, p.31.
116   John Ferris (ed), *The British Army and Signals Intelligence During the First World War* (Stroud, Sutton, 1992), p.5.
117   Corcoran, "Wireless".
118   Corcoran, *Daredevil*, p.2.

Appendix:
Order of Battle of the British Expeditionary Force, August 1914

A Note on Formations Listed

This order of battle is provided as a reference for readers who may not be familiar with the composition of the BEF in 1914. It lists the organisation of the BEF in August 1914 and includes the composition of III Corps (formed at the end of August) and IV Corps (formed in early October). As the chapters of this volume make only passing reference to the Indian Corps, it has been decided to omit an order of battle for this formation, which arrived at the end of September.

Comprehensive orders of battle for 1914 may be found in the relevant volumes of the Official History.

A Note on Unit Strengths

The British cavalry division of 1914 had a paper strength of 9,269 all ranks and 9,815 horses, supported by 24 13-pounder guns and 24 machine guns. An individual cavalry brigade numbered approximately 1700 all ranks.

A British infantry division of 1914 had a paper strength of 18,073 all ranks and 5,592 horses, supported by 76 artillery pieces (54 x 18-pounders, 18 x 4.5-inch howitzers, and four 60-pounders) and 24 machine guns. An individual infantry brigade numbered approximately 4000 all ranks.

An infantry battalion consisted of approximately 1000 men, divided into four companies of approximately 250 men each.

A British aeroplane squadron consisted of 12 aircraft.

ᴏᴏᴏᴏᴏ

General Headquarters (GHQ)

Commander-in-Chief: Field Marshal Sir John French
Chief of Staff: Lieutenant-General Sir Archibald Murray
Sub-Chief of Staff: Major-General Henry Wilson
GSO1 (Operations): Colonel George Harper
GSO1 (Intelligence): Colonel George Macdonogh.
Adjutant-General: Major General Sir. C.F.N. Macready
Quartermaster-General: Major-General Sir William Robertson

ᴏᴏᴏᴏᴏ

Cavalry Division

GOC: Major-General Edmund Allenby
GSO1: Colonel John Vaughan
NB: The Cavalry Division was expanded into the Cavalry Corps on 9 October 1914. This new formation was created primarily for organisational reasons. Allenby was promoted to Lieutenant-General and became corps commander. The corps itself consisted of the original 5 cavalry brigades divided into 1st Cavalry Division (GOC: Major-General Henry de Beauvior de Lisle) and 2nd Cavalry Division. (GOC: Major-General Hubert Gough). 1st Division contained 1st and 2nd Brigade; 2nd Division contained 3rd, 4th and 5th Brigade.

1st Brigade:
GOC: Brigadier-General C.J. Briggs
2nd Dragoon Guards
5th Dragoon Guards
11th Hussars

2nd Brigade:
GOC: Brigadier-General Henry de Beauvior de Lisle
4th Dragoon Guards
9th Lancers
18th Hussars

3rd Brigade:
GOC: Brigadier-General Hubert Gough
4th Hussars
5th Lancers
16th Lancers

4th Brigade:
GOC: Brigadier-General C.E. Bingham
Composite Regiment of Household Cavalry
6th Dragoon Guards
3rd Hussars

5th Brigade:
GOC: Brigadier-General Sir Philip Chetwoode
2nd Dragoons
12th Lancers
20th Hussars

ooooo

I Corps

GOC: Lieutenant-General Sir Douglas Haig
CoS; Brigadier-General John Gough V.C.

1st Division

GOC: Major-General Samuel Lomax
GSO1: Colonel R. Fanshawe

1st (Guards) Brigade
GOC: Brigadier-General Ivor Maxse
1st Coldstream Guards
1st Scots Guards
1st Black Watch (Royal Highlanders)
2nd Royal Munster Fusiliers (Replaced by 1st Cameron Highlanders in September 1914)

2nd Brigade
GOC: Brigadier-General Edward Bulfin
2nd Royal Sussex Regiment
1st Loyal North Lancashire Regiment
1st Northamptonshire Regiment
2nd King's Royal Rifle Corps

3rd Brigade
GOC: Brigadier-General Herman Landon
1st Queen's (Royal West Surrey Regiment)
1st South Wales Borderers
1st Gloucestershire Regiment
2nd Welch Regiment

2nd Division

GOC: Major-General Charles Monro
GSO1: Colonel F. Gordon

4th (Guards) Brigade
GOC: Brigadier-General R. Scott-Kerr
2nd Grenadier Guards
2nd Coldstream Guards
3rd Coldstream Guards
1st Irish Guards

5th Brigade
GOC: Brigadier-General R.C.B. Haking
2nd Worcestershire Regiment
2nd Oxfordshire and Buckinghamshire Light Infantry
2nd Highland Light Infantry
2nd Connaught Rangers

6th Brigade
GOC: Brigadier-General R.H. Davies
1st King's (Liverpool Regiment)
2nd South Staffordshire Regiment
1st Princess Charlotte of Wales's Own (Royal Berkshire Regiment)
1st King's Royal Rifle Corps

ooooo

II Corps

GOC: [1]: Lieutenant-General Sir James Grierson (died 17 August 1914)
[2]: General Sir Horace Smith-Dorrien (Assumed command 21 August 1914)
CoS: Brigadier-General George Forestier-Walker

3rd Division

GOC: Major-General Hubert Hamilton
GSO1: Colonel F.R.F. Boileau

7th Brigade
GOC: Brigadier-General F.W.N. McCracken
3rd Worcestershire Regiment
2nd Prince of Wales's Volunteers (South Lancashire Regiment
1st The Duke of Edinburgh's (Wiltshire Regiment)
2nd Royal Irish Rifles

8th Brigade
GOC: Brigadier-General B.J.C. Doran
2nd Royal Scots (Lothian Regiment)
2nd Royal Irish
4th The Duke of Cambridge's Own (Middlesex Regiment)
1st Gordon Highlanders (Replaced by 1st Devonshire in September 1914)

9th Brigade
GOC: Brigadier-General F.C. Shaw
1st Northumberland Fusiliers
4th Royal Fusiliers (City of London Regiment)
1st Lincolnshire Regiment
1st Royal Scots Fusiliers

5th Division

GOC: Major-General Sir Charles Fergusson
GSO1: Lieutenant-Colonel C.F. Romer

13th Brigade
GOC: Brigadier-General G.J. Cuthbert
2nd King's Own Scottish Borderers
2nd Duke of Wellington's Regiment (West Riding Regiment)
1st The Queen's Own (Royal West Kent Regiment)
2nd King's Own Yorkshire Light Infantry

14th Brigade
GOC: Brigadier-General S.P. Rolt
2nd Suffolk Regiment
1st East Surrey Regiment
1st Duke of Cornwall's Light Infantry
2nd Manchester Regiment

15th Brigade
GOC: Brigadier-General Count Gleichen
1st Norfolk Regiment
1st Bedfordshire Regiment
1st Cheshire Regiment
1st Dorsetshire Regiment

ooooo

III Corps

[Formed in France, 31 August 1914]

GOC: Major-General William Pulteney
CoS: Brigadier-General J.P. Du Cane

4th Division

[Landed in France 22/23 August 1914]
GOC: Major-General Thomas Snow
GSO1: Colonel James Edmonds

10th Brigade
GOC: Brigadier-General J.A.L. Haldane
1st Royal Warwickshire Regiment
2nd Seaforth Highlanders
1st Royal Irish Fusiliers
2nd Royal Dublin Fusiliers

11th Brigade
GOC: Brigadier-General A.G. Hunter-Weston
1st Somerset Light Infantry
1st East Lancashire Regiment
1st Hampshire Regiment
1st Rifle Brigade

12th Brigade
GOC: Brigadier-General H.F.M. Wilson
1st Royal Lancaster Regiment
2nd Lancashire Fusiliers
2nd Royal Inniskilling Fusiliers
2nd Essex Regiment

6th Division

[Embarked for France 8/9 September 1914]
GOC: Major-General J.L. Keir
GSO1: Colonel W.T. Furse

16th Brigade
GOC: Brigadier-General E.C. Ingouville-Williams
1st The Buffs (East Kent Regiment)
1st Leicestershire Regiment
1st Shropshire Light Infantry
2nd York and Lancaster Regiment

17th Brigade
GOC: Brigadier-General W.R.B. Doran

1st Royal Fusiliers
1st The Prince of Wales's (North Staffordshire Regiment)
2nd Prince of Wales's Leinster Regiment
3rd Rifle Brigade

18th Brigade
GOC: Brigadier-General W.N. Congreve VC
1st The Prince of Wales's Own (West Yorkshire Regiment)
1st East Yorkshire Regiment
2nd Sherwood Foresters (Nottinghamshire & Derbyshire Regiment)
2nd Durham Light Infantry

ooooo

19th Brigade

[This independent brigade was formed from battalions originally designated as Line of Communication Defence troops on 22 August 1914]
GOC: Major-General L.G. Drummond
2nd Royal Welch Fusiliers
1st Cameronians
1st Middlesex
2nd Argyll and Sutherland Highlanders

ooooo

Royal Flying Corps

GOC: Brigadier-General Sir David Henderson
GSO1: Lieutenant-Colonel F.H. Sykes
2nd Aeroplane Squadron
3rd Aeroplane Squadron
4th Aeroplane Squadron
5th Aeroplane Squadron
6th Aeroplane Squadron

ooooo

IV Corps

NB: IV Corps was formed on 10 October 1914 and consisted of 7th Division and 3rd Cavalry Division. These formations were in turn transferred to I Corps (27 Oct) and the Cavalry Corps (25 Oct) respectively. IV Corps was reformed on 6 November, consisting of 7th and 8th Divisions.

GOC: Lieutenant-General Sir Henry Rawlinson
CoS: Brigadier-General R.A.K. Montgomery

7th Division

GOC: Major-General Thompson Capper
GSO1: Colonel H.M. de F. Montgomery

20th Brigade
GOC: Brigadier-General Ruggles-Brise
1st Grenadier Guards
2nd Scots Guards
2nd Border Regiment
2nd Gordon Highlanders

21st Brigade
GOC: Brigadier-General H.E. Watts
2nd Bedfordshire Regiment
2nd Green Howards
2nd Royal Scots Fusiliers
2nd Wiltshire Regiment

22nd Brigade
GOC: Brigadier-General S.T.B. Lawford
2nd Queen's (Royal West Surrey Regiment)
2nd Royal Warwickshire Regiment
1st Royal Welch Fusiliers
1st South Staffordshire Regiment

3rd Cavalry Division

GOC: Major-General J.H.G. Byng
GSO1: Lieutenant-Colonel M.F. Gage

6th Brigade
GOC: Brigadier-General E. Makins
3rd Dragoon Guards
1st Royal Dragoons
10th Hussars

7th Brigade
GOC: Brigadier-General C.T. Kavanagh
1st Life Guards
2nd Life Guards
Royal Horse Guards

Index

People

Military Units

General